White Nigger

The Struggles and Triumphs Growing Up Bi-Racial in America

Jason C. Bost, JD, MBA

Progress Always,

The author has attempted to recreate conversations, events, locations and occurrences from memory as well as interviews with various individuals. While every attempt at accuracy has been made, some names, places, descriptions and other details may have been changed to protect the identities of some individuals.

Additional Contributing Editors: Elizabeth Martin, Chichi Ofoma & Robin Evenden
Legal Advisor: Chinyere "Chichi" Ofoma, Esq.
Book Cover Artwork idea: Jason C. Bost, Sr., and Michael "Script" Brown
Book Cover Artwork by Michael "Script" Brown
Paperback edition
ISBN-10: 0-9991945-2-6
ISBN-13: 978-0-9991945-2-2

DEDICATION

To Mom, for all your unyielding strength and guidance. There is no question that everything positive in my character came directly from you. Grandma, rest in peace and thank you for showing me the true power in gentleness. Grandpa, for laying the foundation for our future generations. To my children for giving me the strength to remain positive and keep focused on our future. I love you all from yesterday until forever

Table of Contents

WHITE NIGGER

PART I

"People don't realize how a man's whole life can be changed by one book."

— Malcolm X

1 SELF AWARENESS

The birth of my younger sister Nicole was significant for two main reasons; first, it ended my life as an only child and secondly, it introduced me to the concept of racial differences. A few weeks after my sister's birth, my mother visited my school and brought Nicole with her. I was excited beyond belief and couldn't wait to introduce my entire class to my brand new baby sister. I was glowing with pride, and I made sure every one of my classmates stood up so that they could get a better view of her, as I smiled uncontrollably the entire time. I was a big brother and felt like the entire world needed to know.

Later that day, while walking home from school, my best friend Antonio Plecebo told me that Jimmy, one of our classmates, called my baby sister a Nigger. I had absolutely no idea what the word Nigger meant but for some reason, it infuriated me. I did not identify the word with anything related to race, all I knew was that it sounded like Jimmy was trying to disrespect my sister, my brand new baby sister, and there was no way in hell I was going to let that fly, so I headed straight to Jimmy's house so that I could whip his ass!

Sherman Avenue was a small street and our rented house was one of a few very small, single-family houses on my end of the block. Jimmy lived in a trailer located in the trailer park at the other end of the block. Walking past my house on my way to Jimmy's trailer I stopped inside to drop off my book bag, kiss my sister and tell my mother that I would be back.

When I left my house there was a small crowd of kids gathered outside in anticipation of the fight that they somehow heard was about to take place. This was way before cell phones and text messages, so the rumor of the fight had to travel from mouth-to-mouth in the 10 minutes or so that it took us to walk home from school. As everyone followed me down to Jimmy's house, the crowd, growing in eagerness, began to talk louder and walk faster and I could feel my heart starting to pound in my chest.

I didn't need the crowd to hype me up because I was already pissed off but their energy definitely provoked more of my anger, so by the time I got to Jimmy's house I headed straight for his door and kicked it as opposed to knocking, to make sure he knew I was mad. His mother came to the door, looked at the crowd and saw the anger on my face and immediately knew that I was there to fight her son. She said, "I'm not sending Jimmy out there with all you boys. If ya'll are gonna fight, ya'll gonna fight him fair." She made no attempt to understand what was going on or to sit us down and work out the problem, this was how things were handled in our neighborhood and she knew this.

I picked up a rock and told her that if she didn't send him out I was going to throw it through her window. Instead of snatching my little ass up and putting me in my place or marching me right up the street and telling my mother what I threatened to do, Jimmy's mother sent Jimmy out to face me. As soon as he walked out of his door I kicked him with all the force I had, square in his balls and he dropped to his knees, with the wind completely knocked out of him and a look of shock on his face.

Before he could even think about moving I punched him two or three times in his face and kicked him in his stomach as I could feel the rage inside of me growing more intense. I looked up when I heard his mother say "you dirty little mother fucker, I told you to fight fair." Without hesitating, I threw the rock I was holding and attempted to hit her with it, instead missing and hitting their front door. Stunned, she closed the door but continued to watch from the open screen.

Jimmy was trying to catch his breath and was starting to moan when I stood over him and started screaming, "my sister ain't a

Nigger, you're a Nigger" as I hit and punched and kicked him.

At some point his mother came outside of their trailer and grabbed me, moving me off of Jimmy while I swung and cussed and threatened to punch her. By this time Jimmy was crying and had blood gushing from his nose and from a cut on his forehead. She picked him up and they both went into their trailer. I was furious that she stopped me from exacting revenge for Jimmy's disrespect, so I threw another rock at their door, cussing and yelling for Jimmy to come back outside. Antonio and a few of my other friends grabbed me and dragged me down towards my house. The rest of the crowd was silent, stunned at what they had just witnessed and I was still throwing rocks and cussing the entire way home.

This was the first time that I can remember "blacking out", completely losing self-control when anger and raw emotion took over and filled me with pure rage. And this was the first time that my mother talked to me about race and tried to explain that I was not white like she was or white like the rest of my family was or white like most of my friends. This was the first time anyone told me that I was black, or at least that the world would consider me as being black. I refused to listen to what she was trying to say to me not because black was offensive to me, I had no idea what being black meant, but offensive because it meant I was different.

How could I be different? Why would she say this to me and why say it now, right after I spent my afternoon beating the shit out of a kid for calling my sister a Nigger. How could that term really apply to my sister, to me, to anyone I knew? My stepfather attempted to explain it to me but this only made me angrier and less receptive as I had already developed a strong dislike for him in the few years that he had been in our lives. I guess I've always been stubborn, extremely stubborn, and accepting what they were trying to tell me would mean that I was different than my friends and more importantly to me, different than my mother, the woman that raised and loved me and the woman that I loved more than anything.

For the first time in my life, staring back at me in the mirror was someone different than I had always seen. This was the day that I learned that the word Nigger had some sort of attachment to me and my sister and this made me even more angry at Jimmy. Soon after, I was beating him up every day on the way to school or after school if he avoided me in the mornings. Every time I hit him I would hear that word echoing in my head "Nigger" and my anger would intensify.

2 EARLY YEARS

I was born to a 21-year-old unwed white mother and an African American father. Interracial relationships were still somewhat uncommon in 1970, in fact just seven years before my birth, in the historic case of Loving v. Virginia, the United States Supreme Court finally held that anti-miscegenation laws were unconstitutional. Until the Loving case, most of the states had laws that either prohibited and invalidated interracial marriages or made the marriage between a black and a white person a punishable crime. Even in the relatively few states that did not have any legislative barriers to interracial marriages, the social stigma and challenges related to mixed relationships could be overwhelming and frequently led to confrontation or physical violence.

To further put the racial climate of this country in perspective, the world was still reeling from the assassination of the Reverend Doctor Martin Luther King, Jr. which occurred in 1968, just two years before I was born. The US government, headed by President Richard Nixon, was fighting a war in Vietnam as well as waging a war against its black citizens right here on U.S. soil. The U.S. government utilized publicly funded programs such as the Federal Bureau of Investigation's Counter Intelligence Program, or COINTELPRO, to specifically target and disrupt various political organizations deemed to be a threat to the government.

Under the direction of J. Edgar Hoover, black political organizations became the number one target of COINTELPRO, and the program's goals of discrediting and completely destroying these organizations were made clear to the public. This was all during the same political rule that saw good-ole President Nixon almost impeached for his involvement in the Watergate scandal. Nixon and Hoover's roles in the intentional violation of the civil and human rights of black citizens would not be completely understood or accepted until many years later. The war in Vietnam was ongoing and America was experiencing inflation rates that were triple the rates of the previous decade. The "Free Love" and Hippie movements from the 1960's were dying out and America was beginning to get its first real taste of the effects of long-term poverty on urban communities. Racial inequalities were exposed and highlighted throughout the civil rights movement of the 1960's and now the US was forced to deal with open racial wounds and growing dissent from both black and white impoverished communities.

I entered this racially and economically divided country as we all do, totally innocent and clueless about race or hate or the state of U.S. politics. As any child, I understood the basics, I knew that my mother and grandparents loved me and I had no idea that I was any different than any of them until I was introduced to the word "Nigger." Jimmy's use of the word "Nigger" made me aware for the first time in my life, that the world I lived in was made up of groups of perceived inferior and superior people.

Unlike the rest of my peers, friends and family, I didn't belong to any of these clearly defined racial groups; I was not white enough to be considered white and I was not black enough to be fully accepted as black. I was something in between and I would slowly and painfully learn that I would neither be recognized by white society nor would I be easily accepted by black society. I was an outsider always looking in at those that "belonged". Thus my struggle for acceptance began.

My mother was born a few miles outside of Elmira in a small, somewhat rural community. She was the third youngest of five siblings born to my grandparents. My grandfather worked as a postal worker, delivering mail on a rural route which he worked for more than 30 years while my grandmother worked and took care of home and the kids. Their relationship was what most would consider to have been traditional for that time, and although they were not well off, they made sure their five kids ate every day, had clothes for school and were still able to save a little bit of money along the way.

The town my mother grew up in was composed of other similarly situated, working, middle class white families. She went to school through the 1950's and 1960's and, although racially segregated schools were commonplace in most of the United States, she attended schools that were open to blacks. This was prior to any desegregation busing so the absences of blacks in her community meant the absence of blacks in her schools as well.

By my mother's accounts, my grandparents were somewhat

progressive for the time, believing that all people were equal and should be treated equal under the law but more importantly for them, should be treated equal as people and provided with the same support and opportunities made accessible to all the whites in their community. My grandparents' ideology about race and equality were certainly not considered normal for the times, in fact in today's world they would probably be labeled as extreme liberals, which is ironic as to this day, my grandfather is a staunch supporter of the Republican party and most of their principles and ideologies. My grandparent's views had an obvious influence on my mother which was probably a contributing factor to her being involved in an inter-racial relationship, leading to my eventual existence.

Patrick was my best childhood friend since the age of three. More like a brother than a friend, he lived on the other side of town in Elmira in a section of the city filled with double and single-family rental houses and a few low-income housing projects. The majority of Elmira's black families, including his, lived in his neighborhood making it much more racially diverse than my own.

My mother worked as a nurse at the Elmira Psych Center, requiring her to work long shifts on the weekends as well as some overnights, so I ended up spending many of my weekends at Patrick's house. We would wake up extra early on Saturdays so we could watch the Saturday morning cartoons. I loved Fat Albert, the Jetsons and the Land of the Lost, but my absolute favorite was the Super Friends and the Justice League. When they came out with Super Friends Underoos underwear that had the design and color of the various Super Friends characters on them, I begged my mother for a pair of Aqua Man Underoos! You couldn't tell me that I was not Aqua man, I would wear those underwear every day and I remember quite a few times getting in trouble for jumping in the tub with my Underoos on because I was determined to "swim like Aqua Man!"

Saturday mornings at Patrick's house provided me with my first real introduction to black culture, black music and the black fashion scene. Patrick had two sisters that were eight or nine years older than us, both of whom were very much into the whole fashion and music scene of the time. I never really gave much thought about Patrick's family being black, I never looked at them any differently than myself and they never treated me any differently. My comprehension of the differences between their household and my own didn't materialize until I was introduced to black television.

Patrick's sisters ensured that Saturday afternoons were reserved exclusively for Soul Train. Patrick and I would have control of the television all morning, until Soul Train came on, then they would grab a pair of pliers to change the dial on the old TV and wait, eagerly anticipating the start of the show. Every episode would start with a cartoon image of a train bopping to this bass-heavy, funky theme music and then the host, Mr. Don Cornelius, would say in his soulful deep voice, "Soul Train, the Hippest trip in America. Sixty non-stop minutes across the tracks of your mind into the exciting world of Soul." Then he would introduce the guest artists on that particular show and always add "along with the Soul Train dancers". The show's introduction was immediately followed by commercials which were always targeted directly at the black audiences, including ones featuring black hair care products such as Afro-Sheen, or a McDonald's ad featuring a black family portrayed by black actors. I didn't understand marketing at the time but I clearly remember Patrick's sisters having many of those hair products sitting on their dressers and in their bathroom.

The Soul-Train dancers were composed of mostly black dancers, with a few white, Asian and Latin dancers sprinkled in here and there, and they would perform the newest dances while wearing the latest fashions. Male and female dancers wore massive Afros that were meticulously picked and combed into perfectly round shapes, complementing their shiny silk shirts with huge collars, and skin tight polyester bell bottom pants, accompanied by ridiculously high platform shoes. Don Cornelius would always introduce the latest soul and funk records and Patrick's sisters, Reese and Celia, would get up and imitate the latest dances and scream every time one of their favorite groups or singers would begin to perform, all while they both picked their own Afros and talked about which dancers had the best outfits.

Soul Train introduced me to groups like Con-Funk-Shun, and singers like Minnie Riperton, and David Ruffin, while the dancers would do dances like "the Hustle" and "the Bump." I was captivated with the music. While Patrick would usually go off to his room or head outside to play, I would remain in the living room, glued to the television, secretly listening to everything his sisters said, absorbing all the latest slang and watching them try to master the new dance crazes.

Music has always been a huge part of my life, partially because my mother was a huge music fan. Through her vinyl records and 8-Tracks, I was introduced to the Isley Brothers, Earth, Wind and Fire, Kool and the Gang and the Average White Band as well as many of the popular non-soul artists of the day such as John Denver, Linda Ronstadt, Carol King, the Eagles and Barry Manilow. I would often spend hours just going through my mother's albums and listening to them while studying the artwork on their covers and trying to imagine what the artists singing the songs would look like if they were performing that song right there.

There was something about the energy and passion that Patrick's sisters danced with and something about the soulfulness of the music itself that kept me fascinated and ensured that every Saturday afternoon was spent studying Soul Train, studying the black faces moving in unison to the rhythms of the music and studying Reese and Celia's responses to each song. This was the first time that I can remember paying attention to black culture and trying to absorb and incorporate it into myself. I couldn't explain why I felt drawn to it, I just knew that for some reason it felt right, it felt like that was where I was somehow supposed to be. I never experienced feeling out of place on those Saturday mornings, I always felt comfortable and like I belonged. Looking back through eyes that have experienced decades of feeling like an outsider, just the thought of those mornings relaxes me and makes me appreciate the beauty and calmness of life's simpler times.

When I wasn't with Patrick on the weekends I was usually with my maternal grandparents. While my weekends with Patrick would lead to plenty of boyhood mischief and introduce me to black culture, my time with my grandparents reinforced my familiarity to the social norms associated with my family and white American culture. My grandfather was a huge fan of two television shows: The Lawrence Welk Show and Hee-Haw. Hee-Haw used bales of hay and a farm setting as a backdrop while the cast members, usually dressed in overalls and wearing straw hats, would sing country songs and crack jokes. Roy Clark was the host of the show and Minnie Pearl became famous for wearing these big country church hats with the price tag still on them. As much as I enjoyed Soul Train, I also enjoyed Hee-Haw, probably because I saw how much my grandfather enjoyed it and it was an opportunity for us to watch the show together while sharing Planters roasted peanuts and one of those old school glass bottles of Pepsi.

The time with my grandparents taught me the norms and socially acceptable patterns associated with white culture in America, but I never understood it to be a lesson in Americana, I just enjoyed my grandparents and the security and safety associated with being in their home. My grandparents were very typical for their generation, hard-working, middle class people that believed in spending quality time with their family. Their neighborhood was typical for the time, middle class, all white, neat and clean with nicely manicured lawns and neighbors that all knew each other and took the time to walk across the street to speak to one another daily. I do not recall any other people of color in their neighborhood but at the time it was never really an issue for me. I loved my time with them, their house was warm and loving and I can't remember very many times, if any, in which I was unhappy there.

It was not uncommon for five or six-year-old kids to spend all day outside playing during the summer time or on the weekends, with very little to no parental supervision. We knew the rules, be home before the street lights came on, don't go to the Parker's house because their father was always drunk and almost burnt the house down twice because he fell asleep while cooking; don't talk to strangers; stay on our block and don't ride your bike in the street. We would break every single rule almost every single day except for the street light rule. There was no defense to breaking that rule, that one was clear cut, be home or risk facing the consequences. The other rules were easy to break because they were not visible to our parents and they would never know unless someone reported us or someone got hurt.

Unfortunately for us, someone was almost always there to catch us and someone was always there to tell our parents about whatever mischief we managed to get into! Our neighborhood was full of parents that knew other parents and older folks that acted as if they hated kids like us and loved to get us in trouble so it was not uncommon for our parents to get a phone call from a neighbor if they spotted us doing something we had no business doing. Shit, depending on who the neighbor was, we might even get our ass whipped by them first and then have to deal with more punishment from our parents when we got home. The neighborhood watched and policed itself and everyone knew what the rules were, everyone knew that you were supposed to respect the adults and that any adult in the neighborhood had the right to tear your ass up if you misbehaved. And trust me, many of us fell victim to this type of "community policing" so we were all always aware that eyes were everywhere.

Kids being kids, that never stopped us from doing things we had no business doing. Once, while on the four-block walk home from school, I passed a group of older kids throwing rocks at the windows of an abandoned house. My other friends kept walking and encouraged me to do the same but I was fascinated by the way the windows would shatter when someone succeeded in throwing a rock with perfect accuracy through one of the windows. I stopped and watched for a few minutes before I finally got up the nerve to pick up a rock and throw one myself.

My very first toss was a success, the large picture window overseeing the front porch shattered and glass flew everywhere. Even the older kids were impressed! For a minute, I felt like I was the man, until I noticed Mrs. Burns looking out of her screen door staring directly at me. It seemed like everyone noticed her at the exact same time so we all scattered, running in different directions as we headed towards our respective homes.

Mrs. Burns called Tina, my best friend Antonio's mother, immediately after seeing me throw the rock, so within two minutes of my triumphant rock toss through that huge window, and the very second I rounded the corner onto my street, Tina came charging out of her house with a belt in hand and headed straight for me. I looked behind me thinking that she was after Antonio, or his older brother Chris, but by the time I realized she was coming for me it was too late, she had the belt raised above her head and it was already on its way down, headed straight for my back.

"Whack, whack, whack," I couldn't even say a single word before she hit me three more solid times across my legs and backside.

By the time I gathered my senses and my instincts told me to run she had already hit me at least two or three more times, knocking my Spiderman lunchbox from my hand and spilling a half-eaten sandwich and chocolate milk from my thermos all over the middle of the street. I left that lunchbox right there and hauled ass towards home with Tina in hot pursuit, cursing at me the entire time yelling, "You little bastard, you want to break windows? I will break your ass!" I knew the only chance I had to escape Tina and that belt was to find a place to hide so I zigzagged through the neighbor's backyard and headed straight for the fort we built on the side of the doghouse in my backyard.

I stayed in that fort until it was dark, not coming out until I heard my mother calling my name. When I finally emerged she ran towards me and picked me up giving me a huge hug and, wiping away her tears, asked me why I scared everyone like that. Apparently after Tina was unable to find me, she had to call my mother at work. My mother's fear that something might have happened to me saved me from getting any additional punishment; she was so happy that I was safe that the window-breaking incident was not even discussed.

That was how things went in my neighborhood, at any given time any one of our neighbors might catch us fucking up and provide us with a whipping right there on the spot, no questions asked, no worry about what our parent's might say, they would efficiently and unapologetically administer corporal punishment. Because of this "community parenting" approach, our neighborhood was virtually free from the crimes that plague many communities inhabited by younger kids and it was rare that any of us got into any serious trouble. The community took responsibility for its own and everyone contributed to raising the children. It was a literal example of the African proverb that "It takes a village to raise a child," and it worked. We were certainly not angels but we respected our elders and were raised with a sense of community that is now virtually impossible to find anywhere in this country.

With that much supervision you would think that we would never be able to find enough freedom to get into any trouble, but boys will be boys and trouble seemed to have a way of finding us. As the weather would get warmer we would always manage to venture further and further away from our street and into new and unfamiliar neighborhoods. The opposite end of my street ran directly into a busy main road that contained a plaza which had a supermarket, McDonalds and a few other small shops. We were strictly forbidden from crossing that road, or going anywhere near it, so of course we spent a considerable amount of time trying to figure out ways to cross the road without getting caught by anyone in the neighborhood or getting run over by one of the cars as they sped past. Accidents did happen, one of the older kids that lived in the trailer park at the end of my street was hit and killed by a car trying to cross that road on his bike and our mothers would remind us of that any time they caught a whiff of us acting like we might try to venture across it. For young boys with adventure and mischief running through their blood, that street separated us from freedom and independence, so crossing that road became our number one mission in life.

I can't remember the first time we successfully crossed over into the plaza by ourselves but I certainly recall our attempts to terrorize the McDonald's drive through as well as our raids on the P&C supermarket. We would roll up to the drive-thru window on our bicycles making a sound like a car engine until someone would say, "Welcome to McDonalds, can I take your order?" then one of us would try to deepen our six and seven-year-old voices and say, "ah yes I'd like a fart sandwich and an order of shit!" We would all laugh hysterically and haul ass out of there before anyone could catch us, but one day the manager who had grown tired of our games, snuck up behind us and grabbed me and Antonio by our shirts before we could peddle away. He yelled at us and threatened to beat our little asses and we yelled right back at him, kicking and swinging at him until he finally let us go.

That was the first time I can recall feeling the power and sense of security that comes with being with a group of my boys. The more of us that were together, the more courageous we would become, almost as if we were invincible. I would have never attempted that drive-thru stunt by myself and certainly would have been scared out of my mind if the manager grabbed me when I was all alone, but being in a group gave us all courage, made all of us feel that much more tough and probably made the manager realize that he was going to have to back up his words with actions because we were going to stand our ground until he let us go or took things further. This feeling of power generated from hanging with my boys would repeat itself throughout my childhood and into my teen years and would be the catalyst to much of my early troubles.

Those trips to the other side of that busy road also led to my first experience with the police. Four or five of us would head into the P&C Supermarket and steal anything and everything we could get our little hands on. Usually just candy and snacks but eventually we started to follow the lead of the older kids and snatch cigarettes and chewing tobacco. This was before the days of placing the cigarettes behind the counter, they were still accessible and within our reach and anything within our reach was fair game as far as we were concerned.

One day, after we had gotten particularly bold with our thievery, we hatched a plan that involved me distracting the cashier by asking some random questions while Antonio and another friend grabbed some cigarettes and candy. We all waited in line and then when the customer in front of me finished paying for her groceries, I walked to the front of the cashier's line so that my friends would be behind her back. As I rambled off a bunch of questions and gave her my most charming smile, Antonio started stuffing his pockets full of Snickers Bars, M&M's and my personal favorite, Zotz. (Zotz were hard candies that had this powder inside of them that would fizzle in your mouth when you bit into them. I haven't had one in over 30 years and my mouth still waters just thinking about them!)

Antonio also grabbed a few packs of unfiltered Camel cigarettes, which would become our brand of choice, and just as he was reaching for another pack, the man standing in line behind him grabbed him by his collar. Antonio's first reaction was to take a swing at the man but before he could, the man grabbed Antonio's other hand and lifted him off the ground. That is when we realized that he wasn't some random customer standing in line with his groceries, he was store security and he yelled for all of us to stop. Our other friends took off running but I just froze, looking confused as my heart raced so fast that I was positive you could see it beating through my thick winter coat.

The man took us to a room at the back of the store and began to ask us our names, addresses, phone numbers and our parent's names. Neither of us would give him any information besides our own names; I'm sure we were both envisioning the ass whipping we would receive if our parents found out we crossed that street and even worse, were caught stealing. The security guard said he was calling the police and picked up the phone but we both thought he was just bluffing. We had seen Antonio's mother do the same thing hundreds of times; whenever we would do something she felt was deserving of a good ass whipping, she would always threaten to call the police first, then put the phone down and reach for the belt.

We sat there for what seemed like forever before a police officer walked into the room. My heart jumped into my throat and I thought I was going to pass out. We knew we were in deep shit then! Antonio started crying uncontrollably and immediately started emptying out his pockets and saying in between deep sobs, "I'm sorry, I'm sorry, I didn't mean to do it." The officer stood there staring at us menacingly with his hand on his gun before he finally sat down next to us and asked Antonio to calm down so he could talk to us. The only thing that I remember him saying was, "Ok, I am going to let you go this time but next time I'm going to call your parents and you are going straight to jail. Do you understand me?"

Both of us sat up straight and said "Yes sir, we won't do it again." I had never felt so relieved in my life! As the security guard walked us through the store and to the front door, he said, "If I see either of you little bastards in this store you are going to jail. Now take your little assess home." We walked away from the store fast with our heads down, not saying a word and waited until we were sure that no one from the store was still looking, then we both hauled ass home, running as fast as we could.

All of my earliest memories involve my mother or my maternal grandparents; my father was an inactive participant in my life from the age of two or three, so I have no memories of him at all. I saw pictures of him that my mother kept for me, one in particular that I would look at most frequently was my father and I carving a Halloween pumpkin together. I must have been 2 or 3 years old in the picture. My father, a dark skinned large man, had this medium size afro and was wearing a white shirt with a big collar on it, typical of the style in the early 1970's. I was wearing my pajamas and we were both smiling. Looking at that picture always made me feel that we enjoyed being together as we both looked content and comfortable in each other's company.

That picture was really all I had of my father so most of my early thoughts of him came directly from that picture or from conversations that I would sometimes overhear between my grandparents and my mother. My mother never spoke badly of my father in front of me and I am sure that is why, despite him not being in my life at all, I harbor no ill feelings towards him to this day.

I can't recall ever asking my mother about my father but I do remember my grandfather sitting me down one day and asking me what I thought about the man my mother had been dating. I was about four or five years old at the time and I didn't know what to say to my grandfather; I wanted to tell him that I didn't like my mother's new "friend," but I couldn't articulate why I was feeling that way, I only knew that I didn't like him, so I just stared at my grandfather and shrugged my shoulders as if I was indifferent. People tend to discount children and what they feel, in part because children lack the ability to effectively express their feelings and often their feelings manifest themselves in crying or acting out. My inability to express my dislike for my stepfather led to my simple shoulder shrug but my grandfather must have sensed something because he said, "Well I don't like him one bit. Your mother thinks you need a role model that you can relate to but he is not the role model for you."

I didn't understand what a "role model" was or why my mother would feel that I needed one. More specifically why she would feel that he would be the appropriate role model for me. I just knew that my grandfather didn't like him and that provided me with comfort, made me feel as if I had an ally that somehow understood what I felt. Knowing that made me feel safer with my grandfather, like he was able to somehow magically see into my mind and articulate my thoughts in a way I was unable to accomplish. I knew that what he was saying was right but I didn't know how to tell my mother how I felt. She was happy and smiling and as long as she was happy, I was happy, but that happiness would be short lived.

Many years later, when I was an adult, my mother confirmed my grandfather's thoughts and told me that she felt that I needed a black man in my life to act as a role model and help provide me with the cultural awareness that she could never provide. She possessed a smidgen of an idea of the struggles that I might have to face growing up identified as a black man, and she wanted to make sure that I was well equipped to deal with those struggles. She just chose the wrong black man as a role model.

My mother soon married Calvin and he became my stepfather. When my mother asked me how I felt about having the same last name as my stepfather, and now her, I just shrugged my shoulders. But after a few more conversations about the subject, I finally broke down crying and told her that I didn't want to change my name, that I liked my last name. I asked her why I should take the name of a man that was not my father.

I don't remember my mother's response but she asked my stepfather to talk to me and help explain why he wanted to be my "father" and what that would mean to him. This only made me more resistant to the idea and it was the first time I can recall becoming angry with my stepfather to the point where I yelled at him and my mother and stormed out of the room. When I finally stopped crying and just laid on my bed, I could hear them talking in hushed tones in the other room. Calvin was telling her that I would get over it, that I just needed a man in my life because my mother was babying me too much and that she was making me "soft." I was waiting for my mother to defend me, to say I wasn't soft and to tell him that he was not a part of our family, but she didn't say anything. She was silent.

This was the beginning of a very tense relationship between my stepfather and me. He was intent on breaking my mother from her "bad habits" of "babying" and "spoiling" me. I was intent on showing him that she was my mother and that the way she treated me was none of his god damn business. Despite my open dislike for him, we eventually all ended up at some lawyer's office so that my stepfather could officially adopt me. The lawyer asked me if I was happy that we would all have the same last name now and I told him flat out "no." My mother tried to explain her reasoning in the gentle, caring way that was her nature but that didn't matter to me, I did not want to change my name. I was born Jason Hutchings and I felt a loyalty to that name, and strangely to the father that I had never really known. The last thing I wanted was to take my stepfather's last name.

I was determined to not take his name but I was seven years old. I was unable to articulate my reasoning, unable to explain to my mother that I felt a loyalty to my father, and though he was not a part of my life, his name represented me and represented who I was. It was a part of me and I didn't want that to change. My stubbornness on the matter led to a small victory for me. My mother suggested that I keep my last name, Hutchings, as my middle name and I eventually agreed. We signed the paper work and I left the lawyer's office with my new name, Jason Corbett Hutchings Bost.

My stepfather came from a fairly large family and all of his family lived in or close to Elmira so we ended up spending a considerable amount of time with them. His grandmother, they called her Mamma, lived a block behind us, and his sister Renee lived in the housing projects across the street from the psych center where my mother worked. Their proximity to our house and my mother's job, soon made them the go-to babysitters for me. I never really felt like I was welcome at Renee's apartment. She seemed fake and distant and I felt that she was always full of negative comments about everyone, which always made me feel as if I was an outsider. The one thing I did enjoy about going to Renee's house was the opportunities it gave me to spend time with Patrick and Jon-Jon.

Jon-Jon lived in the adjacent housing projects to Renee. His mother would babysit Patrick so whenever I was at Renee's house, the three of us would spend most our time outside together. Jon-Jon was a chubby, red-haired, pale white kid with lots of freckles. No matter what, he seemed to always have a big, dull red Kool-Aid stain around his mouth. He was good natured and laughed and joked all the time. The three of us became inseparable partners and spent hours and hours riding Big Wheels. Jon-Jon was the first person we knew to have a Green-Machine, a Big Wheel that had levers on each side of the seat as opposed to a steering wheel. We would take turns riding that Green-Machine up and down the sidewalks over and over again.

We spent entire afternoons playing GI Joe, Dukes of Hazard and Battlestar Galactica, all using only our imagination, that Green-Machine and whatever sticks or rocks or trash we could find in the parking lot. We were all poor but Jon-Jon was really poor. I remember hearing Renee talk on the phone and saying, "I don't know why she allows Jason to play with that Jon-Jon boy. He's always dirty and his family is white trash." I didn't know what poor meant but hearing her say those things about him made me dislike her even more; in my eyes Jon-Jon was a friend and his mother always treated me like I was her own. When Jon-Jon ate, we would eat. As little as they had, she would always make sure we ate as well. That was the way most of my friends' families were. They would treat all their children's friends as if they were their own children. My mother was the same way.

My stepfather had two more sisters, Gladys and Valerie, both of whom treated me like I was truly their family. Gladys, the youngest of all his siblings, was very much a free spirit. She was light hearted and mischievous and loved to tell me jokes at which she would laugh hysterically even if I didn't understand them or find them funny. She was pretty, brown skinned, short and well-built and she was very popular with the young men in her neighborhood. Gladys introduced me to Afro-Sheen and showed me how to properly pick out my afro. Like Patrick's sisters, Gladys was a huge Soul Train fan and she would always have me stand up so she could try to teach me the latest dances. I loved her and admired her free spirit and rebellious nature.

Valerie was more reserved than Gladys but they both shared the same love of laughter. Valerie introduced me to Bill Cosby albums and Marvin Gaye. I would spend hours laying on the floor in the living room listening to Bill Cosby tell stories about the "donut glazed snotty nosed kid" and we would both laugh out loud until I had tears in my eyes. She taught me how to play Backgammon and Checkers. She would take me everywhere with her, always introducing me as her nephew. Right after my 11th birthday, while Val was nine months pregnant, she took me to every single shoe store in Elmira trying to find a pair of shoes to fit my narrow feet. We spent so much time running around that she went into labor and later that day, my cousin Paul was born! That is the way she has always been, totally selfless and caring.

My stepfather had a daughter from his first wife named Tara. I was about a year older than her so when she would visit with us, we were usually able to participate in activities that we both enjoyed. Seeing my stepfather interact with Tara made me realize that his interactions with me were unnatural and forced. His affection and attention to her seemed much more genuine. My mother confronted him about this on a few occasions which I overheard from behind my closed bedroom door or their closed door. My mother would question him about why he wouldn't take me places or do things with me in the same manner he did with Tara. He would dismiss her comments and chalk them up to jealousy on her part and continue the blatant unequal treatment of us both.

Despite this, I really liked Tara, especially after she confided in me her own secret dislike for her father. He had been married to her mother just prior to marrying my mother and their relationship ended with a lot of arguing and fighting. I remember hearing my mother talk about Tara's mother and comment about how unstable and crazy she was. My mother encouraged my stepfather to seek custody of Tara and from what I recall, he had the opportunity to take Tara full time but he didn't do it. He seemed much more interested in hanging out with friends and going out drinking whenever he could.

My mother was careful about starting an argument with him because any argument often ended with him physically abusing her. He was abusive to us both and it was not uncommon for him to beat me with a belt, or a wooden spoon or anything he could get his hands on. I don't remember the first time I saw him hit my mother but I remember that it happened often enough that it became a usual occurrence and that anytime voices became elevated, I would get tense with anticipation that soon he would raise his hand against my mother. To protect me, my mother would usually make me go outside to play or send me to a neighbor's house. When I would return, the house would sometimes be a wreck, furniture overturned and dishes broken and my mother would be crying as she nursed whatever injury he had just inflicted upon her.

I would spend hours in my room with my fists clenched so hard that my nails would cut into the palms of my hands. As I cried, I would try to gather up the courage to open my door and confront him, to yell at him "stop hitting my mother" but I just couldn't do it. My six-year-old mind could not formulate the courage to stand up to this grown man. I was painfully aware of the anguish my mother was suffering, and knowing that I could do nothing about it made me feel powerless which in turn made me angry, extremely angry.

There were so many instances of abuse that they all just seemed to blend together, but there is one instance that will forever be a part of me. It was a hot summer day and my mother kept pacing back and forth in our house, obviously irritated and upset about something. I overheard her on the phone with someone discussing that she found out my stepfather had been cheating on her with a woman down the street. Apparently, my mother had confronted the woman and the woman confirmed it so she was waiting for my stepfather to return home from work.

My mother told me to go outside and play but I made excuses as to why I had to stay home. I felt like I needed to protect her and that if I left, things could only get worse. I think my mother may have felt the same way because for some reason she let me stay and every so often she would sit down and hug me. In those brief moments it felt as if her stress had dissipated. My stepfather eventually came home and before my mother could even confront him about the affair, he opened the door, headed straight for my mother and started choking her, both hands around her neck, lifting her completely off the ground. He yelled at her, "What the fuck is your problem? Why are you starting trouble with Ellen? You need to learn to mind your fucking business bitch."

My mother's face was turning a reddish-purple color and she began to frantically struggle to get free. She looked at me as I stood in the living room, my eyes wide open in fear. At that moment I could see my mother's eyes asking me for help, asking me to do something, asking me to stop him from killing her but I stood there completely frozen. He must have seen the same thing in her eyes because he looked into the living room for the first time and saw me standing there he hesitated for a moment.

I snapped out of my frozen state and rushed over. Balling my little hands up into fists, I began hitting him in his legs with everything I had in me while simultaneously screaming at him to let my mother go. He was stunned for a moment and released his grip enough to enable her to slip free from his hands and slump down to the floor. He made a fist and pulled his arm back to punch me but my mother leaped from the floor and grabbed his arm while pushing me behind her at the same time. She pushed me towards the open front door and yelled at me, "Go to Antonio's house and call the police. Hurry and go now and stay there until they come."

Before I could make it to the door, my stepfather closed it and said in a calm, relaxed voice, completely out of place for that moment, "Go to your room. Your mom and I need to talk, everything is going to be ok, she is just upset." I looked at my mom for guidance as to what I should do as he was holding her by the wrist so she couldn't get closer to me. My mom, fearing that he might turn his anger towards me, told me to go to my room and that she would be ok. I slowly walked towards my room, never taking my eyes off him until I was standing inside the door to my bedroom. He followed me, bringing my mother with him by her arm and closed the door to my room.

I stood there, stunned at what had just taken place and fighting back my intuition which was telling me to go to Antonio's and call the police. I knew it wasn't over, I knew that both of them, for very different reasons, were attempting to remove me from the situation and my gut was telling me to run, run out the front door and run all the way to Antonio's house and not to look back or stop until I got there. But I was a child and I knew that I would have to get past him in order to make it out of the door. How could I make it past him when I hit him with all my might and he was able to simply ignore my attack, able to calmly talk to me and act like he hadn't even felt my hands as they struck his leg, as if I was a breeze of wind that could easily be ignored. So instead I ran to my bed and cried into my pillow, hitting my bed as hard as I could and cursing as I cried.

I don't know how long I stayed in my room but eventually I was drawn out by the muffled sounds of my mother's cries for help. I stood with my ear on my door, holding my breath while trying to make out what she was saying. I had to convince myself that I needed to open that door, that my mother needed my help. After a few minutes of weighing the consequences of opening that door, my instinct to protect my mother kicked in and I found the energy to exit my room.

As I walked towards the living room, the muffled sounds became louder. As I turned the corner into the living room, I could see my stepfather's feet and legs on top of my mother's feet and legs as they both lay on the couch. I entered the room and froze as I saw him naked, on top of my mother, covering her mouth with his hand and saying in a quiet, evil, menacing tone, "You do what I tell you to do. You mind your fucking business and listen. Do you understand me?"

Furniture was pushed out of place, lamps were knocked over and their clothes were scattered around the living room, with my mother's ripped shirt hanging off of her body. She looked up and saw me standing there and her eyes widened and got bigger than I'd ever seen anyone's eyes before. She struggled and bit his hand, he removed it enough for me to barely make out what she was saying, "Jason," she struggled and grunted, "please go call the police right now. Tell them he is hurting me," moving her head to try to free her mouth from under his hand, "tell them he is hurting your mother."

I didn't know what to do, I only knew that my mother was being viciously assaulted and she was in desperate need of my help. I started to walk towards the telephone in the kitchen when my stepfather told me to stop and go back to my room. "This is none of your business, go back to your room and your mother will be in there in a few minutes." Then he whispered something into my mother's ear, I could only make out a little bit of what he said, something to the effect that if I touched that phone he would beat the shit out of me. I froze not knowing what to do or how to proceed. My heart was caught in my throat and my eyes were beginning to blur with tears, my mind told me to go get the phone, to call the police, to help my mother, but my legs wouldn't move. My body refused to respond. Before I knew what was happening, the phone was in my hand and I was standing on my tip-toes reaching my finger towards the rotary dial when my father said, "Put that fucking phone down and mind your business."

I looked and saw him whisper something else to my mother as he viciously pushed his hand over her mouth. When he slowly moved his hand away, my mother said, in between sobs, "Go to your room, mommy is ok, we are just going to talk and I will be in your room in a few minutes." I wiped the tears from my eyes and my vision cleared enough for me to see both of them looking right at me, my stepfather as he lay on top of my mother, holding her arms down with the weight of his naked body pressed fully on her, and my mother as she lay there unable to free herself, face red and bruised and tears running down her cheeks. I wanted to stick my finger in that rotary and pull it down so that I could alert the police but fear took over and I found my emotions at odds with the life lessons that had always been instilled in me; respect your elders, follow their directions, do as your told.

I stood there with that phone in my hand for what seemed like an eternity before finally hanging it back up and slowly walking back to my room. I felt sick and dizzy and I could feel the anger raging inside of me. That was the first time that I thought about killing anyone. I seriously considered running into the kitchen, grabbing a knife and plunging it deep into his neck until the blood would ooze from him all over my mother and eventually drip down to the floor. I could see it clear as day but I just couldn't gather up the courage to leave my room. I couldn't let go of the fear that engulfed me, I couldn't make my 6-year-old mind convince my little 6 year-old legs to leave that room, so instead I just lay on my bed and cried.

3 COUNTRY LIVING

My stepfather, along with hundreds of others, was laid off from his job as a tool and die machinist. He eventually found a job in upstate New York, in a small rural town about thirty minutes outside of Rochester. His mother had purchased a home in the next town over so we packed up and moved upstate. I remember my grandmother being sad about us moving farther away. She never said it directly to me but I could tell by the way she talked to me that it was bothering her so of course, it bothered me also. Antonio and the entire neighborhood came out to wave goodbye to us as we drove off and headed to our new home.

Country living was a serious change of pace. Our house was located directly across the street from a cow pasture in which the farmer kept all his heifers. Heifers, for those that are about as "farm oriented" as I was, are female cows that have yet to give birth to any young of their own. Our rented home was a huge old farm house that was built in the 1800's and had a large red barn which was separated from the house by about 50 feet of unpaved driveway and parking space. The house sat on at least 20 acres and our closest neighbors were more than a mile away in either direction.

The house had 4 large bedrooms on the second floor, my room was huge, so big that when I would play with my toys on the dark wooden floor I could hear an echo bounce off the bare walls. The doors creaked whenever they were opened or closed and the house was so drafty that if the wind blew hard enough outside, the thin, see through curtains that hung from most of our windows would move as if they were a flag hung high on a flag pole.

By the time of our move, my sister was three or four years old and my mother had given birth to my brother Calvin, named after my stepfather. We left Elmira in the middle of my fourth-grade year and I transferred into my new school, where I knew no one and where I was the only person of color in my class. I always had an easy time making friends. Most of my peers liked me immediately and I usually ended up being the leader amongst them, not because I was the smartest or loudest of the group and certainly not because I was outgoing but because I was easy to get along with and I always managed to make everyone around me smile. I was actually a very shy kid. I've never enjoyed meeting new people in large groups and I've always shied away from situations in which I was the center of attention. But inside my own groups where I was comfortable and knew my peers, I would open up and allow them to be close to me and myself to be close to them.

Within a few weeks at my new school I had made a bunch of new friends and became especially close with a few of the boys that rode my school bus to and from school each day. The Smith boys and I became instant friends, they were the sons of the family that owned the house we lived in as well as the cow pasture across the street, and they had a large dairy farm where their own huge, old farm house was located. Their bus stop was the one right before mine when we were heading home and the one right after mine when we were headed to school in the mornings.

Occasionally when my mother had doctor's appointments with my little brother, I would get off the bus at their house and stay with them for a few hours during the week. These visits introduced me to life on a farm. As soon as we got off the bus, we would drop off our books in the house then head to the barn that housed the cows. The boys would prepare the electric milking machines while their father and a few farm hands would begin to round up the cows.

As each cow entered the barn, they would move quickly to a large trough filled with grain and begin to feed. The boys and I would then lock the cow's heads into a gate so that they could be milked. The machines used to milk the cows were stainless steel pots with hoses connected to tubes attached to the main pot. Each hose had a stainless steel suction cup that was placed on the cows utters by hand, this was our job. The machine would suck the milk from the cows utter then run the milk through tubes to huge storage containers in another area of the barn. The milk was then pasteurized and afterwards transferred to another storage container to be cooled and loaded onto large tanker trucks for delivery.

When the cows were all milked, they would release the cow's heads and the cows would be herded out through the back of the barn back to the pasture. As soon as the cows made their way out of the barn, their chores were done and we would usually have an hour or so to explore the farm before it was time to head into the house to do homework and eat dinner. We would climb to the top of one of the barns and make forts out of hay, play hide-and-go-seek in the cornfields across the street and venture into the huge silos where the grain was stored, bounce balls off of the walls and make weird noises then laugh at the echo. I loved playing on that farm but I could never get over the smells of the dirt and grime. A few hundred cows create an unforgettable smell, especially inside a confined space. I would always have all kinds of hay and grain and dirt in my hair when we would play, which I hated, but I loved exploring the farm and all the adventures we would have.

Every morning the Smith boys would be up by 4 a.m. to do their morning chores before they headed off to school. I learned that farming was extremely hard work and I also learned how much I enjoyed consuming something that I had helped nurture or harvest. The milk that came from those cows tasted better than any other milk I've ever experienced! The vegetables from their small garden, which we all helped plant and pull weeds from, appealed to me and I actually enjoyed eating them. Their parents were always busy doing work on the farm, cleaning, cooking, repairing the house or farm equipment. I can't recall ever seeing their father sit down, except to eat. Between the smell and dirt of the farm and the amount of work I witnessed the Smith family put into their farm, I knew that farming was definitely not the life for me.

My friends from the next bus stop after mine, the Denis's, had a pig farm and cultivated huge amounts of land to grow corn. I would usually play with them on the weekends, helping them feed their pigs and then spend hours and hours exploring their hundreds of acres of land. I discovered that pigs will eat anything. When the boys told me this I didn't believe them so we would experiment by throwing things into their pens. To test the theory, we threw rotten potatoes, chicken bones, dead birds and frogs into the pen. The pigs would scramble and push each other out of the way as they rushed over and ate it all. They had pigs that were almost as tall as I was, and had to weigh at least 600 pounds. We would pick up the piglets so we could hear them squeal and call for their mothers.

After we fed the pigs we would head over to a pond adjacent to the cornfield, so we could catch frogs, skip rocks and occasionally go fishing. We would round up bunches of frogs then subject them to all kinds of torture to see what would happen. We would throw them in the air as high as we could to see who could make their frog's guts splatter the farthest. We would throw them as hard as we could onto a barbed wire fence, seeing who could get the frog to stick on the fence. We tied M-80 firecrackers on the frog's backs, lighting them then running like hell before the frog exploded, sending frog legs and guts all over the place. We had the most fun using the frogs for target practice with a pellet gun. We tied them to a fence post and we all took turns shooting pellets at them, measuring our success by the amount of damage each shot would inflict.

One time we decided to play hide-and-go-seek in the corn fields. I took off running, determined that no one would find me, not considering that I had no idea where I was headed or how to get back. When I realized that I had probably run too far, I turned around and tried to head back in the direction that I had come. After walking for what seemed like an hour, I started to yell hoping that someone would be able to find me. No one answered back and panic set in.

Eventually I found a small hill and was able to barely see over the cornstalks and figure out a way to get out of the field. I was at least 5 football fields away from the road, but it was not one that I recognized. I made it to the road and realized that I was on the complete other side of the farm. It took me 2 hours to walk back to my house and I made it home just before dark. Frustrated and angry at my friends for leaving me out there, to this very day, I suck my teeth and shake my head in disgust every time I drive by a cornfield!

For a prepubescent boy, country living was a lot of fun. There was always an animal to torment or some new property to explore and I could go fishing anytime I wanted. By this time, Patrick and his family had moved to Rochester, New York, which was only about 45 minutes away, so he would often come spend the weekends with us out in the sticks. We found a pond that was about a half-mile walk from the house. We would take some snacks, grab our fishing poles and a tackle box, throw the poles over our shoulders and walk down the gravel stone road to the pond. In order to get to the pond, we had to climb through an electric fence which was never a problem as we were both skinny and pretty agile.

One day, after making it through the fence, Patrick announced that he had to urinate so he put his fishing gear down and unzipped his pants to relieve himself. I did the same except I said, "Hey, let's pee on the electric fence!" Patrick said, "Naw man, I'm not doing that, you can do it but I'm not." I gave him a look of disgust and said, "Man you're a chicken! You're afraid of a dumb fence? Well I'm going to do it," and I aimed myself directly at the fence and began to pee.

Patrick was watching in anticipation and I just gave him a disgusted look, as if to say "See, told you nothing would happen," when I felt a slight tingle. I said, "oh man, I just felt a . . ." and before I could finish my sentence a jolt of electricity shot up through my urine, through my penis and hit me in my stomach like a body punch from Mike Tyson, lifting me completely off my feet and knocking me flat on my back. I lay there, piss all over my pant leg, moaning and saying, "My dick, my dick, I think I broke my dick!" Patrick looked at me in shock and then busted out laughing hysterically, to the point where he fell on the ground as he pointed at me and reminded me, "I told you, I told you not to piss on an electric fence!" I eventually got up and shook my dick until I was convinced that it wasn't broken, zipped up my pants, gave Patrick the middle finger then started to laugh myself. To this day, Patrick will still bring that up and we both laugh until he cries.

By the time that first summer rolled around, a bunch of my friends were beginning to prepare for football practice. I had always played sports, my mother got me involved in baseball and bowling when I was four or five and I played every year, usually making the little league all-star team for baseball. My mother felt that sports were good for me and she would work hard to make sure I was kept busy and actively involved in some sort of sports year round. Seeing most of my friends preparing to play football, my mother asked if I wanted to play as well. My only real interest in playing football was the uniform. When she told me that I would get to wear pads and a helmet I was in!

My first days at football practice were very different than anything I'd ever experienced. The coaches were always yelling at us to get up or get down or run faster or push harder and everyone seemed to know exactly what to do, except for me. I was totally lost. It took me a few weeks to figure things out and by the time I did, we were fully suited up and ready for our first day of full contact in pads. We were doing the "monkey drill" where two players lay on their backs, tops of their helmets touching, one with a football and the other on defense. Laying parallel to the players are a row of tackling dummies and when the coach blows the whistle, the player with the ball has to try to get up and run by the defensive player before he tackles him.

They matched me against the biggest, strongest kid on the team, a big country white boy named Billy. Billy lived around the corner from my stepfather's mother's house in Newark and he was my closest friend in her neighborhood. Billy was soft spoken and reserved but on the football field, he was a monster! This was his third or fourth year playing and he was the star of the team, playing running back on offense and middle linebacker on defense. As we prepared to get down on the ground for the drill, I smiled and looked at Billy waiting for him to smile back but he just looked right through me with a look like he was going to try to kill me.

The whistle blew and before I could even fully stand up, Billy drove his shoulder into my stomach, wrapped his arms around the back of my thighs and knee, lifted me at least a foot off the ground and then, using all of his weight, slammed me onto my back. I let out a low grunt as the ball came flying out of my hands and everyone standing around us let out a collective "Oooooohhhh." I lay there staring up for what seemed like an hour before I tried to get up and when I did, I took a deep breath and I realized that I couldn't exhale. Panicking, I took a huge gulp of air and tried again but nothing would come out, the air was stuck in my lungs. I rolled over onto my side and I could feel the tears starting to flow down my cheeks.

One of the coaches came over and took my helmet off and said, "Relax Bost, you just had the wind knocked out of you. Relax and you will be able to breath soon." I thought I was going to die! When I finally caught my breath, it was time for wind sprints. Billy came over and asked if I was ok then ran the sprints with me. The whole time I was thinking that I wanted to rip his head off and I was already daydreaming about laying his big country ass out. I gained a whole other level of respect for Billy; that's the funny thing about young boys, the more physically dominant we are, the more we tend to respect each other. Actually, this respect for physical dominance seems to be a trait that stays with boys even as they grow into men, and is exhibited in man's fascination with sports and war, and an overall respect for another grown man, simply because they are able to physically best someone else.

I didn't start to come into my own on the football field until the season was almost over. Eventually I gained enough understanding about the game and what was supposed to take place, that I was able to slowly build some confidence, and with that came more playing time. My aggression seemed to grow in amounts that mirrored my confidence and soon I was laying into dudes and knocking the wind out of them, just like Billy had done to me. On the football field, aggression is feared, admired and rewarded and I had finally found a place where my anger could be unleashed without ever having to express a single word about why I was angry. I was finally able to break away from that shy kid that didn't know the difference between a running back or a corner back, and become a leader on my team, strictly through the application of aggression and athletic ability, and my teammates and coaches encouraged me to do so.

Our entire team was white; white coaches, white players, white cheerleaders, white parents, white fans at all the games. My stepfather, when he did attend the games, was the only person of color in the stands. I remember one of my teammates asking another teammate who the Nigger in the stands was there to watch. My other teammate, knowing that he was a part of my family, just-nodded his head towards me and they both looked at me slightly embarrassed and wondering if I heard them. I did, but I said nothing, I just pretended like I didn't hear a thing while my mind started racing, once again thinking about that word and how it applied to me.

I cringed in the rare occurrences that my stepfather would attend a game, not because of his race or the fact that I might hear the word "Nigger" a few more times, but because of the amount of abuse I'd witnessed him inflict on my mother and all the whippings he handed down to me. I never trusted him, I always watched him out of the corner of my eye and his presence alone was enough to make me anxious. My aunt Val, his sister, attended many of my games and I was always happy and proud that she was there, never feeling the anxiety that was a consistent reminder of my stepfather.

On February 6, 1981, my mother gave birth to my brother,

Calvin. Calvin was born healthy but after a few months he was diagnosed with Sudden Infant Death Syndrome, or SIDS. SIDS causes babies to stop breathing, often resulting in death or severe brain damage if the infant is not revived in time. While getting ready for school one day, my mother started screaming in a panic, "Call the ambulance, he's not breathing, he's not breathing."

When I went into the kitchen, my mother was holding Calvin and his face was turning a dark purple color. She started to perform CPR on him and in between breaths, she instructed me to call the ambulance, and told me what to tell them, then had me wait outside and guide them into the house when they arrived. By the time they got there, my mother had successfully resuscitated my brother and he was again breathing. We still rushed him to the hospital in the ambulance and stayed there until they transferred him to a hospital in Rochester, which was more equipped to address his issues.

When he finally returned home, he was given a heart monitor which would beep loudly if his breathing was interrupted. Even with the heart monitor, I would often go to his crib and place my hand on his chest or just watch his chest moving, listening and watching intently to make sure he was breathing. Later in life I would find myself watching my own children as they slept, looking to make sure their chests were moving and constantly placing my hand on their back to make sure I could feel them breath. My brother had at least two more episodes from which my mother had to revive him, one time we were alerted by the monitor and the other time my mother was holding him in her arms when it happened.

When he got a little older, his monitor would often go off, everyone would rush to his crib and he would be standing there, holding the wires he had just pulled out and smiling! He knew that if he pulled the wires out, the monitor would sound and everyone would come running and he approached it as if it were a game, laughing and giggling every time!

Eventually, my brother's health issues coupled with my stepfather finding a new job, led us to move to Rochester, a small city in western Upstate New York, located directly between Buffalo and Syracuse. My brother was seeing a specialist at Strong Memorial Hospital, one of the best hospitals in the area at that time, and it was around this time that the doctors found a large tumor on one of his kidneys. We soon found out that the tumor was cancerous and at the age of three, Calvin underwent major surgery to remove his kidney and then began chemotherapy treatments to help battle the cancer.

4 ROCHESTER

While my mother was busy attending to the needs of my very sick little brother, I was trying to adapt to my new environment. We moved into a house on Winbourne Avenue, in the Westside 19th ward neighborhood during the middle of my fifth grade school year. I left a rural school in Newark, where the only things I had to worry about was hearing the occasional use of the word Nigger, and entered a city school, where almost all of the students were black and where everyone knew each other and had grown up together. I was once again an outsider, but this time it was different, unlike my move to the rural school, very few of my peers accepted me as one of them, they tested me from day one.

Entering that classroom for the very first time was like culture shock to me. As I entered the class and was introduced by my teacher, who, unlike the student body, was white, I glanced around and saw the only faces that were smiling were the girls. They started giggling and whispering as all the boys gave me their hardest looks while checking me out. I wanted to turn around and run out of that classroom, run all the way home to my mother and tell her that this was not the place for me, that they had made a mistake. But I just sat down, put my head down and tried really hard not to make eye contact with anyone.

The girls in the class went out of their way to say 'hi' and introduce themselves, then run off and giggle. I wasn't into girls yet so their actions did more to embarrass me than anything else. The boys all watched as the girls would giggle and talk amongst each other about the cute new boy in class with the curly hair. So of course, within the first few days at my new school, the testing of the 'white boy' began.

One day, I was walking through the hallway, in a single file line with the rest of my class. As another class passed us heading the other way, one of the boys timed my steps perfectly, placed his foot out in front of me and tripped me, making me stumble into the boy walking in front of me. Everyone in his class laughed and pointed as I stumbled into one of the main boys giving me dirty looks the entire week. He angrily turned around and said, "What's your problem white boy? Push me again and I'm going to fuck you up." The other boys in my class snickered, slapping each other high-fives and instigated the situation by whispering in tones loud enough to ensure everyone could hear them, "Oooooooh, you better be careful Dominique, that white boy is going to beat you up!" To which Dominique replied, "oh, so you think you're tough? Today after school I'm going to beat your ass."

My heart raced as I looked around trying to figure out what to do. My instinct told me to punch him in his face right there, take my fist and try to knock his teeth down his throat, but my mind wouldn't let me do it. I couldn't formulate the courage to swing at him. Why did this boy want to fight me? What did I do to him? This was new to me, I didn't understand the rules or the social norms and why they were calling me "white boy?" I'd never been called that before. I'd been called black boy or a Nigger, but never had I been referred to as a white boy. My mind was racing, my heart was pounding and I was unable to speak or act, I just stared at the floor and continued to walk with the class.

For the rest of that day I had a sick feeling in my stomach as anxiety took over. Most of the boys in the class would look at me and pound their fist in their hands and point at the clock as they laughed and slapped each other five. For the first time I wasn't sure what to do. This was the first time that I had to deal with feeling like an entire classroom was out to get me. Feeling like I had absolutely no one to turn to and nowhere to go.

A few of the girls in my classroom told the boys to chill out and eventually one of the girls told the teacher that the boys were planning on fighting me after school. The teacher eventually pulled me out of the classroom and asked if I was okay. What was I supposed to do? Where I came from we never told the teacher on each other, that was a no-no and a surefire way to get your ass beat! I wanted to say, "I'm scared, I don't want to fight" but I couldn't bring myself to say anything so instead I just shook my head yes or no to her questions, fought back the tears and denied that anyone was planning on fighting. She knew better and kept me after school to "help me with some work." By the time I left the school, everyone was gone and I was able to walk home without a confrontation, but I knew the next day would bring more of the same.

I remember coming home and my stepfather asking me how my day went. I wanted to tell him what happened, the last thing I wanted was to tell my mother. She would get too upset and worked up about it, but telling my stepfather was not an option either. I had no trust in him and I knew there was nothing positive that could come from me sharing my fears with him. He would have told me to man up or beat me for not standing my ground with them, or would have told me that I needed to stop being soft and be a man. How could I get him or anyone to understand that being soft was not the issue? That it is hard to be a man when you have to face an entire classroom full of people that are threatening to beat you up? I didn't know what "being a man" meant but I did know that if it meant being like him, that a man was something I wasn't interested in becoming.

Eventually, after they got to know me, I became fairly popular with most of the kids at school. However, the real hard asses, the boys that thought they were super bad and worked hard to make sure everyone knew it, took an immediate dislike to me. I became the target of their taunts and eventually their physical assaults. In retrospect, I understand their position. I was the new kid, the pretty boy as some called me, that all the girls giggled about. All the kids that used to idolize the tough acting boys were now focusing their attention on me. When you're young and lack the proper guidance, insecurities that are a part of every pre-teen's ego become exaggerated and you become hypersensitive. Their defense against these insecurities was to attack anything that did not make them feel superior, anyone that took the social focus off them was seen as the enemy, and what better way to bring the focus back to them than to put their envisioned enemy on the spot. Especially if that enemy was different than them in some easily identifiable way.

I was aware of what people wore and how I dressed for the first time. Not because I cared about it, but because boys in school would crack jokes, something we called "drilling", on anyone that came to school with pants that were too tight, or shoes that everyone knew once belonged to an older brother or hair that was out of place. Lunch time was the most feared time of day. That was when the kids that could drill the hardest would move from table to table and pick out people to drill on. Anytime they would come to my table my heart would race and I would silently pray that they skipped over me.

Pre-teen years are filled with insecurities and uncertainties, and having someone expose things that you were already insecure about to an entire group of your peers can be devastating. I remember wearing a brand new pair of sneakers to school and never thinking twice about how they looked until my boy Richard drilled on them and said they looked like ugly ass snow-shoes that an Eskimo threw away. Everyone laughed and pointed at my sneakers. I spent the rest of the day looking at them trying to figure out why he said what he said. Often there was no real logic behind it. Many times the drills didn't even relate to the person or the topic at hand. If they were funny and people laughed, the insecurities would take over and do the rest. After that day my mother had to fight with me to wear those sneakers again even though no one said another word, I hated those sneakers and couldn't wait until the day that I got some new ones so I could throw them away.

After a while, I got pretty good at drilling and was able to hold my own with the best of them. However, it never failed, as soon as I would start getting the best of someone, they would immediately make a "white boy" comment. This only intensified after my mother showed up at the school a few times and my classmates got to see her. Then the white boy comments came almost daily and the wannabe hoods became much more aggressive, trying to instigate fights almost daily. They would rarely fight each other as deep down, they were really just scared kids trying to look tough. But an opportunity to fight a white boy was something that all of them wanted to take advantage of.

White kids were seen to be weak, less aggressive and usually easy victims to bully or to pick on as there were only a handful of white students at the school. So even if they stood together, they would still be vastly outnumbered and easily defeated in a conflict. Most of the white kids avoided the hoods and stayed to themselves. I avoided the white students like the plague, to be identified as being white or as rolling with the white kids would have meant even more torment and opened me up to more instances of fighting or being jumped. Most of the fights between the black hoods were head-up fights, one-on-one where the strongest, best fighter would win. Fights with the white kids always ended in four or five black kids jumping one white kid. I don't think I ever witnessed a single head-up fight between a black and white kid in elementary school, not once.

I wanted to shed anything that might associate me with being white, anything that might open me up to the vicious attacks that the white kids had to endure. I started to find excuses for my mother to not come to the school and tried to limit any opportunities that my classmates might have to be able to associate me with having any connection to the white world. My mother was always actively involved in my life, always signing me up for sports and activities and taking me everywhere. I began to wish she would just stay home and stay away from all the school events, the parent teacher conferences, anything where she could be identified as being my mother.

This in turn led to instances where I would embrace my stepfather's presence, however rare, at events and school gatherings. For my classmates to see that the man they all thought was my father, as being black, meant less torment for me, more acceptance and less chance of having to worry about being jumped. As much as I despised him in general, I grew to appreciate his presence in those situations and for the first time started to look to him for guidance to help me navigate this new world I had entered, looking for him to show me how a black man was supposed to carry himself. Unfortunately for me, my grandfather was right when he said that my stepfather was not the one that should be acting as my role model. In retrospect, he succeeded in demonstrating everything that a father, husband and more poignantly, a man should not be.

I was given the honor of being a school crossing guard. They gave me one of those orange vests with "Crossing Guard" written in big letters on the back and I couldn't wait to put it on. I was proud and walked with my chest out a little further until my first day on the corner, right next to the school, when a group of the wanna-be-thugs stopped on my corner waiting to cross. As soon as I held up the bright red "Stop" sign that all the crossing guards carried, I heard, "Look at the white boy, trying to be a teacher's pet," followed by loud laughter and finger pointing by everyone. That was my first and last day as a crossing guard. I felt stupid for being proud and cursed myself under my breath for feeling good about doing something that I thought was helpful. I vowed to never again put myself in a position to feel humiliated.

My mother realized something was wrong, I was always sad and withdrawn and rarely did I play with any friends from school.

Instead I spent most of my time with the girl that lived next door. We would play music, do arts and crafts and spend hours outside playing in her backyard. She helped me rediscover my love for music and we would listen to her father's cassette tapes in her basement and write down the lyrics to songs by groups like the J. Geils Band, Olivia Newton John, and Hall and Oates.

All of my free time was spent with her, and my stepfather suggested to my mother that it was weird that I wasn't spending that time playing outside with boys my age. His concern was not based on the troubles I was having at school that neither he nor my mother were aware of, but rather he expressed his theory to my mother in a conversation I overheard when he said, "I think that boy might be a fag or something. He never plays outside doing any boy shit, he's always up underneath that neighbor girl, playing dolls or something."

Of course, my mother was much more in tune with her eldest child and had long suspected that I was having some issues at school. When she approached me to talk about my time with the neighbor girl, she was much more gentle and focused on the unknown issues at school. I again dismissed her concern as being nothing but I did explode about what I overheard my stepfather say to her. She was stunned. She had no idea I overheard the conversation but she said, "You know he can be a jerk sometimes, don't worry about what he said." Conversations like that kept me close to my mother and acted as a reminder that we were on the same team, that for whatever reason this man was in our lives, she was not going to let him come between us. Despite our conversation, my stepfather convinced my mother that I needed to do more "manly" things so he signed me up to play football that summer and my journey with the Southwest Colts began.

My stepfather knew the head coach for the Pop Warner football team in my neighborhood so he took me to the field and introduced me to the coaches and told them about my experience playing the previous season. A bunch of the dudes from my school were playing on the team as well and a few of them nudged each other when they saw me and said, "Look at the white boy trying to play, we are going to eat his ass up." The team had already received their equipment and everyone was already engaged in full contact practice. Since I started late, I had to wait a week before I could get my gear and start full contact.

Because I was the new kid, the coaches immediately put me into the Monkey drill, the same drill in which Billy knocked the wind out of me the previous year. They matched me against Junior Praylor, one of the hardest hitting kids on the team, gave him the ball and blew the whistle. As everyone gathered around to watch, I could hear whispers of "Get that White Boy Junior" and "Lay his white ass out Junior." My heart was racing as I waited to hear the whistle blow and when it finally did, I jumped up, planted my shoulder cleanly into Junior's stomach, wrapped my arms around his legs, picked him up off the ground and slammed him down, hard on his back. The ball came flying out and I jumped off Junior, grabbed the ball and ran it the other way while he lay on the ground trying to catch his breath!

Everyone's jaws dropped. The coaches looked around stunned and slapped each other high fives and then the "Ooohs" and "Aaaahs" started. Eventually everyone started saying, "Damn, Jason laid him out" and "Oh shit, that dude can hit." After that day, there was no more talk about "white boy" this or "white boy" that, unless it was a player from another team or one of the guys on our team that was trying to get under my skin or simply hating on me.

That day they put me in the Monkey drill with damn near every one of the hardest on the team, Clinton Morris, Jack Dees, and Eric Granison. I held my own with all of them. By the end of the day, I had earned the respect of the entire team and quickly earned a reputation as someone that would lay your ass out on the football field.

Through football I was able to meet many of the guys that would be attending my new 6th grade school. #3 school, which everyone called Interim, was located in the Cornhill neighborhood, close to downtown Rochester. Because the school was not in my district, everyone in my neighborhood that attended Interim had to catch the city bus downtown and then transfer to another city bus that would take us directly to the school. Taking public transportation was my first real taste of freedom, and my first exposure to many of the young thugs from all over the city.

Every school day, kids from all over the city would catch the various city buses from their respective neighborhoods downtown on East Main Street. All the kids headed to my school would congregate by the bus stop on the corner of Clinton Avenue and East Main Street to try to be the first on the bus in order to get a seat. These trips downtown was my first experience with the serious beef between the West side and the East side. I heard small talk during some of our football games that "We hate those mother fuckers from Baden Street" but I never heard any reasons for it and just assumed it was a sports related rivalry situation.

There were fights almost daily, usually head-up fights between two dudes over some girl or because one of them called the other one a name or some other trivial issue. But sometimes a real beef would start and involve ten or twenty or even fifty guys from each side of town. Rarely did these large rumbles take place because of a spur of the moment occurrence. They were usually the result of an event that was instigated over a short period of time in which each prospective combatant had enough time to spread the word and gather their peers from their neighborhoods.

This was the early 1980's, I wouldn't say that Rochester had a serious gang problem. It was much more neighborhood based wherein groups of dudes that hung out together would usually back each other up during conflicts with those from outside their neighborhoods. It was not uncommon for adjacent neighborhoods to have beef with one another and frequently, fights would break out inside those neighborhoods. But whenever someone from any part of the Westside had a beef with someone from any part of the Eastside, the various neighborhoods would unite and each group would represent their entire side of town as one collective military type unit.

Most of the guys in these neighborhoods grew up with each other from birth or had known each other for years. I was the new kid on the Westside. Except for Patrick, I had only known my new friends for a few months to a year at most. This made me an outsider amongst those in my hood and meant that I had to worry about beef with those that didn't know me, even in my own neighborhood. I had earned respect on the football field amongst my teammates but there were plenty of young wannabe gangsters that had no idea who I was. They only knew that I was some light skinned new kid with no real ties to the area, thus with no real backup, so to them I was a potential victim waiting to happen.

My neighborhood was called the 19th Ward and consisted of mainly wide streets lined with full grown trees and large houses, most built in the 1920's and 30's. The houses in the area were sought after for their hardwood floors, stained glassed windows and really large amounts of floor space. The majority of houses had a driveway and a garage, a front yard large enough so the houses would sit at least 10 feet or more away from the sidewalks, and the backyards were usually good sized as well. Most of the yards were well manicured with neatly trimmed bushes and carefully tended to flowers and occupied by what would be considered middle class homeowners and working class tenants.

Some of the streets in the 19th Ward were nicer than others and for the most part, the well-maintained and manicured homes lay in the fifty or so blocks between Genesee Street, Thurston Road and Brooks Avenue down close to Arnett Boulevard. There were some rough streets to the west of West High Terrace composed of more double and multiple family houses, in more disrepair and occupied by lower income families. And most of the streets that ran between Genesee and Plymouth Avenue were the same, with Jefferson Avenue being what most would easily identify instantly as the hood. The farther down Genesee you went, moving east and closer to Chili Avenue and East Main Street, the more "hood" the area became, with scattered multiple unit apartment complexes, a few hole-in-the-wall bars and a low-income housing complex.

There were two high schools in the neighborhood, Joseph C. Wilson Magnet High School, where I eventually attended, and James Madison High School. Madison was almost exclusively all black and had a long-standing reputation for being one of the worst schools in the area. In 1975, a student shot a hall sentry when he tried to break up a fight triggering media attention from all over the country and further strengthening Madison's notoriety.

Our football team would practice at the Wilson High School field, which was located at the Arnett YMCA on Arnett boulevard off Genesee Street, and our games were usually held at the Madison High School field which sat between Genesee Street and Jefferson Avenue.

While there was a diverse mix of white and black working class residents in the middle areas of the 19th Ward, the neighborhoods on the other side of Genesee street were almost exclusively black and living well below the poverty level. Most of the kids on the football team came from the poorer areas and our games were always a big draw for the entire neighborhood. Most of the time, our home games would be free from any type of violence or conflicts off the field, but when the teams from the east side would come to play, there was almost always an incident, especially when we played the east side's Baden Street teams. One time, a game was interrupted when gunfire broke out as rival groups from both sides of town faced off, eventually leading to guns being fired close to one of the end zones while we were still on the field playing! The crazy thing is, after the crowds of young thugs that were responsible for the gun fire ran off in different directions, the referees blew their whistles and the game picked up right where we left off, like nothing ever happened!

Eventually things got so bad that the police started to work security for the crosstown games to make sure that no fights broke out. Many of the suburban teams refused to play us at home, partially because we would whip their asses so bad on the football field, but also because they were legitimately concerned about their safety off the field. Ironically, I remember feeling secure knowing that our entire neighborhood was out there watching our back and the intimidation factor towards the other team seemed to give us all a boost of confidence going into those games. Being young, the thought never once crossed my mind that a stray bullet could easily have struck anyone of us. Instead we reveled in the fact that other teams were afraid to play us at home and we embraced our serious home-field advantage.

The potential for violence outside of the field was not the only intimidation factor involved. Our Midget level team made up of the oldest kids, and our Junior Midget teams, both went two consecutive seasons without losing a single game, and both of the teams I played on went two seasons straight not allowing an opponent to score a single touchdown or field goal! Our neighborhood may have been full of gangsters and gangster wannabes but we also had some serious athletes and knowledgeable, dedicated coaches to help guide us.

One coach in particular, who everyone called Tootsie, was the roughest, hardest, foulest mouthed son-of-a-bitch you can imagine and we all loved him to death! Coach Tootsie was light skinned with what looked like an old burn or birthmark that discolored half of his face. He would grab me by my face mask, get right in my face and yell, "Bost, you fucking bastard, get your pussy ass up and hit someone like you mean it! You ain't no goddamn man, you hit like a bitch!" Then he would have us do the drills over and over and over again until we did them right.

Tootsie would always point me out and say, "Goddamn it, that Bost has heart! Now that's how you lay a mother fucker out!" Tootsie's approach would definitely be considered inappropriate by today's standards, but I never felt intimidated by him, only inspired. He helped make me a tougher, more focused player on the field. More importantly, off the field, he reinforced ideas of respect and taught me that I could push myself and accomplish things that I never imagined were possible. Last I heard, Tootsie had just turned 80 years old and he was still giving every single day to the kids from our neighborhood. How can you repay someone like that? Hopefully these words will begin to suffice and one day he will smile knowing how much of a positive impact he had on all of our lives.

While I earned everyone's respect on the field, off the field was a completely different story. I was cool with most of the kids on my team and there was a group of us that would always hang together outside of football. Clint Morris and Junior Praylor both lived on West High Terrace, one street over from my house on Elmdorf Avenue, so if I wasn't hanging out with Patrick then I was hanging out with them. Junior lived with his older brother Vincent and his dad, who was a coach for our team, Clint's mother was the team manager and was a constant figure at all of our games, cheering louder than anyone and attempting to inspire us with her support.

Many of the parents from our neighborhood were actively involved with the team. They would work selling hot dogs and soda at the games, help set up the field, transport us back and forth to practices and games and host events to help raise money for the team. These were the working-class parents, the parents with what most would have called "good jobs" at that time, most doing manufacturing work at Xerox or Kodak or IBM, all companies that were headquartered or started in Rochester. Single parent homes existed but they were not the norm at that time. Most of us came from a household with two parental units, and those of us that didn't, came from homes where the primary parent had a "good job." There were some on the team, maybe 30 to 40 percent, that came from what would be considered to have been "poor" or impoverished households, most with a parent or parents that were involved with drugs, unemployed or simply unable to hold down a job because of mental health issues.

While none of us considered ourselves to be poor, in retrospect, we were definitely what would now be called working poor. The manufacturing jobs barely paid a living wage and just provided enough money for some to purchase houses within the city. They would not be considered even close to middle class wages by today's standards. Alcoholism and drug use was commonplace, even among those of us coming from "traditional" two parent households. There were a few fathers that would show up to the games stumbling drunk, reeking with the smell of Wild Irish Rose, and we all saw plenty of fights between parents at our games and practices, but this wasn't unusual to us. This was just another day, just how things seemed to flow. It was our normalcy and it was all that most of us had ever known.

But I knew that there was another world. I knew that not everyone lived like this, I knew that not every football game ended with someone fighting in the stands or shots being fired. I witnessed life from a very different perspective prior to moving to Rochester. My previous experiences and lessons were in serious conflict with my new environment and laws that were required to survive within it. I experienced poverty before, I experienced violence and all the elements that come along with living in an impoverished environment, but those experiences were in mostly white or somewhat equally racially mixed environments. This environment was black, almost exclusively black, the rules were foreign to me and I was learning that my previous instincts could not be trusted.

Adolescence can be problematic for most as we begin questioning ourselves. Early planted seeds of self-doubt begin to receive nourishment and often grow uncontrollably into complex emotional gardens. A new environment with new rules, an environment in which most of your peers treat you as an outsider and mentally and physically attack you, further irrigates those seeds until they grow into a burdensome bush with tangled branches adorned with pain inflicting thorns.

The uncertainty and self-doubt associated with the pre-teen years was magnified for me as I was once again forced to confront the fact that, in the eyes of my peers, I was different than they were. My white friends were white, my black friends were black and I was both, yet neither at the same time. Most of my friends from the football team were sincere and genuine with their questions regarding my race. Usually, when we were alone, they might say, "Why is your mom white?" or "What are you? Are you white or black?" These questions immediately made me uncomfortable. I didn't have any answers, I didn't know why my mother was white, I only knew that she was my mother and I didn't know why my father was black. I damn sure had no idea what that made me!

I was fortunate enough to find a few good friends that seemed to be wise beyond their years and had very little interest in my racial composition. They asked an occasional question about my mother or father but it was no different than the inquiries I made about them or their families. Their questions came from a place of deeper learning, from a true curiosity about who I was and why we seemed to get along so well.

I never had a problem making friends, people, both old and young, have always seemed to enjoy my presence and usually within a few minutes of meeting me, most people feel comfortable and at ease. My mother told me that this was always the way people were with me, that babies would smile at me, strangers would start conversations with her about me and that girls of all ages always went out of their way to babysit or to simply say hi. She said she had never seen anything like it before. Now of course a mother's opinion of her child has the risk of being slightly biased, but at the risk of sounding completely full of myself, I would agree with her early descriptions and go so far as to add that those experiences have continued well into my adult years.

With my ability to meet new people, making new friends should have posed little to no problem for me, and it didn't, until we moved to Rochester. I found that the smile that always preceded my introducing myself to someone new was often greeted with a frown and a sucking of one's teeth or a hardened stare, especially from older guys. Before I could say anything they would greet me with a, "What you looking at white boy?" or "What you smiling at nigga?" I had no idea how to respond or why anyone would go out of their way to make someone feel so uncomfortable. Being friendly was in my nature and everything that I was taught supported this nature; be polite, make eye contact when you introduce yourself, be kind to people. None of this seemed to apply in my new world, and my adolescent struggles made me question myself. So of course I felt like I was the problem, like I was the one who was wrong and I realized that this new world was not going to change to accommodate me. Internal change was essential for my survival.

The bus rides to school provided an opportunity to study the cool dudes, the gangsters and the wannabes. I would sit on the bus and quietly listen to every word that they said, observe the way the older hoods dressed, walked and talked, even their body language. I would secretly imitate them, changing my position in my seat to mimic the way I saw them sitting. Whenever anyone would catch me looking at them, I would quickly dart my eyes towards the ground or look out of a window, do anything I could to avoid hearing someone say, "What the fuck are you looking at white boy?"

In the mornings, as we all congregated downtown waiting for the transfer bus to take us to school, I would meet up with some of my friends from the football team and practice some of the new slang I'd picked up on the bus; I would find ways to slowly inject my new vocabulary into conversations saying things like, "Yo that hat is fresh," and "Yo, chill Nigga." The term "Nigga" was used in almost every sentence to mean a variety of different things. "What's up my Nigga?" was a way we would greet each other, or "Yo, that's my Nigga right there," would be used to let an outsider know the person being referred to was a friend.

The word was used so frequently and so often that I quickly forgot about how I had once beaten the shit out of a kid damn near every day because he referred to my sister as a "Nigger." But there was a definite distinction in who could use the word and any one considered white could catch a serious beat down for including it in their vocabulary. A few times, when passing a rival group of teenage boys from across town or outside of our neighborhood, someone would stop us if they heard me say it, and say, "Who the fuck you calling Nigga white boy? We should fuck you up right now." Both groups would stop walking and generally, before I could even say a word, someone from my group would say, "he ain't no white boy mother fucker, keep it moving, you don't want none." After hard looks were exchanged and fingers were pointed, everyone would continue on their way but someone would always yell a warning to me and let me know that if they caught be by myself, it would be on and popping.

Besides the trips to and from school, #3 school was a much more accepting and much less hostile environment compared to #37 school. The school was extremely diverse with students and teachers representing a true cross section of the racial and socio-economic spectrum. The majority of students came from homes in which the parents were actively involved in their children's education and as such, pushed hard for their kids to get accepted into the school.

It was not a traditional public school in the sense that only those in the neighborhood could attend. Instead it was a magnet school that had much higher academic standards and meant students had to take tests and be placed on a list from which they were chosen, in order to attend. The school's curriculum was focused on technology and they were one of the first schools in the country to provide computer classes. Ours was the first to have computers in our classroom and we all took computer classes on the brand new Radio Shack TRS-80! In about 15 minutes, we would write programs that would use all of the memory in the computers and they would set aside 10 minutes at the end of each class for us to save our work onto cassette tapes. It is laughable now but at that time, those computers were cutting edge and we all felt special to have been chosen to participate in those classes.

The focus on higher academic standards helped take away some of the negativity generated by academic success that would often come from my peers. School was not considered "cool" and most of the cool kids, the kids that everyone looked up to and admired, worked hard to at least portray an image that school was "whack" and uncool. This was certainly the case at #37 school, where consistently doing your homework would mean that someone would call you out for trying to "act white" and eventually lead to someone challenging you to fight. The belief was that if you were concerned with school and academic success then you were "trying to be white" and everyone knew that whites in that setting were bound to get their asses kicked.

Most of us at #3 School knew that we were there because we

had earned the right to be there, and the racial and economic diversity, as well as the focus on academics, took away some of that "trying to be white" stigma when anyone showed success in the classroom. However, there were still plenty of knuckleheads at the school and plenty of wannabe gangsters to challenge anyone they thought were weak.

Before attending #3 school, my short time at #37 school made me self-conscience about participating in the classroom and definitely made me think twice before I answered a question that might provide my classmates an opportunity to perceive me as trying to be "white." I learned fairly quickly that the white kids caught hell and the quickest way to draw unwanted attention to yourself was to "act white."

While #3 school was racially diverse inside of the classrooms, outside of the classrooms, in social settings, the school appeared just as segregated as any school you might imagine existed in the deep-south during the 1950s. This became apparent to me during the first school dance I attended. The dances were held inside the school gymnasium, which had a large sectioned wall that could be pulled out to divide the gym into two equally sized separate gym rooms. Both sides of the gym were decorated identically, with colorful streamers hung overhead, connecting the basketball rims at all sides of the gym, and student created posters hanging on the walls representing some of the anti-drug slogans being promoted at the time by Nancy Reagan's "Just Say No" campaign.

Walking into the gym created an unanticipated racial epiphany; the social division that I previously was only subconsciously aware of was now laid out literally, in black and white. One side of the gym contained all but a handful of the white students and the other side was almost exclusively black and Latino. While the scene shocked the conscience, it was somewhat understandable once you heard the music blaring out of the speakers in the separate sides. The white side was playing records from AC/DC, Metallica and Journey and was filled with giggling white girls, adorned in black lace gloves, skin tight Jordache jeans and t-shirts that exposed one or both of their shoulders, all dancing among themselves in the center of the gym. Gathered around the walls of the gym in small groups, were their white male counterparts, wearing AC/DC t-shirts, spiked wrist bands, and ripped jeans with chains dangling from the wallets in their back pockets. The "white" side of the gym was policed by almost all white teachers and the parents of the students, who were obviously also all white.

The speakers on the other side of the gym were vibrating to songs by hip-hop groups like Run-DMC, Whodini and the Fat Boys, and R&B groups like New Edition, the Gap Band, and of course Michael Jackson and Prince. The Black and Latina girls congregated in small groups spread out in the middle of the gym, wearing the same styles as their female counterparts on the "white-side" of the gym, except every single girl on this side of the gym was wearing a shirt covered in Michael Jackson, Prince or New Edition buttons. Just like on the other side, the male students all hung around the wall of the gym in small groups, watching the girls dance and teasing each other about being scared to go dance with one of the girls. The boys were wearing shell-toed Adidas or suede Puma sneakers with fat shoe-laces that matched their tight-fitting polo shirts and colored Levi jeans.

As any pre-teen would do, I advocated fiercely for my mother to just drop me off and not chaperone the dance as she had intended on doing. Entering the gym, I felt an immediate sense of self-consciousness as the internal conflict of my own racial identity seemed to be magnified 100 times by the literal division of the races in each separate side of the gym. I was incredibly thankful that I did not have to walk into that divided gym with my mother as most of my friends were on the "black-side" and I know my mother's white skin would have subjected me to spoken and unspoken ridicule from my peers. While my friends all knew that my mother was white and my father was black and seemed to accept me without looking at me as being different than they were, I knew that my mother's presence would surely create issues with those outside of my circle and I was certain I would find myself once again attempting to protect myself from those looking to jump a "white boy."

I felt guilty for feeling relieved that my mother hadn't come in with me. I knew she only wanted to see me enjoy myself, and as much as I said I didn't want her coming to any of my events, I enjoyed having her there, knowing that I had someone on the sidelines or close by that was there for my support. Part of it was just adolescent rebellion but a larger part was knowing that her presence may draw attention to the fact that I was racially different than my peers, that they could justifiably call me "white boy" and that I would have to deal with the physical and emotional consequences of their taunts and attacks.

Dealing with my heightened insecurities caused by the racially divided gym was bad enough, but my true fear was that one of those girls that would always giggle and say hi whenever I walked by might work up the courage to walk across that gym and ask me to dance in front of everyone! As much as all of my boys bragged about what girls they were going to "get with" and what they planned on doing to those girls when they "got with them," most of us were scared as hell to do anything that might actually give us an opportunity to get close to a girl. But that fear was no match for the hormones that were now starting to heavily influence my body and my thoughts.

My heart felt like it would beat right out of my chest when I would look up and see a group of girls looking in my direction, a part of me prayed they wouldn't say anything, but another part of me was begging for a chance to talk to one of them, for a chance to "get with" one of them, despite not knowing what "get with" meant.

It was at these early dances that I started to realize that I was pretty popular with the girls. Girls had always made themselves comfortable around me and I always had plenty of female friends, but the dances were the first time I noticed them really "noticing" me, and it was the first time that I realized that I was starting to "notice" them as well.

5 HIP HOP

The dances would consist of my group of friends talking amongst ourselves and watching the girls as the girls talked and watched us. I had no idea how to dance with a girl, especially not to a fast song, I'm pretty sure most of us didn't. But what we all knew how to do was B-Boy or breakdance and pop-lock. We would spend hours practicing almost every day, lugging big pieces of cardboard boxes downtown with us. Someone would always have a boom-box with them, a huge radio that they would carry on their shoulder, Run-DMC blasting out of the speakers. We would put the cardboard down on the ground, while someone would hold the radio, rarely putting the radio on the ground because everyone thought that contact with the ground would drain the batteries faster, and then all of us would take turns showing off our moves.

The break-dancers, we called B-Boys, would bop to the beat and start to showcase their legwork as they eventually made their way down to the ground. Some B-Boys were known for their footwork, using intricate moves to kick one foot up in the air while the other one stayed on the cardboard and their hands would move in unison to the music. Some B-Boys were known for their ability to incorporate their legwork into elaborate routines where they would do flares and moves that made them look like Olympic gymnasts. Others were known for their ability to spin on their backs, round and round, over and over and then turn their back spins into what we called windmills. They would grab their crotch with their hands, spin off their back and shoulders and flip themselves from their back to their front, over and over again. Some B-Boys even had head spins in their repertoire and would go from a headstand into a series of spins on their head until they eventually removed their hands from the ground and would literally spin using nothing but their head and neck.

The best B-Boys could incorporate all the elements into a routine; legwork, backspins, jump up to more legwork, then bust out a few flares into some windmills and end in a B-Boy pose and the crowd that would always gather to watch would go wild! Then there were the pop-lockers, dudes that would move their bodies stiff like robots or look as if their arms and legs were liquid, with no bones or joints in them. If you could pop-lock and breakdance, you were truly the shit, especially if you could do it with your own style, unique to anyone else's. Originality was the most important aspect of B-Boying, anyone seen duplicating the moves of another one was deemed to be a "biter" and biting someone else's moves was considered to be a crime punishable by serious ridicule or sometimes even an ass whipping. But most of the time, if you had an issue with someone, you would simply battle.

Battling was how everyone earned their reputation as a B-Boy with the crowd's response determining the winner. The breakers each took turns on the cardboard or floor, showcasing their moves and pointing out their opponent. Sometimes, entire crews would battle each other, with members of each of the crews taking their turns to come out into the center of the circle that would form around them, and give the audience their best moves. Pop Lockers would usually battle other pop-lockers Someone busting a windmill from one crew meant the breaker with the best windmills from the other crew would come out and show their best moves.

The biggest battles always took place at the roller skating rinks. Skating rinks were where everyone went on weekends and each side of town had their own respective rinks. Friday nights were usually spent at USA Skates on the Eastside of town and Saturday nights were for Olympic Skates, on the Westside of town. People went skating for three things; so that guys could meet girls and vice versa, to breakdance or battle, or to fight.

Everyone would be dressed in their best outfits. Girls would wear skin tight Jordache Jeans, suede boots and sweatshirts with their names or their boyfriend's names on the back. Dudes wore fresh suede Adidas with fat colored shoe-laces, breaker belts labeled with their names or nicknames across the front on the belt buckle. In the winter time everyone wore Shearling sheep skin coats or bomber jackets with fake fur linings around the hoods. The breakdance crews would have on matching sweatshirts with the name of their crews on the back and their nicknames on the front or down the sleeves of their shirts. It seemed like everyone called themselves "Ski," Jay-Ski and Tee-Ski or they would take their first name and just use their last initial, like Billy B. or Sam T. The really cool dudes would have original nicknames, like "Cheese" or "Big Bully" or "Smash" and everyone would be strutting around like they were the "Baddest" thing to ever walk the earth.

Most of us didn't go to actually skate, we went to socialize and wait for the fights to break out so we could all watch. There were however, some serious skaters, girls and guys that moved smoothly on skates. They would weave in and out of the slower moving skaters, perform tricks and skate backwards or do the latest dances, all while going as fast as they could around the rink. They made it look so easy that every once in a while, after watching them, I would be convinced that I could skate and I would grab a pair of rented skates and hit the rink. Usually not soon after, my ass would end up hitting the floor! Skating was definitely not my thing so I stuck to just hanging with my crew and watching the older kids talk to girls and fight.

I was shy around crowds or people I didn't know, and lacked the confidence to get involved with the larger B-Boy battles that took place. We were still younger than most of the serious B-boys so most of us would just watch admiringly as the really "fresh" breakers got busy. Fresh was a term we used for everything, but mostly to describe something we thought was trendy or stylish or just plain cool. We would say, "Yo, that outfit is dumb fresh" or "Damn, did you see his windmills? They were fresh to death." And if something was not up to par or we felt that a move was weak, we would say, "That shit is whack." Many fights were started because someone called someone else whack, or accused someone of biting someone else's moves or rhymes.

We did not know it at the time, but we were in the midst of a cultural revolution. The Bronx had just given birth to Hip Hop a few years earlier and the brand new Hip Hop culture associated with it, permeated every aspect of our life, from the slang we spoke, to the music we enjoyed, to the rhymes we all wrote and practiced, to the B-boy battles we participated in. Hip Hop became embedded in our DNA. It was not a way of life for us. It was life itself!

We lived by the principles taught by the culture and spread by the lyrics in many of the songs we enjoyed. Hip Hop consisted of five basic elements; Emceeing (and Beatboxing), DJing, Graffiti art, B-Boying, and knowledge of culture. My first real introduction as a participant in the culture was through B-boying, but I soon discovered Graffiti and my life was dominated by practicing breakdancing and creating new drawings, called "pieces," in my art books.

Graffiti and witnessing a school bully get his ass beat while at

#3 school, led me to meeting Reggie. Reg was short and thin, medium complexioned with a smile that you could see coming all the way down the hallway. His homeroom was down the hallway from mine and we would see each other in passing but never really hung out or spent much time socializing.

One of the older bullies who was about twice the size of Reg, took things a bit too far and pushed him into a locker. Reg spun around off the locker so that he was standing directly in front of the older student, and snuck him in the eye with a left hook that was so fast that no one saw it coming! The older dude fell back, slumped over and slid down the locker to the floor, holding his eye with a totally surprised look on his face. The only one that looked more surprised was Reggie. He kept looking down at his left hand, which was still balled up in a fist, and looking at the older student's eye, as it grew more and more swollen until it completely shut in just a few seconds.

There were only a few people in the hallway when it happened but everyone let out a collective, "Daaaaaaaammmmmnnn" followed by finger pointing at the dude's grossly disfigured eye and loud laughter. Reg, having no idea what to do next, just shrugged his shoulders and started smiling his regular, big ass goofy smile, bopped down the hallway and headed straight for the principal's office. I had to go to the office for something unrelated and when I saw him in there I slapped him a high-five and we both looked at the older student as he sat across from us and laughed. He looked up, holding a bag of ice on his swollen eye, and said "What the fuck are you laughing at?" Without missing a beat, Reg said, "Laughing at you, you one-eyed Cyclops looking sucker," and we busted out laughing some more!

As I waited for my turn to see the principal, I was doodling on a piece of paper, nothing fancy, just drawing my name in some graffiti style letters. Reg looked over and said, "That's fresh. I write too." "Writing" was what we called creating graffiti style artwork. Soon after that we started hanging every day, writing graffiti, drilling on people and just hanging out in general.

We also shared a love for Hip Hop music and we would spend every Saturday night listening to WRUR, the local college radio station, which showcased Rochester's only true underground Hip Hop radio show. DJ Rondell Claiborne had a show on WRUR and we would get blank cassette tapes ready and tune in so we could record our favorite songs. Listening to those radio shows was more like an event, something that we would look forward to all week. We would sit down, listen to the show, talk and design new graffiti pieces. Hip Hop bonded us for life. Our similarities strengthened that bond and our differences seemed less significant because we shared the same passion for a culture that we were helping spread and develop.

While we spent most of our time doing graffiti and practicing breakdance moves we also started to make some time for our growing interest in girls. My experiences at the school dances and skating opened my eyes to the fact that girls were really starting to occupy much more of my thoughts. Actually, they were starting to dominate all of my thoughts. It seemed girls that I previously never really noticed before, had developed breasts and hips overnight. Now the tight designer jeans that they wore really accentuated their hips and thighs, and I started to really notice the way the jeans would hug their behinds and the way their t-shirts now seemed to be completely full and form fitting. It was as if I went to sleep one night and woke the next morning dead smack in the midst of puberty. Most of my friends were going through the same thing. Our conversations were now dominated by discussions about which girls had the best bodies and rumors about which girl was known to be sexually active or who had given who a blow job behind the bleachers on the football field. It seemed like every conversation would eventually lead to some sort of sexual discussion, that every single one of our thoughts was somehow focused directly on our growing sexual desires.

It was around this time that I started to become more self-conscience about my clothes and how my hair looked. I distinctly remember starting my 7th grade year with a pair of plain Levi jeans, a pair of sweatpants, a couple different T-shirts, a sweater and one pair of Kangaroo sneakers with the zipper on the side. I created a schedule for myself so that I could mix and match my clothes to create the maximum number of different outfits throughout the week. This system was working fine for me until I found myself engaged in one of our daily drilling sessions during lunch time. I was drilling this dude about this raggedy wig his mother would always wear and everyone was dying laughing. Just before the bell rang to signal the end of the lunch period, he stood up and said loud enough for the entire lunch room to hear, "Ah nigga at least my momma can change her damn clothes. You just mad because all you have to wear is those same dusty ass sweatpants with that same ugly ass T-shirt every day!" Everyone from my table, the lunch table behind mine, and what felt like the entire lunch room started cracking up laughing and pointed at me saying, "Damn, Jason's sweatpants are dusty!"

Normally I would have a comeback for any drill that anyone could throw my way, but I just looked down at my sweatpants as I could feel the embarrassment rushing over me knowing what he said was true. I felt exposed, like everyone was now aware of my secret, the fact that I only had two pairs of pants, and that now all eyes were on me and my clothes. I had been drilled before for many things, my hair, the fact that I was knock-kneed, my mother's station wagon, and sometimes I would think about those things. I would usually try to just laugh at myself and accept the humor in what was being said, but this was different. Puberty and hormones coupled with the insecurities associated with that time in a young person's life made those words stick to me and I became so self-conscience that I didn't wear those sweatpants again for at least a month, which meant that I had to wear my same pair of jeans every day.

Patrick was in the same boat as I was. He had only two or three pairs of pants himself, so we started sharing each other's clothes so that we could make it seem like we had more options in our wardrobes. It worked out great for Patrick, I was taller and heavier than he was so he could put on a belt and roll up the bottom of my pants to make them fit him perfectly. I, on the other hand, had to squeeze into Patrick's pants and wear boots to cover up the fact that the bottom of the pants sat about 2 inches above my ankle, creating what we called "high waters" and definitely drawing unwanted attention that would lead to someone else drilling me about my pants. This was the first time that we were forced to confront the fact that our families didn't have much money and that there were things that we now wanted that our families were unable to provide.

My insecurities led to me avoiding that lunch table at all costs for at least the next few weeks, and it wasn't until a girl that I had a huge crush on asked me why I didn't sit at the table anymore during lunch, that I finally got up the nerve to go back and sit there again. She told me she would save a seat for me and that she had something she wanted to tell me. For the rest of that day all I could do was day dream about what she would say to me. I envisioned myself sitting next to her and her wrapping her arms around my neck as she pulled me closer to her so she could whisper her secret into my ear. Just that simple thought was enough to make me completely forget about any of the embarrassment from before and my imagination started to really run wild, with me daydreaming about kissing her and touching her plump, firm breasts.

When I finally made it to lunch, I looked towards the table and saw her sitting there with a few of her friends. They were all looking towards the door and when I entered they all started to giggle and whisper to each other. My heart beat faster and faster the closer I got to the table. She moved the lunch tray she was using to save my seat and looked at me with a shy confidence as I sat down next to her. My heart was now beating so hard that I could hear my pulse throbbing in my ear-drums, my mind was racing with thoughts of what she was planning on telling me. She said, "Hi Jason," and all her girlfriends started to giggle and whisper among themselves again. I was not the type to be at a loss for words, but I was so uncomfortable that I did not know what to say, so I just looked at her, and for the first time, I noticed how unbelievably beautiful she was. Her skin was the color of light brown sugar and her lips were plump and perfectly shaped, her eyes twinkled as she smiled at me and I found myself once again day dreaming about her, only she was sitting right there, right next to me.

She leaned over to whisper in my ear and I noticed how good she smelled, not like perfume, just clean, and fresh, exactly the way I thought a beautiful girl should smell. I inhaled deeply, really savoring her aroma, and held my breath as she began to speak slowly and softly into my ear, "I just wanted to know if, ummm, if you liked me because I like you and, ummmm, I want you to be my boyfriend." I paused for a moment and just looked at her, saying nothing, trying to gather my thoughts, I wanted to jump up and shout, "HELL YEAH I'll be your boyfriend," but I kept my composure, swallowed hard to keep down the anxiety building up in my chest, put my arm around her and whispered back in her ear, "Yes, but only if you'll be my girlfriend."

As we whispered back and forth, her girlfriends were sitting on the edge of their seats, biting their nails, shoulders hunched tightly as they looked at our faces for any sign indicating what my response was. She looked over at them and showed them a big smile then they all giggled loudly and grabbed her, taking her out of the lunch room so she could share the details with them. Reg and Patrick and a few of my other boys were sitting at the table and Reg came over and gave me a high five and said, "Oh shit, you're the man!" I was riding on a high that I had never felt before and I wasn't really sure why. I had no idea what a boyfriend was supposed to do or what I was supposed to do next, I just knew that one of the prettiest girls in school liked me and let me know it and that was good enough for me.

It seemed that a lot of my friends were getting into girls at around the same time. We were all finding ourselves attracted to girls that just the year before we didn't even realize existed. A lot of the girls had started to "like" boys the year before, but most of us were so oblivious to them, that it was embarrassing once we realized later that they were giving us open opportunities to "like" them back. This was a brand new world for us but the dudes that were older than us had been actively pursuing girls for the past year or two, and they loved sharing their exploits and providing us with tips whenever we were around. There is a huge difference in maturity between a twelve-year-old 6th grader and a fifteen-year-old 8th grader. We would watch the older dudes in awe as they bopped through the hallways, wearing designer jeans, and talking to every girl that walked past.

I started to study them, watch the way they walked and emulate the way they talked, thinking that if I acted more like they did, that I would be able to get with the older girls in the school. A lot of them were fully developed, I mean bodies that put grown women to shame, and the rumors were that a lot of these girls, actually most of them, were more than willing to have sex. Some of the older girls would see me in the hallway and say to their friends, "Oh, he is a cutie" or "If he was older I would show him a thing or two." While I was secretly praying one of them would approach me, I was still far too shy to say anything to any of them, and besides, almost all of them had boyfriends that were 8th graders, and a few had boyfriends in high school.

That never stopped a couple of my boys from trying to get with them. My boy Peter Campbell, we became close because his birthday is just three days before mine, was confident and aggressive with the girls. Pete was skinny as hell, brown skinned with a long jheri curl and he was always joking around and laughing with or at someone. He would bop down the hallway and bump into one of the older girls, brushing his hand against her breasts or pretend like he was falling down and reach up and grab her ass, acting like that saved him from falling. Most of the girls knew what he was doing and they would either laugh it off or occasionally, one would slap him hard, or invite him to fight. Pete didn't care, either way he would laugh and say, "Damn girl, thank god you had those big ass titties or I would have fallen straight on my face!"

Eventually, everyone started to grab and grope girls in the hallways, especially the girls that didn't protest. Those would be the ones that would be targeted as potential girls to "get with." The girls that would punch you, slap you or seriously get upset when they were touched would usually be left alone or put in the category of "girlfriend material" as nobody wanted to seriously get with any of the girls that all of us could touch. In retrospect, this was a form of sexual assault at its worst, and was definitely harassment, but I think we viewed it as a physical form of flirting and we used it to figure out which girls would probably be willing to let someone get a kiss, or grind up on, or maybe even have sex. It was a way to thin out the herd, isolate the individuals that we thought we had the best chance of having sex with and then focus our individual energies directly on them.

Looking back, it is easy to see how a young girl with insecurities would allow boys to touch her under the guise of playfulness. Adolescence is a confusing time for everyone, and a young girl who is unsure of her self-image may welcome attention from boys, even if it is inappropriate or harmful. Reflecting back to this time in my life has reminded me of the importance of raising strong minded, confident and self-assured young ladies and making sure that they are aware of their true value and that their bodies should be respected at all times, by everyone. As a father, I know that if I saw one of these little dudes grabbing my baby's body parts, I would seriously have to restrain myself from breaking his little ass down!

Most of the older dudes would talk about how fine "red-bone chicks" were, and make fun of the darker skinned girls. There was a clear preference for red-bones, light skinned girls, over darker skinned girls. This was usually the case with the girls as well. They would openly make fun of each other or boys for being "dark as the night" while they would talk about how fine this light skinned boy was or how cute this yellow dude was. The racial preferences of most of my peers placed me at the top of this racial hierarchy with the girls, and made me a target for the dudes. This skin color preference was not just present in my peers, it seemed to permeate most of the Black and Latino neighborhoods, and it was not uncommon for darker skinned Puerto Ricans to be called "Niggers" or "Darkies" and treated as if they were second class citizens within their own communities.

Girls also introduced us to the concept of "good hair," hair that was curly and not thick, tight, kinky or "nappy." Every day a girl would ask me if they could touch my hair or they would comment about how I had good hair, sometimes calling it "baby hair." Of course, I loved the attention and never objected to anyone running their fingers through my hair, but I also noticed all the dirty looks I would get from the dudes with natural style hair, what many would have considered to be nappy. I soon found that the fascination with "good hair" went beyond the girls in my school and extended to their mothers and grandmothers. On more times than I can recall, a girl would introduce me to her mother or grandmother or older sister and the first thing that they would say was, "Mmmm, mmmm, mmmm, you have some good hair!"

All the importance placed on hair contributed heavily to me wanting to get a jheri curl, a popular style at that time worn by both black men and women. A jheri Curl was a chemical perm that gave hair long, loose curls that would be moisturized with curl activator products like CareFree™ Curl Activator. CareFree products came in a plastic yellow spray bottle, labeled with red lettering, and would be sprayed onto the hair to make the curls appear shiny and give them a moist, greasy feel. Curls were so greasy that they would leave greasy marks on furniture, clothing or anything that the hair came in contact with. Even though it was expensive to get the perm itself, and the products to maintain the curl were also costly, artists such as Michael Jackson, Lionel Richie, and later Ice Cube, made the style fashionable with black folks throughout the country.

My hair was naturally curly, slightly tighter than most Jheri curls but I didn't need any chemicals to maintain the look. Of course I wasn't satisfied with my curly hair, I wanted my hair to hang similar to the way Michael Jackson's hair would hang down over his forehead and dangle as he moved his head. I convinced my mother to let her sister, my Aunt Sandy, to give me a perm so that my hair would dangle like Michael's hair. I spent many mornings soaking my hair with activator and every night was spent sleeping with a plastic cap on my hair. Some of the older dudes would wear their plastic caps all day long, taking them off only occasionally to spray more activator in their hair and shake their heads so that everyone could see their curls fling around their heads.

If you had money, you would go to the salon to get your perm done professionally, but most people couldn't afford to go to the salon so they would buy a box kit which enabled them to do their perms at home. Now some box curls, if done correctly, would look just as good as a professionally done perm, but far too many ended up with patches of hair either not permed, over processed, or simply all dried out. If you came to school with a bad box perm, you would be drilled endlessly for months, as you either had to cut your hair or wait a few months for the perm to grow out before you could attempt to try it again. Chemical perms damaged hair, led to split ends and even caused some people to lose their hair all together. Yet people would still scrape together the $80 or so it cost to get them done, spend five or six hours in the hair salon and come out with a head full of greasy curls, swearing that they were doing something big.

At the end of the day, most of the major players and popular dudes had Jheri curls, and the girls would talk about whose curl was the longest and who had the best curl. Many of them would say, "I know he will make a baby with some pretty hair," and "You can tell his baby will have some pretty skin." By the ages of 12 and 13, they had already been completely brain washed into believing that attributes that were considered less black and more white were more desirable, that lighter skin was better and that natural, Afro-centric hair styles were unattractive. This was advantageous for light skinned guys like myself, especially if you had "good hair," and at that age, we lacked the self-awareness to understand the deeper meaning in their preferences. All I knew was that the girls loved me, loved my hair, loved my skin tone and I found myself the center of a lot of female attention. For the first time since moving to Rochester, I began to embrace my racial differences, at least with the girls. But as soon as I started to become somewhat comfortable within my own skin, something would happen to remind me that for a lot of my peers, I was simply that "pretty white boy" and was therefore considered a target for attacks and ridicule.

At the same time that my popularity with the girls was growing, I noticed that my friends were starting to spend less time hanging with each other, and more time chasing or hanging out with girls. The boys were becoming much more physically playful with each other. Slap-boxing and wrestling matches became more common and tempers would flair much faster, often leading to real physical confrontations. It was obvious that our growing sexual awareness was also somehow directly linked to our increased aggression. Years later I would understand that this is often attributed to an increase in testosterone, that aggression is a normal side effect of male hormonal changes, but at the time, I could care less why it was happening. All I knew was that my desire for female companionship was at an all-time high and that feeling on the edge and uptight was becoming the norm.

Right before our summer vacation, actually, right before we were all getting ready to get on our buses on the very last day of school, that pretty girl from the lunch table pulled me to the side and said, "I don't think this is working out, I think we should break up." I wasn't too upset with the idea; she had rebuked damn near every attempt I made at any type of physical interaction. I had pretty much already moved on and started hanging out with a few girls that seemed to be a bit more aggressive and open to a more physical relationship, but we just had not made it "official." Her same girlfriends stood around and watched us as we talked, still whispering to them-selves and giggling upon her return. But this time, I noticed one of them really giving me the eye, and she made sure that I saw her staring at me. Patrick said, "Yo, Linda is really checking you out!" I nodded my head at her to acknowledge that I saw her and she smiled flirtatiously and gave me a wave goodbye before she started to walk home. I watched her as she walked, my eyes shifting back and forth with the sway of her hips, noticing every curve in her fully developed body and memorizing her well-shaped legs and short, confident stride. And just like that, I was completely over my lunch table sweetheart and all seemed right with the universe!

Most of the girls around my age were just beginning to physically develop, but a few of the girls seemed to change into physically fully-grown women, seemingly overnight. One day you're sitting in class next to a girl that you joked around with and looked at strictly as a 'homie' or a friend, and the next day, POOF, your homie is now looking like a curvaceous, grown ass woman. Puberty was rough on us boys, dealing with uncontrollable erections that literally popped up with no warning and at the worst possible times, and testosterone increases that could change harmless play fighting into a full blown "I am going to try to kill you" fist fight in the snap of two fingers. But as rough as the boys had it, the girls had it even worse. Hormonal changes sent many girls into emotional roller coasters. Tears would flow easily and it seemed that the girls were operating on hair trigger tempers that rivaled and even surpassed those of their puberty stricken male counterparts.

Girls were considerably more aggressive than most boys at that age and were already focused on trying to get a "boyfriend" so they would actively compete for the attention of the popular boys and the boys they considered cute. My decent looks, "good hair" and light skin along with my quick wit and accomplishments on the football field, combined to make me extremely popular with the young ladies. My neighborhood was known for having attractive girls and my front porch became the hang-out spot for many of them, while I was still a little shy, I quickly became friends with many of the most attractive girls.

Although our neighborhood was fairly diverse, there weren't many white kids my age so the majority of my friends in the neighborhood were black. Besides the geographic limitations to establishing white friends, I found myself extremely uncomfortable hanging out with the white kids at school because I knew that it would bring on ridicule from others and they would drill me and start calling me white boy again so I made a purposeful effort to keep distance, at least in public, between myself and my white friends and of course this carried over to my interactions with girls as well. While my summer got off to a great start, things would quickly change and take my entire family down a brand new, unplanned course.

6 THE LAST STRAW

My little brother's illness and subsequent treatment kept my mother pretty busy. When she wasn't working, she would spend her days running my brother back and forth to the hospital for chemotherapy and checkups. The chemotherapy made Calvin extremely sick. He would sometimes vomit all day long and rarely moved off the couch or the bed. But every once in a while, maybe once or twice a week, despite his sickness, he would jump off the couch and start to run non-stop, from one side of the living room to the next, over and over and over again, touching one wall, bouncing off of that wall and running straight to the wall on the opposite side of the living room. He would smile and laugh the entire time he ran. It usually lasted five to ten minutes, and then come to a sudden stop, lay back down and go back to being sick. We would crack up laughing, mouths hanging open in amazement at how such a sick child could have these sporadic spurts of super intense energy, all while undergoing chemo and recovering from major surgery! Later, when Calvin was diagnosed with Attention Deficit Hyperactive Disorder (ADHD), it all made more sense. But in that moment, it appeared to be some sort of miracle, and all things considered, it really was miraculous.

Calvin's treatment led to his already skinny three-year-old frame becoming extra frail and he soon began to lose his hair. For a few weeks, the hair on the top of his head remained intact while the rest fell out, giving him a chemotherapy induced Mohawk that looked just like Mr. T from "The A-Team". My mother would sit on the couch and hold him in her arms while he slept, stroking his head and she would cry when she looked at all the hair that accumulated in her hand. She seemed to take my brother's illness personally, as if there was something that she did to make him sick. While she wept and all of her time was consumed with taking care of my brother and trying to make sure my sister and I didn't feel neglected, my step father took advantage. He would spend extra time away from the house, sometimes working overtime but usually just running the streets.

My mother was so worn out from taking care of my brother

that she seldom had the energy to confront my stepfather about his whereabouts or to argue with him when she did confront him. This also meant that he now had to occasionally take me to football practices or run me to various events. My mother would usually attempt to send me with him, in part because she was still very much intent on seeing us develop some sort of father-son bond, but also because I believe she felt that if I was with him, he wouldn't be able to sneak around and visit any other women. Unfortunately, she was wrong on both fronts as I had become even farther removed from him and he had no intention of letting my presence interfere with any plans he may have had to visit other women.

On occasion, I would actually enjoy venturing out with my stepfather. Through him I was introduced to the old school black barbershops. All the barbers were almost exclusively black or Latino men, most older then my stepfather, all holding electric clippers in their hands that hummed and buzzed on and off while they stood behind their red and white metallic, cushioned barber chairs, tilting their customer's head from side to side making sure that each side was perfectly uniform with the other.

Some of the older customers would get their hair trimmed into perfectly rounded, low laying afros with long side burns venturing half-way down their cheeks. The younger dudes would usually shave all of their hair from the bottom of their neck up to about their ear, then the hair would slowly increase in length until it was short enough to brush it down in a style called a fade. The barbershop always smelled like cheap cologne and barbacide, the blue liquid next to each barber's chair that they used to sterilize their razors and other equipment. Almost every barbershop had a television that didn't work and most had a radio sitting on top of the television, playing all the latest music featured on the local black radio station.

These trips to the barbershop were also my first introduction to hearing how grown men engaged in conversations with each other about women. Except for Saturday mornings when a lot of single mothers would bring their sons in for haircuts, the barbershops were almost always exclusively teenage and adult black men. Conversations would usually start when one of the patrons would ask a barber if they remembered so-and-so, almost always using physical descriptions of the woman's body to assist in describing the woman in question. They would say, "Yeah man, you remember Stacy from Arnett Blvd.? You know, pretty light skinned Stacy with the big titties?" or "You remember Lynn, the thick chocolate chick that walks like she throws down in the bedroom." Another way they would identify women is by naming the man that the woman used to date. "You remember Tonya, Peanut's old lady" or "Didn't Chuck used to hit that?"

My stepfather would always engage in these conversations, describing women in these same ways and making comments like, "Man she is fine, I would put a hurting on that." Occasionally, one of the patrons or a barber would look at me and then look at him as if to say, "Hey man, isn't that your son sitting there? Maybe you shouldn't be talking about other women like that in front of him," but he would pay them absolutely no mind and continue to talk about these women as if I didn't know he was married to my mother. I truly believe that he thought that he was helping me become a man by talking like that in front of me, that he believed he was in some way teaching me what being a black man was all about. Instead, he was only fueling my resentment towards him and further assisting me in supporting my position that he was all wrong for my mother and damn sure not worried about my best interest.

It was during these barbershop outings that I began to understand some of what my parents would argue about. There was almost constant conflict in our home. So much so that at some point early on in my life, I taught myself to zone out when they argued, to take my mind someplace else so that I didn't have to hear the yelling or hear the slaps or thuds when my stepfather would physically attack my mother. I would usually close the door to my room, turn on my radio and get lost in whatever song was on at that moment. Music became my savior and acted as a security blanket, comforting me from the ongoing drama in my household.

One night after running around with my step-father all day, sitting in the car while he ran into and out of various strange apartments and houses, my mother got into a huge argument with him, probably about his whereabouts earlier in the day. Dishes were broken, furniture was knocked over and I once again found myself trying to find enough courage to confront him. As I sat in my room listening intently I made up my mind that this couldn't go on any more, that I was going to stop it myself if needed and that the next time he put his hands on my mother would be his last time. I sat in my room, fists clenched, heart racing and occasionally got up and paced back and forth, repeating to myself over and over, "I'm going to kill him, I'm going to kill him." As the voices down stairs got lower and lower, I laid down on my bed and eventually fell asleep, but I woke the next day reminding myself that nothing had changed, that no matter what, he would never again hit my mother.

After that blowout things calmed down for a little while, my stepfather spent most of his time trying to prove to my mother that things would be different, that he was again magically transformed into a new man, something I'd seen happen plenty of times before. It was old to me but somehow my mother seemed to at least half-way accept it. I don't think she ever fully believed him but I now understand how some relationships work and how a person will want something to be what they want so badly that they will look the other way when given even the slightest hope of change.

For the next few months the arguments and fighting subsided and on the surface the house was unusually calm. But the strain of my brother being sick and the years of being in an abusive relationship were taking their toll on my mother. She had always been happy and easy going, quick to smile and share a laugh but now she was more distant, spent a lot of time lost in her own thoughts. Smiles seemed to be more forced and her hugs seemed to be more for her own benefit than mine. She would wrap her arms around me and I could feel her fighting back the tears while she would whisper to herself, but out loud so that I could hear it, "Everything is going to be alright, we are going to make it just fine." While I believe she was attempting to comfort herself and also somehow ease the tension she must have felt growing inside of me, her words and hugs acted to reinforce my position that I would make sure my stepfather never put his hands on my mother again.

I awoke a few nights later to a loud crash downstairs in the kitchen followed by my stepfather yelling. My heart started racing as I tip-toed to the edge of the stair way, listening intently to what was being said. As the tears welled up in my eyes and trickled down my cheeks, my hands balled up into fists so tight that I could once again feel my nails digging into my palms, I shook my head and whispered through tightly clenched teeth, "I am going to kill you, I

JASON BOST

am going to kill you."

As their voices quieted down, I paced back and forth between my bedroom door and the top of the stairway, hands to my sides, fists clenched, trying to summon up the courage to go downstairs and confront him before things got out of hand and he put his hands on my mother. After a few minutes went by, seeming like hours, I sat back down on my bed, heart starting to slow, finally unclenching my fists when I heard a sound that sounded like a sharp thud, almost like a heavy book falling off a tall shelf onto a wooden floor. Then I heard my mother scream, "Stop it, stop it, leave me alone," followed by my stepfather's voice repeating "I told you to sit the fuck down, I am sick of your shit." One or two of the chairs at the kitchen table sounded like they were knocked over and another dish broke while I heard another sharp thud and more yelling.

I rose off my bed, tears now streaming down my face, and ran to the top of the stairway, continually repeating "I'm going to kill him, I'm going to kill him." I walked back to my room to look for something that I could use as a weapon, reaching first for my baseball bat, grabbing it and walking back to the stairway, then going back to my room and putting it down as my heart raced, all the while continuing to say out loud, "I'm going to kill him." I picked up a steel afro pick that had 15 to 20 long metal combs protruding from it and a handle that enabled the person using it to grip it in their hand similar to a pair of brass knuckles. I slowly put my hand through the pick and gripped it so tightly that I thought it might break and just stared at it, feeling the cold steel handle in my hand. I slowly walked to top of the stairs and gazed down to the bottom of the steps, which now appeared to be ten times longer than I could ever remember them being. I could feel my heart beating in my hand as it gripped the pick tighter and tighter as I descended each step.

Their voices were now clear and grew louder as I turned the corner of the stairs and slowly walked down the narrow hallway towards the kitchen where I could see my mother on the floor, hand raised above her in an attempt to protect herself from his punches and slaps while he stood directly above her, hand raised and ready to punch her again. Before either of them saw me I shouted "STOP IT!, PUT YOUR HAND DOWN!" Startled, my stepfather stood up straight with a stunned look on his face and my mother said, "Jason go back upstairs, everything will be alright."

I just stood there and shook my head, holding my hand behind my back, I said, "No, I'm not going upstairs, this is it. I am tired of this, get away from my mother." My stepfather raised his eyebrows as if he was amused and just stared at me. I said "Leave my mother alone, I'm not playing with you." Before he could say another word, I gripped the pick even tighter, took two quick steps towards him, and tried to plunge the pick into his neck. He put his hand up just in time to shield his neck from the blow but the pick struck his hand and the shock of what just happened knocked him off balance. Before he could recover I swung wildly, thrusting the pick at him again, this time striking him in his neck. He regained his balance and stood up, infuriated at my attempt to protect my mother. He swung at me with a slow, drunken uppercut that I quickly dodged then I countered with another thrust of the pick, again striking him on the side of his face.

Reaching towards his face, he wiped away the blood that was forming on his cheek, looked at it in his hand then said, "Oh you think you are a man, I'm going to kill you. I'm going to beat you down like a fucking man." My mother jumped up, eyes bulging from her face in horror and disbelief, and attempted to position herself between him and me. Enraged, he charged forward knocking my mother down and lifting the kitchen table with one hand as he swung at me with the other. I ducked under his arm and tried to move out of the kitchen and towards the narrow hallway leading to the living room and stairs when he caught me, grabbed me by the neck and eventually wrapped both of his hands around my neck, attempting to choke me while saying, "Now mother fucker, who is the man now? I'm going to kill your punk ass."

I swung the pick towards his ribs with an uppercut but it got caught on the doorframe and fell from my hand. My mother was now grabbing on his arms attempting to free his grip from my neck and the family dog, a large German Shepard, started barking at my stepfather and moving in between us as well. I managed to break free from his grip and run into the living room where we knocked over a coffee table and a few lamps before I was able to open the front door and run out onto the porch. As I moved onto the front porch towards the stairs leading to the sidewalk I turned around realizing that my mother was still in the house, only to hear her yell "Run Jason, run, don't come back here, run now."

71

Our neighbor directly across the street, Mr. Dinkle, was a police officer with the Rochester Police Department. I'm not sure if he was home and heard the commotion or if one of our other neighbors heard it but before I made it even ten houses up the block I saw police cars racing towards our house. Tears were now streaming down my face as I started to cry uncontrollably. Eyes clouded by the tears and unable to run any further, I stopped in front of my classmate Anna Marie's house and sat down on her steps. Eventually, I got up the nerve to ring their doorbell, Anna Maria answered the door, seeing me in a ripped shirt, scratches on my face from the fight, tears running down my face, she quickly opened the door and said "Jason what is wrong? What happened?"

I couldn't even speak. All the years of abuse at the hands of my stepfather boiled over and I just began crying uncontrollably. Shocked and not knowing what to do, Anna Maria went upstairs and got her mother and they both stood there, arms wrapped around me, saying "It will be ok, whatever it is, it will be ok." Eventually I was calm enough to tell them what happened, Mrs. Webster went outside and looked up the street to see all the police cars, she came back in and said "Your mother is alright, she is ok baby. I'm going to let them know you are down here." I said "No, I don't want them to know I'm here, I just . . ." tears building up in my eyes again, unable to complete my words, she said "Ok baby. Don't worry, whatever you are going through you are safe here. We will figure this out but you stay right here until we do."

The fight with my stepfather led to my mother finally leaving him and moving us temporarily in with Patrick's family while she tried to find a new place of our own. Patrick lived with his sisters Reese and Celia, his mother and Celia's toddler son Marcel, in a small three-bedroom duplex on Brookdale Avenue on the southwest side of the city. The family that lived downstairs had recently moved out so my mother was able to rent the apartment and we moved in after a few weeks.

Having Patrick's mom and sisters around must have helped alleviate some of the stress my mother felt from our move and her newly established status as a single parent. Although she had always really been a single parent even when she was with my stepfather, the reality of single parenthood was starting to hit home. She was always sensitive but now she would cry at small things like the time she burnt a pizza in the oven because she was trying to bath my brother at the same time. Or when we ran out of sugar and she asked me to run upstairs and borrow a cup, tears just began to flow and she would quickly rush off to her room or the bathroom and close the door in an attempt to disguise her sobbing. I am sure I added to her stress with my attitudes and demands as I was dead smack in the middle of my own pubescent influenced emotional issues.

Despite the emotional ups and downs our household was experiencing, there was a sense of calm and comfort and an overall influx of positive energy that replaced the tension and negative vibes associated with everyday life with my stepfather. My mother understood that we had some serious struggles ahead of us and she was desperately looking for a second job to help pay the bills, but even with the growing financial obligations, she seemed to be much more at peace, which in turn comforted and put all of us at ease.

While my mother worked and tried to keep things together, I was busy chasing my adolescent urges and trying to pick up where things left off before the big fight with my stepfather. My mother and I were in constant conflict over the telephone as it was now almost always glued to my ear. When she was home the phone would ring non-stop from the various girls that were now injecting themselves into my daily life, and when she was at work she could never get through on the phone to check on us as the line was always busy. I remember quite a few times being on the phone for hours and eventually hearing a long "Beeeeeeeeeeeeeep" followed by an operator saying "Hello, we have a request from your mother to clear the line. Please hang up the phone so she can get through!" This was way before call waiting or two-way lines so my mother had to call the operator and ask them to interrupt the call which cost an additional fee and always gave her one more thing to be upset with me about.

I always had female friends and talking on the phone was nothing new but talking to girls on the phone was different now. It morphed from innocent chit-chat to full-fledged flirtation heavily infused with sexual undertones. A couple of my 'friends' were definitely becoming more intimately aggressive as our conversations started to become more and more sexual in nature. Linda in particular really started to peak my interest and soon our conversations led to open challenges on both of our parts. She would say "I bet you don't even know how to kiss" or "I think you are afraid of girls." Of course, I couldn't let her diss me so I would usually retort with, "Why don't you let me show you what I know? Everyone knows that YOU are scared to death of boys!"

Eventually all the talk led to an invitation to come over so we could see who was scared to do what. She told me that her mother worked nights and always slept from 5pm until 10pm, when she had to get up to prepare to leave for work so we would be uninterrupted for the evening. The only problem was that her girlfriend Trina was going to be there. I knew Trina had a crush on Patrick so I convinced Patrick to come with me so that we could both try to get busy with the girls. Patrick had not yet started to talk to girls and definitely had no interest in Trina. I begged him to come along with me for days until I finally promised to take him to McDonalds and he agreed. Patrick was always greedy as hell!

We lied to our mothers saying that we were going to a mutual friend's house then we caught the bus to Linda's house in the Cornhill neighborhood close to downtown. I spent the bus ride telling Patrick about all the things Linda and I talked about and telling him all the things I planned on doing with her. Nervous anxiety made my heart pound so hard in my chest that I was sure you could see it beating right through my large puffy jacket. I had never had any time alone with a girl before and definitely hadn't done any of the things that we talked about doing to each other. Linda had the body of a grown woman, DD cup breasts, and if it wasn't for her round hips and super plump, perfect heart shaped ass, she would probably have been a size 2 because her waist was so small. Just thinking about her sexy walk made me breathe faster and I could physically feel a strong tension in my chest.

When we arrived at the house Linda opened the door and led us both upstairs to a small room where Trina was sitting on a couch watching TV. We all sat on the couch, Patrick on one side of me and Linda on the other and the girls looked at each other and started giggling. Patrick gave me a look like he was ready to go and I gave him a look back that said "Chill . . . don't mess this up for me!" After a few minutes of small talk, Trina asked Patrick if he wanted something to eat and they both went downstairs to the kitchen.

As soon as they left Linda slid closer to me and said "so, I guess you are scared of girls" and sat back daring me to make a move. My heart was beating so hard that I was certain it might explode. I wiped my sweaty palms on my pants and quickly leaned over towards her, she met me half way and we started to kiss. She let out a small moan and moved closer as our tongues met and softly explored each other's mouths. I could now hear my heart beat in my ears, thump-thud, thud, thump-thud, and my breathing sped up until I had to stop kissing her so I could catch my breath. As I pulled away she ran her hands up the back of my neck, through my long curly hair and pulled me back close to her until I was laying down on top of her with one leg wrapped around my waist.

My fear was now completely replaced by an uncontrollable desire to be closer to her and she took my hand and quickly moved it down to her skirt, which she pulled up and then she eased my hand down between her legs and onto the outside of her panties. I could feel her warmth and wetness through her panties which were now completely drenched. We kissed harder and more passionately and she moved her hips to meet my hands and guide my touches to exactly where she wanted them. As both of us struggled to catch our breath, she grabbed my belt and quickly took down my zipper and reached inside, until she found what she was looking for, grabbing it so hard that it hurt.

She squeezed it now with both hands and ran her fingers slowly up and down until I thought I was going to explode then she laid back down and pulled me directly towards her dripping wet panties and I quickly moved her panties to the side so she could guide me into her. As she moved me up and down between her warm, wet lips, my body went numb and my breathing got faster and faster, I moved her hand and tried to do it myself, growing impatient and no longer being able to take not being inside of her. She moaned and lifted her hips up to meet me and after a few moments of maneuvering and trying different angles I could finally feel myself easing inside of her.

We both let out a moan and before I could thrust myself any deeper, we heard her mother's door open and we both froze and held our breath, our hearts beating so loudly that we were certain her mother would hear them from outside in the hallway. The bathroom door creaked and then we heard it close and we both finally took a breath. She moved to wrap her legs around me and the movement of her hips pushed me deeper inside and before I knew what was happening, my heart felt like it was going to explode, my legs got weak and I thought I might faint. Her mother flushed the toilet and in anticipation of her coming back out of the bathroom, we quickly got up and tried to straighten our clothing out just in case she decided to poke her head into the room.

As I tried to catch my breath and gather my senses Linda stood up in front of me and wrapped her hands around me, kissing me and then placing her head on my chest until I wrapped my arms around her and hugged her tightly. I closed my eyes and took a deep breath, inhaling so slowly and deeply that I noticed her smell for the first time, her natural smell that cut through the perfume she was wearing. She smelled comfortable, warm and gentle. She smelled beautiful, like passion, she smelled better than anything I've ever experienced in my life and I was instantly hooked.

After that I made my way over to Linda's house at any and every given opportunity and we were soon announcing to everyone that we were officially a couple. Spending all of my free time with her usually kept me from hanging out in the streets with my boys and minimized opportunities to get into some of the serious trouble that was now commonplace for most of my hanging partners. While I managed to stay out of legal trouble, all the time being spent with Linda eventually led to an entirely new set of issues. Linda told me that she thought she was pregnant.

While my other friends were worried about B-Boy battles and what color sneakers to wear with their Levis, I was contemplating life as a 13-year-old father and worse than that, I was trying to figure out how I would tell my mother if the test came back positive. My mother had ideas that we might be sexually active, every once in a while I would show up with a big hickey on my neck and she would try to ask me about what we were doing and I would always dismiss her inquiries as if she were crazy.

Linda expressed her desire to have a child with me when we first started talking and as our bond became stronger so did her desire to become a mother. I went along with it, never really thinking about what her being pregnant would mean to my life but just happy to be able to have sex whenever I wanted and even more happy that the girl I was crazy about wanted it just as much as I did. So, I was not surprised at all when she called me crying tears of joy mixed with anxiety and proclaimed, "I'm pregnant, I'm pregnant, the test said I was pregnant!"

The words didn't sink in until she said "You are going to be a daddy! I wonder what our baby is going to look like, I know she is going to have pretty hair just like yours!" Daddy? Me? a daddy?? I was only 13 years old and I was going to have a child! For a moment I was excited and I embraced her anxious enthusiasm until I thought about sharing this news with my mother, then my heart sank and I swallowed hard. What was she going to say? How would she respond to the news that her 13-year-old son had a baby on the way?

I don't recall exactly how I told my mother about the pregnancy but I do remember a lot of tears shed by both of us. My mother's came from pure heartbreak and disappointment and mine came from being angry with my mother for not being supportive and scared at what was about to happen. My teenage thought process was centered around myself and I was either unable or unwilling to see what type of effect this would have on my life. My mother called Linda's mother and we got in the car and headed over to her house so we could all sit down and talk.

After talking with each other, our mothers sat us down and told us what they felt was the best thing for us to do in the situation. They both agreed that Linda needed to get an abortion. As soon as the word "abortion" was mentioned Linda burst into tears and started sobbing uncontrollably. Unable to provide any comfort to her, I just sat there, feeling partially relieved but also concerned about Linda as I had never seen her cry so hard or for so long.

7 WILSON HIGH/THURSTON RD.

Joseph C. Wilson Magnet High School was on the Westside of town on Genesee Street, the dividing point for the "hood" and the more desirable 19th Ward. Directly across the street from Wilson High School was the Southwest Boys and Girls Club. The Club was the meeting place for kids from the other side of Genesee Street, which represented some of the roughest neighborhoods in Rochester. Despite the location, the Boys and Girls Club was always considered safe and rarely if at all, did any violence take place at the center. Everyone seemed to respect the staff, most of whom came from the same neighborhood and were once, or were still, actively involved in street life in and around the neighborhood.

Our home on Brookdale Avenue was about a twenty-five-minute walk, or a five-minute drive to Wilson which meant that I would no longer have to catch the city bus to get to school. Not having to catch the bus downtown and deal with the conflicts with everyone from the East side was a relief but going to school in my neighborhood would soon present its own unique set of challenges.

The summer before freshman year was spent attending double session football practices Monday through Friday and then a single session on Saturdays. When I wasn't on the football field I was starting to experiment with alcohol and marijuana. Patrick and his family moved from the apartment upstairs to Herndon, Virginia which meant that my main hanging partner and best friend since the age of three was now gone. While Patrick was not as socially active as I was and was a few years behind me when it came to girls and alcohol, his avoidance of both managed to have a positive influence on me. He kept me from getting into trouble because he was always the voice of reason, the one that would say "Naw man, I'm going home" when we were presented with a situation that might have meant him getting into trouble or doing something he felt uncomfortable doing. With no more voice literally telling me to "go home" and no fear of someone potentially telling on me, I started to embrace my wilder side and alcohol certainly started playing a big part.

WHITE NIGGER

On Fridays after practice a bunch of us would pool our money together and head over to the corner store on Jefferson Avenue so we could buy 40 ounce bottles of Old English, Schlitz Blue Bull or Colt 45 malt liquor. If we happened to have girls with us we would get a few bottles of Pink Champale or a four pack of fruit flavored wine coolers or Cisco, a super strong, syrupy, thick, wine cooler type drink. This was the one store we knew we could buy beer without needing to show ID. The store sat on the corner of Jefferson and Bronson Avenue. There were white metal bars protecting the windows, and the store's outer walls were covered with Colt 45 advertisements featuring one of Black America's biggest movie stars at the time, Billy D. Williams.

Stepping into the store, the floor was always concealed by flattened cardboard box pieces and the walls were covered with more Billy D. Williams Colt 45 malt liquor posters, all featuring sensuous black women hanging over his shoulder while Billy D. held a can or a 40 oz. bottle of Colt 45 with the phrase, "It works every time" printed right under his autograph. There were two or three aisles of chips, snacks, high priced canned goods and grocery items on the aisle shelves and the outside walls of the store, from front to back, were lined with the coolers that kept the soda, juice, and beer ice cold. A clerk was always sitting behind a counter encased by a thick glass with a small square cut out of the middle to exchange money. Behind the clerk was a wall of cigarettes, rolling papers, condoms, and all the candy that was otherwise easy to steal.

Since I looked a little bit older than my peers and was slightly bolder, I was usually the one that would go into the store and make the purchase. I got hassled by the store clerk the first few times but after a while, he knew me by name and never bothered to ask me for ID again. The beer was always sold in brown paper bags which we kept wrapped around the bottles when we drank, partly because there was an open bottle law and the police in the area would harass us, and partly because it was the cool thing to do. Even when we were only drinking a soda or juice, we would keep the container in a paper bag to imitate the older dudes carrying around their 40 ozs and cans of beer.

When we wanted hard alcohol, we would walk up the block to see the bootlegger that sold liquor out of a large hole in a door in the backyard behind Mason's store. You could buy the same thing you bought at the liquor store but they were open 24-hours a day and no one cared about ID. The bootleggers would add an additional thirty to fifty percent on the regular prices of the bottles and unless we could find someone to go into the liquor store for us, we would usually just pay the mark up and accept it as the cost of a hassle-free liquor buying experience.

We each had our preferred drink of choice, mine was Seagram's Gin. Lawrence Pack always got a bottle of Paul Mason brandy. If we were really broke, we would all pitch in and get a few pints of the purple MD 20/20, the choice for winos everywhere! It was a super sweet, super cheap wine that looked and tasted like grape Kool-Aid but packed a punch and would sneak up on you quick. Sometimes we would each have our own bottle of whatever we preferred but most of the time whoever had the money would buy what they wanted and then the rest of us would share whatever they bought. Because of our "share-and-share-a-like" approach to drinking, we all became experienced in the tastes and effects of the various types of liquor and we identified the 'light weight' drinkers from those of us that could 'handle' our liquor.

The ability to drink a lot and still maintain yourself was a valued attribute that garnered respect and admiration from our peers. I quickly established myself as someone that could 'handle his liquor' and soon almost every drinking challenge that was issued was done so with me being the one that everyone else was measured against. Someone would say "Aw Nigga please, you are a light weight, you can't hang with the big dawgs! My man JayBee will drink your light weight ass under the table" and from there it was on. The upside to these challenges was that I almost never had to pay for my liquor. My friends would always provide it so that they could watch their friends pass out or throw up while they tried to go shot-for-shot with me. The downside was that at most parties I would probably end up totally shit-faced and many times, well after the party was over and I was safely home or wherever I ended up, the room would spin and I would find myself hugging the toilet as I threw up and repeatedly chanted, "God please, please stop this room from spinning and let me make it through this, I promise I will never ever drink again!" And as always, despite my pledge to God above, after the next party I would find myself right back in the bathroom, praying and puking!

The only people hanging out on Jefferson Avenue were winos, heroin addicts, cocaine users, whom we called 'geekers', prostitutes and drug dealers. We would usually buy our beer and liquor and head to someone's house to hang out. When the weather was nice, we might hang out on Genesee Street for a little while, a block away from the high school or head to the football field and occupy the bleachers until we finished off the bottles, got bored or had to head home for the night.

While most of us on the football team stuck to strictly drinking beer and alcohol, my friends from my neighborhood around Thurston Road had been using marijuana on a regular basis for some years. These were the friends I would hang with when I left school and was closer to home. Most of them had older brothers or cousins or uncles that were heavily involved in the streets and these older family members would pass down the knowledge of how to succeed in their various hustles. Some sold marijuana, others stole jewelry and clothing from department stores, which we called boosting, and a select few sold cocaine or heroin, but each one seemed to have an area of the streets in which they specialized. My Thurston Road homies all came from backgrounds that gave each one a specific skill set in one or more of these various hustles.

I met Lamont Howard, a dark skinned, good humored, lanky, always smiling brother, through one of my high school friends, Tim Cooke. Lamont lived on Ellicott Street between Thurston and Post Ave, with his mother and his younger brother Londell. Lamont was only a few months older than me but seemed to be decades older when it came to the streets. By the time I met him, Lamont already knew how to roll joints and was an experienced weed smoker and always knew where to get the best weed. Since Lamont's house was central to all of us and his mom never seemed to mind us being there, we would usually meet at his house before we headed out to roam the streets and see what type of trouble we could find.

Lamont grew up on the Westside, around Hawley Street and

Jefferson Ave. before moving to Ellicott Street and he knew everyone on the Westside but was selective about who he actually hung out with, keeping his inner circle relatively small and tightknit. Tim and Lamont were always together, either writing rhymes at Corey McNeil's house or walking up and down Thurston looking for girls. It was rare to see one without the other and never far behind was Londell. Tim was short, bow legged and always laughing about someone or something, even when we found ourselves being chased by the police or fighting a bunch of dudes from another neighborhood, you could always hear Tim laughing in the background.

Through Tim and Lamont, I met Sherrod Allen, Jason Bradley and reconnected with Corey McNeil. Corey was the son of one of the coaches for the Southwest Colts so I knew him prior to hanging out with the rest of my Thurston friends. Corey was the only one in our crew with DJ equipment so we would spend hours in his bedroom, listening to music and practicing our DJ skills while we all took turns saying rhymes on the microphone and beat-boxing. Corey had a nice set up; two technic 1200 turntables and an official DJ mixer with a pair of nice speakers and a few microphones. One entire wall of his bedroom was stacked tall with gray and black milk crates tipped on their side for easy access to the vinyl records stored inside of them. Corey's parents were separated and he lived with his mom but his dad lived right across the street. In retrospect, it was one of the things that kept Corey out of trouble, having his father that close and always around. Lamont, Tim, myself and the rest of our crew all came from single mother households. Corey's father was one of the few fathers that all of us saw on a regular basis and he knew each one of us by our first and last names. His presence deterred us from coming to get Corey when we were heading out to start real trouble and therefore kept Corey out of some of the more serious trouble that many of us would soon find ourselves involved in.

It took me a few months of hanging with Lamont and Sherrod before I found myself growing more and more curious and finally decided to try smoking marijuana. It was never forced on me and there was always a few of us that chose not to smoke while everyone else would take a hit off the joint as it was passed from person to person. The pressure came more from wanting to be like the rest of my peers, from seeing how cool and grown up smoking made the older dudes appear and then seeing the same thing in my peers. It was my opportunity to show the world, and more importantly my hanging partners, that I was down and just as cool as they were. It was also a form of bonding, the same way we grew closer as we passed around and shared a bottle of liquor, sharing a joint and the feelings associated with it brought us all closer together and strengthened our bond helping to solidify our brotherhood.

We would all pool our money together until we had enough to get a dime bag ($10) bag of marijuana, or as we called it, weed. The closest weed spot was off Shelter Street on the other side of Genesee Street but Sherrod had an uncle or someone in his family that sold weed so he always had access to a dime bag or two. The weed came in a small manila envelope about one-third of the size of a regular letter envelope. The envelope was full to the top with enough weed packed inside to make ten thickly rolled joints. Someone always had a brown booklet of E-Z Wider rolling papers, or the more popular Topps brand that came in a yellow booklet with a picture of a red and blue spinning top on the cover. Everyone would take a few papers and start rolling up, licking the small sticky side of the paper with their tongue and sticking two pieces of the papers together to form one larger, doubly enforced paper. Lamont made it look easy, using his fingertips to break up the weed into smaller pieces and removing any stems and seeds from the weed before he created a crease in the middle of the papers and then sprinkled the weed evenly into the papers. When he was done, he would lick the exposed side and use that to stick the papers together, pinching and rolling the papers together with his fingers and gently twisting the ends to make sure nothing spilled out.

Watching Lamont roll joint after joint for months I felt that I was ready to give it a try so I asked him for rolling papers and went to work, licking, crumbling, twisting, licking some more, until I rolled my first joint. Tim and Lamont looked at my creation, looked at each other and busted out laughing hysterically. My joint was enormously fat in the middle and skinny on the ends, looking more like a big jelly bean than a joint! I laughed right along with them and said, "At least I don't have to smoke one of yours, with your crusty ass lips, looking like you just finished eating a powdered donut!" Without hesitation Lamont came back and said

"Ah Nigga please, I know you ain't talking with your yellow ass teeth, looking like you ate a bowl full of butter!" We all broke out laughing as Lamont handed me some matches so we could light up and smoke.

Standing on the corner of Ellicott and Post Avenue, I lit up my first joint, placed it to my lips and inhaled deeply, waited and waited, tried to inhale again and waited some more, but nothing happened. I tried again, still nothing. Lamont handed me his joint, took my joint, pinched it between his fingers and ripped off the end so the smoke would flow more easily from the lit end to the open end and gave it back to me. This time I puffed slowly and took a deep breath, gradually inhaling the warm, sweet, dry tasting smoke.

I held it in my lungs the same way I watched Lamont and everyone else hold it, then exhaled and watched the white, fluffy smoke exit my mouth and slowly rise towards the top of the dull red stop sign on the corner, slowly rising closer and closer to the street lights that were now just turning on. I noticed the sky that was still partially lit from the sun, giving it a light blue and orange hue and sighed as I imagined what the sparsely dispersed clouds suspended above would feel like against my skin. I noticed how warm the air was and felt myself slowly drifting upwards, and closer to the clouds. The cars rolling past in the distance provided a smooth, comforting backdrop like ocean waves, gently caressing a rocky coastline. I felt the heaviness of my lungs as I inhaled, and then slowly exhaled, and could hear my heart beating, boom-boom, boom-bap, boom-boom, as my eyes slowly blinked, opening and shutting in unison with my heartbeat. I could feel the universe softly caressing my spirit with cool, refreshing vibes, I envied my spirit as it smiled at my soul. I was high as hell!

By the time summer ended and I started my first year of high school I again found myself divided as I tried to straddle the lines between multiple worlds. There was the football player and athlete, confident in my skills and dedicated to my team and teammates, excelling on the field, never missing practice and always the first one to jump into a pile to fiercely protect my teammates if an opposing player got overly aggressive. There was the good student, desperately yearning to learn and absorb new knowledge, always ready to take on challenges and demonstrate to my teachers, my mother and the world that I could succeed in the classroom. There was the newly developing street thug, interested only in hanging out and getting as wild as possible with my crew, smoking weed, drinking, and partying. There was the much loved and extremely popular new freshman, always able to make everyone laugh and all the girls giggle, accepted and embraced by the most popular kids in the school. There was the misanthropic, totally depressed introvert, struggling to figure out who he was in comparison to my black and my white classmates, content staying home and sleeping all day. And there was me, a confused individual trying to contain and satisfy all the pieces of my newly developing persona and corral them into one functional being.

Adolescence is a difficult time, insecurities seem to be boiling over and exposed for the world to see, while we struggle to figure out who we are, where our boundaries fuse with our foundation, and what the world is all about. I was racially hyper-vigilant and impetuous towards anyone that even remotely seemed like they wanted to test my "blackness." I was angry and unable to precisely pinpoint where or why my growing indignation manifested, but a tiny part of me knew my anger was rooted in my racial identity, which made me even more angry and built on my ever present feelings of being an outsider.

Sex, liquor and weed all provided temporary relief and outlets for my constant internal struggles, ephemeral escapes from life's intensifying pressures. While I spent more time running the streets around Thurston with my new group of friends, my mother was busy working two jobs and trying to take care of my younger brother and sister. Calvin was finally done with Chemo and was cancer free, which alleviated a lot of my mother's stress and meant that she could focus a little more of her time on what I was doing. While not as involved as she was when I played for Southwest, my mother was in the stands for all my football games and when the season ended, she let me throw a big party for my birthday at our house on Brookdale.

I asked my friend Ulysses, we called him "Tiny Tee," to DJ the party. Tiny lived a few blocks down from my house on the corner of Chandler Street and Brooks Ave. Chandler Street was full of kids my age and I spent a lot of time on the block hanging out with Tim Riley, Ernest "Dink" Kittelbeger, Robert Arnold and Denise Williams and her younger brother Tracy. Tiny had a serious DJ set up in his bedroom and was the first DJ I knew that could mix fluently from one record to the next, matching the tempo and the beats of two records so perfectly that it sounded like it was all just the same song. I would spend hours watching Tiny mix and scratch records and occasionally, Tiny would let me get on the turntables and practice my DJing. I knew if anybody could rock a party, Tiny Tee could, so I made up some fliers using graffiti style lettering and characters and handed them out at school to a few people we knew.

The night of the party, my mother cooked a bunch of chicken wings and assorted food and got me a birthday cake with birthday hats and used streamers to decorate the house. Tiny came early to set up the DJ equipment along with Tim Riley and another one of my friends, Brandon Thorton. Everyone helped move all the furniture out of the living room and into the back bedroom. I knew Brandon from #3 school, everyone picked on him because he was fat and dark-dark bluish black, but he was one of the coolest dudes I knew and he could DJ his ass off! Brandon's record collection was much more extensive then Tiny's and he brought damn near every record he had and stacked them up behind the Turntables so whoever was DJing had easy access to them.

We turned the system on and Brandon started scratching "Peter Piper" from Run-DMC while Tiny and I watched. Brandon had an entire routine where he let the beginning of the song play, "Now Peter Piper Picked Peppers and Run rocked rhymes. Humpty Dumpy fell down, that's his hard time. Jack be nimble, what nimble, yeah he was quick, but Jam Master cut faster, Jack's on Jay's Dick" then the beat dropped. Before the beat would drop on the first record, Brandon switched to the second record that was queued up at the start of the record and he scratched "Now Peter" a few times before he started playing the second record. When the second record said "Run rocked rhymes" Brandon would cut "Peter Piper" on the first record and kept going back and forth, faster and faster until all you heard was "Now Peter Piper" and eventually just "Now" from each record, then he spun around twice and started to do the same routine from behind his back! Then Tiny got on the turntables and used the same records to scratch "Jam Master cut faster, Jack's on Jay's dick" back and forth, faster and faster until he alternated the two records and made them say "Jay's dick cut faster" and then added "that's his hard time."

DJ's would battle this way, using the records to cut and scratch words meant to be a message to the crowd or the other DJ. Brandon switched the records up and put on the start of the Fat Boys record where they sing "The Fat Boys are back, and you know they could never be whack, the Fat Boys are back, don't you know it's the fat boys . . ." And Brandon started cutting "Fat Boys" while he looked at Tiny Tee and we all busted out laughing! These two went back and forth on the turntables until people started to arrive and then they went to work rocking the party non-stop.

Our small house quickly filled up with friends from Southwest and #3 School, my boys from the Wilson Football team and of course my boys from the neighborhood, along with a bunch of girls from the neighborhood. A few of the G-Boys, a loosely formed gang from Genesee Street came to hang out with Lamont which was cool until a few members of the Black Mob showed up as well. Black Mob was another loosely formed gang from the Sawyer street area of Genesee Street, just a block down from where I used to live. I knew dudes from both gangs and was cool with everyone but there was a longstanding beef between the two groups. Someone started to chant "G-Boys" in unison with the music and then a few more people joined in until someone else started chanting "Black Mob, Black Mob" until both sides got louder and louder. Someone eventually pushed someone and they knocked into the DJ table, skipping the record and unplugging a speaker. I didn't realize what happened until the music stopped and I heard my mother telling someone to "Please go outside if you're going to fight."

I heard someone say "Fuck you, you white bitch, you ain't telling me what to do cracker" and then I heard someone else say "Yo chill, that's Jason's mother yo." The angry voice said "fuck you and who the fuck is Jason?" I quickly pushed my way towards the voice and said "I'm Jason and that's my mother, you got a problem?" Recognizing me, he quickly apologized and said "No disrespect, I didn't know they meant you" and he turned to my mother and said "I am sorry Ma'am, I didn't know you were Jason's mom."

We turned all the lights on and told everyone they had to go. As the house quickly cleared, the two opposing sides of Genesee street faced off in the middle of our street, Black Mob on one side, G-Boys on the other, both sides throwing threats back and forth until someone pulled out a gun and waived it in the air. Everyone scattered into different directions, sending most of the girls running back into my house. Tiny Tee, Brandon and my next door neighbor Lenox were the only guys left, surrounded by a bunch of loudly talking girls, all taking a turn using our phone to call their parents to come pick them up. Brandon started smiling and walked over to the turntables and put on one of everyone's favorite slow jam records. The room started to quiet down as the girls looked around at each other. Lenox's sister Candy came over and started to ask me what happened earlier with the commotion and as we talked Brandon came over and said "Are ya'll going to dance or just talk all night?? You look like two squares just standing there!" With that, I grabbed Candy's hand and we made our way to a corner of the living room where we could dance.

Slow dancing was always the highlight of any house party. Usually the DJ would play three or four slow records at the end of the night to slow the pace of the party and let people know that it was time to go home. This gave the guys an opportunity to finally get close with one of the girls and this was usually when you had the best chance of getting someone's phone number. It was always an excuse to grind up on a girl and see if you could get in some make out time that might lead to something else.

I had known Candy since we moved onto Brookdale. She was a grade ahead of me and attended another city School with her brother Lenox. Lenox immigrated from Trinidad after his father, who was also from Trinidad, married Candy's mother. Candy and I would sometimes sit on her front steps and talk while I waited for Lenox to come out so we could all play football in the street. Candy had a caramel complexion and a beautiful smile that lifted her already high cheekbones and made her eyes squint when she laughed. She was thick with wide hips, had long, straight hair that came down below her shoulders and was always smiling and laughing. As I wrapped my hands around her waist and pulled her closer to me she put her arms around my shoulders and laid her head on my chest. Our hips swayed in time to the music as Anita Baker's sweet voice sang "With all my heart I love you baby. . ." I pulled Candy closer to me and held her tighter as she looked up, our eyes meeting and I started to slowly lower my head as she raised hers as Anita sang "Stay with me and you will see, my arms will hold you baby, never leave 'cause I believe. . ." We both closed our eyes, moving our faces closer to each other and just before our lips touched Lenox tapped us on the shoulders and said in a low whisper, "Candy, Mom is here, we have to go, hurry up before she sees you!"

Candy paused and looked at me then pulled me closer to her and whispered in my ear "You owe me a kiss." I pulled her closer and acted like I was going to whisper in her ear, instead giving her a soft, gentle kiss on the base of her neck and whispered back "There is your kiss, now you owe me!" She took a quick deep breath and then held it, closing her eyes as we pulled away from each other. The tension from that moment seemed to linger forever as she reluctantly walked towards the door.

I walked with her and Lenox two doors down to their house, joking with Candy's mother that Candy was the one that started all the commotion earlier at the party. Before they all headed in the house Candy turned around and said, "Make sure you call me tomorrow." I nodded my head to acknowledge that I heard her and turned around to walk back to my house only to see Brandon standing on the sidewalk, smiling a big goofy smile and greeting me with a high five as he said, "You owe me for that one! Man, did you see how I hooked you up??!?" We both busted out laughing and headed in the house to shut everything down and start cleaning up.

Tiny Tee left his equipment at my house for few days so we moved it all upstairs to my room in the attic. We set the equipment up and I stayed up all night spinning records and practicing mixing while Brandon gave me pointers. I stayed in my room for the next three days, practicing scratching and mixing and digging through records. DJ's would take a small sticker or use a marker to indicate the points on the records where the breaks started. A break is basically the point where the DJ needs to place the needle in order to play the best part of the record. True breaks occurred where a record would transition into a drum heavy portion or section of the song where there was usually just an instrumental piece. The DJ would get two identical records and place one on each turntable, playing the break from one first then seamlessly switching to the break on the other record and repeating this process to extend the time of the break and make it as long as they wanted. When Hip Hop started out, MCs would rhyme over these DJ created break loops so the DJ would have to be skilled enough to be able to transition back and forth from each record while making it sound uninterrupted, which is a lot harder than it looks.

I found a copy of T-La-Rock's song "Its Yours" and practiced flashing back and forth to the breakbeat in the record and the part where the record says "DJ Jazzy Jay" and "back to the beat." A year or two earlier the Hip Hop movie "Beat Street" came out and we all flooded the movie theatres to see it. My favorite scene in the movie was the B-boy battle scene in the club where DJ Jazzy Jay is DJing and the two main B-Boy crews face off and start to battle. Jazzy Jay was one of the first DJs to gain international fame because of that movie and his production work on tracks like "Its Yours" and Soul Sonic Force's "Planet Rock." I liked cutting the record because it said "Jay" in it and I would scratch just about any record that I could find with my name in it. Ironically, over twenty years later I would become friends with the legendary DJ Jazzy Jay and spend hours questioning him about the early days of hip hop as I thought back to the day when I stood in my attic learning how to flash using his name off a record that he made!

My time with the turntables taught me a few lessons. First I learned that I really loved playing music. It transported me somewhere else and helped me relax. I also learned that I was not a very good DJ and in order to become a good DJ I would have to practice a lot, so I made up my mind that I would dedicate all my time to the art of DJing and I had every intention of doing so until Tiny Tee came to pick up his equipment. Both Brandon and Tiny Tee would let me come over and practice any time I wanted but usually before I made it over to their houses I would get a call from Candy or some other girl and quickly forget about my dreams to become the next great DJ.

I was always into music and was usually the first person in my crew to have new music as soon as it came out. I would get tapes from NYC radio shows featuring DJs like Teddy Ted and Donald D, Africa Islam's Zulu Beat Show on 105.9 WHBI, Kool DJ Red Alert on KISS FM, Brucie B, Chief Rocker Busy B, Kool DJ AJ, Triple C and many others. These tapes kept me in the loop on the latest developments, educated me on Hip Hop culture, and gave me access to songs that had not made it to mass produced vinyl yet. I soon became the go-to person for anything related to Hip Hop and Hip Hop music. I listened to those tapes so much that most of them would eventually wear down and the tape would break. I would unscrew the tape cover, take out the two reels of tape and put a pencil into the center of the reels to keep them from moving, cut a tiny piece of sticky tape and splice the broken piece of the tape together, screw it all back in place and it was good as new. At least until the tape would pop again!

Listening to those tapes transported me into another world and I found myself fantasizing about being on those radio shows, about being one of those DJs or MCs featured on the shows. I could visualize myself sitting there, talking into the microphone while I answered questions about where I would be performing next or what party I would be DJing later that night. I probably spent more time listening to those tapes by myself in my room than I spent sleeping and I made up my mind that I wanted in, I wanted to a be a part of Hip Hop on a larger scale. And in time I would see my dreams come true.

High school was dominated by glaring contrasts; I yearned to learn and embraced academic challenges but truly feared being called "white" for excelling in school. I had a natural inclination to help people and found great joy in doing so but I didn't want to be viewed as soft or weak. I was angry as hell and wanted to lash out whenever I could but disliked conflict and went out of my way to avoid it when possible. I spent most of my time walking a very thin line between worlds, teetering back and forth and trying to prevent myself from falling more towards one direction then the other.

My circle of friends was extremely diverse, in part because I was very comfortable among both white and black peers, but also because my feelings of being an outsider kept me empathetic to how others felt. I always had a natural curiosity about people and cultures and found myself drawn to people that were outside of my normal circle. While students freely mingled and interacted with each other, as in most high schools, there were definitely distinct social groups or cliques. There were jocks, both male and female athletes from the basketball, football and track teams, many who played all three sports and most of whom were black. There were the street dudes, the ones that could fight and had growing reputations for quick tempers and taking no shit from anybody. We had what I would call the "cool kids" that dressed in the latest fashions, knew all the dances and could fit in with the street dudes and the jocks at the same time. Then we had the nerds, mostly white and Asian kids with a few black kids thrown in the mix, that had no problem openly studying for tests, using the library to do actual school work and were not interested in impressing jocks, street dudes or cool kids.

We had the hard-rock, heavy metal heads, usually white males. There were a few black kids and one or two bi-racial kids, that would wear heavy metal t-shirts with bands like Black Sabbath, Metallica and AC/DC. The heavy metal heads wore ripped jeans with studded belts, black motorcycle style boots and chains attached to their front belt loop linked to the wallets in their back pockets. In contrast to the heavy metal heads, we had B-Boys and B-Girls, at the time almost exclusively all black with a few Latinos. They were heavily ingrained in Hip Hop culture, wearing colored Levi's or designer Jordache or Guess jeans. Adidas or suede Puma sneakers, always laced with thick shoe laces that would match the Levi's or Polo shirt color and add a Kangol hat or some thick Gazelle style glasses to make their outfit complete.

While many would mingle with others outside of their peer groups, everyone spent most of their time within their own circle. My ability and reputation on the football field granted instant access to hang with the jocks and my dedication to Hip Hop culture also made me a part of the B-Boy clique and of course my Thurston Road crew was always around providing strong ties to the streets. I spent a lot of my time with my neighborhood friends and my close friends from the football team but in school I would bounce from group to group, spending time with the various friends I had inside the various cliques.

While I felt pretty comfortable around most of the various groups, I purposely distanced myself from the heavy metal heads. Inside their group were two or three black and one bi-racial dude. While the black heavy metal heads would often catch flak from the other black students, often being called "sell outs" or "white wanna-be's," the bi-racial guy was generally left alone by other black students. Occasionally he might catch some subtle remarks from some of the more rural minded white students, saying things like "We are glad you joined the right side," or "It's better to be with us then with them," but that was rare and far in between. It was much more common for one of my black friends to pull me to the side and ask me "How did you end up being black and he ended up being white when you are both mixed?" I never knew how to answer those questions and they always made me feel very awkward, until I started hanging out with Timothy Ragland.

Ragland, or Rags as we called him, was from Scottsville, a rural outskirt of a suburb about 20 miles to the southwest of the city. Scottsville consisted of a lot of farmland, cow pastures, cornfields and white folks, rural white folks, the kind that didn't necessarily welcome blacks and especially didn't embrace interracial relationships or the byproduct of those relationships. Ragland's parents were married and together for at least 20 years when I met him. His mother, who was white, was an executive in the hotel industry. His father, a black man from Alabama and former Green Beret, worked as one of the first black managing executives for a major corporation in the Rochester area.

Ragland spent his entire life attending schools in Scottsville until high school when he joined the Urban-Suburban program. The purpose of Urban-Suburban was supposed to be "to voluntarily reduce isolation and segregation of academic opportunities." This meant that the only students eligible would be minority students in the city that could move to suburban school districts where students of color were seriously under represented. White students in suburban districts could also apply for the program, enabling them to enter the Rochester city schools which had an overwhelming majority of students of color. It was highly unusual for any white student to want to attend a generally lower ranked, more problematic city school, and the program provided this opportunity clearly to maintain the appearance of equality. I seriously doubt that at that time anyone ever thought a suburban student would want to attend a city school.

In order to qualify, the program looked at a student's grades, behavior, attendance and teacher comments. Perspective students underwent an interview process. The program also required a commitment by the student's parents to attend monthly meetings with or about the schools. Wilson was considered one of the top public high schools in the area at that time and was one of the only schools offering computer classes. Ragland's parents felt that experiencing diversity would be beneficial so they applied for and got him accepted into the program.

Ragland was a product of his environment. Until high school he was surrounded by white, rural peers, so he listened to rock music and dressed and talked just like his white suburban friends. He was a darker caramel complexion, much darker than me to the point that no one would ever confuse him for being anything but black, big, about six feet tall and easily weighed two hundred and fifty pounds, and he was strong, country farm, white boy strong, so he was a natural on the football field. We met through football and became friends after the school year started and we both ended up in the same homeroom.

Freshmen year our homeroom teacher was Ms. McClaney, an older black woman that had been teaching English for over twenty years. She was stern and had a reputation for going off on students, sometimes they said for no reason. Most of the students were not big fans of Ms. McClaney but I appreciated her brash style and was always the first one to bust out laughing when she went off on someone, making comments like "See, I told you that Ms. McClaney doesn't play that but you said you were going to do it anyways!"

My comments would make her even more upset at whomever she was chastising which would just encourage me to say something else. One time, a friend came into our homeroom to hand a late assignment to Ms. McClaney. She was already irritated that the assignment was late and was quietly scolding him before telling him he could go. As he walked towards the door I said in a purposefully loud whisper, "Dude did you just suck your teeth at her??? Man, you better hope she didn't hear that!" Before my friend could respond, Ms. McClaney stood up from her desk and yelled "Come get this assignment. You are getting a zero for this. I will teach you some manners. I am sick and tired of you kids acting like there is no need to respect your elders. You going to learn a lesson today!"

I turned my head away from Ms. McClaney to hide my laughter and the rest of the class let out a collective "Ooooh" before they all busted out laughing. Ms. McClaney scolded the entire classroom for laughing and as she did, I stood by her side shaking my head, serious look on my face and said "I am ashamed of all of you, you think education is a damn joke!" Half of the class sat there with their mouths open while the other half laughed even harder. Then I said "Ms. McClaney can I leave now, I am disgusted by their behavior and could really use some time away from them right now!" And to everyone's astonishment she said, "I know how you feel. I am truly disappointed in them. Go ahead and leave and I'm sorry you had to hear that!"

As I left the classroom Ragland looked at me with his mouth wide open in disbelief! As soon as we saw each other in the locker room before practice he said "Thanks a lot, now she is making the entire home room write a paper on respect!" With a completely straight face I said "Damn, I'm sorry dude!" then I yelled "Sike!" and we both busted out laughing. "I owe your ass BIG time for that one!" he said as he put his arm around me and we walked out of the locker room towards the practice field, both cracking up the entire way to the field.

One day during practice, Ragland was called to the office for an impromptu meeting with the principal and his counselor. They told him that he would not be able to attend Wilson because he did not qualify for the Urban-Suburban program. On the application Ragland checked off the box indicating that he was white, if he had checked the box indicating that he was black then he would not have qualified for the program as the program's intent was to increase racial diversity. Adding another black kid to the city schools would have defeated the purpose of the program's intent. The administrator told Ragland that he lied on the application, and that "anyone could see that he was clearly black!"

Ragland's mother had to come to the school to verify his "whiteness" in order for him to remain in the program. I can only assume that when they saw his white mother come in that their pasty white faces had to turn bright red with embarrassment. They tried to explain their reasoning, saying that the school system considered him to be black even though his mother was white but said despite what the district would think, that he could stay in the program and that they wouldn't take any steps to have him removed. When Ragland told me about it I just listened, and for once I was at a complete loss for words. Not being able to articulate what I felt at that moment or even knowing who to articulate my feelings to. I just shook my head and we both looked at each other, partly laughing and partly wanting to cry.

My mother moved us to a large duplex with three bedrooms and a large, unfinished attic that I would soon use as my room. The house sat on the corner of Genesee Park Blvd. and Woodbine Ave., a few blocks from our place on Brookdale. The move was definitely uplifting for my mother as it seemed to represent a fresh start. She was now permanently working as a nurse for the Rochester City School district and was focused on getting us into what she felt was a better neighborhood.

I was happy for the additional space even though the move meant that I would have to walk a few extra blocks to hang out with my boys on Thurston. I was more concerned with the inconvenience of not having Candy two doors down anymore. Candy's father was super strict and made it clear to me that he did not want me in their house at all with or without supervision! He didn't even want us sitting outside on the front steps and if he was home when we were outside, he would call Candy inside and loudly tell me to leave, making sure that I heard him. Candy's mother was much more laid back but kept a watchful eye on her while being more willing to allow us time to hang out in the house as long as she was home and her father didn't find out.

Casey, Candy's older sister, lived with her two young sons above a storefront on Thurston Road. Casey's husband, who everyone called Jet, was about ten years older than us and grew up close to the corner of Seward and Genesee Street and ran with the Black Mob, the loosely organized "gang" that interrupted my house party. Jet and Casey had an on-again-off-again relationship, he would be around for a few weeks or a month and then he would be gone again. When he was around we didn't say much to each other but always seemed to get along. Candy spent a lot of time at Casey's apartment on the weekends, usually staying overnight to babysit so her sister could go to work or occasionally go out. Casey let me come over and stay with Candy when she was there so her apartment became the one place we knew we could get some one-on-one time away from the watchful eyes of her mother and stepfather.

On the weekends when I wasn't staying at Casey's and spending time with Candy, I was usually hanging out with my boys on or around Thurston. We were now smoking weed and drinking every time we hung out and the more we drank the wilder we usually became. Considering that none of us had jobs or had yet gotten serious about making any money, we were always broke and trying to come up with ways to get alcohol and weed. We would often gather outside of the 7-Eleven on Thurston and Flanders street and hang out there until the manager would run us off.

He was just doing his job but we took it personally, especially when the older dudes congregating outside the store would say things like "Damn, ya'll little Niggas let dude disrespect you like that? Man, I bet he won't tell none of us to move! He knows he will catch hell over this way!" They were just trying to mess with our heads and over time it eventually worked. One day we decided that the manager was going to pay for his apparent disrespect. Lamont and Tim went into the store while the rest of us stayed outside creating more noise than usual to make sure he came out to confront us. As he came out of the door to chase us away, Lamont and Tim came up from behind him. Tim went low and grabbed his legs and Lamont pushed him until he tumbled to the ground. Before he knew what was happening, kicks and punches were coming from all directions and all he could do was cover up until the feet and fists stopped flying. One of the other employees in the store came outside screaming "I called the police, they are on their way." Sherrod shouted "Bring your ass out here if you want, you can catch some of this ass whopping too! I'll tell you what, come fuck with us again and see what happens!"

Someone yelled out "po-po is coming, let's bounce" and we all started to scatter in different directions. Lamont, Londell and I ran up Thurston and then down Sawyer before we saw the lights of the police car behind us and heard "Stop running mother fuckers. Freeze god damn it." Hearts racing, we dipped through a backyard and over a fence into the adjoining backyard as we laughed and Lamont said "Yeah ok, catch me if you can chump!" We zig-zagged through another back yard and onto Enterprise Street where we ran through another yard, avoiding a dog, slid behind a garage and ran through a few more yards until we got to Lamont's backyard. We knew those streets and backyards like the back of our hand and there was no way anyone, especially the police, had a chance to catch us in our own neighborhood. We all bent over laughing and walked onto the front porch and went into Lamont's house, peeking out of the front window every now and then to see if the police were on the street.

After that, we became bolder with our activities in and around 7-Eleven. The next time we got together in front of the store we all expected to see the police show up or for the manager to again try to run us away but nothing happened so a few of us headed into the store. While I talked to the employee at the cash register, Londell, Sherrod, Lonnie Harper and a couple others made their way into different aisles, spreading out to make it impossible for the cashier to see everyone at the same time. I kept asking for things that were on shelves behind the cashier and as he would turn to get them everyone would quickly stuff their pockets full of items. We all left the store and walked down Flanders Street until we were out of eye sight of the store and everyone started to empty out their pockets. Sherrod pulled out packs of Bubblicious Bubble Gum, Now & Laters, Pop Rocks and Whistle Pops, and Londell and Lonnie had their pockets filled with bags of Wise Potato Chips, Spicy pork rinds and Doritos.

We all grabbed a few items from each other, walked and ate our bounty as Lamont and Tim drilled each other with Lamont saying "Nigga you was so scared to take anything that I could see your hands shaking all the way across the store!" And Tim fired back "Ah Nigga please, you should have stolen some damn deodorant with your musty ass!" We all laughed as we made our way through the neighborhood looking for some more trouble to get into.

Eventually we got so fearless that four or five of us would walk into the store, head straight to the back coolers where the beer was kept, grab as many forty ounce bottles as we could carry and walk right out of the store, not even trying to hide them. On the few occasions when the manager did call the police, we always made sure to return to the store and throw a few rocks or a brick through the window as a reminder that he had just made a big mistake. Eventually, after the threats and the beat downs and the inability of the police to catch us or do anything, he just gave up and turned his back the other way whenever we would come around.

As we experienced more success evading the police and running wild through our neighborhood, our activities became more and more audacious. Double-Day's bar was a few blocks down and across the street from 7-Eleven. Friday and Saturday nights the bar would be packed with middle-class white folks, usually in their twenties or early thirties, all out to drink and party. One late weekend night, we were walking past the bar when we heard someone yell out "Hey Niggers" followed by laughter from inside the bar. Tim said "What the fuck did that cracker say? Did he just call us Niggers?? Man, we got to fuck him up!" We all kept walking to the corner and out of eyesight of the bar then Jason Bradley went back and yelled "Bring your ass outside so I can show you who the Nigger is mother fucker!"

A lone white man in his early thirties came out of the door as his friends tried to stop him and made his way closer to the street where Jason was standing. Surprised that anyone dared to come outside, we split up, a few of us headed around the corner of the bar while a few walked behind Jason and into the parking lot of the bank across the street. I doubled back and walked closer to the entrance of the bar until I was a few feet behind the man and stood with my back leaning against a tree in front of the bar. We moved so quickly and so quietly that the man didn't even realize he was surrounded but the other patrons in the bar saw what was happening. Jason said "Who is the Nigger now?" Before anything could happen, someone came out of the bar and said "take that shit across the street or I'm calling the police."

Jason started to back up into the street as he said "You're lucky mother fucker you were about to get your ass kicked." Surprising all of us, the man followed Jason across the street and said "You can't kick my ass, I will teach you mother fuckers a lesson!" As soon as he got into the bank's parking lot, Tim rushed him, bent down and grabbed his legs, picked him up and slammed him hard onto his back. "Ooooooh, yeah mother fucker, who is the Nigger now?" Seeing us start to close in on him, the man jumped up and tried to take a swing at Londell but before he could fully regain his balance, Tim grabbed him again, picked him up almost over his head and slammed him to the ground even harder. The man let out a loud grunt as the air left his body and the impact caused Tim to lose his grip, allowing the man to slide out and ease his back up against the wall of the bank.

He somehow managed to stand up and before Tim could react, the man was on top of him, pulling his arm back and getting ready to punch Tim as he said "I got you now you bastard." I made my way closer to where the man was standing over Tim and before anyone else could react I punched the man square on his chin, wobbling his legs and forcing him to fall backwards. Before he could regain his footing, I unleashed three or four more punches, hitting him in his nose then his forehead, knocking him further backwards and finally delivering one last blow to the chin that sent him straight to the pavement face first. Tim jumped up and everyone yelled out "Ooooooh shit, you got your ass knocked the fuck out! Who's the Nigger now mother fucker??" As he laid on the pavement dazed and half out of it, Tim, looking like an NFL field goal kicker, took one or two steps towards him and kicked him in the head as if his head was a football, lifting him up off the ground and smashing his head against the brick wall of the bank. Blood was gushing from his head and nose as everyone jumped in and pummeled him with fists and feet. He curled up into a ball and tried to protect his head and body but blows were coming from every direction, hitting his body with repeated dull thudding sounds.

Watching from across the street, someone from the bar yelled out "Ok, that is enough, we called the police. Stop it before you kill him!!!" Tim was irate, he was kicking the man over and over again with such force that we all stopped to look at him in shock. Lamont finally grabbed Tim and said "Chill, that's enough, dude is done man, he is done." Looking down at the man's lifeless body, blood pouring from the cuts on his head, mouth and nose, we all froze for a moment. It seemed that we were all thinking the same thing. We may have just killed somebody, and I paused looking for any signs of life.

The sounds of sirens in the distance slowly moved closer and became more intense as the man started to move and moan loudly. Lamont grabbed my arm and said "Come on man, we got to bounce. Let's make a move man." Jason Bradley said "I bet you won't call us Nigger again!" and laughed as we all ran down the side streets and disappeared into backyards, high fiving each other and discussing who hit him the hardest and who inflicted the most damage.

This became our normal hang out activity; roam Thurston

until we found some trouble, run from the police, get drunk, smoke some weed and repeat. This pattern was echoed repeatedly in neighborhood after neighborhood throughout the entire city. We were always looking to jump somebody and white boys were the number one target. Beating down white dudes was a game that everyone seemed to be playing and they almost never had a fair chance. Just like in grade school, there was no such thing as a fair one-on-one fight against a white boy. Everyone wanted a piece of them and anyone standing on the sidelines, not participating was considered to be suspect and would be drilled so unmercifully that it seemed that they would be shamed for life.

It was during times like this that I tried to forget about who I was, that I tried to forget that my mother was white and that I was in-fact half white. I would get caught up in the moment, the anger, the hatred that came along with growing up poor and in this jungle-like environment that consumed all of my peers and seemed to push us all over the edge. None of my friends ever looked at me as being anything but what I was and in their eyes, I was the same as them, I was another black boy growing up in the neighborhood.

I tried to forget, tried to force the memories out my mind about my early days at #37 school when they called me "white boy" and how lost I was trying to figure out why everyone wanted to pick a fight with me. I instead allowed myself to focus on my anger, an anger that grew from places I didn't fully understand but to me felt like it must be related to my racial identity. I was now an active participant in the exact same system that seemed to advocate violence against people like, or perceived to be like me. The love and acceptance I received from my crew was genuine and deep. Coupled with the attention I received from the girls and the popularity in school, at times I felt like I was on top of the world. But there was always something or someone that was there to remind me that in their eyes, I was an outsider, a white boy or in some cases a black youth, that needed to be put in his place.

8 KARMA

Even though I had a number of really great teachers that took the time to work with me and would often pull me aside to talk with me and share their confidence in my abilities, I started skipping most of my classes. There were a few classes that were engaging enough for me to actively participate in and through one of these classes I managed to get nominated for a position as a student court judge.

Student court was established to provide students with an opportunity to have their disciplinary actions heard in front of a panel of their peers. The student judges would determine innocence and guilt and hand down punishments accordingly. When I first heard about it my initial thought was that it would be a great opportunity to help my friends get out of trouble and it also seemed like a great way to make some money. I figured we would be able to hand down not-guilty verdicts for friends and take money from those we didn't know in order to "fix" their verdicts and get them off easy. After going through training sessions and watching a few sessions of the student court we were finally given our chance to act as judges.

I sat on a panel with Reg and my football teammate Lawrence Pack. We heard three cases, all involved students whom we knew, each appearing for a different offense. Once we heard their charges, they were allowed to present their case while we asked questions and then convened privately to determine the verdict and if need be, the punishment. As soon as I put the judges robe on and sat down on the bench a transformation took place. It wasn't just me, it was all of us. Our initial idea that everyone would be walking out of there not guilty was replaced with a seriousness and professionalism that seemed to come out of nowhere. We handed down three guilty verdicts with accompanying punishments that were much more severe than any of us expected.

I had a strong sense of pride sitting on that court and came away from the experience wanting to do more, wanting to achieve a level of success in school that I hadn't wanted before. It felt good to hear the praises of the supervising teachers and see the respect that came from my peers for doing something positive. I also found myself interested in the law and for the first time I allowed myself to think about doing something bigger in life, like maybe becoming a real judge, and the idea stuck with me until I found out that being a judge meant first being a lawyer, and that being a lawyer meant at least seven years of college. Seven years sounded like an eternity to me so I quickly dismissed the idea and went back to flirting with girls and cracking jokes on freshmen.

Like many of my peers, I lacked the patience for long-term goals and I thought that immediate financial success was the answer. I saw a focus on academics as meaning four years of high school, then another four years of college, and then finding a job and putting in another ten years there before I could finally buy a fancy car or a big house or have the nice clothes that all the girls seemed to love. I thought that if I could find a way to make all that money today then I could have all those things and at the same time bypass college and a good job and maybe even bypass high school. Besides, isn't making money the entire point anyway? Isn't the idea of a good job based on the idea that the good job will put good money in your pocket? This was the reasoning that I used to justify not caring and to help erase any of the internal resistance I may have had to my own poor choices.

Wilson was actually full of talented educators, most of whom genuinely cared about the students and took education very seriously. Wilson also had a large number of students that were academically competitive and seemed to be already focused on college and their future careers. There were many times when I looked at those academically driven peers and envied them, their focus and maturity. There was a large part of me that knew that I could do what they were doing, that I could succeed in the classroom and achieve good grades but I was still very much caught up in trying to prove that I was tough and not some nerdy white boy. My years spent trying to emulate the examples set by my stepfather, the thugs and the cool kids around me created behaviors that were becoming entrenched in my thought process and were directly competing against the time, energy and effort that would be required to succeed in school.

While I was busy trying to fight against the system, Candy was accumulating academic awards and recognition at her new job, which rewarded her with a day off and a bonus check and to celebrate she wanted to take me out to eat. We met at Reggie's house and decided to walk the fifteen blocks or so back towards Thurston to the restaurant she choose for us to eat at. We held hands as we walked, laughing and talking and enjoying the beautiful weather, taking a short cut through Aberdeen Square, by #16 school. As we approached the square, composed of a large section of green grass acting as a divider for the two streets running on either side about two blocks long, we turned the corner and encountered a group of eight to ten young dudes, all my age. We walked through the group, two of them stepped in front of us as the others slowly eased their way behind and each side of us eventually stopping our progress.

I wasn't really worried as I knew a few of them, Darnell who lived across the street from me when I lived on Elmdorf, and his cousin Raylondo, and I saw most of the others guys around from time to time but didn't know them on a first name basis. Raylondo, standing in front of us said, "Look at the white boy, holding hands with a sister like that shit is cool. That shit ain't cool white boy." Sensing that things were about to get ugly, I eased Candy closer to a tree until her back was against it and moved in front of her to try to act as a barrier against them.

I could hear whispers coming from some of the other dudes saying, "Wait a minute, isn't that Jason? Dude is cool man, he's from the other end of Thurston." While someone else said, "I don't know that white boy, he ain't from our neighborhood so fuck him." Raylondo chimed in, "What the fuck you going to do white boy?" and as I made a fist in preparation to swing at him I felt a punch land to the back of my head, knocking me forward and closer to Raylondo, who quickly threw a series of punches towards my head. I ducked the punches, bent down and grabbed Raylondo, wrapping my arms around his legs and quickly picked him up, slamming him hard to the ground and landing on top of him.

As I was positioning myself to pin him down with my legs so I could hit him, someone tackled me from the side and knocked me off of him then I was pummeled with kicks from all directions. "Yeah white boy, stay down mother fucker," and "Oh shit, we got his white punk ass now," was heard as they continued to land kicks, trying to go for my head which I instinctively covered. Someone said "Chill, chill, what are ya'll doing, that's enough."

And as quickly as it started, I looked up to see them all running in different directions, the same way we had always done whenever we jumped someone. I sat there for a moment, trying to regain my composure when I looked up to see Candy standing there with her hands over her face, mouth wide open, tears running down her cheeks as she looked at me. I stood up, brushed the dirt off of my shirt and pants and wiped off the blood that was trickling from my nose. She said in almost a whisper, "Jason? Jason? Are you ok? Why did they do that? What was that all about? Are you ok??"

I shook my head and shrugged my shoulders in anger and embarrassment, not knowing what to say I just put my arm around her and said, "I'm alright, I'm alright, don't cry, you see I'm alright." As we continued walking Candy pulled some tissue out of her purse and I stuffed it into my nose to help stop the bleeding. Seeing the concern on her face, I jokingly said, "I would have beat them down but I didn't want you to think I was some sort of savage or something!" She looked at my slightly bruised face and gave me an uneasy laugh while I continued to move the tissue in my nose to make sure it was effectively stopping the bleeding. As we walked down Thurston, past the 7-Eleven, past Double Days and all the various spots that we always hung out, smoking weed, drinking and jumping other people, I couldn't help but think that this was payback for all those times I participated in jumping someone, that the universe was now balancing things out by handing me a humbling reminder that what goes around comes around.

When I got to my house, my mother saw my face and immediately started peppering me with questions, "Are you ok? What happened? Oh my god Jason, let me look at you." "I'm ok mom, I got jumped, it's no big deal, just a bloody nose." She then turned her questions to Candy, "What happened? Are you ok? Did you get hurt too?" Candy explained to her what happened and I think for the first time my mother realized that the world I was living in was considerably different then the world she envisioned. She saw me becoming more defiant and difficult but I think she chalked that up to simple adolescence, to the changes associated with becoming a teenager. This seemed to open her eyes a bit to the types of things that I may have been involved in, to what I may have been experiencing on a daily basis.

She looked at me differently, with a concern that came from somewhere new and she hugged me and said, "Who did this to you? Please tell me what happened?" I brushed off her questions and tried to show her that I was tough, that I could take being jumped like a man, that it was nothing for her to worry about, but part of me that was slowly being buried deep inside wanted to cry, wanted to tell her all the things that I've seen and done, wanted her to know that I was tired of being called white boy and that I was tired of having to prove that I was tough. A part of me desperately wanted to just run away, just go somewhere safe, find a place where I could be accepted for who I was and not persecuted for who others thought I was.

But I swallowed hard and pushed those feelings down, kept them in check so that I could stand tall and portray what I thought was the stance of a man. The streets were teaching me that being a man meant not crying, that being a man meant that you never took shit from anybody and if someone disrespects you, you put them in their place immediately no matter how large or small their slight. The "real men" that everyone admired had lots of girls, wore the latest fashions, were feared by everyone and respected for their ability to fuck someone up quickly. The real men that were respected showed no fear, they were courageous and were everything that was the opposite of what the hood felt was white. White men were looked upon as weak, as physically inferior, as the prime example of what not to be. The ultimate diss was to have someone say you were acting white, it meant that you were weak, you were not respected, that you had no style, that you were trying to be something that the hood despised and worst of all that you had no respect.

At the same time, I was feeling vulnerable and wanting to welcome my mother's embrace, I started to get angry, remembering them calling me white boy as they kicked and punched me. "Why did they do this to you Jason?" I wanted to shout out, "WHY? WHY? They did this to me because of YOU! They did this to me because you are white and they think that I am white, they did this to me because I am not them!" I wanted to tell my mother everything that I had gone through, tell her about my first day at #37 school when I was tripped and called white boy and tell her how I was picked on for raising my hand and knowing the answer to questions in class. As she hugged me, I was torn between hugging her back, enjoying the comforts and security of being close to my mother, and wanting to push her away and get as far away from her as possible. The moment seemed to encapsulate the feelings of being an outsider, the emotions associated with being a bi-racial teenager struggling to find himself in a world that showed no interest in accepting anyone that fell outside of the clearly defined boxes we were all expected to fit into.

My inability to articulate my emotions often led to feelings of anger and the behaviors associated with being angry. The only person that even hinted that they might understand what I was going through was Ragland, but even his experiences seemed to be different than my own as his identity was rooted more in rural white culture and he seemed perfectly fine wearing ripped jeans, fastening his wallet to a chain on his belt and listening to Metallica and Bon Jovi. I was drawn to Hip Hop culture, colored Levi's, suede Puma's with the fat shoe laces, Run-DMC, Whodini, the Fat Boys, Public Enemy, and R&B groups like DeBarge, New Edition, Cameo and Ready for the World. Although we were different in many of our cultural attractions, we had far more similarities than differences.

When our parents first met, they were thrilled to see that we both had a bi-racial friend. Both of our mothers worried about the struggles that we would have to face and seemed to find relief in the hopes that we would be able to commiserate with one another about our experiences. Ragland's father was a bit more pessimistic in his views of our friendship, and while he too was thrilled that Ragland found someone like him to hang out with, he had a much more in-depth understanding of the types of struggles we would face in a world that looked at and treated black men like criminals from birth.

My 16th birthday brought with it two goals; to find a job and second, I wanted a car. I had always found ways to make money, from my first few years in Rochester when I would get up early, grab a shovel and go door-to-door asking neighbors if they needed their driveways and sidewalks shoveled, to getting my fist paper route a few years later. I was always drawn to having my own money and loved having a few dollars in my pocket just so I could spend it if I ever decided that spending it was what I wanted.

I learned a lot about running a business from those paper routes. I learned about collecting debts and how difficult it can be to track down people when they owe you money and I also learned that the people that paid got the best service. I learned how to budget and estimate profits and I learned how to save money and plan for future purchases. As much as I enjoyed the responsibility and the little bit of money that I was making, I hated hearing my friends tease me about delivering those papers and eventually I quit but that little taste of working for myself and making money stuck with me.

It had been years since I had a paper route, as my birthday approached, I began looking for job opportunities and a few days after I turned 16, I landed my first job washing dishes at the restaurant inside of the Radisson Hotel next to the Rochester Institute of Technology. Despite my mother's hectic schedule working multiple jobs and taking care of my brother and sister, she always made sure I got to work on time and would pick me up whenever I was unable to catch a ride home with someone else. Initially I worked on the weekends but quickly picked up hours during the week filling in when someone called in sick or when they fired someone.

I didn't mind washing dishes, except for the pots and pans there wasn't much washing by hand. The busboys and wait staff would bring in dishes from the restaurant on trays, throw away any remaining food and place the dishes on a large counter which had a rack on top of it that held containers where the dirty glasses would be placed. I would take the dishes, spray them down and load them into two-foot by two-foot racks before I pushed them into the large machine that washed and dried them and then take them out of the machine and stack them in preparation to be put back into circulation. The entire process, from rinsing the dishes off, to loading the machine, to emptying the machine took maybe two minutes.

I hated just standing around waiting for the machine so instead, I would help the servers clear off their trays, which they loved as it meant they had more time to spend with customers in the dining room. Eventually, the servers started to tip me out at the end of each night, $20 or $30 each, and that extra money from five or six servers added up quick and helped me bring home sometimes an extra $300 to $600 a week on top of my regular pay check.

When the other dishwashers found out I was getting tipped

they were pissed and there was a big issue between them and the servers. I somehow managed to stay out of it but it got so bad that most of them were fired or ended up quitting. Most of the wait staff and all of the cooks were white while many of the dishwashers and maintenance workers were black. There seemed to be an air of tension always lingering between the two sides. The white cooks would have their radio blaring on the cook's line, playing classic rock from groups like Led Zeppelin, Ozzy Osbourne, ZZ Topp and Pink Floyd. I knew a lot of the songs they played from my days in Elmira. One of the first albums that I asked my mother to buy for me was Pink Floyd's "The Wall." I played that album non-stop and I would listen to Ozzy Osbourne with Antonio and Matthew's older brother who was a huge Ozzy fan.

While Pink Floyd played on one side of the kitchen, on the other side, behind the dishwasher where I worked, the maintenance and dish staff were playing Hip Hop and R&B. Atlantic Starr, the S.O.S. Band, Billy Ocean, Bobby Brown, Dougie Fresh, the Beastie Boys and the 2 Live Crew would blast from the speakers while we bobbed our heads, rapped and sang along and danced while we worked. I would sing along and bob my head and then take the clean dishes over to the cook's line where I would nod my head in approval of their tunes and grab a quick listen to some of those same classic rock tunes that were a part of my earlier life.

I found myself moving between both worlds without putting forth much effort and it was the first time that I felt like I had an advantage among the people that were around me. My easiness around the wait and cooking staff along with my laid back personality and sprinkles of charm made communicating with everyone comfortable and I soon became the intermediary between the two opposing work forces. I would pass the concerns of the dish staff to the head Chef and he would tell me the issues the cooks were having and without really knowing what I was doing, I would work towards negotiating a truce between the sides.

The head Chef started having me assist with chopping lettuce and vegetables and doing other prep work that was normally assigned to the prep cooks. When the sandwich and salad cook didn't show up to work one day, I was asked to fill in and spent the day making turkey club sandwiches, cobb salads and shrimp cocktails. I caught on so quickly and worked so fast that the following week he put me on the prep cook schedule and asked me if I knew anyone that was interested in picking up some of my hours washing dishes.

Reg had been looking for work and was one of the few friends that I thought would be responsible enough to show up to work and actually work when he was scheduled so I brought him in to meet with the head chef and get him on the schedule. I trained him for the next few weeks and then he took over my position washing dishes and I started as a prep cook/sandwich cook on a regular basis. When a few of the other dishwashers quit, the chef again asked me if I knew anyone else that was looking for work and soon, most of the dish staff was composed of my friends. I brought in Tyrone Scott and Tim Riley, my two homies that were a part of the break dancing group the "Ultimate Rockers" and performed in the talent show at #3 school with me. Eventually it didn't even feel like work anymore, we would play our music, talk, laugh and hang out as if we were on our own time, but I always made sure that I got my work done and tried to make sure that they did the same.

Soon, during dinner rushes and when things were really busy, I was asked to help out on the main cook's line, at first just placing garnishes on plates and helping out on the frying station. The cook's line was fast paced and required communication between the head chef and the other cooks in the various stations on the line. The wait-staff would bring the customer's order into the kitchen written down on a small piece of numbered note paper and place it on a wheel located at eye level to the Chef. The chef would look it over and then call out what had to be cooked at each of the various stations before he would place the order on a small rail above where the food was being plated. Usually, the Chef would also oversee or help out on the grill where steaks, burgers, fish or chicken were being cooked while one or two sous chefs would handle orders that were cooked in pans, such as shrimp scampi, pasta, and seared dishes. A senior sous chef would back up the head chef at his station and also run the broiler, basically an overhead box with a hot flame coming from the top that was used to broil things like swordfish or prime rib or melt cheese over items like French onion soup, potato skins, and nachos. The assistant chef also supervised the fry cook at the fry stations where multiple large industrial sized deep fryers, with two large steel woven baskets suspended over each, were used to deep fry French fries, chicken wings, seafood and other unhealthy tasty foods and appetizers.

The chef would figure out how long each food item would take prior to calling them out so that he could time the entire meal perfectly and have it all come out, piping hot at the exact same time. This was no easy task as there might be twenty or thirty orders being worked on at one time with many different orders headed to the same table and of course everyone at the table wanted their food to come out hot and at the same time. The chef would have to know each server's tendencies and how long they would normally take from the time they picked up their appetizers, until the time they usually picked up their entrées and factor that into when he told the other cooks to start on the order in each of their stations. I never knew how much work went into getting a meal from a customer's order to a kitchen and then back to the table but I was developing a new respect for the process.

Within a few weeks I had mastered the fry station and was soon trained on the grill, practicing creating perfect diamond shaped grill marks on hamburgers and grilled chicken sandwiches during slow lunches before being taught to expertly cook a steak, from red and bloody rare, to well done, depending on the customer's preference. After mastering steaks, I started working the line during the busy dinner rushes and Sunday brunches and soon learned to work each station on the line as effectively as some of the cooks that had been doing it for decades. Within a few months, when the assistant chef called in sick on a Saturday night, the busiest night of the week, Jackson, the head chef, gave me a shot at running the broiler and backing him up and after seeing me hold my own, he officially promoted me to line cook and started scheduling me to work the assistant position when the assistant chef was not on the schedule.

I also started delivering room service orders on the weekends and busing tables during Sunday brunch. When a customer finished their meal and left, I would clear off the tables, wipe them down and then replace the linen table cloth and add new place settings, glasses, etc., in preparation for the next customer. While the customers were still eating, I would sometimes refill their water glasses and bring them coffee when they finished their meals. For my efforts, I was paid minimum wage and I received tips from the wait-staff. I quickly learned to flip the tables of the wait-staff that tipped the best first, and to make sure that their tables always had water and coffee without them having to ask.

Initially Sunday brunch had two to three busboys, but I worked so fast that eventually I was running the entire dining room by myself, which meant that I got to keep all of the tips instead of splitting them equally with the other busboys. The Wait-staff would usually tip me out about 10% of whatever they made that day with their tips being about $300 on a slow day and up to $700 on a good brunch. With eight to ten servers working a brunch, I was bringing in $300 to $700 myself for four hours of work. With my weekly salary from the kitchen, the automatic 20% tip from my room service deliveries and my busboy tips, I was bringing home between $750 and $1500 a week, which was serious money for a sixteen-year old in the mid 1980s.

Eventually I started closing the kitchen on Friday, Saturday and Sunday nights. I would be the last cook in the kitchen and was responsible for making sure the kitchen was cleaned, prep schedules were ready for the next day and the preparation of any late night orders coming in from room service or the bar area was completed. Closing also meant that I was usually working with and directly supervising at least one of my dishwashing friends. As soon as the Chef and other cooks cleared out, I would throw a couple of filet mignons on the grill and whip up some shrimp scampi or one of the other dishes that I was now experienced at preparing and we would eat like kings! Sometimes, I would fix the bartenders some food and in exchange, they would bring us beers on tap and shots. Leaving work with a belly full of gourmet food, a buzz from the drinks and a pocket full of money made me feel as if the world was mine and soon I was working forty to fifty hours a week and spending more time at the hotel then I was at school.

It was becoming common place for me to miss at least two to three days of school a week because I was either too tired to get up after working all night or because I just didn't feel like going. My mother was now working as a school nurse in the city school district and she would receive a call from the central attendance office whenever I was late or not in school, which was pretty much every day. My discontent with school was growing almost as quick as my mother's frustration and led to many arguments between us, most of which resulted in me leaving the house for a few days until things cooled down. I would stay at Reg's house or if it was a weekend, at Candy's sister's house and then go back home when things calmed down.

Despite my declining interest in school, my mother was pleased with my desire to work, which was helping me develop a true sense of pride in earning my own way. Besides putting money in my pocket, working full-time reduced the time hanging with my partners on Thurston and limited the amount of trouble I could get into. By this time Lamont, Sherrod, Tim, Londell, Lonnie and the rest of my boys were easing their way into activities that could have sent all of us to prison for a long time. Our early days of jumping drunk white dudes and raiding 7-eleven morphed into robbing those same drunk dudes for their wallets and car keys, stealing their cars and venturing into new neighborhoods across town to see who else could get robbed. The more brazen the activity, the more respect we generated from each other and the rest of the neighborhood.

Everyone knew I was working and when I told them I could get them jobs working with me, a few of them reached in their pockets and pulled out wads of cash and said "Nigga, does it look like I need a job working all the way out there with you? I ain't working for those crackers, that ain't for me bro." I said, "Well if you change your mind, let me know, now pass that weed so I can hit it before Lamont puts his crusty, dusty, chalk board looking lips on it!"

Lamont would fire back, "Fuck you, you light bright, Prince looking want-to-be, your momma likes these lips!" and we would all bust out laughing as we passed around weed and used sips of the forty-ounce bottles of Old English to chase down the guzzles we all took from the rotating bottles of E&J Brandy or Seagram's Gin. Although I wasn't around as much as I used to be, it was those times that made me still feel like we were family, like nothing had changed but time and like nothing would ever change .

Hanging out in Corey's bedroom as he and Tim practiced for an upcoming talent show; I sat on Corey's bed listening as they worked on their routine, checking out the large posters of Run-DMC and Whodini, and the small pictures of the Fat Boys, the Beastie Boys and others, cut out from magazines and carefully placed throughout the room. The entire room, from the records stacked up in milk crates to the speakers blasting the sounds of Tim rhyming on the microphone, to Corey's scratches, everything was Hip Hop. We were all laughing and so caught up in the moment that nothing else seemed to exist, life was good and we were just enjoying being alive, until Sherrod came and stuck his head in Corey's open bedroom window.

"YO, YO, did ya'll hear about what happened?" Sherrod asked as he yelled in a voice that was trembling and totally uncharacteristic for him.

"Naw man, what's up? What's going on man??" I said.

"Lamont. Its Lamont. Somebody...he was...man he was downtown and that dude Drew...man he got fucked up real bad, Lamont got stabbed man and he ain't going to make it."

The entire vibe of the room changed from the warm, bright and colorful, music filled party, to a dreary, dimly lit, black and white, motionless box. I slowly stood up from the bed as Tim peppered Sherrod with questions, "When did it happen, who was there, where is Lamont now, who is with him?" I could hear the questions but they all blurred together and Sherrod's answers were unintelligible as we all looked around at each other, mouths wide open and not knowing what to do. We stood there, stunned for what seemed like forever until anger finally broke through and slapped us back into the moment. Tim was the first to shout "Yo we got to get that mother fucker. Go get everybody together and we got to find that motherfucka, he ain't getting away with stabbing Lamont! Fuck that."

Before we could make any type of move Sherrod said, "He's at the hospital, I'm heading back over there now, I'll call ya'll and let you know what's happening," and he left. Tim headed to his house and I headed to mine, in a bit of a daze and not knowing what was going to happen.

As I walked home I thought about all the crazy things Lamont and I had done together, all the jokes we cracked on each other, all the times he made me laugh when I was going through something and didn't feel like laughing. Lamont was the glue that held all of us together, he was the reason that we all became friends and the reason that we all remained friends even when we had problems with each other. He had a gift for bringing people together which was why he was the only one out of our entire crew that had free reign in every neighborhood on the Westside. Despite his wild side, out of all of us, he was the peacemaker, the one that could defuse any situation and calm opposing sides down with a few words. He grew up around everyone in the G-Boyz and the Black Mob crews and everyone from every neighborhood respected him, which was why this just didn't make any sense.

Shortly after I made it my house Tim called, "Yo Jay, Lamont...Lamont is dead bro. He's dead man. They killed him, he didn't make it." His words hung in the air for what seemed like forever as I held the phone to my ear, listening intently for him to say he was just joking but knowing that what he said was real. I physically sensed it, that feeling you get deep in the pit of your stomach almost as if someone has just punched you and knocked the wind out of you, but you can breathe, and every breath deepens that feeling and starts to push on the back of your eyes until tears form and start streaming down your cheeks.

The time from that phone call to the funeral was a blur spent mostly smoking weed and drinking with my hanging partners. It was the first time I remember going to a funeral. Walking into the funeral home, the walls were covered in dark wood paneling and there were dark wall-to-wall carpets that were dark and dingy and looked like they had past their prime about a decade ago. I slapped a few of my friends up and we hugged each other as I walked towards the room in which Lamont's body was being presented. Over the quite whispers and muted conversations, you could hear sobs coming from various corners of the room as depressing, old school church spiritual music played softly over speakers in the adjacent hallway. Sherrod was just walking back from viewing the body, tears running down his face, openly crying when he grabbed me and hugged me and said in his loud, brash voice, "Yo Jay this is fucked up man. They killed my brother Jay. They killed our brother man."

Not knowing what to say I just hugged him back until a few of our other friends put their arms around him and took him outside. As I slowly walked toward his open casket, I glanced over at the large blown up picture of Lamont placed to the side, he had a jheri curl and was wearing a bow tie and looked like he was about

12 years old. I could feel my heart beating faster and growing heavier with each heartbeat and I inhaled deeply trying to hold off the tears that I felt starting to swell in my eyes.

When the line finally moved up enough for my turn to say my last words to Lamont, I stood there trying to accept that he was actually the one laying in the coffin. At first it didn't seem real, he didn't look real, he was dressed in a suit and tie and his hands were gently folded over each other just below his chest. His eyes were closed and his face was much lighter than usual with a powder like dust covering it, for a second I breathed a sigh of relief thinking to myself, "Wait a minute, that's not Lamont!" then a woman's scream shattered the moment and brought me back to reality, it was Lamont and he was really laying in a coffin in a funeral home. He was really gone.

I don't know how long I stood there but eventually one of my boys put their arm around me and gently pulled me towards the back of the room. As I walked down the aisle, chairs on both sides of the room full of people young and old, I felt the tears running down my cheeks. I wiped them away on the sleeve of my shirt and headed outside to get some air, seeing Tim and the rest of my crew gathered together, I headed over towards them and we all hugged each other.

Despite the utter pain we were all feeling, we also felt closer than ever before. There was a love between us that was never previously expressed and now we stood around hugging and consoling one another, visually showcasing the bond which was created over the years we spent running around Thurston raising hell. It was a feeling of belonging, a feeling of true love and family and a feeling that we all embraced but knew that we never wanted to feel again, at least not under similar circumstances, but we all knew that this wouldn't be the last time we mourned for each other. We had a growing feeling that this was what our life was destined to become, that one day soon, each one of us would be laying in that box in preparation to be set in the ground for all eternity. While we couldn't express those feelings at that time, we definitely all shared the same thoughts, thoughts that would become commonplace in our minds throughout the rest of our early lives and for some of us, all of our lives.

PART II

"To stimulate wildly weak and untrained minds is to play with mighty fires."
–W.E.B. Dubois

9 COCAINE

Lamont's death effected all of us in different ways, Sherrod became even more wild than before, Tim retreated deeper into music, Lonnie became more quiet and reserved in general but started to run with a crew that was into robbing drug dealers, Londell was just lost for a while, and I withdrew from my crew and started to figure out ways to find my own path. There was a mythical statistic that everyone in the neighborhood would quote, something to the effect that the average black man in America's life expectancy was only supposed to be twenty-one years. I don't know where that came from or how it spread so far and so fast but any person of color was sure to bring that "statistic" up in a conversation about life. Another "statistical" saying was that there are more black men in prison then in college. Seeing and experiencing the actual truths associated with inner-city impoverished living, crime, arrests and incarcerations of black youth, violence, and unemployment all acted to reinforce those urban statistical myths and lend strong support to the possibility of their truths.

We had all seen the police jumping out of their patrol cars and randomly picking out someone to beat down with nightsticks, steel toe boots to the face and fists, in order to, "Set an example for the rest of you monkeys." We had all seen or participated in violence within our own neighborhoods. We had all watched the politicians on TV discuss poverty as if it was a nasty growth created by the impoverished themselves, that needed to be eradicated by any means necessary, including the death or destruction of the impoverished. And now we had all seen one of our own die violently in the same manner in which the police, politicians and media continued to tell us was commonplace. How is a young black man not supposed to believe that they won't live beyond the age of 21, that we were all destined for prison or a coffin?

At that time, I didn't realize the forces that worked to teach and train me that my life was destined for failure and I had no insight into what options were available to overcome what I was now seeing as being the inevitable. My mother believed in honesty and hard work, in education to assist in getting ahead, in surviving by putting in time to make your situation better. I saw my mother as a woman, a white woman that knew nothing about what I was experiencing growing up as a bi-racial black man and whose advice often conflicted with what I saw and knew to be the truth as related to the streets. She had great advice for someone living in her world, for white American's living in white America. But I was not living in white America, the closest I came was my job and even at work there was a small grey area that separated the white management from the black workers, though I was able to straddle that area with one foot in either world, always feeling like I was never able to fully gain acceptance on either side.

I felt that it was time for me to move onto something bigger, to earn the respect associated with being a man in the hood so I set out to follow the examples of those that I had been taught to admire. It was time for me to get my hustle on. Many of my friends were starting to make money, the squares had jobs while the "respected" thugs were hustling. Some sold weed, some were now doing robberies, some were stealing cars and a few were selling cocaine or heroin. My man Victor Speight, a year or two ahead of me, had a miniature bartender kit that he carried around with him and a larger kit in his locker and he would sell shots and mixed drinks to anyone that wanted one for $1 a shot. Another friend, Craig Bell, everyone called him Puba, sold high quality weed in $5 nickel bags, $10 dime bags, and sometimes sold joints for $2. Weed was easy to get and easy to sell because everyone smoked, from the jocks to the nerds to the white boy hard rock heads, almost every social circle smoked weed, so it was the obvious hustle for a lot of my friends trying to make a few dollars.

The problem with weed was that while everyone could get it, everyone didn't have access to the good stuff. It was easy to find an ounce or two of some dirt weed, dry and crumbly with a lot of seeds and stems in it and it gave you a headache high. You could get a dime bag of dirt weed that was the size of half of an average letter envelope and plump as a pillow, full of seeds, stems and shaky, super dried up weed. The real smokers stayed away from it and would only buy the good stuff while the new jacks and those that didn't have access to anything better would gladly dish out $10 for a mediocre high.

With everyone selling weed, the only ones making any real money were the ones selling large quantities, pounds of weed, and the ones that were selling the really good, high quality stuff. Puba had the good stuff and he had access to pounds of it through one of the largest weed dealers in the area, a Jamaican born immigrant that everyone called Selector. Selector owned a nightclub out in the suburbs that held large reggae parties in a traditional Jamaican dancehall style. The club had huge speakers that lined two opposing walls from the ground to the ceiling that would blast out reggae and dancehall music during the weekly weekend parties, while a small bar served dark Guinness beer and shots of liquor. Puba eventually became Selector's right hand man and the two worked together to open a Jamaican style restaurant.

The restaurant sold traditional Jamaican cuisine like stew chicken, curry goat, homemade beef patties, rice & peas, and ackee and salt fish and drew a loyal following for their food but it was the marijuana being sold from the back of the restaurant that really drew the customers. Puba brought his older brother Greg in to help prepare food, sell meals and eventually sell weed from the back of the store. Puba sold weed on the same corner as the store when the store closed, and became the main supplier to everyone in our school.

I tried my hand at selling weed here and there but I always ended up smoking most of it and I would eventually give up as the competition was too intense. I didn't mind standing on a street corner to sell it, in fact being seen on one of the corners known for weed sales was a reputation builder, but I didn't have the patience to fight with three or four other dudes and run to cars to try to sell a $5 or $10 bag of weed. I watched them do it and thought that there had to be a better way to make more money than doing what everyone else was doing.

I was still working at the hotel and making pretty good money doing that but I wanted street money, money that also brought what I thought was the necessary respect from my peers in the streets. I decided that cocaine was the future of drug sales. There were not many people selling coke and the ones that were selling it were making a lot more money than their weed-selling contemporaries. I saw the effects of heroin and most of the people that I saw selling heroin were dope-fiends, heroin users themselves and I damn sure didn't want to be associated with them. Everybody was starting to use cocaine; rich, poor, white, black, young and old, everyone was either sniffing it, lacing their joints with it and making what we called "wu-lees" or some were even shooting it up. It was a glamorous drug and Ronald Regan's "War on Drugs" only helped sensationalize cocaine. The nightly news would occasionally show piles and piles of cocaine sitting next to stacks and stacks of hundred dollar bills confiscated in raids.

The irony of the Regan's "Just Say No" campaign was years later, it was discovered that President Regan himself, the same President modern day republicans consider to be the greatest thing that ever happened to American Democracy, was trading cocaine for guns in what was eventually called the "Iran Contra Affair." Mr. Regan and his homies in the CIA put together a system in which they helped import cocaine into the United States in order to circumvent Congress and fund weapons that the US was secretly providing to support two separate wars, one in Iran and one in Nicaragua. Cocaine started flooding the United States, dropping the price of the drug and making coke easily accessible. While I was not aware of the politics behind the scenes, I did recognize the potential and was convinced that cocaine was definitely the future, now I just had to find a way in.

After weeks of hearing me talk about my cocaine plans, Reg hesitantly told me that Vic, a mutual friend of ours, had quickly transitioned from selling a few bags of weed into making thousands of dollars a week selling coke and was looking to expand his business. I went to see Vic at the apartments where he set up shop on the corner of Thurston and Chili Avenue, and told him that I was ready to get my hands on some coke to sell myself. While I knew how to break down weed from an ounce into smaller, $5 and $10 bags to sell in order to try to turn a profit, I was unfamiliar with cocaine and had no idea what it cost or how it was sold.

Vic took me to meet his business partner Ozell and they both schooled me on how cocaine was purchased, broken down and sold. Vic and Ozell were both the same age as me but were years ahead when it came to hustling and were the only friends I knew that were already involved in the cocaine game. We sat down at the kitchen table in one of the apartments that they rented and Vic opened a kitchen cabinet and pulled out a sandwich bag of white powder that was buried deep inside a box of cereal while Ozell went to the refrigerator and pulled out a box of baking soda and a large plastic jar containing some more white powder. They sat the powder on the table, pulled out a plate, some razor blades and a large plastic bag containing hundreds of tiny smaller plastic zip-lock baggies.

Vic grabbed the bag from the cereal box and handed it to me, he said, "

open it, lick your finger and taste it, that is pure cocaine." I licked the tip of my finger and dipped it into the bag, pulled my finger out and looked at the crystalized, yellowish white powder on my finger tip before cautiously placing a little of the powder on the tip of my tongue. My tongue immediately got numb and the powder left a slight metallic taste in my mouth. Ozell laughed at the face I made and said, "Yeah Nigga, that's that good shit! Ha ha, these geekers love that shit man! Watch, you going to have them going crazy!"

Vic pulled a metal screened flour sifter, measured out a couple of tablespoons of the cocaine and added a couple of tablespoons of the other white powder from the fridge and sifted them together onto the plate along with a tablespoon or so of the baking soda. "What is that for? What does the other powder do?" I asked, as I carefully watched his every move.

"That is cut, you use it to stretch the coke and make more money. We can double our money off this if we add equal amounts of this cut and baking soda to the coke." Vic said. Ozell smiling the entire time he spoke, added, "this is what makes the money! Turn an ounce of coke into two ounces of coke and they love this shit! Ha ha!"

"You can cut it with anything, baby powder, baking soda, aspirin, anything but we like to use this here procaine shit. It numbs your mouth like cocaine and if they cook it up, it doesn't fuck up the cook." Vic added, "It costs a little more but I never get any complaints when I use it, they always come back for more."

Ozell took the sifted powder on the plate and mixed it some more using a playing card before taking a razor and using it to cut up some of the slightly larger chunks of the powder before picking up the card again, folding it and then scooping up some of the powder, opening one of the small zip lock baggies and adding the powder to the bag until it was about half way full. Vic gave me a card and some bags and we all repeated the process repeatedly until we had bagged up all the powder and had roughly 300 small baggies in front of us.

They counted them out and placed most of them back into the cereal box, while Vic took ten of them and put them to the side and Ozell took about twenty of them and put them in a potato chip bag before opening the door and heading out to the hallway where three or four customers were already lined up waiting for him. Vic gave the ten bags to me, "These are dime bags, take these and keep two for yourself and bring me back $80. I'm telling you right now, don't give any of these geekers this shit on credit, you ain't ready for the shit you have to go through to get your money, that shit just ain't worth it!"

My heart racing, I quickly grabbed the bags and asked, "How much coke did we just bag up?"

"That was an ounce, an ounce is 28 grams we can get it for $1000 but if we cut it and bag it up like we just did, we can turn that $1000 into $3000!" he replied.

"Come back with that and I will give you twenty dimes next time. You got a spot to work out of or you want to hustle here with us? Man, its plenty of customers around here, you will get that off in no time. Zell already hit three of four licks when he went out the door! I'm telling you this money comes quick!"

I hadn't even thought about where I would sell it or who I would sell it to, all I was focused on was getting my hands on some coke. Not wanting Vic to think that I couldn't move what he gave me I said, "Naw man, I got a spot but if its slow I might head back this way."

"Cool, see you later man."

I stood up and stuffed the baggies in my pocket and headed out the door. Having no idea where I was going to go to sell the coke, I headed towards Genesee Street hoping that I could sell a few bags by the corner where Puba hung out. I spent an entire afternoon up there with no luck, the corner was booming with customers for weed but no one was looking for coke so I headed home to get ready for work. This cycle repeated itself continuously for a few days before I finally went back to Vic after not selling a single dime. I was not going to tell him I didn't sell it and post up at his spot in order to get rid of it, I knew that wouldn't look good so instead I gave him $80 from out of my pocket and said, "Man they loved that shit! I would've come back the same day but I've been busy as hell so today was the only chance I had to come see you." Ozell looked at me surprised and with his usual smiling, laughing self, said "Oh shit! Jay ain't playing around, you really trying to get that money! My Nigga, man that's what's up!"

Vic took me inside and started to hand me the twenty bags he promised before but I stopped him and said, "This is cool but I'm really not trying to be working for anybody like that. I need my own. Let me buy some weight from you so we can really get this money coming." Vic looked at me surprised at first, then a big grin slowly grew on his face and he said, "Man you are serious?! Cool, I can front you an 8-ball, just bring me back $150." Seeing the slight look of confusion on my face he added, "An 8-ball is 3.5 grams, its 1/8th of an ounce. If you add some cut and bag it up right you can bag up $300 off of it. Here is some cut and some bags to get you started. Remember how we did it before? And throw it on this scale right here to make sure the weight is right."

I sat down at the table and turned on the digital scale, placed the small baggie on the scale and read the weight, it was 3.5 grams exactly so I grabbed the plate, razor and other materials to mix the powder together and went to work packaging it up. When I finished I had thirty-two small baggies ready to go, I cleaned up the plate and packaging materials and put five baggies in my hand and the rest I stuffed in both of my socks before heading out into the hallway. The building housed about twenty apartments, mostly one bedrooms and studios with a few two bedroom units on the second or third floors. There was an identical apartment building directly across the street called the Apollo which was also low income and housed mostly young single mothers, crack-heads and dope fiends, all of whom were on some form of public assistance.

As I made my way towards the front of the building where Vic and Ozell were standing, Vic called me over and pointed to a fifty something year old man standing next to him wearing an old black leather looking jacket with ripped pockets and some dirty suede Puma's that looked like they had seen much better days. Vic said, "This is my man Sammy, Sammy needs three but he only has $25. You want to work with him?"

Looking Sammy up and down I noticed the intense, straight

ahead glare in his eyes, he was focused and his right arm was twitching, slowly at first but then faster as he awaited my response. "$25 for three? Aight man, I got you." Sammy damn near leaped in the air as he handed me the money. I started to count it when Vic said, "Naw man, don't count it out here, go inside the hallway. Next time, have him give you the money inside so no one can see what you are doing."

We headed into the hallway where I took the money, two crumpled up $10 bills and five singles, and as I counted it, Sammy watched intently as his arm started twitching again. Ozell came inside with us to watch and make sure there were no problems. I opened my hand and gave him three of the baggies and watched him as he picked up each one, plucked it with his finger to shake it down so the powder settled at the bottom of the baggie and then compared them to each other. Shaking his head displeasingly he said, "Naw man, this bag right here is short, I need me something bigger then this man. Let me get another one."

I opened my hand and let him pick the one he thought was bigger, which took more shaking of the baggies and more comparing. Finally satisfied that he had the three biggest baggies, he put the baggies in his mouth under his tongue and damn near ran out of the door towards the building across the street. Ozell started laughing and said, "Man why did you let that mother fucker pick the ones he wanted? Next time tell him to take it or leave it. Trust me, his ass will take it!"

I shrugged as if to say, "It's no big deal," and Ozell still laughing added, "You got to watch these crack-heads man, they will try to switch the bags and give you back some bullshit if you let them. Dude tried that shit on me once, took one of my bags and tried to sneak me back a bag he made up with some bullshit cut in it! I had to fuck his old ass up quick fast man!"

Opening the door to the building, Vic yelled down the hallway, "Yo, I'm sending two more your way," as he moved to the side, two more customers walked down the hallway to where we were standing. Ozell pointed to me as they both stopped, looked me up and down and one of them said, "Man I don't know this dude. You sure he ain't Po-Po? He looks like he the police."

Laughing hysterically, Ozell said, "Man shut the fuck up. Do you want to cop or not? Get your money out or walk your ass back out that door."

"Give me two fat ones, here" handing me $20 and extending his hand waiting for me to drop the baggies inside his waiting palm. I gave him two and then looked at the other customer, a thirty something woman that looked and smelt like she hadn't washed her body or clothes in weeks. She said, "Give me five" and handed me a wad of crumpled up bills. "Hurry up man, I got to go, the police are out like crazy today," she said as she frantically looked around, hoping that her warnings of the police would somehow make me forget to count the money she handed me which I soon discovered was only $30.

I handed her three baggies and she said "Wait a minute, I said five man, this is only three."

"Bitch, you only gave me $30, you get what you pay for. Now take your ass out of here before I change my mind."

She took a step back and just looked at me and before she could say anything Ozell busted out laughing, "Oh shit, Jay put your raggedy ass in check!"

She said, "Come on Zell, you know me, you know I bring customers through here all the time, hook me up this time and I'll be right back with the white boys that always spend all the money. You know the ones from way out in the country? Come on please? Please?"

Ozell looked at me as if to say it's up to you and I quickly said, "Bring that money back and then we'll see what I can do alright sweetheart? And take a shower or something, you look like you might be fine if you took care of yourself."

She smiled and said "Oh I see you got some shit with you! I like me some light skinned men. I'll be back to see you, but I only want to see you, I ain't fucking with you no more Zell!"

"Ha ha, bye bitch, get to stepping hoe!" Ozell said as he bent over and grabbed his stomach with laughter. "Jay, you gonna have these coke hoes going crazy! Man, go ahead! Get that money!"

I stood around for a few more hours and sold a few more bags before I had to leave to go to work. I smiled the entire way to work thinking about how I had just sold my first few bags of coke and how easy and fast the money came. I knew I was on to something big and my mind was racing trying to figure out how I could get the rest of the bags off without having to sell them at the Apollo or anywhere near Thurston. I wanted to show Vic, and more importantly, prove to myself, that I could make things happen on my own but I had no idea how I was going to do it, all I knew was that I would find a way to make it happen.

When I got to work, Junie, one of the few black busboys, pulled me to the side and told me that he saw me on Thurston earlier and he asked what I was doing by the Apollo? He had a half grin on his face and before I could respond he said, "Let me find out Jason is getting his hustle on! I know what they do over that way."

I thought I was busted and my heart started racing at the thought of someone at my job finding out that I was involved in anything having to do with drugs. Defensively I said, "What where you doing over there? I thought you were from cross town?"

"Naw man, I'm from Chili Ave, my grandmother still lives around the corner from the Apollo and I know those dudes that be over there selling coke." He bent down and looked around playfully as if he was trying to make sure no one heard what he was about to say, but making sure I saw that he really didn't care if he was overheard and whispered, "Man you got some coke???"

"Naw man, I don't know what you're talking about Junie."

"Aight man, you don't have to get all defensive, I was just kidding...unless you DO have some coke?" and he broke out laughing as he walked away.

The rest of that night Junie would come to the kitchen and make little inside jokes, hinting that he wanted some coke until finally I pulled him to the side and said, "How much do you want, show me the money or shut the fuck up. I'm getting sick of your jokes man."

A huge smile came over his face and he said "Let me get eight dimes, I will give you the money as soon as they tip me out tonight."

"I don't have any on me but I got you when we finish work." Junie was a good-humored dude, always joking around and laughing and flirting with the waitresses and bartenders. He was in his early thirties and had worked a number of odd jobs before getting a job at the hotel. We never hung out but he definitely looked like the type that wouldn't say no to a good party. As soon as our shifts ended, he took me home where I had him park on the next block over so he wouldn't see where I lived and so no one saw me with him. I went into the house, grabbed eight dimes and came back around the corner where I hopped back in the car and showed him what I had.

"I never bought anything from you before, can I try one to make sure it is legit? Come on man, I'm buying eight from you" he said as his eyes got bigger and sweat started to form on his forehead. I thought about it for a minute, then said, "Give me the money and I'll give you nine for $80, I don't sell any bullshit." He gave me the money and I handed him the eight baggies and told him that I would give him the other one when I saw him at work the next day. He immediately opened one of the bags, poured some onto a book he had in the car, divided the powder into two lines, rolled up a dollar bill into a straw and quickly snorted what was on the book, a line into each nostril.

He blinked his eyes and wiped the water from them, made a few snorting noises and then said, "Oh yeah, that shit is good. You got a lot of cut on it but its good. Make sure you bring some to work with you." He laughed and added "Oh shit, Jason is a coke dealer! I would have never known. You look like a straight square laughing with those white folks at work. Here man, you want some?" He asked as he poured the rest of the bag onto the book.

"Naw man, I don't fuck with that."

"Smart man! That's how you make that money, don't get high on your own supply!" he said and started laughing hysterically at his own words before he inhaled the rest of the coke.

The next day I gave Junie the extra bag I promised him and he immediately asked me for two more bags promising to pay me as soon as his shift ended. I gave him the two bags and a few hours later he asked for two more. I noticed the banquet manager, a tall, deep voiced white dude in his early forties, watching us talk from the other side of the kitchen. I asked Junie if he noticed him watching us and he started laughing loudly and said "Of course Fred's watching us. He's waiting to hit this coke man!"

"I told you not to let anybody know!"

"Man chill out; these white mother fuckers out here snort way more coke than I do. You need to thank me for turning him on to you. He is going to be your number one customer, watch, you will see!"

He headed towards the back of the kitchen and the manager followed. When they both came out a few minutes later, their eyes were glossy and Fred was talking louder than usual, barking out commands to the banquet staff as they prepared for an event. Fred made sure to come over to where I was working and speak to me, something he almost never did before, and he nodded his head letting me know that he thought the coke was good. I nervously nodded back, looking around to see if anyone else saw us communicating.

Before the night was over, Fred came to me, slid a fifty-dollar bill in my hand and motioned his head towards the back of the kitchen were the walk-in coolers and freezers were located. I waited about five minutes then went back there making it look like I was grabbing food needed on the cooking line. I went into the cooler and handed him the five dimes, looking around nervously he asked "Do you have more? I'm going to need about five more before I leave and another ten tonight after I get off work." I told him I didn't have that much but I could get it for him when I finished work.

At Vic's advice, I bought a beeper when I got those first few bags from him and I gave Fred the beeper number, told him to put his number in with the number 1 behind it so I knew it was him and told him to hit me if he needed anything since he got off work a few hours before I did. Like clockwork, as soon as I got home my beeper went off with a number one behind the number. I called him back and he said he needed ten and he would meet me wherever I was. I told him to meet me on a corner a few blocks from my house in ten minutes. I jumped in his car, he quickly gave me two crisp fifty dollar bills and snatched the ten bags from my hand before saying, "We're going to keep this between us right? This is nobody's business at the hotel, shit half of them snort coke too so they can't judge me but I'd prefer if it stayed between us."

"No problem, I don't like people in my business either. Hit me anytime you need something, I got you." I said as I exited the car and took the long way home, making sure he didn't follow me or see where I was headed. About an hour later, he beeped me again and we repeated the transaction same as before. I told him that I was out and wouldn't be back on until tomorrow so he would have to wait until then if he wanted some more. His eyes were glossy, pupils dilated, his hair was disheveled and he barely looked at me when he said, "Ok, I don't need any more anyways. I haven't partied this hard in a long time. I'm not use to being able to get good coke that fast! It's better that you are out man, it's better that you are out." He said the last few words as if he was talking to himself and then he drove off.

I had officially just sold my first eight-ball and I did it on my own. I counted the money over and over again, and although I had made more money busing tables in a single day, that money felt heavier to me, it looked greener, it smelt better, for some reason that money seemed more real and I was ready to make some more, a lot more.

I went to see Vic the next day, gave him the $150 that I owed him and gave him another $150 on top of that and asked him to give me two 8-balls, which is the same as a quarter ounce, and told him that I would give him the other $150 back as soon as I flipped it again. He handed me the quarter ounce and told me to that he would only charge me $250, and if I wanted a half ounce, $450.

I went to the corner store on Chili Avenue and bought a bottle of cut, some razors and a bag of baggies and headed home to mix and bag up in preparation for work later that night. I added the cut and mixed it together and bagged up about sixty dimes, I took twenty with me to work and hid the rest, along with the empty baggies, cut and razors behind a lose board in our garage and I headed off to work.

Junie and Fred bombarded me all night, first one then the other, two for Junie, four for Fred, until I was sold out. Once I got home they both paged me and by the end of the night I had sold everything again. I went and saw Vic, gave him the money I owed him an extra $450 and bought a half-ounce from him. Bagged up and kept repeating the process for months.

By the time my Junior year rolled around, I was making good money from my job and supplementing whatever I made with the money from selling cocaine. Having my full-time, forty plus hours a week schedule cut back to around thirty hours a week gave me time to pursue my true passion, girls. Candy and I were still seeing each other but our relationship was slowly fading as she focused more on school in preparation for entering college after her senior year. The new school year meant an influx of new faces and plenty of girls that none of us knew or more importantly, knew us. One of the new girls, a cute, dark skinned, honey, gave me her number and I called her the next day.

We talked on the phone for a few hours and a few hours more the next night. She told me that she had just turned sixteen and had transferred to Wilson from Marshall High School and that she was now a Junior and scheduled to graduate with my class. She invited me over to her house on a weekend when her parents were working and she was home babysitting her younger twin brothers. She gave me her address and I told her that I would see her around 11pm just to be sure that her parents were both gone to work. I left my house and headed for the bus stop to catch the 2 Thurston downtown so I could transfer to the crosstown bus that would take me to Clifford Ave, a few blocks from her house.

I was a little worried about being so far from my own neighborhood by myself, and I knew that if I ran into the wrong crowd, I would have to fight or run for my life but that did not stop me, I was young, horny and dumb and there was no way I was going to turn down some guaranteed new sex! I exited the bus about ten blocks from where I was supposed to get off and decided to take the side streets to try to avoid being seen. As I got closer to her block I noticed a group of dudes about three blocks ahead moving towards me so I quickly turned down her street, crossed to the opposite side of her street and purposely walked right by her house so I could look in the driveway and make sure the cars that she described as belonging to her parents were gone.

Seeing no cars and noticing the group of guys turning down her street and heading my way, I crossed the street, went to the front door and got ready to knock but before I could, the door opened and she stood there, peaking out of the door making sure it was me. My heart raced as she opened the door, told me to take my shoes off and let me into the living room. I looked around to make sure the coast was clear as there was a part of me that was unsure if she was in some way trying to set me up. I heard a lot of stories about guys going to meet girls somewhere and being robbed and beaten so it was not out of the question.

The house was small but very well decorated with thick, cream colored, wall-to-wall carpet everywhere. She hurried me upstairs into her parent's room, quickly moving past her little brother's room so they didn't notice me. The upstairs was small, four doors all close together with her parent's room in the front of the house, her room at the rear corner and her brother's room right next to her parent's room, separated by a bathroom.

She quickly closed the door and told me I could sit down on the bed, which took up almost all of the room. It was a king sized waterbed with a mirrored headboard and padded sides. As I sat down, the bed wiggled and jiggled under my weight and I struggled to get comfortable, looking up at her for the first time and noticing that she was wearing a thin robe and it looked like there was nothing underneath! She said, "Take your coat off and get comfortable, I will be right back, I have to make sure my brothers are going to sleep." I watched her as she walked out of the room, she was short, maybe five foot three and had a chocolate complexion, she didn't have much of an ass but she had the thickest, sexiest thighs that I'd ever seen. She turned around and caught me checking her out, and smiled slyly as she left the room.

As I laid back on the bed and tried to relax I looked over and saw myself in the mirror on the headboard and thought, "I am going to tear this pussy UP!" My heart was now beating out of my chest with nervous anticipation, partly from being in a strange house and in her parent's bedroom and partly from the sexual tension that was rising inside of me, feeling like I was going to burst from within.

A few minutes later Heather came in and laid down on the bed, exposing one of her perfectly oiled legs, making me forget all about the risk associated with being in her parent's bed. I laid down next to her, heart racing, wanting to touch her but too nervous to make a move, and she leaned closer to me and kissed me, which led to more kissing and my hands finally getting a chance to feel those thighs and caress those breasts that were now popping out of her bathrobe.

After the second or third time round, we finally fell asleep, only to find myself awoken by the sun coming through a crack in the curtain. I turned my head slowly and was startled by a face that was staring right back at me. I jumped up and started to reach for my clothes when I realized that it was Heather's little brother, sitting on the pillow next to me, and now laughing because he scared me.

I breathed a huge sigh of relief, put my clothes on and cracked the bedroom door, carefully listening to see if I could hear any voices coming from downstairs. After a few minutes, her little brother handed me one of the toys he was playing with and I sat on the bed and played with him, heart starting to race again as I started to figure out potential exit routes in case one of her parents was home. I had already determined that if I had to, I could jump from her parent's bedroom window into the front yard but I would have to jump far enough to miss the bushes that lined the front of the house. Besides their front bedroom window, I was trapped, nowhere to run or hide and nothing that I could do except face whatever consequences might be headed my way.

Just as I had made up my mind to try to sneak down the stairs and head for the front door, the bedroom door slowly opened and, holding my breath, I stood up and eased my back towards the window until Heather appeared and said, "My father should be home soon. You should probably get going." As my heart raced I thought to myself, "I will never do this again, this is crazy as hell!" She walked me downstairs, gave me a kiss at the door and I headed out into the bright sunshine, quickly making my way down the street, around the corner and up the next block to the bus stop, looking around semi-paranoid in my attempts to avoid being seen by her father, or anybody that might want to test me because they recognize that I was not from their neighborhood.

By the time I made it home I had forgotten all about the fear associated with feeling trapped in her parent's room and the tension from being across town and in a new neighborhood. My mind was busy being occupied with thoughts of the things that we did in that waterbed and how I needed to figure out a way to make it happen again. Before I could put a plan together, she called and we set up a time to meet again, this time at my house, and just like that, our one-time thing became an every-other-day-wherever-whenever thing.

Sometimes, when we are headed in a direction that is destined to bring us to difficult times, we receive signs or an intuition, to turn around and head the other way. I kept getting these signs with Heather, like the constant nervous feeling in my stomach, but I shook them off and kept doing what I was doing and after a few weeks she called me crying, she was sobbing so hard that I couldn't make out what she was saying. "Calm down, I can't understand what you are saying, what happened? Take a deep breath and tell me what happened?"

She eventually calmed down enough for me to hear, "I got my period today...I'm not pregnant."

Confused as hell, I asked, "Well, isn't that a good thing? Wait, you told me you are on the pill right? You are on the pill aren't you??? Then why would you think you would be pregnant? And why are you upset about not being pregnant?"

My heart dropped to my stomach as reality set in and I thought back to our initial conversation, when I asked her if she had any condoms or if I needed to bring some and she told me she had some if I wanted to use them but she was on the pill and we didn't need them. When I got to the house that first night I asked her where the condoms where and things just got hot and heavy without her ever answering me. And I thought about each subsequent time that I asked her if she was sure she was on the pill and she repeatedly reassured me that she was on the pill.

Crying more loudly again and almost as if she was talking to herself, she said, "I want my baby...I just want my baby. It's not fair, it's not fair."

My nervousness now turning into anger, I yelled, "I asked you a question. ARE YOU ON THE PILL OR NOT??? Answer me??"

Controlling her sobs, she sheepishly replied, "I told you yes, but I might have missed a couple days so I thought that maybe I was pregnant but I'm not so you don't have to worry and I won't miss any days again. I don't want to go through this again."

Still not sure what the hell was going on, I told her that we would talk later and quickly got off the phone. The one thing that I knew just couldn't be true is that she actually wanted to have a baby, so I worked hard to dismiss that idea as it just didn't make any sense. I called Reg and told him what happened and we both figured that if she wasn't taking the pill and she didn't get pregnant after all the sex we were having then I probably wasn't able to make a child. I thought back to something I heard somewhere about microwaves causing infertility in men and tried to convince myself that all my days spent standing in front of a microwave, waiting for food to warm up, must have led to a decreased sperm count, or maybe even made me infertile. I ran my theory by Reg and he laughed but he said he heard the same thing, so maybe it was true.

I don't think we actually believed this to be true but it helped to clear my conscious and settle my nerves and provided an excuse to get right back at it with Heather. No protection and fucking like rabbits soon led to the inevitable pregnancy. Sixteen years old and once again I found myself facing a pregnancy, I couldn't help but think back to how hard it was to tell my mother about Linda's pregnancy and this time I would have to explain how a girl that I just met came up pregnant.

I sat down with her at my mother's house and we talked about the pregnancy and what we should do, well I talked and tried to pretend that I was seriously considering what our options were when I knew what I wanted and she knew what she wanted and we both wanted something completely different. I knew that there was no way I was ready to be a father, especially with a girl that I barely knew and was not even in a relationship with. She knew that the one thing that she had wanted for a long time was to have a baby, and she didn't care about how old we were or anything else for that matter.

The more I talked, the angrier I became as I was now realizing that this was her intent the entire time. She was never on birth control. I thought about the time she called me crying about not being pregnant and I realized that was not some emotional babble. She was really upset about not being pregnant. The more I thought about it, the more irate I became until I finally exploded. Yelling at the top of my lungs, spit flying from my lips, hands flailing, pacing back and forth, I angrily shouted, "Get the fuck out of my house bitch. You set me up! Get out now!"

Crying and trembling, she slowly made her way to the stairs and walked down, pausing to look back, tears racing down her cheeks, "Why? Why are you doing this to me? I am pregnant with your baby, why would you yell at me?"

Stunned and at a complete loss for words I just stood there looking dumbfounded. What was she talking about? 'Pregnant with my baby?' As I stood there she made her way out of the door, slowly opening the door then looking back at me before closing it behind her as she left. For the next few hours, I sat down and thought about what she said, the words playing over and over again in my head, "I'm pregnant...I'm pregnant with your baby."

I had waves of nervous anxiety that were quickly replaced with anger and then back to the anxious nervousness. Eventually I calmed down enough to get mad at myself. Not for allowing myself to get into this situation but for losing my cool and kicking her out. I thought that if I had just remained calm and talked rationally with her that she would see that this was a bad idea and that there was no way that we could have a child now. I spent the next few weeks trying to talk to her. At first yelling and arguing with her, which just led to crying on her part and more anger and frustration on mine. Then I tried taking a new approach, I empathized with her, showed her that I understood her feelings and desire to have a child and tried to gently influence her to rethink things. By the time I realized that nothing was going to change her mind, she was already a few months pregnant and starting to show.

After I thought about how things initially played out with us, how she told me she was on the pill but then cried when she found out she wasn't initially pregnant, and the way she was glowing and smiling when she told me that she was pregnant, I knew that I was played. The more I thought about it, the more angry I became and the more resentment I felt towards her and the situation in general. There wasn't much that I could do except to accept that this was happening and that regardless of being only 16 years old, I was going to be a father.

My friend Randy Jones had a 1982 red two door Buick Skylark with a super loud, custom made, booming sound system in the trunk. We went everywhere in that car with Randy. To basketball courts way out in the suburbs. To the malls, to parties all around the city. We would pile in the car, he would throw in a cassette of Run-DMC or Dougie-Fresh, turn the volume up as loud as it would go, and we would just cruise the streets. Randy had every Richard Pryor live cassette, and when we weren't blasting the latest hip hop, we would ride around and crack up laughing as we listened to Richard Pryor. After Randy graduated, he signed up for the Marines and was quickly scheduled to head out to boot camp and right before he left, I bought the car from him.

I put it off for as long as I could but I knew that it was time to tell my mother about Heather. In my mind, it was simple, I had the words all planned out and I was ready to tell her but as I tried to talk, the words got caught in my throat and I couldn't seem to get them out. Before I could even get the words out, she looked at me, disappointment and hurt showing on her face and in her eyes, as if she knew what I was about to say. "Mom, I got a girl pregnant, she is going to have a baby."

"No, no, no why Jason? Why are you doing this now?" she said, more to herself then to me. Shaking her head, she said, "Who? Who is the girl? How far along is she?"

"Its Heather. She's four months now" I said, barely lifting my head to look at her.

"Well, what are you going to do? I'm not taking care of a baby. This is your responsibility so what are you going to do?"

"I'm going to do what I'm supposed to do" I said, not really knowing what I was supposed to do or what those words really meant. I spent the next few months in a daze, going to work, hanging out with my friends on the weekends, smoking weed, drinking, trying anything I could to help escape the quickly approaching reality of teenage fatherhood.

Heather told her parents around the same time I told my mother and needless to say they were heartbroken by the news. I sat down and talked with her mother a few times and even though she was extremely disappointed, she was always respectful towards me and greeted me with open arms, going out of her way to make sure I felt comfortable in their home. I was unable to articulate my appreciation at the time but her demeanor really provided some much needed relief to some of the stress and tension I was experiencing. Heather's father went out of his way to not be there whenever I was coming over. Probably to help keep himself from trying to strangle me but he was also respectful and did a hell of a job biting his tongue as I could sense the anger and frustration he felt towards me.

I was unable to get over my anger and feeling like I was 'tricked' into fatherhood and my patience with Heather was almost non-existent. She kept lying to me about things that made no sense to me. She lied to me about who her homeroom teacher was. She lied to me about what classes she was taking. She lied to me about being a Varsity cheerleader even though she knew that I knew all the varsity cheerleaders. They were small things but they just didn't make any sense. Why lie about something that she knew was so easy to find out about? Anytime I confronted her about anything, she would break down crying and tell me I was upsetting her. I was perplexed, frustrated and stressed out and I finally said 'fuck it.' For the sake of the baby I just stopped confronting her with these seemingly petty issues. Since pregnancy was no longer an issue, we continued to sleep together on a fairly regular basis and that seemed to help ease some of the tension. But then my anger would get the best of me and I would become cold and distant which always led to more crying and tears.

Despite the fragile state of our relationship and all the tears, Heather invited me to join her and her family in celebrating her 17th birthday at her house. I stopped and picked up some roses and a card and headed to her house, arriving just in time to be ushered through the kitchen and into the living room where everyone was preparing to sing "Happy Birthday." I sang along, watching Heather as she rubbed on her huge belly and bent down to blow out the candles on her cake.

As she took a deep breath and leaned closer to the cake, preparing to blow out her candles, I stopped singing. I felt a large lump swell in my throat and the bottom of my stomach felt like it was about to drop. I leaned closer and looked at the cake to see "Happy 16th Birthday" written across the top. I quickly stood up and looked at her as she laughed and smiled with her family. Feeling my face turn red with anger, I backed up and went out onto the back porch to try to get some air, I clinched my teeth and quietly mumbled to myself, "she's 16??? She fucking lied to me about her age???"

Now many of her previous lies made sense. Telling me that she was in a different homeroom so I wouldn't know she was actually a freshman and not a transferring junior like she said. Telling me she was taking classes that she wasn't taking so I wouldn't know she was actually a freshman. Jumping in as soon as her mother tried to mention her age to me. Quickly cutting her mother off with instant tears and crying so that she never had a chance to tell me how upset she was with me for impregnating her then fifteen-year-old daughter!

The more I thought, the more my lividity increased. I eventually went back into the party and asked Heather to come outside so we could talk. Smiling from the birthday attention and glowing from the pregnancy, I looked at her and contemplated not saying anything, knowing that she would probably burst into tears and leave me looking like I was the biggest asshole in the world in front of her friends and family. But I couldn't hold it. As soon as we were on the porch, away from everyone I said, "Why the fuck did you lie to me about how old you were? You told me that you were sixteen, the same age as me, you told me that you were a Junior, the same as me. Why did you lie about that?"

Without hesitation and still smiling she said, "I didn't lie to you, they made a mistake on the cake, I am really turning 17."

Stunned and not knowing what to say I just looked at her, biting my lip hard trying not to burst out screaming at her. I just shook my head and calmly, gently said, "Please stop, please. We have a child on the way, you don't need to keep lying to me." Surprised at my own calm demeanor, I paused and waited for her response.

She replied just as calmly, "Let's talk about this later, I didn't lie to you, I'm going back to the party" and turned and walked back, leaving me standing there, stewing in my own emotional hodgepodge. My anger quickly faded into an all too familiar feeling of utter despair as I realized that I was going to have to deal with her for many years to come, and for the first time the true reality of how my life was changing hit me and hit me hard.

Even though Heather was pregnant with a huge belly, I was still seeing Candy, who knew about the pregnancy and was definitely not thrilled about it. We were spending more and more time arguing and fighting and eventually one of our arguments escalated into her slapping me and me returning her slap with one of my own. I immediately felt horrible for hitting her but justified it in my mind because she hit me first. Upset, she confided in her sister what happened and her sister confided in her husband who told Candy that he wanted to see me so he could "Teach me about hitting girls."

I was irate. How could this dude confront me about a slap when everyone knew that he beat the hell out of Casey on a regular basis! I got Puba and one of my other friends and we discussed heading to Jet's house to confront him. My other friend, Wade, pulled out a .22 caliber pistol from his front pocket and said, "I got your back, let's go."

Guns were just starting to become more common place among my crew and it wasn't the first time that I had seen one but it was the first time that I ever considered using one to start or settle a beef. Puba was known to carry guns. Usually shotguns that he would tuck under the long trench coats he would wear, even when the weather was muggy and hot. Whenever anyone saw Puba with a trench coat on, we all knew that usually meant he had a shotgun under there and everyone would stay clear.

My heart now starting to race, my intuition telling me to stay my ass right at home. All in direct contrast with the words that flew out of my mouth, "Yeah man, let's go find that nigga." Puba and I got into my car and Wade got into his mother's car and he followed us to Sawyer street, where Jet's mother lived and where Jet could usually be found. As we drove up the street Puba said, "I don't trust Wade, you sure he's down?"

"I guess we are about to find out now" I said, heart feeling like it was going to explode out of my chest. All my time hanging with my partners on Thurston, fighting and jumping people taught me how to harden my thoughts in preparation for a conflict. I learned how to shake off that feeling in my stomach that was trying to warn me that something bad was about to happen. I learned to empty my mind of thoughts of fear and focus strictly on anger and pain in order to convince my mind that what I was doing was justified. I had been training myself to overcome the 'flight or fight' response to situations that all of us feel when confronted with immediate, imminent conflict and danger, so that any desires I might have to rely on the flight response would be suppressed and my fight instincts would take over.

I watched all of us go through this process. Suppressing the flight instinct in order to commit acts that our minds, hearts and instincts told us were wrong, as we drew from the anger and hurt and pain we all felt at one time or another and channeled that anger into action. I watched some of my friends completely black out. Their eyes becoming cold and lifeless as they clinched their fists in preparation to attack. I was learning to shut down my natural instincts to help, to laugh, to love, and was drawing heavily on my anger and stress, which seemed to be multiplying by the minute.

As we pulled up in front of his mother's house, a few houses down from the corner of Sawyer and Genesee street, I noticed a few guys standing on the corner. Some were holding 40 ounce bottles wrapped in brown paper bags and others looking out for the police while still others passed drugs off to customers with one hand and collected money with the other hand. This was Black Mob's corner. Most of their members were three or four years older than us and came from Sawyer and neighboring streets. I knew most of the younger members from school, Southwest Colts football and from when I lived a few streets down on Elmdorf, and Puba knew everybody on that end of Genesee.

I parked the car, got out and quickly walked across the street to Jet's mother's house and rang the doorbell. I looked over to Wade who was parked behind me and had gotten out of his car and was leaning against his driver's door, hand under his shirt. He gave me a quick head nod letting me know he was ready. Jet's mother answered and I asked for him, when he came to the door his eyes got wide and he said, "Jason? What's up?"

"I heard you were looking for me? Well here I am mother fucker, what's up now?" Completely surprised, he said "Oh yeah, Ok, what do you want to do?"

My instincts told me to talk to him, ask him why he was telling people he was looking for me and try to work this out before things went too far but I shook that off and drew on my anger. "Bring your punk ass outside and stop hiding behind that door and I'll show you what's up." He looked around to see who else was with me and seeing Wade standing by the car and Puba standing by my car he said, "I see you brought your boys with you. That's how this is going down?"

I looked back at them and held a hand up indicating that they should stay where they were and said, "Naw Nigga, this is all me and you."

He stepped outside and off the porch into his front yard, "We don't have to do this you know. I'm just not cool with you putting your hands on Candy, man that shit wasn't right."

Heart racing I said, "Mind your own fucking business. Am I checking you about you putting your hands on Casey? You shouldn't have been running your mouth about looking for me. Here I am, so fuck this talk, what's up?"

As the last word was leaving my mouth, Jet rushed forward, putting his shoulder into my stomach and tried to slam me to the ground. I spun around, moved to the side and hit him with an uppercut that landed clean on his jaw, standing him up and knocking him backwards. As he fell back, he reached up and grabbed my shirt, pulling me closer to him and into the bushes that covered the front of the porch. I swung again with another upper cut, barely missing him and then followed that up with a left hook to his nose that connected.

Seeing his eyes start to water up and the dazed look on his face I moved closer, throwing a series of punches to his face that were mostly blocked by his arms which were now covering most of his head. "Jet why are you fighting with that boy?" His mother said from inside the screen door on the porch, "Ya'll stop before someone gets hurt out there." I glanced up to see where his mother was standing and noticed that the dudes that were on the corner had now made their way to the front yard and were slowly starting to circle us. As one or two of them drew closer, I heard someone say, "Fuck that white boy up" and then someone else say, "Naw man, that's Jason, he's alright."

"Fuck Jason, I don't know his ass, this is our hood man fuck that."

As I looked around to make sure no one moved closer, I stumbled on a hole in the yard and Jet rushed forward, using my loss of balance to eventually knock me to the ground. We wrestled for a few minutes until someone grabbed my leg and someone else grabbed my arm, enabling Jet to get on top of me until he was sitting on my chest. "You fucked up now Jason, I got your ass now" he said as he pulled his arm back in preparation to rain down punches on my unprotected face. "Alright, this shit is over with, its done," Puba said as he quickly moved towards Jet and pushed him off of me. Seeing a few kicks come my way I covered up and then Puba pushed his way through the small crowd that was quickly closing in on me, got me up onto my feet and we stood back-to-back, throwing a few punches at the couple of dudes that were trying to come our way.

While I was on the ground, I looked up, waiting to see Wade come out with the gun and start clearing people out but instead he got into his mother's car, started it up and pulled off, tires screeching as he drove away. Most of the guys stood and watched as they knew Puba and they knew me but the few older dudes that didn't started saying, "Someone go get the tools, I'm going to teach these young boys about coming down this way with this bullshit."

Before anyone had time to do anything else, Puba and I made our way back to the car and took off. We rode in silence for a few minutes until Puba finally busted out laughing hysterically. He was laughing so hard that tears were starting to run down his face. I looked at him confused, "Man what the fuck is so damn funny?"

"You are one crazy mother fucker," he said between deep laughs. "I never seen anyone go to someone's house and beat their ass in their own front yard in front of their momma! You are my Nigga for life!" he said. "But yo, what the fuck is up with your boy Wade? Man, that nigga left us, that shit was whack."

I just shook my head. I was hurt because I trusted him and he let me down but more so out of disgust as I thought about how badly that situation could have turned out if Puba wouldn't have come through the way he did.

"We should go find his ass and fuck him up for that man," Puba said, looking at me for confirmation. I thought about it and said, "Naw man, fuck him. I just can't believe he left me out there like that, but fuck him." Shrugging his shoulders, he reached for the volume on the radio and turned it up until the speakers in the trunk started rattling the entire car, then he lit up a fat joint and we headed to his house on Hawley Street, a few blocks away from the high school.

Puba lived with his mother and his young niece, Shayvone, in a cramped two-bedroom apartment on the third floor of a house on Hawley Street, about half way up the block between Jefferson Avenue and Genesee Street. We parked in front of the house and made our way up the three flights of stairs and into the apartment, making our way to the back bedroom where Puba cleared off a bunch of clothes scattered in piles on the bed and lifted the mattress, exposing an arsenal of guns. He reached for a sawed off shotgun along with a black .38 special. He tucked the revolver in the back of his pants and set the shotgun on the bed while he looked for his boot length trench coat. "Yo man, what's all this for?" I asked, not quite sure what he had in mind.

"We need to go see your homeboy and straighten his ass out. Man that was fucked up, we could have got our asses lit up out there like that," he said as he put the trench coat on and placed the shotgun into the inside pocket, which he had modified specifically to hold the shotgun.

Shaking my head slowly I said, "Naw man, I told you, let it go.

I just know I can't fuck with him like that again."

He starred at me for a long time, eventually sucking his teeth before taking the trench coat off and putting the shotgun back underneath the mattress. "I'm keeping this .38 with us just in case those Black Mob niggas decide to get stupid."

I headed to the bathroom and cleaned off some of the blood that dried underneath my nose and wiped some of the dirt from my shirt. Looking in the mirror I saw that I had a slight bruise underneath my eye from one of the kicks that landed on my face but other than that I was in good shape considering what just took place. Puba came into the bathroom and smacked me on the back of my neck and said, "Ha ha, they bruised up the pretty boy's face!!" I immediately turned around and threw my hands up and we started to play fight. Me swinging wildly with a left hook to his head while he ducked and countered with a couple quick punches to my stomach. I jumped back and we threw a few more fake punches, purposely hitting nothing but the air in front of each other, before we both busted out laughing.

Puba pulled out a bag of weed that had to weigh at least a pound, rolled up a few spliffs, three times the size of a regular joint, stuffing each with an entire dime bag worth of weed. I put Eric B. and Rakim's "Paid In Full" cassette into the cassette player and we sat back and smoked spliff after spliff, until the entire house was full of smoke. Nodding our heads to the beat, we repeated every lyric of every song in unison with Rakim's mono-tone, conversational rap. The music and the weed transported us to another place. A place where drama was replaced with rhythm and the monotone cadence of Rakim's rhymes, and the throbbing of my knuckles from repeatedly striking them against Jet's hard head was replaced with the throbbing bass on each song on the tape. We smoked and played that tape over and over again until it was dark and I finally headed home. My emotions dulled from all the weed but still feeling anxiety about the fight and knowing that Heather was going to give birth any day. Life was growing more and more complex by the moment and I was nowhere near close to possessing the tools necessary to cope with the new layers of stress that were piling on top of one another, slowly suffocating me and making it feel as if I was carrying the weight of the world on my shoulders.

10 A SON IS BORN

I would spend hours laying with my head turned towards Heather's stomach, talking to her belly as I gently rubbed and played with the growing child inside, exchanging gentle pushes in return for kicks and punches from the baby. In these moments Heather was in heaven, a smile drifting across her face that was large enough to be felt. I found myself slowly growing closer to her and for the first time really noticing her. She had beautifully shaped light brown eyes that sparkled when she laughed and a glow that was now radiating from her entire being. While I was still leery about the lies she told me and the fact that she still refused to admit that she was almost two years younger than me, I was finally starting to accept that she was going to be the mother of my child.

I was at work when I got the call that she was going into labor and was headed to the hospital. The world seemed to slowdown and my thoughts became louder and more pronounced. For the first time the fear that I worked so hard to suppress came rushing out, moving faster than everything around me and took over my entire body. I felt my legs get weak and my arms felt as if they each weighed two hundred pounds as I leaned back against the wall and tried to gather myself. Slowly, the sounds of the kitchen began to creep back in and the movement in the distance came back into focus.

I saw the servers bringing orders to the line cooks and watched as Reg and the other dishwashers laughed and joked around as they quickly unloaded the server's trays. "I'm about to be a father", my heart raced as I mumbled those words out loud for the first time and as if magic, hearing those words come from my own mouth seemed to speed up my heart beat until it was now racing and beating so fast that I had a hard time catching my breath. I told the Chef that she was about to have the baby and I had to leave and then I told Reg, who quickly removed his apron, throwing it on the ground and said, "Man let's go!"

We jumped in the car and drove from the restaurant in Henrietta all the way across town to Rochester General Hospital.

We spent the entire ride not saying a single word. I was unable to speak as I struggled hard to keep my emotions and thoughts in check. I was torn between being excited at the birth of my first child and being paralyzed with fear at the prospect of being a father. For the first time I thought about my father, about how I had no idea what type of father he was or even what type of person he was beyond the pictures and few stories that came from my mother. I had brief moments of envying him, that he was free from the responsibilities that came with feeling the way I was now feeling. Then those thoughts were replaced with the overwhelming emotions of my true inner spirit, gently reminding me that being a father to my child was the only thing I could do. I knew anything else would destroy me because I would have to fight against all my instincts in order to not be there.

I drove in silence while Reg just rode, looked out the window and let me tangle with my thoughts until we finally arrived at the hospital, parked the car and went to the front desk to get visitor passes. The rest of the time was a blur. I remember holding Heather's hand and watching her cry and scream as the doctors encouraged her to stay calm and push. I remember the way her mother gently caressed her hair, projecting a calmness into the room that relaxed me and seemed to have a similar effect on everyone else. Bright lights, doctors and nurses hustled in and out of the birthing room. Muffled chatter from the doctors were broken up by loud screams and grunts from Heather and then the room slowed down. The noises became muted as I saw a little bit of hair and the top of a head starting to make its way out.

The blood and fluids coupled with the unique smell of childbirth and the sounds and lights all started to blend together and I started to feel light headed. One of the nurses touched my arm asking if I was alright and her touch seemed to wake me, enabling me to shake off the light headedness. I brought myself back into the moment just in time to see the doctor ease a child gently into his arms as a nurse wiped away blood and fluids from the baby's face. Her mother started smiling, kissing Heather on her forehead she said, "You did it! You did great! I am so proud of you!"

As the nurses worked to clean the baby up, a voice finally said, "It's a boy! You have a beautiful baby boy!" A boy! I have a son? I felt the tears swelling up in my eyes and before I could fight to push them back, they were rolling down my cheeks. I was a father. I now had a son and I was a father! That feeling overtook all the anxiety, all the anger, all the fear that had dominated my thoughts for the previous nine months, completely erasing all the negativity and replacing it with pure joy. I was so lost in my own thoughts that the nurse had to ask me three or four times if I wanted to hold him before I heard her. Hold him? Hold my son?? I didn't know what to say. I wanted to hold him more than anything in the world and I reached my arms out as she gently placed him close to my chest, taking my hand and placing it underneath his head to make sure I supported him properly.

I looked down into his wet, wrinkly face, expecting to be overwhelmed with emotions but instead I felt blank. At that moment my entire being just went blank. People talk about finding Nirvana, a mental state in which you are able to free your mind of any and all thoughts, a sort of spiritual oneness with the universe, and for a brief moment I was there. My mind was completely free from all thoughts, emotions, sounds, the only thing I saw was my son and then with a deafening "wooosh," reality smacked me in the face and the first feeling that crept back into my mind, seemingly directly from my heart, was fear. I was afraid in a way that I had never been before. Not like a fear of the dark or even a fear of failure, it was a deep, dark, all consuming fear that momentarily paralyzed me as I stood there, staring at this face belonging to a brand new life that I helped create. I wondered what in the fuck I was supposed to do now.

They cleaned him up and moved him down to the maternity ward, where Reg and I stood outside, staring through the glass window into the large yellow, brightly lit room lined with row upon row of newborn babies. My mind was racing. "You good man?" he asked. "Yeah man, I'm good," I replied, knowing it was a lie and being unable to even make an attempt at disguising the worried look on my face.

"So how does it feel?" Reg asked in a completely genuine tone, as if he was truly intrigued by what new fatherhood might feel like.

"Feels like . . . man I don't know how it feels," I said, shaking my head, disappointed that I couldn't give him the insight that he was obviously searching to find. How was I supposed to tell him that it felt empty, that it felt uncomfortable, that I was scared as hell and had no idea how to be a father. I wanted to say all those things but all I could eventually muster was, "Fuck it man, let's go to the store so I can grab some flowers for Heather and smoke a spliff. I need some smoke bad as hell right now."

"I hear you, let's go grab a drink and celebrate! You're a Dad man!!!" Reg said as he put his arm around me and we walked down the hallway towards the parking lot. Those words kept ringing in my head, over and over, "You're a dad. . .You're a dad. . . You're a Dad." As soon as we got to the car, I pulled out a spliff and lit it up immediately, inhaling as deeply as I could. I hit it a few more times than nudged Reggie and tried to pass it to him, even though I knew he didn't smoke. He gave me the same "Nigga are you crazy" look he always gave me when I tried to get him to smoke weed and as always, it made me bust out laughing.

We headed to the store to get some flowers and hit the bootlegger to grab a bottle of E&J brandy and a 40 ounce of Old English. I dropped off Reg and dropped the flowers off at the hospital, then I picked up Puba. As we passed the bottle of E&J back and forth, every few swigs Puba would make a toast to my new son, then we would chase the swig of E&J with a gulp from the 40 ounce and then follow that up with two or three hits off of one of Puba's famously large spliffs. Eventually, I was so high that I just passed out, waking up hours later still holding the bottle of E&J in one hand while Puba was knocked out in the chair next to me, still holding the almost empty 40-ounce bottle.

I eventually made it home, cleaned myself up and headed back to the hospital. Heather was exhausted but woke up immediately when I entered the room. I sat on the bed next to her and we talked, really talked for the first time in months. I could see that her eyes lacked the fear that I was feeling, her smile and glow supported everything that she said about being so in love with our child. I was envious of her ability to be so optimistic about everything, about the way she seemed to be truly happy and I was searching for something inside of me that would help me understand why I didn't feel that same optimism and joy.

When they brought our son back into the room, he had a nametag attached to his leg. Seeing my namesake spelled out for the first time sent a chill up my spine as I sat up a little straighter and felt my heart start to fill with pride. Ready or not I had a son and regardless of the fears or doubts I was experiencing, he wasn't going anywhere. I knew that my life would never be the same again, but I had no idea how much it was going to change.

I was already starting to feel the stresses associated with teenage fatherhood. I continued working at the hotel, picking up more hours now on the weekends and day shifts whenever school was out. I started spending more time with people from work, hanging out after work in the parking lot or at a co-worker's house, getting drunk, smoking weed and usually selling whatever cocaine I had to the same co-workers I drank with.

Lucy, one of the bartenders that worked the weekend shifts, started buying a lot of coke from me, usually ten to fifteen dime bags each shift and eventually ended up owing me a couple hundred dollars for coke that I gave her on credit. I could see that there was no way she would be able to pay me back and the last thing I wanted to do was to have to fuck somebody up at work, especially a woman, so we worked it out so that she would sell coke for me, earning $10 from every $100 she sold to go towards repaying what she owed.

Lucy did coke with a few of the hotel's bar customers, sometimes asking me to watch the bar for her as she slid off to the bathroom so they could share a quick snort. Most of the bar customers were corporate types, and business travelers and many worked for the airlines. The hotel had contracts with a few of the airlines and the stewardesses and pilots would stay there during layovers. I quickly discovered that the airline folks enjoyed doing coke just as much as the bartender, and soon she was selling a few hundred dollars-worth of coke a night, most of it just to them.

As the word spread, more hotel customers started buying from Lucy. First just the regulars, then a few airline staff, then a couple business travelers. She went from selling a few hundred dollars a night, to sometimes a thousand dollars or more a night. Business was booming. I continued working as a cook, busing tables for Sunday brunch and delivering room service on the weekends and stopped selling to the few managers and servers that I was selling to before. Lucy was now selling to everyone and I tried to make it look like I was no longer involved, keeping my hands as clean as possible and distancing myself from Lucy the best that I could. But trying to keep a low profile with a cokehead is an improbable task.

We set it up so she would drop money off in the cooler, usually underneath some vegetables or other produce that I knew no one would touch that day. Then pick up a package of pre-bagged coke, usually in bundles of 30 bags, twenty-five she would sell for me, and five she would keep for herself. The weekends got to be so busy that she was making three or four trips a night back to the cooler and I noticed that people were starting to get suspicious. One day I caught one of the cokehead servers in the cooler, lifting up produce and going through boxes of food. He jumped when I opened the door and tried to play it off but I knew that he was in there looking for the stash. Despite these type of instances and my instincts strongly telling me to chill out, we kept on selling coke until I had graduated from buying $150 eight-balls, to big eights and quarter keys, four and a half ounces and nine ounces respectively.

While business was booming, my relationship with my son's mother was struggling. I would come by her house and see my son almost daily, dropping off diapers, formula, clothes and whatever she said he needed and spending a couple of minutes or a few hours with him. When we started arguing she would threaten to keep my son from me and I would try to diffuse the situation by trying to be close to her which usually led to us having sex. The sex led to expectations on her part of us being together and those conversations led to more arguments and anger on my part as the feelings of being set up and lied to would resurface and dominate my thoughts.

I would sit down and talk to Reggie, venting about the relationship and trying to bounce ideas off of him on how to deal with things. Reg had stopped working at the hotel but we still hung out almost every day, usually drawing graffiti, listening to music or double dating. Before Heather got pregnant I would sneak into her bedroom window and stay the night with her, usually the same nights that Reg would do the same thing at his girl's house. Both of us telling our mothers that we were staying at each other's houses.

I asked Reggie to be Jason's Godfather, not in the religious sense but as sign of our brotherhood and because next to Puba, I viewed him as my closest friend. In my mind he was as close to family as you can get. He would often come with me when I went to visit my son at Heather's house or hang out with my son whenever I picked him up for the day. When things got ugly with Heather and myself, sometimes he would act as the go-between, calming her down and helping me keep my anger in check which was cool for me because the less I had to deal with her meant less opportunities for arguments.

I brought Ragland over to Heather's house so he could see my son. After hanging out for a little while, my son fell asleep so I headed upstairs to put him in his crib while Heather and Ragland talked downstairs. As I turned to leave her room I noticed a piece of paper sticking out from underneath her pillow. I moved the pillow and saw a handwritten letter and a few pictures. I picked up the pictures and my heart started to race as I saw Heather in the picture with Joe, a guy she was dating before me. I looked closer to see that Joe was holding my son in one arm and his other arm was wrapped around Heather. A few people told me that they thought that our son might not be my child, they said Heather was still seeing Joe. I thought about it for a while but after seeing my son and his resemblance to me, and having Heather and her family reassure me repeatedly that she was not seeing anyone else, I let it slip to the back of my mind.

Seeing the picture brought back all those rumors and conversations and I immediately felt like a fool. Heart feeling like it was going to beat out of my chest, I quickly opened the letter and started to read, each line making me more and more angry.

> I wish I was Jason's father, I would treat him and
> you the way you deserve to be treated. Jason doesn't
> know what he has in you, you need a real man by
> your side. I am tired of daydreaming about kissing
> your soft lips and feeling your body close to mine, I'm
> ready to take this to another level, I hope you give me
> that chance.
>
> Love and kisses always,
>
> Reggie

I paused for a minute, rubbed my eyes, held the letter closer to my face and squinted to read the signed name at the bottom of the letter again. Reggie??? Looking at the handwriting I immediately recognized it and realized that the letter I thought was from Joe was actually from Reg, my best friend, my son's godfather. I was furious. I don't even remember walking downstairs. My next memory was hearing Ragland's muffled voice as he grabbed me saying, "Jay, Jay, come on man, you're going to kill her Jay...Jay... Jason!"

Slowly coming back, I felt Ragland's hand on my wrist and his arm around my chest as he tried to pull my hands from around Heather's neck and lift me from on top of her. Both of my hands were firmly wrapped around her neck and I was squeezing so hard that her eyes were bulging out of her head and she was unable to breath. "You fucking bitch, you want to fuck with Reggie? You and Reg want to play me like a fool? I'm going to show you bitch, I'm going to show you," I shouted, squeezing harder and harder.

"Yo Jay, chill man! Chill! You are going to kill her man," Ragland yelled as he worked to tighten his grip on my wrist and pull me away, finally lifting me off of her and removing my hands from her throat. He pushed me towards the door and kneeled over Heather, shielding her from me and helping her stand up. Her legs were wobbly and her eyes were watery and red and she gasped for air as she stood up. I started to move towards her again and Ragland turned, wrapped his arms around me in a bear hug and whispered in my ear, "Jay you're scaring me man. You don't need to do this, this isn't worth it man."

Something in his tone snapped me back, brought me into the moment and I looked around realizing what had just happened and felt a numbness take over my entire body. Heather started to cry hysterically and sat down on a kitchen chair, sobbing. "I'm sorry, I'm sorry, but you didn't want me. You didn't want to be with me. I'm sorry Jason, I'm so sorry."

I turned and walked out of the house and as soon as I got to the car Ragland came out. He was talking to Heather, trying to soothe her and as he explained later. Trying to convince her not to call the police. He got in the car and we drove, in silence, no music, no conversation, nothing but my thoughts and the streets ahead of me. Driving always helped me think, helped to clear my mind and relax my spirit so I drove for a long time until Ragland eventually said, "Are you ok?"

"Naw man, I'm not ok," and I proceeded to tell him what I saw in the pictures and more importantly, what I read in that letter. Ragland couldn't believe it. He said there was no way that Reg would do that, there was just no way. I reassured him that it was his handwriting, I knew it well from all the time we spent doing graffiti together and the years we spent in the same classes in school.

Sensing what I was feeling, Ragland said, "Look man, take some time and think before you say anything to Reggie. You need to calm down. I never saw you like that before. You blacked out on her. Man your eyes were blank. You scared me dude." I thought to myself, "I'm going to kill that mother fucker."

I thought back to the time I was on the bus coming home from school and some dudes were on the back of the bus mumbling to themselves about how they were going to jump me when I got off. How Reg, hearing what was going on, grabbed me and made me get off the bus with him by his house. I thought about all the times we spent laughing and drawing and just kicking it, talking about every and anything. Then I thought about those words in that letter. About how he said I was a bad father. About how he said he should be with Heather and I could physically feel my heart break. I had nothing but love for Reg. I looked at him like a brother and he was the last one that I would ever think would go behind my back. I shook off the pain and allowed anger to take over, focusing on how and when I would get him back.

Heather told her mother what happened and she in turn called my mother. I will never forget the way my mother looked at me after hearing that I put my hands on her. There was a look of disappointment that ran so deep in her eyes that I could physically feel it take hold across my entire body. I could see her eyes speaking to me, saying "You saw your mom get beat, how could you do that to any girl?" Her eyes gave me insight into how much pain she had been carrying as a result of my recent life choices and it crushed my already bruised and battered heart.

Heather's mother came over and sat down with my mother and I to discuss what happened. They listened as I told them about how she was trying to keep my son from me and how much we argued about everything. While I danced around the real issue, never revealing the pictures or the letter, they just listened until I was done. Heather's mother calmly said, "I understand that you guys are going through some things and I will talk to her about keeping the baby from you, that's not right, but let me be perfectly clear on one thing, it is not ok for you to ever put your hands on her. I don't care what she does. You can come talk to me, you can talk to your mother, but don't ever put your hands on her. I can't allow that to happen to my daughter." Despite her anger with me, she remained calm and came at me with understanding and wisdom I was far from being able to comprehend. She realized that this was going to be a long journey with many more problems to come, and that we were far too young to comprehend the depths of that journey so she led by example.

Hanging my head in shame, unable to even look at my mother or Heather's mother I nodded to let them know I understood. I felt disgusted with myself for allowing my anger to get the best of me, for attacking my son's mother the same way I saw my mother get attacked. I knew how it made me feel and the last thing I would ever want would be for my son to feel the same way I did when my stepfather was beating my mother. I made a vow to myself that I would never again put my hands on another woman, no matter what happened.

When my senior year rolled around I found myself with no interest in school. The only reason I went to school my junior year was so that I could keep playing football. My grades had gotten so bad that it was looking like I might not be academically eligible. We started double session football practices as usual and although I was physical there, my mind was someplace else. I was caught up in thoughts about my son. About the heat that was growing more intense at work around my drug sales. About the recent betrayal from Reggie and Wade and about what the hell I was supposed to do with my life after high school was over. My mind seemed to always be cloudy which was made worse by my daily weed sessions and almost daily alcohol use.

Football was still an escape for me and I was able to harness all my built up frustrations, pain and anger and channel it directly through my pads and into my opponent. I had always been aggressive with sports, but my aggression reached another level and it was not uncommon for me to deliver a tackle to someone that was so vicious that it would knock them or myself unconscious. After every hit I would get up expecting to feel better but instead found myself being filled with even more anger and rage.

My ability to let off steam on the football field quickly disappeared as right after the season started I was declared academically ineligible. My coach set me up with a tutor and all I had to do was attend weekly tutoring sessions. The tutor would sign off on them and I'd be allowed to continue playing until the next marking periods grades were released. I didn't have the energy or the focus to follow through with the tutor so I was no longer able to play. With more free time on my hands I started spending more time with my newest girlfriend, usually going to her house after I got off work, bringing her gourmet meals I prepared at work. Filet mignon, shrimp scampi, crab legs, prime rib, pasta alfredo; anytime I learned a new recipe I would grab some to-go boxes and come by her house so we could eat and she could critique my new creations.

I really enjoyed cooking, the kitchen was busy and kept my mind off of my stresses and it relaxed me and allowed me to express my creative side. I would often re-create recipes from work in her kitchen, cooking for her and her mother, and I quickly learned that women really like a man that knows how to cook! Once I figured that out, I damn near lived in the kitchen!

My friend Tim Riley, bought a brand new Suzuki Samurai, a small four-wheel drive two-door truck with a vinyl, removable top. It was one of the hottest cars out, especially after EPMD mentioned it in one of their rhymes. Everyone wanted one and Tim was the first one around our way to have one. When I wasn't working, we rode around in his truck all day, laughing at how the girls would watch as we drove down the streets. I made up my mind that I had to have one too, so shortly after Tim bought his, I bought mine. A brand new 1987 Suzuki Samurai right from the dealership.

Tim's was baby blue with a white vinyl top and he had "Timmy" on the side of it in plan dark blue lettering. Mine was white, with white rims, a white top and black trim. I took mine to the custom car shop and got a series of black lines added to both sides with "JayBee" written across the lines in black. We would follow each other all over the city, always riding one behind the other, turning heads everywhere we went and attracting an entirely different level of girls.

With an unlimited supply of money to spend, a brand new car and an already easy way with the ladies, I was soon meeting women that were much older than I was and they began to introduce me to concepts and ideas that I had not yet thought about. Weekend trips and romantic getaways. Quick trips to Niagara Falls for dinner or just to walk along the falls or checking out a play at the theatre. I was starting to realize that the world was a lot bigger than I thought and just as I was settling in to my new lady friends, I got a phone call from a friend of mine that worked in the front office at my job saying we needed to talk but not on the phone. I immediately got that feeling one gets when they know something isn't right. My gut told me what she was going to say before he even said it.

She said if I was involved with any type of drug activity at the hotel that I needed to stop because the police were asking questions and they were starting an investigation. I heard later through some customers at the bar, that a few of the airline workers got caught with some coke at an airport check point and they told the agents at the airport that they supposedly got it from the hotel bar.

I thanked her for passing on the warning and called Lucy and told her to meet me at Genesee Valley park, around the corner from my house. We sat and talked, just general conversation as I tried to feel her out and see if she was wearing a wire or acting unusual in any way. She didn't set off any of my mental alarms so I told her that things were getting hot and I wouldn't be able to supply her anymore and I suggested that she didn't sell anything else.

The incident shook me so much that I didn't go back to work. I just stopped going. Never called, never went back, just quit. I cut off all ties to all my old customers, got a new pager and got rid of the old number and stayed clear of the hotel. Not only did I no longer have a regular job but I also lost all of my cocaine business, all in one clean sweep. I had enough money to last for a little while but I knew that I needed to find another job or figure out another place to hustle and do so quickly.

Between fatherhood, legitimate paranoia from the job scare, losing my job and my erratic sleeping patterns, my mother began to suspect that something deeper was taking place. One morning I woke up to her standing over my bed, yelling as she pointed to the bag she was holding in her hand. I rubbed my eyes, trying to wake up and figure out what she was yelling about and slowly gained focus on the baggie in her hand. It was one of the bags I used to give Lucy, with about thirty dime bags of cocaine and a few dime bags of weed.

Stunned and at a loss for words she sat down on the bed and quietly said, "Get out. I can't take this anymore, you have to leave here right now. You brought drugs into my house, what if your brother or sister would have found them? What if the police would have come in here? You put us all in danger, I love you but you have to go Jason." She got up, walked out of the room and hung her head as she walked down the hallway towards the end of the stairwell before stopping, turning and saying, "I mean it, I want you out of here right now."

I grabbed a few of my clothes, stuffed them in a bag, took my car keys off the table and left the house with no idea where I was heading. I decided to get a hotel room and try to figure things out so I drove out to one of the hotels in the suburbs, got a room, laid down on the bed and tried to think but the more I thought, the more my head spun. I finally went to check Puba out and get some weed to clear my head. I told him what happened and he said, "You know she is right man. You can't have that shit in her house."

"What? Man, fuck you. You have more guns under your mattress than a gun store and you're going to lecture me? Fuck you," I said, half joking but half serious. He passed the spliff and just shrugged his shoulders as if to say, 'yeah, you're right.'

As we smoked I sat back and thought about where things were with my life. I thought about my son and the drama with Heather, about Reggie and how that whole situation went down. I thought about the hotel, about my mom and my current state of homelessness, about the fight with Jet and how I was now constantly watching my back because of the threats made by some of Jet's older homeboys. It seemed like every day that went by brought a new set of problems that piled on top of yesterday's bullshit and built upon the shit from the day before that. With no solutions at hand I was starting to feel like I was carrying the weight of the world on my shoulders, and my back, as strong as I thought it was, felt like it couldn't take much more.

Candy was now a freshman at the college. Sometimes when I worked late and had to be back to work in the morning, I would stay with Candy in her dorm room because it was close to work. With no place to stay, Candy invited me to bring my stuff to her room and leave it there and stay there with her for a little while until I figured out what I was going to do.

The dorm experience was cool. It gave me an insiders perspective to college life and I was around so much that everyone just assumed I was a student. I even went to a few of the larger lecture classes and sat in the back, listening and watching as the professor taught and the students took notes. While there were moments that I felt like college could be for me, I quickly lost those thoughts whenever I managed to make it to my own school. I had pretty much stopped going to school all together, only showing up once every 10th day or so to make sure that they didn't mark me as a dropout. Until my senior year, I was able to skip classes and fake it through the year and always managed to do well enough on my final exams that I would get the credits necessary to pass the class, but I had fallen so far behind that relying on the finals to get me through was no longer a viable option. If I wanted to graduate, I was going to have to put in some serious work to make it happen.

Standing by the back door of the school, I looked outside and saw my brand new car sitting in the parking lot. I put my hand in my pocket and felt the knot of hundred dollar bills. I looked down at my pager and saw that I had just received a text from one of the older women that I occasionally hung out with and said, "Man fuck this shit, what do I need school for? I have it all!" While my instincts were telling me to turn around and put in the work that I knew I was capable of doing, my pride and ego told me to keep walking, screamed at me 'fuck that school and those squares, you don't need them.' As was becoming my habit, I ignored my intuition and everything that my mother worked so hard to instill in me and instead embraced the anger associated with my pride and kept it moving. Just like that, I had officially become a high school dropout.

Puba and I started hanging almost every day, and on the weekends we would go hang out with Puba's brother Greg as he DJ'd at this small hole in the wall bar on Genesee Street called Jenks & Jones. Jenks & Jones was always dark. The walls were covered in old school wood paneling with a dark wood L-Shaped bar to the right of the entrance way. There were a few round tables scattered throughout the small front area and bottles of liquor adjourned the wall behind the bar. The back wall behind the bar was covered in small square mirrors, all placed together to look like one larger mirror. Christmas lights hung overhead year round and no matter what time of day or night, there was always one or two regulars, usually old black men in their late fifties or early sixties, sitting at the bar, head hanging low, drunk as hell from spending an entire day sipping on watered down liquor.

The DJ booth was set up in the very back of the bar, slightly hidden by the bathroom that jetted out and acted as a dividing point for the front of the bar and the back. While everyone knew that Puba and I were underage, no one ever asked for ID as we were always recognized as Kevin's 'cousins' or G's 'little brothers.' I would walk in, nod to the bartender, walk to the back and slap up Kev or G, sit down listen to some music and eventually order a drink or two. Kev would always roll up a fat spliff and we would hit the bathroom to smoke then come out and order some more drinks and repeat until Puba and I would damn near stumble out of the bar.

At the bar, I would stand behind the DJ booth and watch G as he mixed and scratched records, soaking up everything he was doing. I was mesmerized by his ability to mix two records together in perfect timing so that they sounded like one brand new remixed record. Eventually, as I began to understand the music and art of mixing, I would dig through the crates and hand G records that I thought would blend well with whatever he was playing. We would pop a cassette tape in and make live mix tapes of all my favorite records, mixed and scratched live from the back of Jenks & Jones. Soon, Puba's friends from Shelter Street, Big Darryl along with his younger brothers Derius and Deidrick and their cousin Paul Griffin, were coming by the bar asking G to make them customized mix tapes as well. G had no interest in doing the tapes but I stayed on him, handing him records and popping in cassettes when he wasn't looking, recording those live sessions and handing out tapes when we finished.

Besides music and DJing, I really went to the bar to drink. Puba and I would order triple shots of Bacardi 151 proof rum, the same rum that the bartenders would use to light drinks on fire when they wanted to impress a customer, and we would chase the shots of 151 with champagne. We all kept pockets full of money so we started buying cases of splits, smaller sized bottles of Great Western Champagne. The bartenders would put the entire case on ice and we would use a split of champagne to chase down one of the shots of 151. After one or two shots, a couple of bottles of champagne and a few spliffs, G would usually be slumped over a table in the back while Puba and I would keep drinking, buying drinks for everyone and cracking up laughing as the old heads would pass out trying to hang with us.

With no job and no school, I had a lot of free time on my hands, most of which I spent riding around the city with Tim in our Suzuki's and occasionally venturing out to explore Buffalo or Syracuse, both only an hour or so away from Rochester. I also started to figure out a new plan for hustling. I saw how quickly the money came from selling coke. I had the contacts and the know-how, I just needed to find a new location from which I could apply my trade.

All the traffic coming in and out of the buildings led to numerous police raids so Vic and Ozell moved away from the apartments on Thurston and started venturing out to other areas of the city. They had already established themselves on the streets and had a few other dudes working for them, selling from a couple of drug houses they set up. There was really no room for me to get involved with what they were doing as I was well beyond the stage of working for someone else and my entrepreneurial instincts were quickly evolving. We still hung out all the time. Most nights you could find Ozell standing up in the back of my Suzuki as we drove through the city blocks, music blasting from the large speakers installed in the back, while Vic sat in the passenger seat, bobbing his head in unison with the music.

I tried a few more spots out. Puba's corner on Genesee and Kirkland and a spot around the corner from the apartments on Thurston. But I wasn't comfortable with being out in the open where everyone could see me and where I was easily vulnerable to the "Jump out squad." They were a group of police officers on the city's anti-narcotic task force that would pick random corners, sneak up on them from all different directions, and search and harass anyone standing on them. I learned how to only bring a few dime bags at a time and stash them in places far enough away from me where the police, if they decided to jump out on the corner, couldn't pin them on me, but close enough so I could keep an eye on them and make sure that they wouldn't be stolen by any of the geekers that were always watching.

I went from making thousands of dollars a night at the hotel and never touching anything to standing on corners with three or four other dealers, making a hundred dollars and trying to avoid the police. After a week or two of playing the corner, I knew I had to find an inside spot to work so I started to branch out, network with other drug dealers I knew and see what they had going on in their perspective neighborhoods.

As I looked to branch out, a friend of mine turned me on to three brothers originally from New York City. Shawny along with his younger brother Quan, and older brother Clayton, had built up a steady business, mostly selling large amounts of cocaine to independent coke dealers such as myself. I headed to the Downtown Motor Lodge on the corner of South Avenue and Mt. Hope. The Motor Lodge was a low-cost hotel frequented by prostitutes turning quick tricks, drug users, drug dealers and teenagers looking for a quick, cheap place to have sex. Quan led me to his room where we sat down and waited for Shawny.

While waiting, someone else knocked on the door, Quan answered and a stocky, gruff speaking dude came through the door. I immediately recognized him, it was Tim Brown, one of the dudes that used to try me when I first got to #37 school. He ended up going to #3 school with me and we eventually became somewhat cool. Since I knew him in fifth grade, Tim was always a thug. Rough and wild, he earned a reputation for being able to fight at an early age and quickly earned the respect of the older thugs. "Oh shit, Jason?" he said, surprised to see me sitting there. Laughing as he slapped me up. "What are you doing here? Let me find out Jason from #37 school is hustling now!"

As he sized me up I could see the wheels in his head turning. Tim had also developed a reputation for robbing people, especially other drug dealers and I picked up on his vibe immediately. "Man where you hustling at? We need to get some money together."

My instincts going wild, I said, "I'm here and there man, just trying to make a few dollars." Tim laughed and said, "Man cool out. I'm not trying to beat you up or anything. This ain't #37 school!"

Noticing the tension building in the room Quan put his arm around Tim and said, "I got your page, Shawny will be here in a minute. Let me get that money now." Pulling out a wad of singles, five and ten dollar bills, Tim handed the money to Quan and watched as he counted. "Yo man, what the fuck is this? I told you I don't want no dollar bills. Take this shit back and get some twenties or something, "Quan said in a thick New York accent, shaking his head and handing the money back to Tim.

"Come on man, that's all I got right now. What difference does it make, it's all money man," Tim said as he laughed and put his arm on Quan's shoulder. Just then the door to the room opened and Shawny stepped into the room. He walked in and slapped up Tim, not taking his eyes off me the entire time. "What's up, I'm Soldier," he said to me while flashing a warm smile as Quan said, "Yo, this is JayBee. Spanky's people."

Shawny closed the door, locked it then reached into his sock and pulled out an eight-ball for Tim, placing it into Tim's hand and pointing to a digital scale that was sitting on a large TV stand, next to a television set. Tim quickly went to the scale, placed the eight-ball on top, picked it up and said, "3.6 grams, good looking on the extra as always!" Shawny reached down into his other sock and pulled out another clear plastic baggie, wrapped in a tight ball with the top of the plastic cut off so that the coke was gathered into a small compact ball. He handed the ball to me and motioned for me to place it on the scale. I put it on the scale and saw '7.2 grams' appear on the scale read out. I nodded my head and put the bag in my front pocket.

"You might want to throw that under your nuts," Shawny said. "It's been crazy hot around here. Police ran up on us yesterday, searching our pockets and shit."

I quickly removed the bag from my pocket and put my hand down the front of my pants, placing the bag underneath my balls. Then I wiggled around and straightened my pants until it felt comfortable. Shawny gave me his pager number and said to hit him when I was ready to re-up. We slapped each other up and all headed out towards the parking lot, looking around to make sure there were no unmarked police cars or suspicious people watching before we got into the car and drove off.

I soon started hanging out with Shawny and Quan and we quickly became close. Shawny had a genuine and sincere nature that I respected. He spoke to people with a confidence and charm that you would expect from a seasoned politician and with that, commanded respect from everyone. Quan was less political in his communications. He had no problem telling someone off and was much more likely to become openly agitated by people. In many ways they were polar opposites. Quan was flashier and was always fresh from head to toe. If he got a scuff mark on his sneakers he would throw them out and pull out a new pair, while Shawny was content wearing the same thing he wore the day before as long as he had money in his pocket he was cool.

We eventually went into business together, setting up shop in this small apartment behind a large apartment building right off of Jefferson Avenue near the corner of Main Street. You had to walk between two house in order to get to the apartment making it impossible to see from either of the main roads. We went inside the house and Shawny gave the woman that was living there a couple bags of coke and a few dollars for letting us work out of the house. We counted all the coke, which was already bagged up into large dime bags and put the majority of it in the garbage can in the kitchen, keeping ten or fifteen bags out within easy reach. Putting the majority into the garbage was a way to try to limit what the police might find if they ever raided the house, hoping that they would be too lazy or disgusted to thoroughly check through the garbage, and to hide it from any potential stick up kids that might try to rob us.

Shawny showed us the window that we were going to sell

from and then headed out. Ten minutes later there was a tap at the window. I went to the window and he was standing there holding two twenty dollar bills. He handed them to me through the window and said, "Let me get four of those fat ones!" I handed him four of the fattest bags we had and he quickly gave them to the large, dark skinned person standing next to him, whom I looked at for the first time. The person that I thought was a man was actually wearing a short mini skirt, high heels and a blond wig which was in direct contrast to their dark brown, almost purple black skin.

Seeing the confused look on my face, Shawny started to crack up laughing and I heard a voice deeper than my own come from the person in the wig saying, "Hey sweetie, what's the matter? You never seen a tranny before? We don't bite baby, unless that's what you are into, with your fine yellow ass!"

I didn't know what to say. My instincts told me to reach through that window and try to grab his neck but Shawny was laughing so hard that I eased up and just shook my head and started laughing myself. After they left, Quan told me that there was a boarding house around the corner that was full of transgender prostitutes, men that dressed in woman's clothes and turned tricks with other men. Most of their customers, or tricks as they called them, were white men from the suburbs and many of them also liked to get high.

A few minutes later Shawny came back with a different transgender woman, this time buying five dimes. And a few minutes after that, he came back with another hooker and she bought seven. After a few hours Shawny came back with four take-out containers of food, one for each of us and one for the woman that lived in the apartment. I watched the way he talked to the customers. It was different than what I had seen before or even done myself. Most of the time we called them geekers, took their money, yelled at them and occasionally beat them up if they did something we didn't like, but Shawny dealt with them like they were people. He laughed and joked with them and thought enough of the woman in the apartment to bring her food and included her when we all sat down to eat. He spoke to the customers as people first and not geekers. Within three hours we sold everything we had, all 150 dime bags were gone and now the trans-hookers were begging us to come back soon. That was how I envisioned my dope house business operating and I realized that I could learn a lot from this brother.

Every few months or so there would be a major drug bust in Florida or New York City or even locally, and the coke supply in Rochester would dry up. We would end up paying more money for lower quality, less potent cocaine. Whenever a drought would hit, Shawny would head down to New York City to buy coke from his connections in the Bronx. Shawny took me with him a few times to meet his connects in the city. While most people would do anything to keep others from knowing who their connect was, and thus forcing others to buy directly from them, Shawny was open about it and lived by the philosophy that if we all were making money it would be harder for us to fall.

I had hustled up enough money to buy a few ounces so Shawny and I put our money together and made our way to the Bronx to see Shawny's cousin Kwame. Kwame, or Sin-Q as everyone called him, was moving a lot of weight in the Bronx and through a few smaller cities up and down the east coast. He had organized a solid crew and they branched out to other east coast towns like Springfield, Mass., and some towns in Maryland as well as Rochester.

Kwame lived in the Soundview section of the Bronx in one of the large, identical seven story brick projects located in the center of the horseshoe shaped road that ran through the center of the projects. The entire neighborhood was notorious for violence and, through Him and his crew quickly developed a reputation for being the go-to suppliers to buy weight in the city. For years, the Dominicans in Manhattan, specifically Washington Heights, had dominated the cocaine trade and were considered to be everyone's first choice when buying weight but Kwame was running with one of the biggest dealers in the city and together, they were starting to shift the power structure in the New York City drug trade.

Eventually Kwame brought an entire crew up to Rochester to help him set things up and linked up with Terrell Wyatt and a few other dudes. Terrell, Tee for short, was a lanky, jheri curl wearing, fast-talking, always smiling brother who was born and raised in

Rochester. He came from a family that had long ago established themselves in the streets of Rochester. Through Shawny, Kwame linked with many of the midlevel dealers in the city. He was soon providing many of the dealers cocaine on consignment, collecting the money from the proceeds after they had sold the coke, and then re-supplying them when they were ready.

Getting drugs fronted to you was the quickest way for someone to establish themselves in the game. All you needed was a connection that trusted you enough to give you a package to get you started. This allowed people with little money but the desire and means to sell drugs, an opportunity to hustle even if they didn't have the cash to invest in buying the product. In return for the credit, the dealer supplying the drugs would expect a slightly higher payment, usually an additional ten or sometimes even twenty percent on top of the usual price. Thus a half ounce of coke that would normally cost $500 would be given on consignment for $550 or $600, increasing the dealers return for the additional risk associated with giving someone their product before they got paid.

Providing coke on consignment also meant that an out of town dealer such as Kwame, could quickly build up a loyal customer base of mid-level dealers even in areas where they were not well known. The down side to providing coke on consignment was the risk that the person receiving the credit might run off with the product or end up in a situation in which they lose the product or find themselves going to jail. It was well known that consignment was serious business for the providers as well as the recipients of the credit. It was not uncommon to see a geeker getting brutally beaten for owing someone $5 and not paying the debt off on time, so you can imagine what would happen if you were late or failed to pay a few hundred or a few thousand dollars.

If you were in the business of providing credit to anyone at any level then you had to make sure that you were willing to assault them or, depending on the amount of money owed and the manner in which they didn't repay, you had to be prepared to kill someone. Letting someone go that owed you money was a sign to everyone else that you were weak and might encourage others to try to short change or not pay you. More often than not, they would make an example out of someone owing money. Many times viciously battering the debtor in a public setting to make sure that everyone got the message, "Pay me what you owe me."

Even before Kwame and his crew put in any work or made examples of anyone, they were respected solely because they came from New York City. New York City was held in mythical standards as the toughest stomping grounds where only the rawest and realest hustlers and thugs lived. Anyone coming from 'the City' as we called it, gained instant respect. Just hearing a New York accent was usually enough to make someone think twice about engaging in a conflict with that person. I noticed this with Shawny and Quan. While they had both attended high school in Rochester, their accents and their ties to NYC made them admired among their peers and added to their developing aura.

Quan had a style that was different than everyone else's. He used slang terms that were different and slightly more in tune with the language used in a lot of the rap songs of the time. He always had a fresh, brand new pair of sneakers, urban designer jeans and rocked brands that were only known by those truly in tune with high end fashion. Quan walked with a bop in his step, in a style called 'pimping,' where he would hop slightly on his left foot while he quickly dragged his other foot up, hunching one of his shoulder forward and slowly swinging the opposite arm forward and backwards, in unison with his bop. His slang, dress and walk commanded attention from everyone, especially in Rochester, where he made sure everything about him said, "I'm from the Bronx!"

Kwame carried a similar style walk but was subtle in his dress, preferring to utilize a more low-key look which was less likely to draw attention to himself. While Kwame and Shawny were comfortable laughing and joking, Quan was more serious. He preferred grimacing and made it clear that he had no interest in playing around with anyone and he was always quick to check anyone that thought otherwise. Quan had also developed a respected reputation for his skills as an amateur boxer. He was known for possessing serious one punch knockout power and was admired around the boxing community for going toe-to-toe during sparing sessions in the gym with some of Rochester's boxing legends, including future world champion, Charles "The Natural" Murray.

Within a week, Kwame had supplied most of the Westside of Rochester with coke and not soon after, had to start chasing a few dudes down that were late paying back the money from the fronted coke. Kwame quickly developed a reputation for being willing to work with just about anyone that Shawny or Tee recommended and just as quickly set the tone for anyone that was slow paying him back for fronted work. One day, we were all standing in front of Tee's mother's house when a dude walked up to Kwame and asked to speak to him privately. The dealer said he wasn't able to pay Kwame what he owed because someone robbed him and took all of his work. Kwame signaled to Madman, a short, round, dark skinned brother with a slight overbite and strong accent, and Madman quickly & quietly moved in behind the dude. Before he knew what was going on, Madman pulled a black nine millimeter handgun from his coat pocket, raised it above his head, and hit the dude in the head with the handle of the gun repeatedly until he dropped to the ground, clutching his bleeding head.

Madman cocked back the gun and put the barrel against his head and Kwame said, "Check this out, you can go get the mother fucker's that robbed you and get my coke back or you can go get my money, it is up to you, but either way you are going to pay what you owe. Do you understand?"

Holding a hand up over his head as if to signal to Madman that he surrenders, he said, "Yeah man, I will get your money. I was trying to tell you I would get your money but you didn't even give me a chance to finish what I was saying."

Thud, thud, thud. Madman hit him with the handle of the gun three more times, until he was laid out flat on the ground. Bones started to cry, in between sobs saying, "Man please don't kill me, please don't kill me. I will get your money. I swear I will get your money."

Kwame nodded to Madman and Madman grabbed him then used the back of the dude's shirt to wipe the blood from the handle of the gun and then placed the gun back into his coat pocket, taking a few steps back from but never taking his eyes off of him. Kwame helped him up off the ground and said, "Damn dude, I really don't want to have to kill anybody up here but you understand that I do need my money right? This shit ain't personal man, this is business you know?"

His head now gushing with blood from two or three large cuts around his forehead and nose, he walked backwards down the street until he got to the corner and then he turned the corner and ran as fast as he could. Madman busted out laughing. "Man that mother fucker damn near pissed himself! Let me find out these niggas up here is soft or something," he said, looking at Kwame and then Shawny. Shawny quickly moved towards Madman, grabbing him and putting him in a head lock, both of them laughing the entire time as Shawny said, "Nigga ain't nobody up here soft, they just scared of that gun your black, crusty ass pulled out!" Everyone started laughing as they playfully slapped boxed with each other.

Needless to say, the word quickly spread that anyone dealing with Kwame or his squad needed to come correct. Despite the warnings, there was always someone trying to get over in one way or another so Madman and the rest of Kwame's muscle stayed pretty busy for the first few weeks.

We stuck with the neighborhood around Jefferson and Main street for a while, switching apartments whenever we felt one was getting hot or whenever we caught a police car watching or looking to hard. We just packed up and moved to the next spot. Shawny would hit the streets and let them know where we were at and within minutes the new spot would be moving just as fast as the previous. As Shawny made his rounds, Quan and I usually worked in the house, talking shit and smoking weed.

Kwame made a few more runs back and forth to Rochester but eventually decided to move on to another town that was closer to home so him and his squad packed up and went to try their luck in Poughkeepsie, New York. When it came to coke, the 80's were like the wild-west, everyone was getting rich, especially when crack hit the streets. There was always plenty of money to go around but New York City dealers soon discovered that taking the drugs away from the New York area and into smaller communities meant that one could double or even triple their profits so they started moving all up and down the east coast. Towns like Poughkeepsie and Springfield were within a few hours of NYC but were full of crack and cocaine users. The local dealers usually lacked the connects to keep the streets supplied and were also intimidated by the boys from New York. Homicide rates were growing in the larger cities and it was a lot easier to go out of town, double your money and deal with less savvy police forces and less violent competition.

Quan was the first person that I saw roll a Blunt instead of a spliff or a joint. He would take a Philly Blunt cigar, lick it and then split it from end to end. Then empty the tobacco contents of the cigar into the garbage and replace the tobacco with marijuana, lick the Blunt again and reseal it back together. Rolling a Blunt, like rolling a joint was a true art form. After a few weeks of sitting in coke spots with Quan, I was able to roll a Blunt like a pro and we started having contests to see who could roll the best and the fastest. We would usually smoke them as soon as we could roll them, often rolling ten or fifteen Blunts and chain-smoking them back-to-back.

We smoked so much weed that our favorite weed man would find us wherever we were at and bring us ten dime bags at a time. When Shawny saw how much weed we were smoking he suggested that we just start buying ounces or a quarter pound instead of wasting all that money on dime bags. We took his suggestion and we were easily going through an ounce or two of weed every day. While we were busy smoking weed, Shawny was busy trying to figure out how we could increase our income and after a few months of testing the waters himself, he decided he wanted Quan and I to try out the new town he and his partners discovered. He said in just a few days we could make ten times as much money as we were making in Rochester in an entire month. That was all I needed to hear!

11 THE FALLS

Niagara Falls, like New York City, was quickly shifting from powder cocaine to crack. Before crack, geekers would buy powdered coke, empty it from the small baggies into a test tube or cooker where they would add water and baking soda and boil it until the powder turned into a yellowish, thick substance. They would take the yellowish blob, twirl it around a metal stick and remove it from the water. Within thirty seconds to a minute the blob would harden. Then they would take a razor and chip the hardened pieces off, placing them into a pipe and smoking them. Crack was basically that hardened product ready to smoke so that they no longer had to go through the process of cooking the coke themselves. It was pre-cooked which made the entire process a lot faster.

Recipients of New York State's welfare program received welfare checks around either the first or the fifteenth of each month. The recipients would head off to a check cashing spot and then practically run to get their favorite high, flooding the liquor stores, weed spots, crack and coke dealers and heroin peddlers with more business in one or two days then they'd see all month. There was an excitement around the first and fifteenth that could only be compared to Christmas time as a kid. Everyone moved faster in anticipation of receiving their piece of the state provided financial pie. Hip Hop groups like Bone-Thugs even paid respect to the bi-monthly pay days in songs like "It's the First of the Month!"

Shawny started making moves around Niagara Falls with his partner Wes and Flint Street Brown. Flint Street was a Rochester street legend who leveraged connections he and another Rochester drug dealer had in Florida with the Columbian drug cartel to corner the cocaine and crack market in Rochester, Buffalo, Syracuse, Niagara Falls and parts of Ohio. Flint Street was also a pimp and was known to always keep a bunch of young, attractive women close at all times. He was always driving the newest exotic car and was one of the first people in Rochester to have a Rolls Royce. Wherever he went, people noticed.

Wes was Flint Street's right hand man and Wes invited

Shawny to partner up with them in Niagara Falls. After spending a few weeks in the Falls, Shawny quickly realized that there was plenty of money to go around and in order to effectively monopolize every dollar moving in and out of the Falls, more man power was needed. Wes, Flint Street and Shawny had already established themselves as the 'go-to' suppliers for all of the street level dealers and Shawny quickly recognized that selling slabs along with larger quantities of weight would enable everyone to double or triple their profits.

'Slabs' were pieces of crack cut in to rectangular half a gram and gram pieces that were sold for $50 or $100 respectively. Selling Slabs meant that we could make $350 off of each eight-ball, in Rochester an eight-ball was being sold for $150 and in Niagara Falls that same eight-ball would be sold wholesale for $200 to $225. Thus an ounce of crack in Niagara Falls sold as slabs would bring back up to $2800 and a kilogram would bring back more than $100,000. Flint Street was getting a key of cocaine for $15,000 and sometimes less, depending on how many were taken at a time so a profit of $85,000 or more could be made off of each and every key.

With every corner of the Falls covered, it was easy to sell three or four keys a day during the two or three days around the first and fifteenth, which meant that hustling for just six or seven days out of the month could collectively bring in considerably more than a million dollars in profits.

Shawny took me to a house on Columbia Avenue, near the corner of Genesee Street, where we went inside and he introduced me to Flint Street and Wes. Wes, short, stocky and dark skinned, who dressed like a preppy white dude from the suburbs, greeted us with a big smile as he gave Shawn a hug and said, "Man are you ready? We are about to get paid in full!!!" Shawny smiled back and said, "This is JayBee, Quan's partner. He is making the move with us to the Falls."

"JayBee, I've seen you around. You drive that white Suzuki right? That shit is dope! I hope you're ready to upgrade that bad boy to a Ferrari cuz that is how fast that money comes in the Falls," Wes said, laughing loudly and slapping me on the back.

Flint Street came into the room, a dark skinned, heavyset brother with a neck full of gold chains of various sizes and styles. His wrists were covered in bracelets and what looked like a diamond encrusted gold Rolex. Damn near every finger on his hand was covered in large gold rings covered in diamonds. If I had to guess, I would say he had to have been wearing at least $250,000 in jewelry as he just lounged around the house. I had never seen anything like it before so of course as he spoke I listened.

Wes and Flint were heading up to the Falls to get things set up and Shawny, Quan and myself would follow a few days later. Flint Street said, "Man I've been doing this for a long time and I have never seen a town that generates so much money so fast! It's a slow town, they are way behind us in the way they move and do things but you got to keep on your toes. It's hot as hell up there and they are already starting to look at us."

Shawny gave us the details on what he experienced in the Falls. He stressed to us repeatedly that we needed to stay on our toes and always watch each other's backs. He would be rolling with Wes overseeing things in one of the larger neighborhoods that they had already locked down and he had a neighborhood that he wanted Quan and I to run. They called the neighborhood 'Vietnam' because of all the crack heads walking around, looking like zombies and the large number of vacant lots and decrepit looking houses. Vietnam was one of the biggest money making spots in the Falls and Shawny estimated that if we set it up right, we could pull in $100,000 to $200,000 in a single day from that four to five block neighborhood alone.

After a few days of planning, we jumped in my truck and made our way up to the falls, making sure to take the back roads into town. We went into a small apartment where Wes greeted us and brought us into the kitchen. The kitchen table had a couple large one-gallon sized zip lock bags, each full to the top with prepackaged eight-balls, and quarter ounces. On the counter behind the table sat a few more gallon size zip lock bags, each containing what had to be thousands of pre-cut slabs of crack. Wes and Shawny went in the other room with two of the bags, divided up the work, stashed the bags behind a ceiling panel and we all headed out to get an overview of the city. Before we left, Shawny pulled me to the side and said, "Listen, you are a good dude, that is why you are here with us. I needed someone that I could trust to have Quan's back the same way Wes and I have each other's back. I know you will look out for Quan as a brother and I appreciate that. We are going to make a lot of money together and we move like a family, you are family now, you know?"

Wes drove as Quan and I sat in the backseat and Shawny sat in the passenger seat. We pulled up to a small housing project and before the car stopped rolling, three or four dudes came up, slapping Shawny five and asking if they were back on yet. Wes told them that they would be back through in about an hour and to sit tight. As we pulled away Wes said, "Each one of them is waiting on a quarter key, and they will go through that today and be right back tomorrow to buy another quarter key a piece! Welcome to the Falls!" We made our way through block after block, with each stop seeing the same sort of requests as the first. I realized that they had not exaggerated about the type of money that was being made in the Falls, if anything they down played what they thought we could make.

After a day of riding around, learning the neighborhoods, meeting who was who around town, and re-supplying every mid-level dealer in town, we went back to the house. Wes came in, reached into his pocket and pulled out a knot of money so big that it took two hands to hold it all together and placed it onto the table. He reached into his other pocket and did the same thing, then into his back pockets. He lifted his shirt and took money from inside of his waist band, then bent down and took a wad of cash from both socks and finally lifted off his hat and removed the cash that was placed there. By the time they were done, the entire table was full of wads of money that were so large the rubber bands holding them looked like they were about to burst.

We sat down and started counting, placing the money into shoeboxes until each was full and then placing the shoeboxes into a removable panel in the ceiling. By the time we were done counting all the money, it was time to make another run to drop off more coke and pick up more money. This continued for at least 24-hours straight until we finally crashed for a few hours, took showers and got prepared to head out again. This time, Shawny was taking us to Vietnam. Everyone decided that Quan and I were ready to run our own neighborhood so we jumped in the car and headed across town.

We drove through the neighborhood once or twice as Shawny pointed out which of the houses had been raided by the police, who the best customers were and which yards to cut through if the police came through the block. We parked a block away and walked through some backyards and a few vacant lots until we reached the center of the street where we stood around a large tree and scoped out the area. The tree provided the perfect cover as standing on either side of it disguised you from being seen from the main streets but allowed you to see everything that was coming from every direction. As we stood there, three or four crack heads came up to Shawny asking him if he had anything. He took two crisp fifty dollar bills from them, reached into his sock and gave each one a slab, as they inspected it they both smiled, "Man this shit is official! Good looking out Soldier, we will be back for more in a minute."

Within minutes we had sold a few thousand-dollars-worth of slabs. Shawny left to head to the spot to get some more and drop off the money. By the time he arrived back, Quan and I had sold out and there was a neat and orderly line of crack heads forming that went almost to the end of the block. Shawny started laughing, "Man you guys ain't no joke! You lined these mother fuckers up and got them looking like they are waiting for school lunches!" We went to work, collecting money and serving out slabs until it was time to re-up again.

A young dude came up to Shawny and started telling him about some recent robberies around the neighborhood. He said a couple of dudes were driving up to drug dealers, getting out of their car, pulling a gun and robbing them. Shawny said, "Man I wish a Nigga might try me! I would grab that gun and use it to bust a couple of caps in his ass!" The young dude said, "Man just be careful out here, shit is getting crazy."

"You want something to eat or drink? I'm going to run into the store up at the corner and grab something to drink," Shawny said.

"I'll take an orange soda," Quan said, and I added, "Yeah, me too. That sounds good."

It was one of those extra hot days at the end of summer that makes everyone appreciative of another warm day but anxious and tired from the heat. Shawny turned and walked past the few houses towards the bar, looking back at us and laughing as he turned the corner. Quan and I put our backs against the tree, tired from the heat but also being cautious and wanting to make sure that no one had an opportunity to sneak up behind us. There was a stillness in the air, something that one would usually dismiss as an aftereffect of the humid summer afternoon but that, along with the story the young dude had just told us, made us both uneasy and on edge.

After a few minutes we heard a loud "BOOM" that sounded like a blast from a shotgun, and then silence. Complete silence. We both got down low and started looking around to see if we could figure out where it came from and we noticed two figures crouched down low, walking really fast across the vacant lot in the opposite direction of the corner. Looking closer I saw that one of the figures had what appeared to be a long barrel shotgun, which he was carrying close to his body as if he was trying to conceal it from being seen. Then I heard someone shout from the corner, "Yo, Yo, your brother was shot! They just shot soldier man, hurry up they shot him."

Quan looked at me and said, "What the fuck did he say? They shot my brother?. . ." I looked back towards the two dudes quickly moving past the other side of the vacant lot and my instincts told me to go after them. I knew that if someone had really shot Shawny that it had to be them. Almost as if he read my mind, Quan took a few steps towards the vacant lot and then I grabbed his arm, "Chill man, we don't have any guns on us, they have a shotgun, that ain't the move man. . ." and before I could finish saying anything else we heard someone else yell, "They shot Soldier, oh shit, they shot him."

We looked at each other and started to make our way towards the corner by the store, staying low and moving cautiously, continually scanning the area for any potential shooters or danger. As we got about two or three houses from the corner we saw Shawny walking around the corner and my heart felt like it leapt from my chest as I realized that he couldn't have been shot. He didn't look like he was hurt and I didn't see any blood or evidence of any sort of wound. He was standing up, holding his right arm with his left hand and slowly walking towards us.

We sped up our pace and by the time we got a few feet away, he looked at us, dropped down on one knee, and fell down onto his back. We both ran to him, Quan saying, "Shawny, yo Shawny, you ok man? What happened?" I knelt down beside him and noticed blood coming from his white wife beater and as his arm fell from in front of him, I saw a large piece of the inside of his forearm missing, exposing tendons and what looked like bone. As I looked closer, I saw a grapefruit sized hole in the right side of his stomach, just below his rib cage that was outlined with deep dark red blood.

"It hurts man, it hurts," Shawny said in a hushed whisper, struggling to get the words out as he desperately tried to catch his breath. "Call the fucking ambulance, call the ambulance! These mother fuckers shot my brother," Quan screamed in a panic, "They shot Shawny. They shot my brother!"

As my heart raced and I tried to figure out what I could do to help, I took the shirt Shawny had tied around his waist and tied it around the top part of his arm, trying to create a tourniquet with the hopes of stopping the bleeding that was coming from his arm. Quan sat down on the sidewalk next to Shawny and put his head in his lap saying. "Stay with us brother. Shawny you hear me? Stay with me." Shawny, his eyes shut tightly and grimacing from the pain, moaned and struggled to catch his breath as I applied pressure to his arm and continued to yell for someone to call the ambulance.

We sat on that sidewalk for what seemed like hours, feeling totally powerless, unable to stop his pain and not knowing what else to do to help. Someone came and suggested putting his feet up but when we went to move his legs, he moaned in pain so we just let him rest where he was. Everything seemed to be moving in slow motion. I could hear voices around me but they sounded muffled and I couldn't focus on what they were saying. The sun still beamed down on me and I could feel the heat radiating back up from the sidewalk but my body felt cold, my mind numb and my thoughts were muted and jumbled. The only thing I could hear clearly was the moans coming from Shawny, and Quan yelling for someone to get help. When the ambulance finally arrived, Shawny was still moaning and when the EMT asked him what happened he just kept saying, "It hurts, it hurts, man please stop the pain, it hurts."

As they loaded him into the ambulance, I asked them where they were taking him and they told us the name of the hospital. I don't remember how we got to the hospital but the next thing I recall was entering the emergency room and being taken to a smaller room where doctors were furiously working on Shawny, placing IV's in his arm. They put a brace around his neck and his legs were covered in a blanket. We could hear him yelling, and the doctors talking loudly to each other as everyone rushed around before they wheeled him into another room.

Eventually a doctor came out and told us that they were working to stabilize him so that they could air lift him to the trauma center in Buffalo. I watched as Quan paced back and forth, shoulders hunched forward, head down, shock and complete disbelief engulfing his entire being. "They shot my brother yo. They shot Shawny. He's going to make it. My brother is strong as hell. He's going to make it," he kept repeating, looking at me but really talking to himself.

The next few days blended all together into a blur. My next vivid memory was standing next to Shawny's mother by his bedside in the hospital in Buffalo. She was holding his hand, IV's connected to it, laid gently to the side of his body, his other arm bandaged and a large bandage covering most of his upper body, from his waist to just below his chest. There were tubes running in and out of his mouth, which was tapped closed, some of them used to drain blood and fluids from his stomach and lungs and others used to pump his lungs full of air.

"Look at my baby," his mother said in a low whisper as she slowly shook her head. "Look at my son. He's in too much pain right now. This is too much for anybody to handle." A nurse came in and told us that she needed to check his wounds, Shawn's mother said, "I need to see them, is that ok?" The nurse, sensing that saying 'no' was not an option, nodded and slowly lifted the blankets off of him, then carefully lifted a corner of the large white bandage covering his stomach. As she slowly pulled back the bandage, parts of it stuck to the semi-dried blood that had formed around the edges of the wound, until enough was lifted that I could see that they had not sewn up the wound, instead leaving it open because as the nurse stated, there was too much swelling to properly close it and they might need to go back in at a moment's notice to operate again.

I closed my eyes and turned away. Sensing my uneasiness, Shawny's mother put her hand on my hand, gently squeezed it and said, "It's alright baby, it's alright. He can't feel anything right now, it's alright."

They kept him in a coma for the next few days, the doctors all commenting that they were surprised he had survived and saying the longer he was able to make it, the better his chances of survival. They said he was going to lose his arm and had already lost most of his large intestines, a large part of his stomach and he'd lost enough blood to fill his body three or four times over. They said he would have a long, tough road to recovery and that his life would be forever different. At some point a few days later, a Doctor came into the waiting room and said, "I'm sorry, but he didn't make it," and just like that, he was gone.

The weeks following the funeral were spent in a daze. Quan was hurt, seriously and deeply hurt in a way that I could see but not fully comprehend. We spent days that turned into weeks smoking weed from the time we woke up until the time we went to sleep, riding around listening to one song over and over again. Soul II Soul had just released a cassette single for "Keep On Moving," a mid-tempo, smoothed out R&B track that sounded like it was meant for the customized, bass heavy sound system in my truck and the lyrics seemed to speak directly to Quan and the situation at hand.

We would drive around the city, sometimes for hours straight, not saying a single word as we passed blunts back and forth, letting the bass vibrate through our spirits as the lyrics spoke to our hearts:

Keep on moving,
Don't stop like the hands of time
Click Clock, find your own way to stay
The time will come one day. . .

We stopped by the liquor store and grabbed a liter bottle of Seagram's Gin, we called it Knotty Head because of all the bumps covering the bottle. Stopped by the corner store and grabbed a couple of 40ozs of Old English and a box of blunts and headed out to one of the more secluded Lake Ontario beaches on the outside of the city. We parked, rolled up, cracked the bottle of Knotty head and used the 40ozs to chase the liquor as we drank it straight from the bottle, passing blunts back and forth until the sight of the water, the bass from the song and the lyrics all blended together seamlessly, erasing time and submerging the pain beyond our reach.

Why do people

choose to live their lives this way. . .

We got out and walked down to the water, finding a couple of large rocks to sit on and starred out upon the small waves as they moved slowly, crashing gently onto the rocky shores.
Keep on Movin
Keep on moving don't stop no . . .

Water has always relaxed me, enabled me to temporarily escape my stresses and paint tranquil images across my mind. I didn't know what else to do to help Quan deal with his pain. I just knew what worked for me and hoped that it would also somehow help him as well. It did seem to momentarily help him escape but eventually we had to come back to reality. I kept hearing Shawn's voice in my head: "I needed someone that I could trust to have Quan's back . . . I know you will look out for him as a brother . . ." That was the last conversation we shared, and those words just kept ringing in my ears intertwined with the constant visions of him laying on that sidewalk saying, "It hurts, it hurts." I wasn't sure what we were going to do but I knew that I felt like I had a strong responsibility placed on my shoulders and years later, Quan would confide in me that Shawny had told him the same thing. Shawny said I was a good dude and told Quan to stay close to me. Those words and that experience forged our brotherhood and set us up for what would take place in our near and distant future.

Weed, women and alcohol dominated my time in the few weeks and months after Shawny's death. Not fully understanding the effect it had on me, I found myself more easily agitated and my ability to focus on any one task was greatly diminished. I was torn between trying to find a regular 9-to-5 type of job and continuing on my path towards the streets and selling drugs. Niagara Falls showed me two things; first that the game I chose to get involved in was for keeps and death was a big part of that game; and secondly, that I could get rich quick if I had a plan and I used my head.

Being eighteen and feeling like my life was already destined to be short, I found myself being heavily drawn to the streets. But the values that my mother had instilled in me were calling me, trying to gently tug me back to the square life, constantly whispering into my conscious, "It's not worth it, that is not your true path." When the whispering got louder, I would light up a blunt, twist open a bottle or bury myself deep inside of a woman, sometimes I would do all of the above.

The pattern was becoming a part of my regular routine; visit with my son, argue with his mother, smoke, drink, fuck, repeat. The only constant thing in my life besides the weed and women was my son. I found solitude and comfort in spending time with him and no matter what I was going through, he would always manage to put a smile on my face. I would take him everywhere with me and crack up laughing as people would marvel at the fact that he never smiled, unless he saw me. I started to feel a connection with him that wasn't there at first and that connection was pushing me closer and closer towards following my mother's voice in my head that was always telling me to do the right thing. I loved that little dude more than I could ever imagine and that love was in constant contradiction to the anger and pain I felt towards the rest of the world.

12 JOSEPH & CUBA PLACE

A few months after Shawny died, Quan and I were both picked up by some detectives and taken to jail in Niagara Falls. They held us for an entire month without telling us why or providing us with any information, only saying that we were being held because of the investigation into Shawny's death.

At the end of the month, an investigator came and talked to us, asked us some questions about what we saw. We told them the exact same thing that they already had in their report, that we didn't see who did it and could only describe what happened after we heard the gun shot. Disappointed in our information they let us go and we made our way back to Rochester.

My thirty days gave me plenty of time to think and instead of having a jail cell influence me to move in another direction, I felt more rebellious against the system. Shawny's death only worked to reinforce what everyone around me was always saying: "Life is short…Live for today because we are not promised tomorrow…Get rich or die trying…Real niggas don't let anything stop them from getting money…" I decided it was time to get back on some sort of serious hustle. Quan and I had spent a lot of time hanging out with Tee at his house on Thomas Street on the Eastside of Rochester. Tee was a true hustler, always had his hands in something that would generate a profit, usually weed or coke. At that time, Tee was selling weed from his house at night and spent the day selling weed up the street on the corner of Joseph and Cuba place.

Cuba place was Rochester's most well-known open air weed market. Cars would drive down Joseph, turn down Cuba place and wait for one of the six or seven dudes standing on the corner to come to their car and sell them weed. There was so much traffic on Cuba place that there were always at least five or six different hustlers standing there. All with their own weed or selling weed for the Jamaican's that owned one of the stores on the corner. Even with all the competition everyone would still be able to sell $1000 to $2000 worth of dime bags a day.

Tee introduced me to his people on Cuba Place and I spent

the next few weeks learning how things moved on the corner. I also learned more about the "Jump out squad," the police task force that was put together to try to reduce the flow of drugs moving into and around the city. The Jump out unit would pull up in a couple of unmarked cars, three or four to a car, quickly run towards whoever was standing on the corner, grab them, force them to the ground and rough them up while they searched them. They would usually jump out on Cuba place at least once a day. When the weekends came around they might jump out three or four times and they would sit at the end of Cuba place and wait for cars to come down so they could stop the cars and search the occupants, hoping to find drugs. Despite all their efforts, within a few minutes after the officers left it was business as usual.

It was not uncommon for the officers in the Jump out Squad to kick, punch and beat the hell out of whoever they decided to harass. Everyone on the block was always ready for the police and usually kept their stash of weed hidden somewhere close so that the police wouldn't find it on them when they jumped out. Some people would use crumpled up potato chip bags thrown on the ground to look like garbage. Others would put it in cracks in the building or around the corner under rocks in the vacant lot. Anywhere they could get to it quickly but where it would be far enough away that the police couldn't effectively charge them with possession if they found it.

Eventually everyone started taking turns standing a few blocks down from Cuba place in all directions and yelling when they spotted the unmarked cars approaching. Two or three dudes would work the corner for an hour or so then switch off with the ones playing look out and continue to do this throughout the day. After a while, it became a very rare occurrence for the police to actually find anything on anyone so out of frustration, the beatings administered by the officers became more frequent and more severe. Years later, most of the members of the Jump out Squad were investigated for various misconduct and civil right charges and a few ended up being convicted and going to jail. Actually, the Chief of Police at the time, Gordon Urlacher, ended up being indicted for stealing money and drugs from the police custody rooms. The corruption was rampant and started from the top all the way down but was especially felt and experienced by those in the impoverished neighborhoods.

I learned a few things from hanging on Cuba place. First that I was not going to sell weed on that block. There were already too many people up there running to cars, all with their hands out showing the customers the bags of weed. Being seen out in the open like that was something that I had no interest in doing. Second, I learned what the police looked for when they stopped you and where they looked. I kept a bag of penny candy on me to help soothe my sweet tooth and every time they searched me, they would reach into the bag or empty it out, pick through the candy and when they saw that there was nothing illegal in the bag, take a few pieces of the candy, unwrap it and pop it into their mouth before they let me go. They each had their own preference but none of them ever took the Bazooka Joe bubble gum. It was usually stale, hard and wrapped in a paper wrapper that twisted at both ends.

I also learned that getting caught with drugs on you was a sure way to go right to jail, but putting your weed in a stash spot could get you robbed so fast that you might not even see who did it. Geekers were always watching to see where someone put their stash and as soon as no one was looking, the more brazen ones would try to sneak into the vacant lot or pick up the potato chip bag and make off with whatever they found. It was risky as hell and they knew that if they got caught the entire block would catch them and beat them mercilessly, possibly even to the point of hospitalization or death, but their desire to get their next fix was so strong that they didn't care. It was a daily occurrence to see a geeker or dope fiend get caught trying to raid a stash and get the shit beat out of them. Funny thing is that usually meant that no one was looking and while one was getting beat down, another one would make a run for another stash at the same time!

I also knew that there was a lot of coke around the neighborhood and competition for customers was fierce. Most of the coke dealers were offering buy-two-and-get-one-free sales to entice customers to buy from them. The problem was that most of them had the same coke and were cutting it so much to make up for the buy-two-get-one specials that it was all pretty much garbage. The customers still came because they didn't have any other options and they were addicted, they had to have their hit.

I took all my observations and decided it was time to give Cuba place a try, but I wasn't going to follow everyone else. I had a new plan. Wes fronted me some work, he offered more but I knew I wasn't ready for it so I settled on a quarter ounce of coke and agreed to pay him back as soon as I sold it all. While everyone else was putting cut on their coke and trying to double their money, I decided to leave mine raw, not putting any cut on it. Even though I knew I had to pay Wes $250 for the quarter ounce, I bagged up thirty dime bags, effectively setting myself up to clear only a $50 profit. When I told Tee and Quan what I was doing they both said I was crazy and Quan decided against working the package with me, opting to continue to work with Tee instead.

My plan was simple. I would refuse to take any shorts, I wouldn't give any of the geekers that brought me customers a fee, I would sell my dimes for $10 each and happily make $50 profit. I knew that my bags were twice the size of everyone else's and I knew that my coke was twice as potent because I didn't hit it with any cut. Instead of following the other dealers I was going to bring all the customers to me and rely on high volume sales to make up for my slim profit margins. It was risky because no one that I knew had ever done it before but I knew that if it worked that I would flip so much work that my suppliers would all be fighting to drop their prices and give me however much I wanted, on credit, and that no one else would be able to compete so I could take over the entire Eastside of town and eventually, if I played my cards right, the entire city.

I had my plan but now I had to figure out a way to exist on that corner without getting caught by the Jump outs. I bought a big bag of penny candy and took out all of the Bazooka Joe bubble gum. I untwisted each one, placed a bag of coke inside and tightly re-wrapped them, making sure that the bag was completely concealed inside then I placed them all back into the bag of penny candy and put the bag in my front coat pocket. Sure enough, I wasn't on the corner for more than twenty minutes before the Jump outs came, roughed me up, searched me, went inside the bag of candy, stole a few pieces of the good candy and left the Bazooka Joe right in the bag! As soon as they left I cracked up laughing, "Enjoy the candy you stupid mother fuckers!"

It took about three days of trying to convince one of the main runners that my coke was real. We all called her E.T. because she walked hunched over with a limp and had boney, super skinny fingers reminding us of the character from the movie "The Extra

Terrestrial (E.T.)." She was convinced that it had to be what the geekers called a "Bunk bag," a bag that contained fake cocaine, usually baby powder or baking soda or a combination of various cuts all resembling cocaine. She asked for a 'tester' and I continued to refuse, knowing that I couldn't afford to make anything less than the $50 I was already planning. Finally, she decided to give it a try, gave me $10 and said, "If this shit ain't real I'm going to tell everyone around that you are selling bunk and I'll make sure you never sell anything around here again. I said, "Bet, and when you see that my shit is official then you have to bring all your biggest spenders to me!"

She looked at what I placed in her hand and said, "What the fuck is this? I don't want that hard ass gum, where is my bag?"

"Open the bubble gum, its wrapped inside," I said. She untwisted one side of the wrapper then looked up at me with a huge smile on her face. "You are one smart yellow motha-fucker! I'm going to call you 'Candy Man' from now on!"

She hurried across the street to a four-unit apartment building, went inside and came back out about 20 minutes later, sweating profusely, her mouth was twisted and she was smacking her lips repeatedly as she tried to talk. I looked at her and started laughing hysterically, "I told you that shit was official! You look a hot mess!" She laughed, handed me $80 and said, "ok, give me ten, here's eighty dollars."

"$80? Get the fuck out of here, take that shit down the block to one of those dudes selling those little, weak ass bags. I don't take any shorts."

"Come on, hook me up, I'm spending all this with you. The dudes up the block will give me ten for eighty."

"Then take your ass up the block."

She shook her head and said, "man you ain't right, give me eight." Then she added, "You know what, I'm not going to call you Candy Man, I'm going to call you Fly. You are cold as hell and don't take no shorts, but your yellow ass is fine as a mother fucker, just like Superfly." I laughed and said, "Whatever, just come back and see me for more!"

We walked to the back of the store and I handed her eight pieces of gum. The owner of the store said, "Don't be dealing that shit in here," and before he could finish I told her to show him what was in her hand. She quickly opened her hand so he could see the bubble gum and then rushed out of the store. He gave me a funny look and said, "Sorry man, you know how this goes around here, I thought you were trying to sell something in my store."

Twenty minutes later she came back for five more, then three, then ten, then twelve, within the next hour I sold everything I had and needed to re-up. I paid Wes for the first quarter, this time I had him front me an ounce and told him I'd be back to see him in a few hours. He looked at me like I was crazy but when I came back again, he said, "Oh shit, JayBee's got a hot spot!!" I said, "Something like that, just make sure you're around tonight cuz I will be back in a few hours."

Within one week I went from trying to convince anyone to buy a single bag off of me to flipping five to six ounces a day and I was only on the corner for four or five hours a day, making sure that I was gone well before the stores closed and the night fell. I was so low key on that corner that it took the dudes selling weed an entire week to figure out what I was doing right under their noses! By the time they knew what was going on, I had already made arrangements to move my sales off the corner and into the apartment building across the street.

E.T. was staying in one of the two units located on the second floor of the building. She shared an apartment with three other people, two females that both worked as prostitutes to support their cocaine habit and a dude that was in his mid-thirties, also a coke head, who was trying to live off his female roommates. E.T. and her roommates were all eager to have me work from their apartment but the male roommate was resistant. The first time I entered the door leading into their unit, I stepped into a large kitchen area and was invited to come sit down in the living room which was just off to the left of the kitchen. There were large windows on both sides of the living room, providing a clear site line all the way down Joseph Ave towards Upper Falls Blvd., as well as a clear view of Cuba place and all the activities taking place on the corner.

Directly off the living room, opposite of the window with the view towards Upper Falls, was a bedroom used by China, E.T.'s roommate. Past the kitchen and the small, elongated bathroom, down a narrow hallway was another bedroom containing a bed and not much else and off that bedroom was a small closet that E.T. was using as her room. The outdated, rundown furniture was accompanied by a few mismatch end tables, a wobbly card table covered in an old bed sheet acting as a table cloth, surrounded by four mismatched chairs forming the kitchen table.

E.T. lived to smoke and shoot up cocaine. Everything that she did was in an effort to get more cocaine and stay high for as long as possible and despite her 'coke first' priorities, she would give the shirt off of her back to anyone in need. I respected her for her character and treated her like the good person I saw in her. I remembered how Shawny dealt with the Transgender women and through him, learned that even geeked out coke heads were people, and respect goes a long way in most circles, especially towards people that tend to get disrespected on a regular basis.

Between E.T. hustling and bringing in all her suburban customers, and my potent and super-sized coke bags, we locked down the entire area in a matter of days. I picked up a couple of hand guns and a shotgun to keep in the spot just in case anyone wanted to try anything. Business started getting so busy that I needed to bring in some help so I got a few of my friends, my man EF and his partner Stone to come watch my back and work the spot whenever I had to make a move. EF, dark skinned, and built like a truck, loved to laugh but would quickly turn from laughing into being serious at the snap of a finger. He lived in the housing projects a few blocks away from Cuba place with his mother and younger brothers, all of whom had a reputation for not taking any shit from anybody.

Stone was a few years younger than all of us, probably fifteen or sixteen years old, short and midnight black. He wore glasses that made him look like a super nerd. Stone was well spoken and loved to laugh and was usually the first one to start laughing whenever anything crazy went down. Both EF and Stone were still going to high school and would come to the spot straight from school, sit down at the kitchen table, take off their book bags, pull out their books, set them right next to the shotgun and do homework as they took turns answering the door and serving customers. We soon had everything running like an assembly line and were clearing ten to fifteen thousand dollars in a single day, just selling dimes. Traffic was so heavy at times that there was a line, ten to twenty people deep in the hallway.

Weekend nights, when the corner stores would close down,

the hustlers from the corner would come up to the spot and we would all shoot dice, drink, smoke and chill. There was a unity between everyone that was unusual, especially considering that everyone came from different areas of the city, some from New York City and Jamaica. Despite everyone working independently, and some working for the Jamaicans that owned the corner store, we all had each other's backs and in all the times we got together to drink, smoke weed and gamble, we never had a single problem among each other. Any issues were usually worked out with a conversation and we all followed the unwritten, unspoken rule that we stand together, respect each other and protect the corner above everything else.

That was part of the craziness of that world. Respect and brotherly love went side-by-side with violence, guns, police harassment, constant intoxication, and eventually became so common place that if someone didn't get beat up or shot at, or if the police didn't jump out and rough up the corner, we felt like something was wrong and out of place. When things got too quiet everyone started to get anxious because we knew something was not right. Living in an environment that doesn't enable opportunities to rest or relax creates individuals that are able to move on instinct, without thinking about consequences or long term repercussions associated with immediate action. When violence becomes a part of your everyday life, you learn to expect it, be ready for it and eventually, you become numb to it, some to the point that all life, including your own, loses value.

G and Puba were still selling weed with Selector across town and making pretty good money, but it was nothing compared to what I was making. G, Puba, and Puba's homeboy St. John and I would get together and shoot dice and I would pull out a knot that was often ten times the size of their bankrolls. They would carry a wad of $1500 or $2000 and I would pull a knot of all hundred dollar bills from one pocket and then reach in the other pocket and pull out another. The knots held in place by a large rubber band and easily containing four or five thousand dollars each. While my previous attempts to turn them on to the money that could be made selling coke had been basically ignored, they could no longer disregard what I was saying as the money was now talking for me.

When I first told them what I wanted to do, bag up $50 profit off of a quarter ounce, they told me I was crazy but now the huge wads of cash helped them understand my vision. I showed them how I was bagging up, turned them on to my connect and within a few weeks, they had the entire Westside locked down, all from this eight or ten-unit apartment building on the corner of Genesee and Bronson. G was living in the building in one of the top floor units and knew everyone in the building, most of whom were coke heads.

Directly across the hallway lived "Shaky" and his roommate Gringo. They called him Shaky because his hands would start shaking really bad as soon as he took a hit of cocaine. We used to crack up laughing, his hands shook so bad that he couldn't light the pipe because the flame on the lighter would go out from all of the hand movement. He would relight it and try again, hands shaking more and more the closer the lighter got to the pipe. Sometimes, when I was bored or feeling especially mean spirited, I would smoke a blunt, give Shaky a bag and let him try to smoke it just so I could watch him and laugh. After a while Puba would yell, "ENOUGH ALREADY, FUCK," and hold the lighter for him, which only made me laugh harder.

Gringo was about Shaky's age, both in their late fifties, and had suffered a series of heart attacks that led to a pacemaker being installed into his heart. Every time Gringo would smoke cocaine, the pace maker would start to beep faster and faster, alerting him that his heart was beating at an irregular pace and initially scaring the shit out of all of us. Eventually the beep from his pace maker was used as an indicator for how good the coke was, the geekers would gather around as G and Puba gave Gringo a tester. Then they would all listen to see how fast the pace maker would beep. The faster it beeped, the more excited and anxious they got in preparation for their own smoking experiences.

Shaky, like a lot of cocaine smokers, would start looking around the table and the floor in the hopes of finding a tiny particle of coke that may have been missed or possibly fallen when he was trying to cut up the coke in preparation to smoke. No one ever found anything, but they would spend twenty or thirty minutes on their hands and knees, head close to the ground or the table, sweating profusely as their eyes rapidly raced back and forth across the surfaces. They would quickly pick up anything that looked like a white crumb, put it into their pipe and attempt to smoke it. To mess with them, I would sometimes take a piece of paper, rip off little tiny pieces, twist them between my fingers into tiny balls and scatter them throughout the floor and table then sit back and Puba and I would laugh our asses off as they picked them up and tried to smoke them. G would shake his head and say, "Man ya'll ain't right. You're going to hell for that man," then he would sit down and start cracking up as he watched the show.

It was not uncommon for me to leave the spot on Genesee Street, go back to my spot on Joseph and walk in the door to find EF butt ass naked sitting in a chair in the middle of the kitchen. He would have one hand on the back of the head of the woman that was kneeling in front of him performing oral sex on him, and the other hand holding a 40 ounce of Old English. Stone would be sitting at the kitchen table doing homework, stopping every few minutes to look up and laugh at EF, who was providing commentary, saying things like, "Uh huh, now lift my balls. . . Yep, now talk to them, tell them you love them baby, talk to my balls."

Tricking off, exchanging drugs for sex, with geekers wasn't new to any of us. Beyond the money associated with selling cocaine, the power that the drug held over people, and gave to those controlling the drug, was in itself intoxicating. There were some very attractive women that were totally turned out on smoking coke and many of them would come to the spot with little or no money with the hopes of exchanging sexual favors for a bag or two of coke. Sitting in a drug house for days on end, drinking, smoking lots of weed, being young and just looking to have some fun made tricking a form of entertainment for us. We viewed it no different than going to a strip club or watching porn, the only difference was that it was live and in your living room and directly involved us.

EF had no problem stripping butt naked and being the center of the show. He would have Stone open the door while he sat there doing his thing and casually take customer's money as they looked at him surprised. EF would reach for their money and say, "Give me the money mother fucker! What the hell are you looking at, you act like you never seen someone getting some head before," then he would start laughing, which of course made all of us laugh.

We continued our stance on taking nothing short of $10 for a bag and there were a number of times when a coke head would come to cop and be short a dollar or less and someone would negotiate with her for her to give head to the entire house and over and over again they would do it! I was watching the small black and white television that sat on the old TV stand in the middle of the living room when E.T. came to me and said that there was a woman at the door that wanted to buy ten dimes but she only had $85 and she wanted to talk to me to see what she could work out. "E.T., you know we don't take shorts, tell her to buy eight and when she gets more money she can come back and buy more later."

But E.T. said she was insistent on speaking to me so I got up and went to the door. I stood there listening to what she was saying, "Fly, I know I haven't been here before but. . ." I stopped her midsentence, looking at her perplexed and said, "Gladys?"

She stopped, looked at me and said, "Jason? You are the one that everyone calls 'Fly'??" Then realizing the awkwardness of the situation, she added, "Oh, I was just coming by here for my friend, she likes to party but you know I don't mess with this stuff like that right?" I looked at her and said nothing, completely thrown off to see my aunt, my step-father's youngest sister, the one that I enjoyed spending time with as a kid and thought she was so cool, the rebel of the family, standing in front of me in shabby clothes, looking to buy coke. I heard the stories about her having a drug problem and knew that she was out there but seeing it with my own eyes in that way stopped me in my tracks and made me think.

I could see her mind working. I could read her thoughts through the expression on her face. She was seriously considering trying to ask me again to get those ten bags for $85 but she caught herself and instead said, "I live right across the street, we should get together and talk sometime." I said, "Yeah, we should definitely talk," then she turned to walk away. As she left EF said, "What the fuck was that all about?"

"That was my aunt! crazy world man, crazy world."

"Damn man, that's fucked up," EF replied, "But you know if

your ass wasn't here I would have had her butt naked in the kitchen, bent over the table!" EF started laughing and I looked at him like he was crazy then started laughing myself. I knew he was trying to break the awkwardness with his comment but what made it funny to me in the moment was that I knew he was being 100% serious and I was glad I didn't have to walk in and see that.

It didn't take long for the spot to start attracting a lot of police attention. From marked patrol cars sitting in front of the house to the unmarked vans that parked up the street but made it obvious that they were watching. I was forced to take time away from the spot, eventually leaving it alone completely except for the few days when welfare checks came out and the flow of business increased tenfold.

Until things slowed down, I hadn't even thought about finding myself a stable place to live. I spent most of my time in the spot and when I left I would hang out at one of my girlfriend's houses. With no real plan or desire to find my own place I started living out of hotels, never spending more than a week or two at one because of paranoia and fears of being watched by the police or stick up kids. In retrospect, everyone that I knew at that time was paranoid and usually with good cause. Staying alert and aware of the police required one to be hyper-vigilant and on point, always looking at new faces as if they were a threat or questioning the motives of the people around you. Paranoia meant that you were always aware of the dangers associated with a life in the streets and paranoia acted to keep you alive but it also created an extremely high level of stress.

Stress, paranoia and the ever-present demand for respect made for an often deadly combination resulting in hair trigger tempers that could erupt at the seemingly smallest slight and often led to friends turning on friends and enemies being hunted down by enemies. Coupled with the known effects of street level paranoia, the emotional and psychological effects could be devastating. There were many stories of successful street hustlers killing a family member or themselves or ending up in a mental ward because they had a breakdown.

I was far from immune to the stress and paranoia and seeing Shawny killed made me much more aware of my own mortality and acted as a constant reminder of the consequences of slipping up even for one second. I was becoming more easily agitated and less likely to laugh at things that I usually found humorous. I found myself snapping and often resorting to violence to settle matters that in the past would have been dealt with using charm and a smile. I needed some down time and the hotels usually offered an escape.

Wes rented me a car and I drove out to the Holiday Inn in Henrietta, a Westside Rochester suburb, rented a room with a Jacuzzi and slept for two straight days. When I finally got up and got moving again, I went and picked up Quan, hit the liquor store, got some weed from Puba, picked up a few Blunts and headed back to the room. Puba's cousin Brian came out to the hotel to drop off some money. Puba and G vouched for him so I gave him a package of fifty dimes, had EF supervise him and put him to work in the spot. He was supposed to bring me back $400 and keep $100 for himself but he came back with a story about losing eight bags and only having $320 because he spent his money already.

My initial instinct told me to fuck him up right then and there, to not say anything and just pick up something and bash him over his head to let him know that I wasn't one to try to get over on. Seeing me reach for the bottle of Pink Champale, Quan eased between me and Brian and pulled me to the side.

"Don't fuck that Nigga up in here, you know they will call the police quick fast on us. Let him go man, that's short paper, just don't fuck with him anymore, lesson learned" Quan said.

I thought about what he said, he was definitely on point about the police and it was only $80 but it was the principal. I took a deep breath and shook my head in agreement with Quan. It was two in the morning and we were out of Blunts so we got in the rental car, me driving, Quan in the passenger seat and Brian in the back seat, and headed towards the 7-Eleven a few miles away. I noticed a police car heading the opposite direction pass us then turn around and start to follow us. I got that feeling in my stomach that I would always get when something bad was about to happen. I looked down at my speed and slowly eased my foot off the gas pedal even though I was only going about 40 MPH in a 45 MPH zone.

Quan, his hand already on the door handle, said, "I got warrants on me, if they pull us over try to get close to those bushes over there so I can bounce."

"Chill, we are straight, there is nothing in the car. We don't drive dirty like that out here, we all know better," I said, looking back at Brian in the rear-view mirror as he wiggled around looking real uncomfortable. We drove for about thirty more seconds when the red and blue lights of the police car came on accompanied by a few blasts from his siren. "Fuck, this is some bullshit, everybody just keep cool," I said.

The officer approached the car and within a few seconds, two more patrol cars pulled up. He asked for my license and registration which I handed him, explaining that the car was rented by my "uncle." He came back to the car, approaching the driver's side window while another officer approached the passenger side and they told us all to get out, searched and cuffed us then placed each of us into the back of separate patrol cars.

From the backseat of the car I wiggled to try to get comfortable despite being handcuffed and watched as they searched the car. After a few minutes, an officer pulled a small bag from the back of the car, called the other offices over and then they high-fived each other. Getting into the patrol car, the officer said, "You fucked up you know that don't you? So you like coke huh?"

Brighton was a Westside suburb known for its large Jewish population, good schools, beautiful big houses and nasty police force. The last thing anyone wanted to do was get caught doing anything wrong in Brighton and here I was being processed and booked at the police station by two of the whitest looking cops I had ever seen. They put us all into one holding cell as they started to process the paperwork. Quan kept saying, "Man I am fucked if they find out about this warrant." Brian was quiet, not saying a word and keeping his head down. I was trying to figure out how they found coke in the car, I knew that all the counts from the previous few days were right on point, with every single bag accounted for so there was no way anything could have dropped in that car.

The lead officer came to the cell and said, "Look, there is no need for all of you to get booked and processed and get arrested, just tell us who's coke it is and we will let you all go tonight. This isn't enough to charge you with a felony, you guys figure it out and we will release two of you and let the other go with an appearance ticket."

After discussing it repeatedly with Brian and Quan and realizing that Brian wasn't going to take the responsibility, I told the officer that I would take the rap, hoping that by doing so, they wouldn't discover the warrants on Quan. The officer typed up a statement, had me sign it and let Brian and Quan go without booking them, then they booked me and gave me an appearance ticket.

Brian and Quan left the police station while I was being booked. I called a cab and headed to the spot. When I got there, I read the police report and for the first time saw what they found in the car: ". . . found in the crack of the back seat where suspect number three was seated, eight small plastic zip locked baggies containing a white powder that tested positive for the substance cocaine." I became instantly furious, eight bags of coke found right where Brian was sitting and he came up $80 short! EF said, "Man that shit is fucked up, that Nigga has to catch it for that." I knew EF was right and felt the same way but my run-in with the police slowed me down so I sat on the couch, lit up a blunt and fell asleep.

13 SQUARE LIFE

The arrest eventually led to a couple of years of probation requiring me to meet with a probation officer, submit to random drug tests and maintain full time employment. While I openly complained about the probation to my friends, there was a part of me that actually welcomed it and saw it as an excuse to ease away from hustling. The streets viewed people with jobs, leading so called 'straight lives' as being unable to demonstrate the toughness and resolve to survive outside of the system. Squares were thought of as being weak and whenever a real street dude ran into a square, the square would always be looked down upon.

I spent the last few years focused on establishing myself in the upper reaches of the street hierarchy, suppressing my empathetic instincts so that I could profit from the addictions and misfortunes of those around me and hardening my heart so I could unleash physical punishment in a split second. While I worked to become what I thought I needed to become in order to survive and succeed in the world I chose to live in, I was straddling another world, the square world that I worked so hard to fight against. I developed two distinct personas enabling me to slide in and out of the square world and the streets, both of which were often in direct conflict with one another. The time spent with my family, my mother's family, enabled me to see white America from an insider's perspective and gave me a level of comfortability within white America that most of my friends did not possess. It was easy for me to get a job. I interviewed extremely well and was able to always find commonality with the interviewer regardless of their race or gender. Being raised around white America also enabled me to communicate with tones and language that was comfortable for white Americans and thus allowed them to see in me a part of themselves.

While I began a job search, my girlfriend's mother pushed me to get my GED. I took the exam in the East High School gymnasium with about two hundred other people of all different ages and races. I sat down in a chair on one of the outer rows and upon giving the signal to start, opened the exam and began. I was the first one to finish, raising my hand so that the proxy could come gather my materials, and then I quietly left.

I was confident that I had passed the exam and left feeling like I had accomplished something. I caught a bus across town to the 24-hour Perkins restaurant for a scheduled interview for a line cook position and they hired me on the spot. They gave me a pair of white pants, a cook's shirt and an apron. I was also given some paperwork to complete and was told to start work the next day. I was on a natural high. In one day I had taken the GED and gotten a job. For the first time in a long time I looked forward to calling my mother, knowing that she was in desperate need to hear something positive about my life.

As I waited at the bus stop to catch the bus back across town, I watched a brand new BMW pass by. It was all black with silver shiny five-star rim. The windows were down and "Strictly for the Ladies" by Lord Finesse and DJ Mike Smooth was blasting out of the high end speakers. The driver was draped in thick gold chains and his female passenger was wearing big gold hoop earrings and bobbing her head to the music. Everything about that car reminded me of why I had spent so much time sitting in dope houses trying to make fast money. I thought about how I must have looked to them, standing at the bus stop, paperwork and uniform in my hand, waiting on a bus to take me wherever I was headed. Everything about me said 'square,' and I dropped my head for a moment, hoping that if they knew me that they wouldn't recognize me. My earlier moment of victory was quickly replaced with feelings of failure and shame for not being able to drive off in my own BMW and for not being able to pull out my own thick gold chains. I knew that I had to focus on getting a job because of probation but I was still not ready to let go of my big money and street dreams.

I eventually found another job at a restaurant up the street from my mother's house which paid more and provided more hours so I quit the job at Perkins and with the relationship with my girlfriend fading, I eventually moved back in with my mother. I got a second job working at another restaurant and was soon working forty-hours a week cooking at one job and another thirty hours a week washing dishes and doing prep work at the other.

I enjoyed cooking, it took my mind off everything else that was going on and provided me with an outlet that enabled me to express my creative side. I quickly learned the ins and outs of the kitchen and was soon running the busiest shifts as the wheel cook. Besides supervising all the orders that came in, the wheel cook ran the kitchen and determined who would work in which station. I was one of the youngest cooks and soon received a lot of push back from the older cooks, some of whom had been there for five and ten years.

While I could handle most of the issues with the older cooks with diplomacy and communication there were one or two that refused to work with me and would purposely mess up orders or work slow when I ran the wheel. The instincts that had propelled me into success in the streets were now in conflict with the expected behavior in my work environment. My anger and instincts were telling me to pick up one of those heavy pans, walk slowly over to the cook with the attitude, cock my arm back and swing the pan with as much force as possible making sure that I knocked his punk ass out. I knew that acting on that instinct would lead to a violation of probation, additional charges, a loss of my job and probably some jail time.

I thought about how to approach the problem cooks for days and eventually pulled one of them to the side before the start of our shift and calmly explained to him that I needed him to keep up with the orders and stop fucking around. He looked at me with a slight grin and said, "Hey man, I'm doing the best I can," then walked away, grin growing wider. I felt the blood rush to my face, my hands clinched tight and I took a few steps towards him before stopping, taking a deep breath and reminding myself of the possible consequences.

Walking the line between what is considered respect in the streets and trying to conform with the rest of America's societal norms was a serious challenge. I had the advantage of having my mother set the tone early in my life, showing me the only way she knew how to live, by the book, and was able to rely on what she had been working to instill in me since my birth. But the streets were always in direct conflict with what she taught me:

Mom: "Be compassionate and caring."
The Streets: "Compassion is for suckers and the only thing you should care about is getting money and respect."
Mom: "Walk away from conflict, a physical conflict is for

those too weak minded to develop a resolution."
The Streets: "Don't take shit from anybody. Knock them the fuck out before they even get a chance to come at you wrong."

It was like the episode of Tom & Jerry I would watch a kid, where the little devil is dressed in red and sitting on Jerry's right shoulder trying to convince him to destroy Tom while the little Angel sits on his other shoulder urging him to turn the other cheek and forgive. This two-way pressure would grow to dominate my life and I would continually find myself being swayed back and forth, pulled and pushed between two competing ideologies as I worked to discover myself.

I was soon served with paperwork stating I had to appear in court for a custody and child support hearing regarding my son. I was furious. While Heather and I often argued about what my level of contribution should be, I always made sure that I gave her whatever she asked for. From clothes to diapers to money for a babysitter, whatever she asked for I almost always delivered. I didn't realize it at the time but the fact that she had to ask me for anything was problematic. While I recognized that my son had needs I can honestly say that I was out of touch with what those needs truly were from both a financial and emotional standpoint.

I was spending as much time with him as I could, picking him up for a few hours a couple of days during the week and then occasionally on weekends. Despite loving him with all my heart, there was a disconnect between us as I struggled to understand how to be a father. The only example of fatherhood I had to follow was what I saw in my step-father and there was no way in hell I was going to emulate him when it came to parenting. I took what my mother had given me, tried to re-package that into my version of what I felt a father should be and delivered that to my son. While I was trying to understand the meaning of fatherhood, I still had no idea what it meant to be a man and I am sure that Heather saw my interactions with my son as being less than what she expected from the father of her child.

My first experience with court was with my arrest so I thought I knew what to expect. I also had plenty of friends to provide first hand insight into the criminal court system, but family court was an entirely different experience all together. As soon as I stepped off the elevator and onto the third floor and into Monroe County Family Court, I heard babies crying, saw girls younger than me walking around with rollers and scarfs on their heads and pregnant bellies bulging. There were couples arguing loudly as deputies threatened to kick them out or arrest them. My heart started beating faster and faster as I walked towards the deputy sitting behind the desk and gave him my name.

"Bost, ok the other party hasn't checked in yet but you can go around the corner and wait by courtroom number three. They will call you when it's time to enter the court room," the deputy said dryly without looking up, as if he had said those exact words thousands of times.

I made my way to the hallway and sat down, taking a deep breath and looking around noticing three or four other dudes sitting in close proximity with the same look of disgust and anxiety on their faces. Though we didn't know each other personally, each one gave me a head nod, something that I had learned was a common way for black men to great each other, sort of a respectful acknowledgment of each-others presence. To this day, especially in predominantly white or non-African American communities, when I see another black man we almost always give each other a head nod, a simple "I see you brother," greeting only truly understood by each other.

I found little solace in seeing others going through the uncomfortable anxiety I was experiencing and if anything, it added to my slowly simmering anger as I realized that this system also seemed to be heavily biased. Black and Latino faces dominated the courtroom waiting areas while almost every Sheriff deputy was white. I watched as the deputies laughed and joked with each other, not necessarily at the expense of us but just in their daily communicative ways, the same way everyone laughs and jokes at work. Their smiles quickly turned to frowns as soon as someone asked them a question. They would provide a quick one-word answer and usually point in the direction that the questioning party should move towards.

The lawyers, most of whom wore cheap suits, were carrying around large outdated briefcases overflowing with files and papers, shouting the names of clients that they had yet to meet. "Are you Mr. Smith? Aaron Smith, is Aaron Smith here?" one would say as another would yell out a different name, eventually freeing up one hand by setting their files down on a chair so they could shake the hand of the client before quickly whisking them off to find a quiet corner of the waiting area to conference. Most of the attorneys were court appointed through the public defender's office and carried huge caseloads which meant they may just be looking at a client's case file for the first time in those few minutes prior to going into court.

Finally, a deputy came out of one of the closed courtroom doors and called Heather's name then mine. She appeared from around a corner and we both walked into court. They ushered us to two separate small tables set up in the front of the Judge's huge, imposing desk and then the Judge quickly asked us to state our names and asked us if we were represented by counsel. I immediately said, "No sir, I don't have a lawyer because I can't afford one but I would like time to get one if that is possible."

The Judge, looking up at me for the first time, said, "You had plenty of time to get a lawyer before today. We will proceed with the child support matter as this court does not provide counsel for these matters, however, you can talk to Mr. Johnson standing by the door on your way out with regards to the custody matter." Then the Judge asked me questions about where I was working, how much I earned and how often I got paid. I answered the questions and he quickly determined how much I should pay. He said that I was in arrears for three months and that they would take an additional sum out of my paycheck every two weeks until the arrears were paid in full, then he said good bye and had us ushered out of the courtroom.

The attorney he directed me to talk with, met me outside, asked me a few questions, gave me his card and said he would contact me to let me know if I was eligible for representation on the custody matter. I tried asking him questions about what had just happened, about what 'arrears' meant and tried to figure out how I could owe money for something that just started that day but he quickly dismissed my questions saying, "I can't answer those questions, I'm not your attorney for that matter and frankly, I have another case I have to sit for now back in the court room. I will contact you soon," then he hurried back into the courtroom, shuffling through papers as he went.

I was lost, confused, furious but overall, relieved that I was done with court for the day. I was given another court date for the custody matter and I headed for the elevator still trying to figure out what the hell had just happened. I met with G and asked him if he knew anything about child support considering that he was already a father and he shook his head and said, "Man they got you too? Shit is fucked up man." He told me that the arrears meant I owed back money for support payments as the court starts counting from the day that the mother files the child support claim, which may have been filed months before the actual court order is entered. I also found out that once you get more than three months behind in child support they can garnish your paycheck and in essence take it all until your arrears are paid off in full or even put you in jail for non-payment. "How does that work man? They didn't even give me a chance to pay anything yet and they are already coming after my paychecks?" I said.

"Yep, welcome to the system my friend," G said, laughing and shaking his head. "Here bro, you look like you could use a drink," he said, passing me the forty ounce bottle he was drinking from. I took a long, deep swig of the ice cold beer and passed it back before heading out, "I have to get to work man, thanks bro, appreciate the info."

A few weeks later I received a call from the attorney's office and was informed that I didn't qualify for representation. They provided me with names of other attorneys to contact. I called the first one on the list and after a brief conversation with a secretary, was told that they would probably require at least a two to three-thousand-dollar retainer in order to take my case. I hung up the phone and didn't bother calling any of the other numbers. When my court date rolled around I just didn't show up. The court sent some more documents which I promptly threw away in an attempt to try and forget the entire situation, hoping that burying my head in the sand would somehow work in my favor. I was wrong. About a year later, when I finally went back to court to try to get my child support reduced, I found out that the documents that I ignored and the court dates that I missed were actually regarding custody of my son. Because I didn't show up, the court granted sole custody to Heather, leaving me with no parental rights beyond what she felt she wanted to provide me with. Fortunately, at least for a little while, things remained somewhat civil between us and I was still able to see my son on a regular basis, although how and what that regular basis would be was completely determined by Heather.

While I was learning about the family court system, working my two jobs and trying to stay out of trouble, I started spending a lot of time with Jennifer. From the beginning, we had a weird, high-strung chemistry. We would either argue and cuss each other out or sit down and engage in deep conversations about our future hopes and dreams. When we were on good terms we couldn't keep our hands off each other, having sex everywhere from the hoods of parked cars in her mother's driveway to empty playgrounds at night in the middle of winter. If we could find a few moments of time alone, it was usually on and popping.

Her ability to discuss academic and current events coupled with her street smarts gave us a lot of common ground and drew me closer to her. She ended up spending so much time at my mother's house, often staying there when I would leave for work, that her and my mother became close and she unofficially moved in. She was the first woman that really pushed me to think about the future, about getting a place of my own and figuring out how to get ahead in life outside of the streets. I was still on probation and knew that catching another charge would probably mean I would be headed to jail. With her support I shook off the ever-present draw of the fast money in the streets and managed to remain focused on going to work and stacking my paychecks.

My mother was finally able to buy her first house, a small two-bedroom house with a large backyard in a neighborhood full of similar houses in Gates, a Rochester suburb bordering the south Westside of the city. Gates was one of the lower priced suburbs, historically composed of a lot of Italian American families and white folks that couldn't afford the slightly more affluent Westside suburbs. My mother worked for many years to buy that house, determined to get my brother and sister away from the inner city influences that shaped my decision making process. A few weeks after moving in, she received an unsigned type-written letter saying that she should "Move back to Genesee Street to be with 'her people' because Gates didn't support Niggers or Nigger lovers."

While my mother was able to shake off the letter as being ignorant, I was infuriated and spent the next few weeks walking around, menacingly looking at the neighbors and trying to determine who may have written the letter. I was hyperaware of the racial issues associated with being bi-racial and had grown accustomed to fighting for my respect so I was damn sure not going to let anyone attack my mother, be it physically or behind a cowardly written letter.

Despite the letter, my mother soon got to know her neighbors and quickly settled in as did my brother and sister. Calvin was soon one of the more popular kids on the block and the doorbell would ring all day long with kids looking to play with him. For the first time since he was a baby, we started to spend time together, usually when my son was at the house with me watching as they played games or ran around chasing each other outside. Calvin was always following me around, trying to hang out with me whenever he could and usually, I would get annoyed and dismiss him, encouraging him to go play with his friends instead.

I eventually found a job working at a tool and die company about twenty-five minutes outside of Rochester. The pay was good and the hours allowed me to continue to cook during the day so I worked both jobs, saving up enough money to finally get my own apartment. Since Jennifer had been staying with me at my mother's house, we decided to move in together and found a two-bedroom duplex across town on Garson Avenue. I quit cooking and took a full-time position at the tool and die shop where I started working double shifts, from eleven at night through three in the afternoon, six days a week. With my bump in pay plus all the overtime, I had no time to do anything except work and sleep. All the time at work gave me an excuse to start slowly trying to ease myself away from my relationship as I was starting to feel a disconnect with Jennifer.

As we were slowly growing apart, I was struggling with the realization that this is what my life was going to look like; Working 16 hour days, having no time to do anything but sleep. The more time I spent working, the more time I spent re-evaluating what I was doing and the more I realized I wanted more from life. I missed the excitement and fast money that came with selling drugs and watched some of my former running partners as they drove by in brand new BMWs and Mercedes, wearing big gold chains and thousand-dollar custom made jackets.

The fact that I had kept a job, maintained clean urine and stayed out of trouble resulted in almost three years taken off my five-year probationary sentence. I told Quan the good news and he came over to the house with a couple of bags of weed so that we could celebrate. We sat in the living room, rolled up a couple of fat blunts and got super high, puffing and passing the blunts back and forth as we reminisced about some of the wild things we had seen and done. He told me that he had been going back and forth to the Bronx and asked if I wanted to go in with him on buying his next package. "Man you know this working shit ain't for you. You're a hustler. I know how you get down in those streets my nigga." He reached into his pocket and pulled out a wad of cash, adding, "See, this is what you are all about! Come on and get this money with me fam, we could run this whole shit in no time. I need my brother by my side fam."

I sat back and let the weed relax and guide my thoughts through memories of what we had previously accomplished. I closed my eyes and saw the stacks of money jam packed into shoe boxes. I thought back to Joseph Avenue and how I turned an eight-ball to a quarter ounce to an entire kilo in just a few weeks. I missed the camaraderie shared between everyone, the way we all had each other's backs and the excitement I felt building something from nothing. I thought about Shawny and how he told me he knew I would have Quan's back and hold him down as a brother.

Then I thought about Shawny laying there on the sidewalk, a hole in his stomach, part of his arm missing and the confusion and pain that came from losing him. I thought about how I managed to find a decent job that enabled me to make more money than most of the adults I knew and how I had to work 16 hour days, every day to make that money. I thought about how proud my mother was that I finally had a place of my own and was working and managing to stay out of trouble. I thought about my son and how we were finally starting to establish some sort of normalcy spending time together even though I was usually exhausted. He had his own room at my house and could now come over and stay the night whenever I was home, which because of work wasn't very often.

Despite knowing all these things and being able to look around me and see the fruits of my hard work, I wanted more. I yearned for the perceived respect that came with fast money. I shook off my instincts, that feeling in my gut that was telling me once again to stay positive, to keep focused on doing all of the things that helped me establish myself in my current life. While everything in me was telling me to stay on my positive path, greed and Quan's words kept ringing in my ears and I kept thinking about Shawny's last words to me, about his faith that I would always have Quan's back and look out for him as my brother. I started to calculate some numbers and figured that all I needed was a few months to make enough money to enable me to walk away from the streets and live life comfortably, happily ever after and once again I was drawn back into the direction I spent the past few years working to get away from.

14 BACK IN THE GAME

Quan and I took a trip to the Bronx to get a few ounces of coke from Kwame. Kwame, along with damn near everyone else was no longer selling powdered cocaine and was moving only crack. Unable to find any powder coke we decided to step into the crack game. "Fuck it, this shit will move fast as hell anyways" Quan said. I was unsure as crack had not hit the streets of Rochester yet. The geekers were still much more comfortable buying their cocaine in powder form and then cooking it into crack themselves.

Despite my reservations, I immediately started to think of ways we could exploit being the first ones to sell vials of crack in Rochester. In Rochester powder coke was still being sold in the tiny clear zip lock baggies. Crack in New York City was being sold in small hard plastic tubes called vials. The vials had a plastic cap on the top that could be easily popped off so the customer could access the small rocks of crack inside. Although most of the drugs on the streets came from the same one or two suppliers, the vials had different color tops to help differentiate who had what crack.

Walking past the corner of Rosedale and Randall Avenues in the Soundview section of the Bronx, a large mural was painted on the corner that said "Kids from Cozy Corner," the nickname for the block where young men would constantly call out "Got those red tops" or "Yellow tops over here," in reference to the cap colors of the vials that they were peddling. Quan said, "Yo, we need to get some vials so that they know our shit is New York City official."

I figured the first ones to have real crack and sell it in vials, were destined to make a killing. I would soon realize how wrong I was. We hit up the corner store and bought a couple packages of the empty red top vials, got a few ounces of crack and headed back to Rochester to set up shop.

I got EF and went about trying to find a new spot for us to work out of. I ran into ET and gave her a sample so she could help spread the word. "What is this? Is this crack???" ET asked, looking perplexed as I handed her the vial.

"Its cooked coke, the same shit you smoke every day but just better, pure and pre-cooked. This shit will save you time, give you more for your money and get you high as hell," I responded.

"Naw man, I don't fuck with no crack! That shit will mess your life up," she said. I looked her up and down, she was wearing a pair of dirty, raggedy jeans, a head scarf that she probably hadn't taken off in weeks, a dirty jacket and a pair of shoes with holes in the soles. She was homeless and spent all day every day trying to figure out ways to get high, yet she was turning down a free high! "I'm straight. I'd rather have some powder so I can cook it myself. I'm not fucking with crack!"

EF busted out laughing, "Bitch, your life is already fucked up! You are ignorant as hell. How you going to decide that today is the day you want to 'just say no' to drugs!" Bending over with tears in his eyes from laughing so hard he added, "You are one ugly, stank, dirty, homeless geeker but you ain't no crackhead!"

ET went off and came back about an hour later with a dude that looked like he was in just about as bad as shape as she was. "Give me three," he said, handing me $30. I handed him three vials and he said, "Wait a minute, what is this shit? Man I don't want no crack, un uh, no way." Dumbfounded, I said, "What the fuck do you think you have been smoking all this time man? This is the same shit you cook up every day except we are giving you more and our shit is better!"

"I'm straight dude, just give me my money back, I don't fuck with crack."

We couldn't believe it. These same geekers that had been cooking up and smoking cocaine for years were turning down our product because it was in vials! We spent four or five days in that spot and couldn't sell a single vial.

Realizing that we couldn't get rid of the vials in Rochester and growing impatient, we decided to head to Syracuse and try our luck there. Not wanting to lose the money I had put in to buy the crack, but more so because I couldn't accept failing at my re-entry into the game, I took another week off of work. Quan and I jumped on a Greyhound bus and took the hour long trip to Syracuse. Once there, we managed to sell everything we had in a few hours which attracted the attention of the local dealers and within a day we found ourselves literally fighting an entire housing project and barely escaping with our lives! I got stabbed in my back and got a pretty nasty black eye but otherwise survived what probably should have been a fatal attack.

Contrary to my instincts telling me to go back to work and leave hustling alone, I used my black eye as an excuse to quit my job and decided to go all in with my crack investment. Everything inside of me told me to leave it alone, to cut my losses and walk away but my pride and ego got the best of me. I felt like a failure. I had a job, made good money, had my own apartment and was finally stabilizing my relationship with my son but I kept measuring myself against what the streets viewed as an acceptable way of life. Even though I was doing better than the majority of my friends that were hustling, I felt that no one would give me any respect if I continued with my square job.

Quan had a friend that was hustling in Buffalo and said he was making a killing so we decided to go up there and see what we could make happen. Buffalo was foreign to us. I hung out there in the past, partying or messing around with girls but never hustled up there and really didn't know anyone there. Similar in size to Rochester and only an hour to the west, we jumped on the thruway with the rest of our vials of crack and no real plan other than to set up shop, get rid of what we had and go back to the Bronx to get some more.

In Buffalo, they referred to crackheads as 'hypes,' and we quickly found out that the hypes were crazy about our vials. Seeing how they responded to the vials and how excited they got when we told them it was from New York City, we realized we needed to emphasize our New York connection. We witnessed Shawny do the same thing in Niagara Falls. He played up the fact that he was from NYC and I watched in awe as dudes would damn near break their necks to try to get down with him.

In the Falls we never called each other by our real names. We figured telling them we came from NYC and giving them nicknames would make it much harder to get a feel for who we actually were and offer some protection in case anyone tried to snitch on us. We were also trying to insulate our families from anything that might happen while we were in the streets. It was becoming much more common for stick up kids to kidnap someone's family member and hold them for ransom, especially in Buffalo. There was an entire crew that just focused on kidnappings and would have no problem heading out of town to snatch up someone's mother or kids and hold them until they were paid a ransom. If you couldn't pay, they would kill your family or chop off a finger or a limb and send it to you to show you they were serious. Quan chose the name Hassan, and I used the name Seauall, pronounced like 'See-all,' both names that became so much a part of us that many people still refer to us by those names to this day.

After stopping random people that looked like hypes, we eventually met someone that directed us to a spot she had on Townsend Street. Townsend, like most of the streets on Buffalo's Eastside, was composed of mostly double unit houses constructed in the early 1900's. Many of the houses were boarded up and there were large empty lots between some of them where other houses once stood before being demolished.

Like Detroit and Newark, Buffalo never fully recovered from the race riots that took place in the late 1960's and many of the streets still bore the scars from those times as old burned out and abandoned buildings seemed to be left as a reminder. While Rochester had pockets of poverty and run down neighborhoods, the entire Eastside of Buffalo looked like one big ghetto.

She guided us past a few boarded up houses and an empty lot to a light green colored house and walked us to the side entrance, pulled out a key, unlocked the door and had us follow her inside. Like most of the houses on the Eastside, the apartment was narrow and long, the walls were covered in dark wood paneling which made the house darker than what it actually was and the entire apartment smelled of weed and cooked cocaine.

We had seen people shot, robbed, beaten down and taken advantage of and we knew that the stakes were extremely high so being overly cautious was essential. Quan seemed to be naturally paranoid and it served him well as his instincts were almost always on point. We made a good team that way. He would question and look and be distrustful of everyone while I could smile and embrace people, sort of a good-cop/bad-cop routine but it was genuine.

We followed her into the living room area. In the center of the room was the original heating unit, a large, brown metal box with a glass window in front of it, enabling you to see the orange flame coming from inside. The emerald green carpet was covered in dark spots and had sections worn down to the wooden floors underneath from decades of use. We looked around and checked out the kitchen which was directly off the living room while two adjoining bedrooms both sat opposite the kitchen. As soon as we walked in the place, it felt right. There were none of the negative vibes you sometimes caught in strange houses. The location was right with a door that couldn't easily be seen from the street and a vacant lot behind the house so people could approach from the front or rear of the house.

We gave each other a head nod indicating that this might be the spot to set up shop. I sat down to talk business with the tenant of the apartment, a thirty something black woman that looked much older than her age. She was wearing a headscarf and a sweatshirt with another sweatshirt on top of the first, a pair of neatly pressed but old jeans and some large, fury slippers that looked like they were as old as the carpet. Before we sat down, the woman that introduced us said, "Now listen, I brought ya'll over here so Im'a need you to hook me up with something."

Seeing Quan stand up and walk towards her with a look of disgust on his face, I quickly stood up and said, "Let me talk with her first and then we will work something out with you. I appreciate the introduction and we take care of those that take care of us. This is a family thing." Quan looked at me, shook his head, smiled and said, "My brother is on point!" then went and started to thoroughly check out the other rooms in the house.

The woman that brought us there stayed on me until I finally told her that I would give her a vial for bringing us to the house. She complained and argued saying it wasn't enough so I took a vial and set it on the table in front of us as we talked. She couldn't take her eyes off of it and within a minute or so sucked her teeth and took the vial. I had learned the power of cocaine a long time before that and knew that very few cokeheads could say no, especially if they could see the product in front of them. They would get more agitated and excited and eventually give in to whatever was being requested. Cocaine was a powerful drug and seeing the effect it had on those who used it acted as a constant incentive to never try it myself. I knew that I could make a hell of a lot of money if I was the seller in the relationship and I saw all the buyers give up everything, their money, possessions, relationships, bodies, dignity, everything just to get a taste of it.

I also gave Lulu, the woman who was giving us her house, a vial and watched as they took out their glass pipes and prepared to smoke. They placed a few small rocks of crack into the tops of the thin tubes, pulled out a lighter, lit the tip and watched the rocks melt. When smoke formed, they inhaled it over and over until it was gone. The familiar smell of burning cocaine filled the air, a thick, sweet, rich smell that reminded me of a much more fragrant, mild scent of burning plastic.

Quan had scoped out the house and was trying to open one of the windows in the bedroom to see if it would work as the point of sale. We didn't like opening doors as it provided too many opportunities for someone to try to rob us so we focused on windows or holes in the doors to receive money and serve customers. Staying behind a door or window also gave us the ability to remain unseen if we chose, which we felt made it more difficult for the police to pin a direct sale on any of us individually.

Lulu came into the bedroom, sucking her teeth, eyes darting around the room and rocking back and forth, "Ya'll have to excuse me but when I get high, if the shit is really good, I start bugging out like this. Yep, yep, uh hmmm, yo shit is really good!"

We both busted out laughing. Quan jumped up and playfully slapped Lulu on the ass. "We know it's good bitch, now get out there and let everybody else know it's good!"

Lulu looked at Quan and started giggling, "Now you better stop that, you know I get a little horny when I smoke too and ya'll fine young asses up in here might make an old bitch do something!"

"You got a fat ass, you bring that money through here and I might let you get some of this dick ya heard?!" Quan shot back, cracking himself up. "Now get out there and get that money."

Lulu put on her coat and headed out to try to round up some customers. We just missed the 1st of the month so we knew it was going to be hard to get things moving right away. After things started moving I jumped on a bus to head back to Rochester to get EF and pick up some guns.

I stopped by Quan's mother's house to check on his mom and sister and let them know all was well. Shatina had always been a bit flirty with me and made it clear that she was interested in me but I had always brushed it off and focused on her as a little sister. She had gotten pregnant when she was fourteen with her daughter Jasmine and I was at the hospital right after her birth, holding Jasmine as Shatina giggled and said, "See, that is your yellow uncle Jason!" Immediately after that, she had two more kids and just like with Jasmine, I visited the hospital after each birth. Quan's mother was aware that we were hustling and would say, "Jason, please take care of my baby. I know ya'll are grown men now and Quan can take care of himself but you both look out for each other out there." I slipped some money to her and told her that we would be back in a few weeks.

I stopped by EF's house and hung out with him and his little brothers for a little while, playing video games and waiting for him to pack a bag so we could leave. EF filled a backpack with a few t-shirts, jeans, underwear and socks and grabbed a large green army duffel bag that we filled with a couple sawed off shotguns, handguns and some ammunition. We headed to the bus station, got EF a ticket, he jumped on the bus, I got in a car and drove back to Buffalo just ahead of the bus. I met him in Buffalo at the bus station, picked him up and we headed to the spot.

Competition for customers was serious business. My philosophy had always been to give customers the biggest bags of the purest product, treat the customers with respect and the product would do all the work. We had something that no one else in Buffalo had, vials, and once we got them coming, the only things we would have to worry about was making the spot secure from stick up kids and staying two steps ahead of the police.

As soon as the word got out that some 'New York boys had that real crack,' customers flocked to the spot. We started making multiple trips a week back down to New York City to re-up. Quan and I usually made the runs together, driving down in cars we would rent from hypes. It was common practice for hypes to rent their cars to dealers for a few hours or a day, usually for $20 or $30 worth of crack. Neither of us had a valid driver license, but that never stopped us from driving any and everywhere. Quan loved renting cars and as soon as a customer came through with a nice car, he would push them hard to let him rent it, often just bullying the car away from them, even when they had no intention of giving it up.

He also loved 'staying fly,' dressing in the latest fashions and making sure that everyone knew he was from the Bronx. It was not unusual for him to spend a few thousand on clothes and renting cars from hypes in a week, discarding the clothes after he wore them, laughing as he said, "Ah nigga, real gangstas don't wear the same shit twice!" I, on the other hand, was content wearing the same thing for weeks. I preferred being understated, usually wearing a black or grey Champion hoodie, some plain Levi jeans and regular white or black Reebok classics. I didn't like to draw attention to myself and would either dress as mentioned or wear clothes similar to what everyone else in the neighborhood was wearing. I found that blending in drew less attention from the locals and more importantly, kept me under the radar of the police.

Our styles definitely contrasted. I was the one that everyone would talk to, try to reason with and enjoyed doing business with. Quan was the one that everyone feared. He was quiet and usually laid back and just watched, always wearing a grimace, never smiling and quick to call someone out for something. Whenever I left for a day or two making a run to New York City or Rochester, I would return to Lulu complaining about Quan not paying her or telling me that he made her feel threatened. EF and Quan often got into it as well. EF was easy going and loved to laugh but his laid back demeanor hid his aggressive side. He wasn't usually the aggressor but would never hesitate to put in work if he felt threatened or if someone got in his face.

EF and Quan had a few standoffs; Quan would tell EF that he was going to 'see him' because he felt slighted and EF sitting back would laugh saying, 'see me nigga, I'm right here.' Quan started spending more and more time away from the spot, usually riding around in rentals, or making trips to New York while EF seldom left the spot, which made for conflict when Quan would return and comment on the way things were being run.

While Quan was loose and care-free with spending, I was more focused on staying on budget and the bottom line. If we bought four ounces of crack to sell, I would calculate exactly how much we needed to bag up, including what we had to pay for the spot and other known expenses and I would add in a little extra in case something unexpected came up. Once I had the bottom line number, I would work hard to make sure we met that mark, not taking any shorts, not even a dollar, and not spending anything more than what we needed until the package was gone.

I started going to the store and buying $30 worth of groceries, usually chicken, a big bag of rice, dried beans, potatoes and other staples that could be stretched to feed everyone in the house for the entire week. My cooking experience came in handy and I was usually in the kitchen every night, whipping up something for the whole house to eat. I used the meals as a time to bring us closer together and make sure Lulu felt like she was a part of the family, always making sure she ate with us or we saved her some food for whenever she returned home.

One time, a neighbor that had been giving her problems well before we arrived, got in an argument with her and smacked her around. When she came in the house upset with visible marks on her face, without hesitation, EF grabbed a gun and went and confronted the dude, bringing him back to the house and making him get on his knees, kiss her feet and apologize. Then he pimp slapped him with the back of his hand over and over again while saying, "Now how does that feel? You like slapping bitches?? I bet you won't come around this way with that shit anymore, now will you?"

"No, I won't, please stop, I promise you I won't do it again," he said, voice trembling and tears running down his face. EF kept slapping him until Lulu grabbed his hand and begged him to stop. Having EF stand up for her solidified her bond with us and proved that our loyalty was extended to her as well.

There were a few local dudes on the block that were hustling as independents. In Buffalo, large portions of the city were controlled by various, loosely organized gangs. The Eastside had been taken over by notorious gangster 'Sly' Green's crew, many of whom came from California and were called 'The LA Boys.' Sly Green had received numerous life sentences for racketeering and murders and had been incarcerated since the late 1980's but it was rumored that he still had control of the streets on Buffalo's Eastside through the LA Boys.

Many of the blocks were run directly by or indirectly through members of the LA Boys or affiliated groups like the Sycamore boys. Townsend Street wasn't considered to be prime real estate and lacked enough of a population of either young hustlers or customers to provoke much interest from anyone other than locals. Until we arrived, no one in the neighborhood was making any real money. Occasionally, someone would get their hands on a potent package or some good weed and for a few days or a week they would attract some business but never for very long.

When a large shipment was confiscated in Miami or coming across the border from Mexico, it made coke harder to find, driving up prices and increasing the level of violence in the streets. When some people couldn't buy what they needed, they would resort to taking what they needed, usually by force which often resulted in someone being killed.

I understood the dry spells and knew how to wait them out when we needed to, but Quan coming up short on his end of the money was more of a problem for me. It was becoming a pattern. When it was time to put money back into the pot to re-up, I was carrying the bulk of the load. Our agreement was to be equal partners, 50/50 split on all profits and 50/50 split on all costs. I was tight with money, setting goals and struggling to reach them while Quan was loose with money, sometimes spending it as fast as it came in, always counting on more money being there in the future and never really planning ahead.

We started arguing on a regular basis. We would sell out of product and I would be ready to move up to buy a larger package while Quan's money would push us back to a package that was smaller than the one we just bought. I wanted to move from a quarter kilo to a half kilo to two kilos, to ten kilos, etc. and was willing to put every dollar I made right back in, knowing that the goal was to accumulate as much weight as possible. Profit margins were much better the more we could buy. We could decrease the prices that we sold to everyone else while still expanding our own profit margins and increasing the number of customers at the same time. My plan was to take Buffalo over and set up spots in Rochester, Syracuse and the Bronx, but we couldn't do that if we kept going back buying four ounces at a time.

Quan always portrayed himself as a baller, even when things got tight, he went out of his way to give the appearance that all was well. At times this worked to our benefit by attracting people to us, like the dudes on the block that wanted to work for us, but it was also counter intuitive to my own ideology. I liked to keep a low profile, making it seem like I had less than what I actually did, in part to avoid problems and in part to encourage people to cut me deals and look out for me. No one wants to give a discount to someone that they think is a millionaire, but on the other hand, no one wants to do business with someone they think is broke either. We always went back and forth on this and it was times like that, when he came up short with his end of the money, that tensions ran the highest because of our philosophical differences and my strong desires to get ahead.

EF and Quan were starting to get into disagreements more

frequently. EF pulled me to the side and told me that he was going back to Rochester. He had been unusually quiet for a few weeks and told me that he was tired of arguing with Quan, but more importantly he was tired of being in the streets. I made a modest attempt to get him to stay but I knew that he was making the right choice. I had learned to bury my intuition and ignore the voice inside of me that was directing me to do the same thing but I hadn't developed the courage to make the change. EF was one of the realest dudes I knew and I didn't want to see him go, but I respected his decision and secretly envied his desire and resolution to change.

I was still making frequent trips back to Rochester to see Jennifer and take care of expenses related to the apartment. Our relationship was fading into a few bi-monthly visits, arguments and tension. I still cared about her but it was becoming obvious that things wouldn't last and instead of just ending things and moving on, we continued with our pattern, increasing the amount of stress in each other's lives.

I would stop by Quan's mother's house and drop off some money for her and Shatina. Shatina got an apartment for her and her kids across the street from her mother on the Eastside. She was becoming much more flirtatious with me, telling me how handsome I was and inviting me over for dinner. I would look at her mother, smile and shake my head, give them both a hug, say goodbye to the kids and leave. Her mother spoiled her rotten, sacrificing everything to ensure Shatina had whatever she needed, which infuriated Quan. He saw the struggles his mother went through and felt like she was taking advantage of their mother and would often end up getting in big arguments with Shatina about how she treated their mom. For as long as I had known them, he always had a difficult relationship with his sister which was growing more and more contentious.

During one visit, in front of her mother, Shatina invited me over to dinner, smiling and giggling as she always did and as usual, I declined. As I sat and talked with her mother, she became more and more persistent until her mother got involved and said "Baby, just go ahead and eat with the girl." I looked at her mother for reassurance and she said, "It's just food, everybody needs to eat Jason, besides ya'll are both grown." I hesitantly agreed and told her I would come by later.

I left and went to hang out with Puba and his cousin Kip. Kip always had some next level weed so we spent a few hours rolling up blunt after blunt and chasing the blunts with shots of E&J Brandy and malt liquor. By the time I left them I was super high, floating on a cloud and in my own world. I was seriously debating whether to go to Shatina's house for dinner or not. I tried to convince myself that it was just innocent dinner. I would eat and leave and she would be satisfied with that but my instincts were on fire and strongly telling me not to go. Once again I suppressed my instincts and headed over to her house.

When I arrived, Shatina opened the door in a silk robe. She gave me a big hug and invited me inside. She had candles lit and the house was full of the aroma from her baked lasagna. She poured us both a drink and came over to the couch where I was sitting, handing me my drink then slowly turning around so her back was facing me, bent over and put her hands on the coffee table in front of me and slowly sat down next to me. I looked at her for the first time; I mean really looked at her, not like a sister but as a woman. She had caramel colored skin that was glistening from the strong, flowery scented oils she had just covered her body with. The tightly tied belt of her robe accentuated her ultra-thin waist and highlighted her curvy hips, and for the first time I allowed myself to notice how pretty she was, looking at her beautiful eyes, high cheekbones and enjoying her infectious laugh.

I caught myself, sat up straight and started to stand up to leave feeling like what I was thinking was wrong. This was Quan's little sister, I was there when her brother Shawny was shot and killed, I knew I was violating every code there was and I felt like I needed to leave. Sensing my uneasiness, she put her arms around my neck, moved in closer and hugged me. She slowly ran her hand up my chest, around my shoulder and up to my face, gently turned me to face her and kissed me.

I realized that the years of subtle flirting had gradually built a growing desire for each other and in that moment, all the pent up passion erupted. By the time I regained my composure enough to process how wrong being close to her felt we were both laying there, sweat rolling down our bodies trying to catch our breath. I knew in that moment that my life would be different. I had that strong feeling in my gut that was reaching up and trying to shake some sense into me yelling as loudly as possible for me to move in a different direction. For the first time in a long time I started to embrace that instinct and almost as if she could read my mind, she wrapped her arms around me and slowly rubbed my chest, whispering to me, "Don't worry, this is our secret. We are both grown so we ain't doing nothing wrong."

I wanted to believe her, take her words and use them to boost up my feelings of defeat and wrongdoing but I knew better. I got up, got dressed, gave her a kiss on her forehead and told her that what we had done was wrong but reassured her that I had no regrets. The reassurance was for her benefit as I was filled with regrets and trying to figure out how I let things go that far.

As my trips back and forth to Buffalo continued, I found myself growing more and more unhappy with my life. I tried to avoid going home so I wouldn't have to argue with Jennifer and would make excuses not to go to Quan's mother's or Shatina's house. I began looking for ways to mentally get away, usually finding an escape in blunts and liquor, and occasionally in the company of a female friend.

Listening to 103.9 WDKX, the local urban radio station, at about three in the morning as I drove into Rochester from Buffalo, I heard a listener call in on the radio requesting a song. The DJ asked her name and when she said 'Amy-Lynn', I immediately recognized her voice. It was my long-time friend from #3 school. Her mother had bought a house right around the corner from my mother's house in Gates and we reconnected a few years back, spending time together and sharing a few intimate moments every once in a while.

Her mother had always liked me and half-jokingly called me her 'son-in-law'. She would often cook me dinner or invite me over for dinner when Amy-Lynn would cook. Amy-Lynn had a daughter that was a few years old and I would laugh and play with her as Amy-Lynn cooked. I was still cool with her older brother Drew and it was not uncommon for all of us to sit down and laugh about old times over a few drinks at the kitchen table.

When I started seeing Jennifer, Amy-Lynn and I stopped hanging out and lost touch for a few years. Hearing her on the radio felt like the perfect opportunity to give her a call and see how she was doing. I stopped by my mother's house and despite the late time, gave her a call. She answered the phone and giggled with excitement when she heard my voice. "Oh my God, Jason, where have you been? You just forgot all about me."

"Never that, you know how life goes, just been busy. How are you? How is your daughter? I heard you on the radio, what are you doing up this late anyways?" I asked.

"Couldn't sleep, a lot on my mind, you know how music soothes me, just like you used to soothe me," she said, lowering her voice to a sexy whisper. "When am I going to see you?"

"Well I'm in town, I'm at my mom's house, we can make this happen right now!" I said, "and why are you trying to give me that sexy voice? You better chill before I reach through this phone and do something nasty to you!"

"Mmmm, mmm, mmmm, you have no idea how bad I want that right now. . ." she said, before being interrupted by a man's voice on the line.

"Who is this? Who are you on the phone with?" the voice said, getting louder and sounding angrier with each word.

"What? Get off the phone," she fired back.

"Answer my question, who are you talking to??" he demanded.

"Hang up the god damn phone, I'm sick of you, do you hear me?" she yelled and then we heard a 'click' sound.

"Is this a bad time? You seem like you have some things going on right now," I said, somewhat amused and curious about the interruption.

"No, it's ok. That was my fiancé, he lives with us. His ass is always tripping about something. Honestly, I am sick of his ass and pretty much over it," she said nonchalantly. "Are you coming over or what? I am ready for that dick!"

"Ah, what about old boy? I'm thinking this is a bad time, we can do this another time, I'll be around."

"Hell no! I've been waiting to see your ass for too long! Give me about 15 minutes and I'll be ready."

"What about your fiancé?"

"Oh don't worry about him, I'm about to put him out right now," she said as his voice could be heard in the background continuing to question her about who was on the phone.

I shook my head, jumped in the shower and laid down on the couch. As I was dozing off the phone rang, "are you ready for me? Come over now, I got rid of him for the night," she said.

"Fuck it, I'll be there in a few minutes," I said, shaking off my sleepiness, I grabbed a few condoms and headed up the street to her house. I circled the block a few times, passing by the house and scoping out the parked cars on the street, trying to make sure that no one was lying in wait or able to get the jump on me from a hidden location.

I parked in the front of the house, walked up the driveway and before I could knock, she opened the door. "What happened to homeboy?" I asked, looking carefully past her and into the hallway.

"I put him out, told him he had to go because I needed some space tonight." She closed the door and quickly wrapped her arms around me, hugging me closely for a long time before taking my hand and leading me down to the basement where we sat on the couch. She told me that she had been engaged for about six months but was in the process of breaking everything off. She said she caught Joe, her fiancé, in too many lies and had discovered that he was 'too soft' for her. "He is nowhere even close to being a real man, you know, someone like you. I know you would never let me get away with all the shit I pull on him!"

"Enough about dude, I came here to get in that ass," I said as I grabbed her by the back of her hair, pulling her down to her knees in front of me as she giggled. "Now this is what the fuck I've been needing," she said. After a few hours in the basement, we came upstairs to find her mother in the kitchen cooking breakfast. "Jason, oh my god, it is so good to see you! Are you hungry? Sit down and let me make you some breakfast sweetie," her mother said, as she greeted me the way she always did, with a big hug and a genuinely warm smile.

She was always positive and took the time to tell me how much she believed that I was going to do great things with my life. As I sat down to eat, I couldn't help but think about how ironic it was that she was busy sharing her positive thoughts about me as I sat there with my pockets full of drug money and big plans to accumulate as many kilos of cocaine as possible.

"Where is Joe?" she asked.

"Oh we needed some space mommy, you know how he gets," she said, winking at me and trying not to laugh.

"Hmmm, well maybe you all need more than just some space. I always tell Amy-Lynn that she could do better, get a young man like you or something!"

Belly full, I gave her mother a hug and said good-bye as Amy-Lynn walked me to the door. Giving me another hug, she said, "You better not go that long without seeing me again." I assured her she would see me again soon then slowly made my way to my car looking up and down the street, behind bushes and trees to make sure that dude wasn't out there waiting.

I ran into her brother Drew a few months later and he told me that Amy-Lynn finally broke up with Joe. He said they had a big argument and she attacked him their garage, throwing the engagement ring in his face and hitting him with punches until Drew ran in and broke it up. Laughing, Drew said, "Man she whipped his ass! I felt bad for dude, but that was on him!"

I started noticing more and more of my friends seemed to be experiencing breakdowns. While I am sure many had some sort of pre-existing mental health issues, the stress and tension associated with the streets can break down even the mentally strongest person. I knew people that were smart, stable, in control and focused, and I watched them slowly deteriorate into walking zombies, talking to themselves or just turn into straight up killing machines. Constantly seeing the people that you love involved with or become victims of violence, police brutality, drug addiction and poverty can create mental scars that can change even the hardest person and break them down.

My own feelings of anger and despair would sometimes dominate my mind, making it almost impossible to deal with everyday stresses like the issues related to my son and the growing strain on my relationship with his mother. I had no idea how to deal with what I was feeling and when I looked around I saw my own situation and feelings as being much better than most of the people around me. I worked to keep my anger and depressing thoughts buried as deeply as I could but that took a tremendous amount of energy which left me feeling drained and worn out. On top of all that I was hiding this secret; the casual relationship I started with Shatina. The efforts it took to conceal it from Quan and the rest of the world was weighing heavily on me. On the rare occasions that we both were at Shatina's house at the same time I always felt awkward and soon things went from bad to worse.

Shatina asked me to come over so we could talk. I thought that this would be a great time to tell her that we needed to stop sneaking around and go back to our 'brother/sister' type of relationship because I wasn't feeling right about what we were doing. Before I could tell her what I was thinking, she said, "I'm pregnant."

My heart felt like it was moving in slow motion, beating so hard that it seemed I could hear it echoing off the walls of her living room and could feel it throughout my head and shoulders. She lifted her shirt and revealed the small outward curve that was now slightly showing on the front of her normally flat stomach. Her normally super petite build gave prominence to the small bulge in her belly and made it obvious that she was indeed pregnant.

My head spinning, I left and headed to my apartment. I knew Jennifer was at her mother's for a few days and I would have the place to myself and I really needed a place to just sit down alone and try to clear my head. On the way in, I grabbed the mail and saw a notice from the New York State Department of Motor Vehicles ("NYSDMV"). I opened it to find a notice of suspension for my driver's license for failure to pay child support. I opened another envelope from the NYSDMV to find another suspension order on my license for failure to pay child support. I threw both envelopes and the remaining unopened mail directly in the garbage can, flopped down on the couch, rolled up three or four blunts and smoked until I passed out. I woke a few hours later to a dark house. When I went to turn the lights on, nothing happened. I went into the garbage and pulled out the envelope from RG&E, Rochester Gas and Electric, to see a 'shut off notice' for non-payment.

I laughed until my laughter turned into tears. First tears from laughing so hard then tears from the stress. My laughter slowly turned into deep sobs and I found myself crying for the first time since Shawny's funeral. I felt all the emotions that I had suppressed making their way to the surface, exploding from my soul through my tears and sobs. After a few minutes, I reminded myself that crying was for the weak. I told myself to shake that shit off and stand tall like a man, wiped the tears from my face and just like that, stopped crying. But the pain was far from gone.

I felt weak for breaking down like that, embarrassed that I succumbed to my emotions and allowed the years and years of anger, torment and pain to come out through tears. Since I was a small child I always heard people like my step father say, "Shake it off," and "Stop crying. Men don't cry," or, "Crying is for little girls," all of this was emphasized even more in street culture. I lit a candle, rolled up another blunt and drank the remaining contents of a litter bottle of Seagram's Gin.

I put five hundred dollars on the table along with the RG&E bill and drove back to Buffalo, suspended license and all, feeling like I really needed to get on my hustle and inspired to get the next spot moving so I could take care of my ever growing list of responsibilities. At least that is what I tried to tell myself. The truth was that I was running from my responsibilities, trying to escape them in the highs and lows of the streets and hoping that I could make enough money to bury my problems even deeper, maybe so deep that they would never again resurface.

15 WALLS

I got back to the spot to find that Quan had once again come up short on his end of the money to re-up. Despite the numerous arguments and discussions about making sure his end of the money was always correct, we still had to go through this almost every time we needed to get another package. I kept putting in extra to make up for his end, which meant that I was unable to reach my goals of buying larger quantities at cheaper prices, and more importantly, that I was unable to save much more than what I was making.

I started to resent Quan. I allowed him to pull me back into the game after I had found a good job and was finally starting to establish myself in the legitimate world. We had split ways a few times prior, usually not for more than a week or so before coming back together and again working towards achieving our 'King of New York' style drug-dealer dreams. I was once again seriously considering going my own way but Shawny's words kept ringing in my ear, "Watch his back like I would watch his back, like a brother…"

I thought about how seeing Shawny laid out on that sidewalk changed Quan, about the pain I saw in his face and still saw in him every day. We had been through a lot of battles together and always managed to come out of them together and stronger. I thought about how he seemed to have a natural instinct for staying alive and coming out of situations that no one else could have ever come through, like that time in Syracuse. I thought about all the ups and downs we saw together, the broke times and the times we walked around with tens of thousands of dollars in our pockets loving life without a care in the world.

Thinking about those times, I realized that they were more a part of me than they were memories, which always made it difficult for me to try to move in another direction. With Shatina pregnant, the guilt was overwhelming. I knew I had to find a way to make our situation work so I buckled down and got to work finding another spot, a brand new one that could help get us both back on top and generate the money that I felt I seriously needed.

I began to spend more time with Shatina trying to figure out how best to handle the situation when I started noticing some things that were troubling. She had a serious temper and when she didn't get her way she had no problem getting really ugly with whomever was opposing her. I had observed this behavior a long time ago from a distance, toward her oldest son's father. I knew him from high school; he was a few years younger than me and overall, a cool, quiet and laid back person. I watched as their relationship fell apart and she started attacking him, first making it extremely difficult for him to see his son then dragging him through court and occasionally trying to get Quan or myself or her oldest brother to beat him up.

I didn't think much about it at the time because all I had to go on was her version of events. However, her version always sounded contrary to what I observed and knew about him. The same thing happened with her oldest daughter's father who I also went to high school with. She laid out a vicious attack on him, coming directly to myself or Quan and telling us stories about how he abused her or wronged her in an attempt to get us to physically hurt him. Quan had grown to know her ways and was usually not drawn in by her stories but every once in a while, she would convince him that some dude did her wrong and he would go on a temporary rampage until he realized that she was exaggerating or that it was bullshit.

I was treading on very thin ice and my attempts at keeping her content were working for the most part but I was slowly losing patience with the entire situation. I was still involved with Jennifer which Shatina was aware of and I knew I had to tell her about the pregnancy before Shatina told her. Shatina had the phone number to our apartment way before we started messing around and would occasionally call me looking for Quan but she started calling me just to talk and probably to try to irritate Jennifer, causing more problems within our relationship.

When I finally sat her down and told her, she was more disappointed with the fact that I had gotten Shatina pregnant than anything else. She kept saying, "Why her? Out of all the women out there that want you, why did you have to mess with her?" and she would shake her head in disgust.

Surprisingly, things got a little better between us after I told her. Our friendship came back into focus, probably because we both realized that the relationship was pretty much over and I think she may have recognized that I needed some emotional support. Despite agreeing that our relationship was over, on occasion, we still allowed ourselves to get physical, each time telling each other that was the last time, then saying the same thing the next time.

A part of me felt relieved that Jennifer and I were over, thinking that I would be able to spend more time focusing on the situation with Shatina and I wouldn't have to worry about supporting Jennifer or paying for the apartment once she moved out. Part of me was sad and depressed that my life seemed to be taking its own path, taking turns and going in directions that I didn't plan and definitely didn't like. As was the norm for dealing with my issues, I rolled up a blunt, puffed it until I was high and shrugged my shoulders, "Fuck it, time to get this money."

16 ANOMIE

Quan and I continued to go back and forth about money until I eventually told him I was going to do my own thing. I never intended to part ways completely, I just needed some space to save enough money to handle my affairs and restore us to a position where we could both succeed. I found a new spot on Fillmore Street close to Sycamore Street, across the street from a small Arab run corner store and a 7-Eleven type gas station.

I took over the upstairs unit in a double unit house. The house itself was old. White paint was chipping off the front porch exposing the worn, original wood underneath while the lime green paint on the house itself was faded and showing signs of deterioration. Entering the shared doorway led to a small hallway giving access to the downstairs unit and a stairwell leading straight upstairs to my spot.

The spot itself had stained and filthy dirty carpets that looked like they had been there for at least fifty years. The walls were at one point painted white but over time, grime and scruff marks had teamed up with years of cigarette and cocaine smoke to create a dirty, beige like color. The carpets and the smoke stained dirty walls combined to give the house a smell like an old musty bar.

There was a huge picture window in the front room overlooking the street, providing a clear view of the gas station, corner store and enabling clear sight all the way to the street light at the corner of Sycamore. There was a new couch that looked out of place in the old dusty house but made for a comfortable place to sit and sleep.

I hit the streets around the neighborhood, spreading the word to all the hypes that there was a new spot and giving a few samples along the way. I once again made my bags almost triple the size of what everyone else was selling and waited for business to come. Quan came through a few times to hang out but usually got tired of waiting for customers to come through and left after three or four hours. I stayed in that spot for three weeks straight, coming out only every few days to use the payphone across the street and to buy the little $.25 Huggie juices and a couple bags of Ramen noodles.

I set a strict budget for myself allowing only $5 a day for food, phone calls or anything else I needed. I knew that it would take some time to get things moving. The customers didn't know me and thought that anyone with bags as fat as mine had to be selling fake drugs. No one had ever seen a dime bag as fat as mine and I was unwilling to give any breaks on the price so it made them skeptical, but I knew that curiosity would eventually break them down and once that first person bought a bag, everyone else would follow, just like my spot on Cuba Place in Rochester.

Sitting in a dirty dope house with nothing to do can make anybody a little antsy, especially with no television. I found a box of old books and started reading. In that box, I discovered books by Donald Goines, who told stories about the streets, pimps, prostitutes, drug dealers, and murderers. His books depicted the urban struggle in a way that I had never heard of or seen before. I was mesmerized by his stories. I would pick up a book and read it from cover to cover and entire days were soon flying by as I found myself yearning to read more.

I read the Autobiography of Malcolm X by Alex Haley and for the first time, started to seriously question my purpose in life. I was captivated by the story of Malcolm Little facing the challenges associated with being black in America and his life of crime and how he eventually found the strength and desire to change his life. I never thought about change as being something internal, something that I could control whenever I wanted to do so. I felt the desire to change inside of me but didn't know how to initiate that change. Through Malcolm X's story I started to peel back a few layers of myself and question what I was doing in a dirty crack house in Buffalo.

The doorbell rang and interrupted my intellectual enlightenment, then it rang again, and again and again. Sitting in that house for all that time finally paid off. Over the next few days I sold everything I had, re-upped and sold it all again repeatedly for twenty or thirty times. The spot was now booming with business and I knew it was time to bring in some help. I reached out to a couple of the corner dudes I met on Townsend Street to put them to work. I had tried out a few of them when we were on Townsend and they always came back correct.

I also brought in Stankman, a skinny, dark skinned dude,

always quick to laugh but unusually quiet, and his cousin Hector. Hector was stocky, solidly built, with a perfectly round head and smile that made him look like he was always up to something. They were both in their teens, both raised in the hood in Buffalo and both scared shitless of Quan. He had pressed each one of them at different times when he thought they were skimming off the bags, a practice that many young hustlers tried on occasion. Skimming was taking a small amount of drugs out of each bag and then using what they skimmed to create a few extra bags for themselves, either to sell or use.

Quan could be an intimidating figure. Between his heavy New York accent, full-time bop when he walked, menacing stare and his 'I don't joke around' attitude, he kept dudes like Stankman and Hector always guessing when or if he would step to them. I used to laugh my ass off watching dudes squirm and get uncomfortable in his presence. Our natural 'good-cop-bad-cop' personas played perfectly when dealing with outsiders especially when it came to money.

I put together a system for running the spot. Someone would walk down the stairs and answer the door while someone else stood at the top of the stairs with an AK-47 aimed right at whomever was coming in. A third person would bring down however many bags the customer wanted and serve the customer. The AK-47 remained pointed at them the entire time, which of course initially made people very nervous but the bags were so fat and the coke was so good that they kept coming back and after a while people acted like it was no big deal.

The word spread quickly among all the hustlers in the area and soon even they were coming to the spot to cop from us. They would buy five or ten dimes from us and then add some cut and try to make back double what they spent. A few tried to post up close to our spot but we didn't even worry about running them off. The customers would take one look at their average size bags and walk right past them directly to where they knew they would get the biggest and best quality.

With the hustlers in check and the stick-up kids knowing that they would have to come with some seriously heavy artillery if they wanted to try to rob us, business was running smooth as hell. Money started pouring in and I was able to take care of some personal needs and focus on setting up another spot. My goal was to stack a few million dollars and get out and I calculated that with one or two more spots moving like Fillmore Street, I would be able to leave the game in the next six months or maybe sooner.

The landlord lived downstairs. He was a cool, older brother that always kept to himself and usually only spoke on Friday nights after he had a few drinks. He was well aware of what we were doing and told me so but he gave off a vibe of an old school hustler and as such, pretty much left us alone and let us do our thing uninterrupted as long as we kept things quiet and calm. On Friday nights, I would usually buy him a bottle of gin or whatever he wanted to drink and share a drink or two with him before heading off to do my thing.

One Friday he asked me to come down stairs so he could introduce me to his daughter. I had seen her a few weeks earlier jumping out of a cab wearing a full length fur coat and watched as the cab driver took three or four large designer suitcases and travel bags out of the trunk and helped her carry them onto the front porch. I said out loud to myself, "Damn, she is bad as hell, I wonder who that is?"

She looked me up and down from head to toe and smiled then he said, "This is my daughter Laura. Come on in and sit down."

This was the first time that I had been inside his house. We usually sat on the front porch or on the stairs inside the hallway whenever we shared a drink or conversed. I sat on the couch and Laura quickly sat down next to me and started talking. She was about ten years older than me; her pretty light brown slanted eyes gave her almost an Asian look and her skin color resembled a dark skinned Native American. She spoke with a raspy voice and confidence that I was instantly attracted to and I found myself asking her question after question, trying to get to know her better.

She was blunt and straight to the point as she told me that she had been all over the world 'working' and was coming back home because she was a few months pregnant and preparing to have a baby. I was naïve to the game so I asked her what type of work she did. Her father and her both gave me a look like I was a square and without hesitation she said, "I'm a hoe."

I was a bit taken aback, not necessarily from her answer but rather from the nonchalant way she said it, almost like saying "I'm a lawyer," or "I'm a teacher," or "I'm a cab driver," she just said it as if it was any other profession. She told me she had been to Hawaii, Alaska, all up and down the west and east coast and had pulled together enough money to buy a house and settle down for a little while until her child was born.

After an hour or so of conversation I got up to leave, explaining that I was on my way out of town for a few days. She stood up and walked me to the door, grabbing my hand right before I walked out and she said, "I choose you. I can tell you need a down ass chick in your corner and I'm going to be that for you. Handle your business and when you get back come see me first, I'll be right here waiting on you."

As I headed out, pocket full of money, enlarged ego from meeting Laura, I was feeling like the dark cloud that was hanging over my head was finally starting to ease away. Jennifer paged me twice back-to-back, which she never did. Figuring that she was probably in need of some money to catch up on some bills and finally being situated with a pocket full of money, I smiled as I walked to the pay phone to call her back.

"I'm pregnant," she said. Pregnant??? My mind started racing, then Shatina crept into my mind. In that moment, I felt like having two women pregnant at once was the ultimate proof of my manhood. In my mind, I was sitting on a throne; the king of my family as each woman sat on either side of me, looking up at me lovingly while I rubbed each of their bellies and soaked up the admiration of my peers. I smiled at the thought of what was to come, completely ignorant to reality and one hundred percent out of touch with how my life was about to change. If ignorance is bliss then I was floating on platinum lined clouds well above the masses, loving life as envisioned within the boundaries of my own mind. Eventually, reality forced its way back into my world and I would find my blissful dreams replaced with overwhelmingly vast amounts of endless stress.

Weeks quickly turned into months and eventually I decided it was well past time to sit down and talk with Quan about his sister's pregnancy. He hadn't been back to Rochester in months and although his mother knew what was going on, everyone was waiting for me to talk to him before they discussed anything with him. I was consistently teetering between states of ignorant euphoria and staunch denial about the pregnancies and I did my very best to suppress any negative thoughts or emotions associated with the situation.

Shatina's was becoming more hostile and was now constantly threatening me with exposing our secret to the world. The first major blowout happened when she asked me for money and I obliged but gave her less than what she had requested. She went ballistic, yelling and screaming and telling me to get out of her house. She threatened to tell her brothers that I was mistreating her and then followed that up with threats to tell her cousin Kwame the same thing. "You know that my family doesn't mess around, they will kill your punk ass if I tell them how you are treating me."

If she was any other woman I would have simply walked away, thrown my hands up and said, "Fuck it, this isn't worth the bullshit," but because of the bond that I had with her family and feeling that I had stepped well over the line by messing with her, my guilt and loyalty wouldn't allow me to leave. I knew it was well past time to tell Quan everything, I owed him that much so I pushed through my feelings of overwhelming guilt and finally told him.

My guilt was slowly destroying me. I had nothing but love for Quan and his family and in the few years that we had spent as partners in the streets I truly looked at him as my brother. As we drove around Buffalo smoking and scouting out the neighborhoods trying to find a new spot, I finally broke the news to him. I was so high and out of it that the conversation was a blur, I only recall the feeling of disgust I had for myself and the regret associated with messing around with his sister that was now dominating my entire being.

He was angry but more than anything I got the feeling that he was hurt. He also looked at me as a brother, and never in a million years could he have imagined me messing around with Shatina. He kept referring to me having a girlfriend and would just look at me and shake his head, not saying anything but written all over his face was utter disappointment.

I threw myself deeper into the streets, telling myself that I was focusing all my time and energy on making as much money as possible but in reality, I was again trying to hide from my problems. All the stress related to the streets coupled with the relationship drama from the dual pregnancies was making me feel tired and my body felt physically heavy. At times, it would take me an hour to find enough energy to get up out of bed in the morning and when I finally did get up all I could think about was going back to sleep.

I started getting intense headaches that would start in my shoulders and gradually the tightening pain would work its way up through my neck and into my head, often making it difficult to see straight and forcing me to wear sunglasses all the time. I would learn years later after finally seeing a doctor, that some of these headaches were migraines caused by the physical tightness in my muscles, all of which were induced by high levels of stress.

I spent the time leading up to the end of the pregnancies in a daze, partially from the stress and constant headaches but probably more so from smoking weed and drinking every day. I would wake up, grab a dime bag of high quality weed, roll it all into one blunt, light it up and smoke the entire thing before I ever got out of the bed, then repeat the process about two or three more times throughout the day. When I finally got up I would take about an hour-long shower, hoping that the hot water would loosen up the tightness in my neck, throw on some clothes and run around picking up money and dropping off work.

Laura, true to her word, did everything in her power to help me and lift me out of my stress. She was always putting money in my pocket, from her savings or from the small hustles she would run. She had boosters, people that stole merchandise, steal for her and she would pickpocket unsuspecting women as they played bingo at the bingo halls. Whatever it was, despite me telling her not to, she would always put some money in my hand. She would cook me breakfast in the morning, put some money in my pocket before I left the house, cook me lunch and then make a huge dinner at night. Without saying a word or applying any pressure, she made sure I was with her every night and woke up with her every morning. She did everything in her power to show me that I never needed to go anywhere else for anything while still giving me space to handle my business with Shatina and Jennifer and never getting overly jealous about me being with any other women.

Despite all her efforts, I still found myself falling into bouts of extreme melancholy and relied more and more on weed and alcohol to make it through each day. The potency of average marijuana was no longer working for me. I would roll an entire dime bag into one blunt, smoke it by myself and find that I was barely getting high. Everyone had basically the same weed so I got in the car and headed to Rochester with Dink, one of my Buffalo homies, to buy some high-end smoke from one of my friends. He had some of the best weed around and normally wouldn't sell anything less than ten pounds but made an exception for me and sold me a pound of some of the best weed I had ever smoked.

I bought a fifty-count case of blunts, rolled up four stuffies and went to hang out with some of my Rochester friends, Puba, Marc Carlos, Paul Griffin and Kip at G's house. We spent the time drinking and smoking until the small room we were sitting in was full of smoke, looking like the thick layers of haze that often fill the Los Angeles skyline on the days when pollution levels are really high.

After a few hours, we said our goodbyes, hit up the liquor store for some drinks and headed back to Buffalo. Dink rolled up another quarter ounce size blunt as I drove with an open bottle of gin between my legs, music blasting, windows cracked, and enjoying the scenery. We came to the toll both at the entrance to the New York State Thruway, I rolled the window all the way down, said hello to the toll both operator as he handed me my toll ticket and we drove off.

About thirty minutes later, we found ourselves sitting in a jail cell at the New York State Trooper's barracks in Batavia, a small town half way between Rochester and Buffalo. The New York State Trooper that pulled us over told us that the toll booth operator had called in to report that I was drinking and driving as he apparently noticed the large bottle of gin sitting in my lap.

Dink was in shock. He had never been arrested before so this experience was traumatic for him. I had already been arrested and did some time on paper along with the month in jail in Lockport so I was much less worried about going to jail. I assured him that county jail was nothing to worry about and assured him that we would get some bail money together and get him out first.

The next day we made a few calls and a few days later had another court appearance and immediately bailed out Dink but not before an article appeared on the front page of the Batavia newspaper saying something about a "Miami to New York" drug network being busted. Then it listed our names and information about our arrest in the article! Dink was from Miami and his identification listed a Miami address so I guess in a small sleepy town like Batavia, a pound of weed on the thruway was big news and the media decided to make the story as big as possible.

I got out a few days after Dink and spent the next year or so going back and forth to court until they finally lowered the charges down to a minor marijuana possession violation and I paid a $200 fine. Fortunately, we had smoked enough weed to lower the total amount to less than a pound which moved the charges from a felony to misdemeanor category. Dink had all charges against him dropped but it was enough to seriously shake him up and led to him being much more cautious about how he moved. I began feeling more and more comfortable with the idea that incarceration was a part of my destiny. I was cautious and spent a lot of time planning ways to protect myself from being arrested but despite my growing intuition and desire to make a change and leave the streets alone, I accepted the fact that the police and prison were just a part of everyday life.

Shatina started to have some complications with her pregnancy. She was in and out of the hospital every week or so and the doctors put her on strict bed rest until it was time for her to deliver. I was running back and forth to Rochester every few days to check on her and help take care of her other kids while she was in the hospital. I had pretty much removed Jennifer completely from my life after she called Shatina and started sharing intimate details of our sex life with her. I think she felt that telling Shatina about our sex life was would make Shatina jealous and somehow lead to her and I falling out but it actually just led to me becoming enraged with her and pushing her farther away from me.

I had always been a very private person. I didn't share details of my relationships with anyone, even my family, and having her tell Shatina about our sexual exploits infuriated me. I started to see a lot of the ways in which Jennifer would try to manipulate me and other people and the more I saw, the less attracted to her I became. I was already stressed out and looking for a way to minimize my stress so I took her conversation with Shatina as being a personal attack against me and used that as an excuse to keep my distance from her.

Between running back and forth to Rochester and stressing

over the pregnancies, business still managed to continue running. I was making more frequent trips to New York city to re-up and started to look at new, less risky ways to transport the drugs back to Buffalo. I brought Quan back into the business and we decided to use his girlfriend to bring the drugs back for us and took her to the city with us on a run.

By this time, the area around Kwame's block in the Soundview section of the Bronx was becoming notorious for drug sales and homicides. Moving in and out of Soundview without being stopped and questioned by the police was becoming more and more of a challenge. Even with the intensified heat, nothing seemed to deter us from our goal of buying more drugs to sell for larger profits in Buffalo.

After buying a substantial amount of crack we wrapped it in plastic wrap, bundled it up tightly and securely fastened it to his girlfriend's body, then we all headed downtown to the Port Authority bus station to head back to Buffalo. Quan and his girlfriend left first and took a separate cab to the Port Authority and I rode down with Kwame about thirty minutes after they left. We knew that the Port Authority had cameras all over the outside and inside and we wanted to make sure that no one knew that any of us knew each other.

The plan was for me to dress like a regular thug, wearing a black hoodie, Timberland boots, army jacket, etc., and board the bus just before his girlfriend. My thinking was that if they were going to stop anyone and search them that they would stop me and not her especially since we would get on the bus as strangers. She was dressed like a college student, back pack with a University of Buffalo hoodie, and she was carrying a few large books to help really bring home the 'college girl' look.

I bought my one-way ticket to Buffalo, put my hoodie up and got into the line to board the bus. A few minutes later I looked back and saw her in line, about five or six people behind me. I scanned the area looking for any signs of police but didn't see anything. There was a homeless dude laying on the ground close to the bus and another homeless dude laying against the wall a few feet away from the bus, totally normal for the Port Authority. As I approached the bus driver I reached into my pocket to get my ticket and before I could pull my hand out, the lady standing behind me grabbed me and the bus driver reached behind him and then pulled out a gun. The homeless bum on the ground jumped up, pulled out a gun in one hand, showed me a badge in the other and said, "Freeze mother fucker, take your hands out of your pockets nice and slowly." Then the other homeless man jumped up, pulled out his gun and two more plain clothes officers rushed in from behind the bus and one more from on the bus itself.

"Down on the ground now," the homeless bum looking officer said. As I lay there, they quickly put my hands behind my back and handcuffed me, then stood me up, slammed me against the wall and searched me. I looked up and down the line of bus passengers and saw horrified looks on most of their faces, especially on Quan's girlfriend. She looked like she couldn't breathe, her eyes were huge and she looked as if she was going to pass out.

"Alright everybody, keep moving onto the bus, we are sorry for disturbing your trip. There is no problem here, please travel safely," one of the officers said as a real bus driver came to the front of the bus and started collecting tickets again for the rest of the passengers. As the police escorted me away from the bus I looked back to see Quan's girlfriend hand the bus driver her ticket and board the bus. I started smiling, thinking to myself that I was one smart mother fucker! My plan had worked, she got on the bus unmolested and the dumb ass detectives stopped me and not her!

"Where are you coming from?" One of the officers asked. "The Bronx. . . Soundview. Why, is that a crime?" I said, with a big goofy smirk on my face. Two of the officers looked at each other and one whispered, "Yep, this is definitely him."

"Oh you think this shit is funny huh? You know why we are stopping you?"

"I have no idea officer, why don't you tell me."

"We know about the murders, all four of the people you shot died, but you fucked up because the rest of them lived you piece of shit!"

I laughed and said, "Whatever man," as they took me to a holding cell in the basement of the Port Authority and unlocked one of my handcuffs then secured it to a large ring on the wall above a long bench. Another officer came in and took my fingerprints while another came in with a camera and took a few pictures of me, then my hands.

They left me sitting on the bench, handcuffed to the wall for about an hour before another officer came in and said, "Well, today is your lucky day. You know they picked you up because four people were killed in the Castle Hill section of the Bronx and you were a perfect match for the suspect. But we ran your prints and looked at the photos and we got the wrong man."

I jumped on the next bus to Buffalo and made it back there about twelve hours after Quan's girlfriend. Quan met me at the bus station, hugged me and said, "You are a mother fucking genius! That shit worked just like you said it would!!!" We both busted out laughing and headed to the house to get back to business.

A few days later I was watching the local Buffalo news when they showed a photo of a young Latino dude wearing a black hoodie and Timberlands, being taken into custody in Buffalo for the shooting of seven people, four of whom died, in the Bronx! I said, "Holy shit, they weren't bullshitting, this shit really happened." My heart started racing as reality set in and I listened as the reporter said, "the 18-year-old suspect, Dionisio Mojico, along with two other men, dressed as Con-Edison utility workers, gained entry to the apartment before they executed three female and one male occupant of the apartment located in the middle class Castle Hill section of the Bronx . . ." I was momentarily stunned and relieved that they had enough information to know that I was not the one they were looking for in connection with the murders. When they showed his picture again, I shook my head and said to myself, "Damn, I need to slow down," then I lit up a blunt, cracked open a 40 oz. and smoked until I didn't feel anything at all but relaxation and relief.

There were so many signs telling me to turn around, to head in another direction, to leave all that street shit alone and move on, but I refused to listen. I was set on making my mark in the drug game and determined to not be labeled a failure or too soft to make it in the streets. I had convinced myself that money would solve everything but more importantly I discovered that I could hide from what I thought were my real problems in the streets. I always had an excuse to smoke weed and get drunk. I had an excuse not to be back in Rochester taking responsibility for my son or the two additional kids that I had on the way. It was much easier to say, "Man, I'm trying to get this money," than it was to actually put in the work associated with being a responsible man, or more importantly, a father.

I had moments of trying to do the right thing, when my parental instincts would kick in and push me towards doing the right thing, whatever 'the right thing' may have meant. Shatina was now going to the hospital at least once or twice a week with labor pains so I took about two months and stayed with her and the kids in anticipation of the birth of the baby. I would go back and forth to the hospital with her, sit there with her for hours until they sent her back home because the contractions would get wider apart then fade away. I finally headed back to Buffalo and a few days later got a page from Shatina's mother. When I called back she said, "Baby, I think this is really it this time. She just went to the hospital again. You might want to get down here as quick as you can."

I had been to the hospital at least ten to twelve times in the previous few months, each time certain that she was about to deliver the baby, only to be sent home just to repeat the process again a few days later. I was in no rush to get back there until her mother called back again and said, "she is seven centimeters dilated, it is finally about to happen!"

I headed down to the bus station and jumped on the next bus to Rochester, caught a cab to the hospital and walked into the delivery room. The doctors and nurses were all smiling as I looked over to see Shatina holding a baby wrapped in a pink blanket. I had missed the delivery of my daughter by about thirty minutes. I couldn't believe that she finally came and I wasn't there after spending all that time for months leading up to her birth running back and forth to the hospital.

Before I had a chance to get upset a nurse handed me the baby and I looked down to see this little, yellowish newborn looking right back at me, moving her head around and trying to see what was going on around her. My heart instantly melted as the doctor said, "She is extremely alert and active. We usually don't see babies move their heads around like that for a few weeks to a month! She is definitely taking everything in!"

Shatina looked at me, tears in her eyes and said, "That's your daughter! She looks just like your yellow self!" I looked at Shatina and for the first time in months felt comfortable around her, felt like I didn't have to have my guard up and I could just enjoy the moment with no worries about arguments or tension. I took a deep breath and relaxed for the first time in a long time feeling like life was good.

17 DOWNWARD SPIRALS

My daughter's birth slowed me down for a few weeks, then the arguments and bullshit started up with Shatina. So once again, I used that as an excuse to head back to Buffalo and hit the streets. A few months prior, I had stopped paying the bills at my apartment despite the fact that Jennifer, large pregnant belly and all, was still living there. Jennifer continued to inject herself deeper into a relationship with my mother and sister, eventually leading to her moving in with my mother after eviction notices were sent to our apartment.

My mother had always been sympathetic to the plights of the women in my life, especially the ones she felt I had wronged. I never shared the ups and downs of my relationships with my mother so she relied on conversations with my girlfriends for insight into my life and relationships. Of course, this led to them presenting very one-sided views of things and despite warning my mother about letting my exes get too close to her, my mother and sister continued to be their 'shoulders to cry on,' causing me to further distance myself from both of them as well as Jennifer.

I jumped on a Greyhound bus and made my way back to Buffalo to get back to hustling and more importantly, escape the growing stress continually swirling in Rochester. I linked up with Dink and set up shop at a new spot across the street from our spot on Fillmore, and next door to the corner store owned by a family of Arabs. Over time I had developed a relationship with the owner of the store. I would occasionally hang out with him when I was waiting on phone calls on the pay phone outside the front of his store and would come into the store once or twice a day to buy blunts or beer.

The local dealers and knuckleheads in the neighborhood would usually hang out in front of the store, running inside whenever the police would ride by or try to run them off the corner. Most of them were buying dimes from us, breaking them down, adding cut and then trying to sell them around the neighborhood.

Muhammad, the store owner, would often park his car in front of the store and then make trips back and forth to the car, unloading merchandise from the car and bringing it into the store. Whenever I was there, I would always give him a hand, then he would offer me some money for helping him and I would always refuse.

Even though I was adding to the destruction of the community through my involvement with the drug trade, I still had a strong sense of community and went out of my way to try to give back in small ways whenever I could. I would have Stankman or Hector or one of my workers grab a shovel and clear out the sidewalk and driveways of the elderly people and single mothers on the block, or buy and drop off groceries to those that I knew were struggling to stay afloat. I would run all the hypes away from the block, partially to keep my spot from getting unwanted police attention but also to keep the neighborhood quiet and safe.

When someone broke into one of the elderly women's houses on the block, I found out who did it, brought them to the house and made them apologize then had them brutally beat down in broad daylight in the middle of the street, sending a message to everyone else that this behavior was not going to take place on my block. I bought her a brand new television to replace the one that was stolen, had her window repaired and gave her some pocket money for her troubles. She was so thankful that for the next few months, every Sunday, she would cook a big dinner and invite me over. She would share stories about her kids and what the neighborhood used to be like when she first moved there over fifty years prior.

Through my interactions with the community I found that many of those in the neighborhood were dead set against drugs and drug dealers but were still willing to get behind me and watch my back. It turned out that the elderly lady that I helped out had a nephew that was pretty high up in the police department so she would occasionally pull me to the side and give me a heads-up when she heard that things were going to get hot around the neighborhood. And she was always right.

Through the neighborhood I met Belinda who had more game than anyone I had ever met in my life. She was short but her thin frame and long legs made her appear majestically taller than her actual height and her thin waist made the curves of her hips look more well- rounded than they really were. She had the softest looking lips I had ever seen and dark, chocolate brown flawless skin that looked just as soft as her lips. She was pretty in a classic way and exuded sexiness that drew men and even women to her. She knew how to use all of her physical assets to persuade people into seeing things her way. On top of her physical qualities, she was very smart, hyper-intelligent and she ran mental circles around almost everyone. On more than one occasion I sat back and watched her tell a man that she was going to have his necklace or that he would give her all the money in his pocket and within a few minutes whatever she said was going to happen, happened! It was the most amazing thing that I'd ever witnessed. This crack head woman, a stone cold crack addict, was able to game people by simply talking to them, never lying to them, always telling them upfront what she wanted and always, always, always in the end, getting whatever she asked for.

Belinda sold her body for money to support her crack habits but she wasn't a traditional 'crack hoe.' I saw the young dudes offer her money or crack for sex and I watched as she talked to them, took the money or crack, left and never let them touch her. She was a master and everyone admired her. If she wasn't on drugs she could have been something big, a natural politician. I could have seen her on television, addressing masses of people and putting them at ease as she sold them whatever dream she felt they wanted to hear.

Belinda would work the hoe stroll down at the other end of Genesee Street, close to Baily Avenue. As soon as the sun set, the three or four blocks on Genesee would be dominated by women walking up and down the street, dressed in skimpy clothes, waving at cars that they hoped would stop so they could hop in, drive around the corner and turn a trick for some money.

Most of the customers were suburban white men, many of them with professional jobs; lawyers, doctors, executives, with pockets full of money. They would circle the block three or four times until they worked up the nerve to stop, or finally found the one they were looking for, pull over, roll down the window and started negotiating a price for what they were looking for. If the women knew the men, they would jump right into the passenger seat and the car would speed off, usually headed to one of the side streets where they would park and handle their business.

Crack and heroin addiction completely changed the prostitution scene in Buffalo. For a longtime, prostitutes made substantial money plying their trade but when the crack epidemic hit they saw their profits shrink as crack addicts began taking less and less money in exchange for drugs, forcing the non-addict prostitutes to lower their prices or be forced out of business. It was not uncommon for the crack-hoes to receive less than $20 a trick, sometimes earning less than $5 on a slow night. There were still a few ladies that held their prices high and demanded much more money, never taking less than $150 or $200 and they were able to bring in a different type of clientele, a much more discrete clientele that didn't mind paying extra because they made their clients feel like it was a secret between only them.

Belinda took me to the hoe stroll with her a few times, asking me to sit in the car and watch her back as she worked. She schooled me to what to look out for from the various tricks. She showed me which prostitutes where doing what and for how much, and turned me on to all the stick up kids and wanna-be pimps that would hang around the area all trying to make a quick buck off of the clients or the women themselves.

She pointed out various tricks and told me what each one was into. Up until that point I had considered myself to be a freak and pretty open sexually but after hearing some of the things that these guys were into I realized that I was lame in comparison! She pointed out a middle aged white guy driving a brand new Mercedes Benz, good looking guy who obviously was making a lot of money. He circled the block three or four times as Belinda told me that the longer he waited to find her the more he would always pay. She said he would pick her up, negotiate a price, usually $500 to $700, then Belinda would take off her shoes, give them to him and get out of the car. She would walk around for the next ten or fifteen minutes barefoot while he sat in his car, sniffed her shoes and watch her walk around. After her feet were covered in dirt she would get into the car, put her feet in his face and then demand that he lick them clean while she said degrading things to him. After he had licked them clean she said she would spit on him and slap him around. The more degrading things she said and harder she slapped him, the bigger the tip.

She showed me another guy that would come wearing his

wife's panties, then ask her to take his pants off and use his belt to whip his ass until it turned bright red. Another trick asked her to sing the national anthem while he masturbated and if he wasn't able to finish before the song was over, he would cry hysterically while she held him. All of the fetish types always paid top dollar and were usually middle aged, successful, wealthy white men. Every single working girl shared crazy stories about white tricks like that, each laughing and shaking their heads as they described their experiences.

Every few hours, Belinda would come to the car, pull out a wad of money and give it me, saying "Hold this for me daddy." Then she would drop her head and smile a shy smile, jump out of the car, and hustle back to the block. After a few trips to the car she said, "You think that's enough money for tonight? I'm tired and ready to go home."

I shrugged my shoulders and said, "That's on you. I'm out here with you until whenever so it's your call." I always brought at least a hundred bags of crack with me to sell to the other prostitutes as well as their tricks and most nights I would sell out within a few hours so any time after I sold out was a good time for me to leave.

Every time I shrugged my shoulders, she would suck her teeth and give me a look of disappointment, then she would say, "Let's go," as she sat in the passenger seat, pouting the entire way home.

"What the fuck is your problem?" I finally asked after a week of going through the same thing every night.

Sucking her teeth, she said, "I've been giving my money to you every single night and you never count it, you never take any of it, you just give it back and we leave. I need you to push me, make me get out there and get that money and then I need you to take care of that money for me and take care of me. You know I'm just going to spend it getting high. I don't want to get high no more, I just want to take care of you and I want you to take care of me."

Surprised by what she said, I just looked at her and said nothing. She said, "You know, you are the smartest mother fucker I've ever met out here, but for someone so smart, your ass is naïve to the game! You got all these hoes out here running to you, giving you all their money, all up in your face and you haven't taken advantage of any of it! You could be the biggest pimp to ever walk these streets and with a bitch like me by your side, there is no way we will lose!"

I thought about what she was now saying and finally realized what she had been doing the entire time. She was grooming me, teaching me everything I needed to know to be a successful pimp, schooling me to the game and putting money in my hand to see how I would respond. Laura also shared many stories with me about her exploits in the streets and told me that she wanted to take me out of town with her so we could get some real money. I was always resistant to the idea. I had 'real' money and I knew nothing about the pimp game beyond what I had read in a Donald Goines' book so I would listen and generally dismiss her ideas all together.

While my ego got a serious boost from her suggestions and I had always admired the flashy characters in movies like "Super Fly" and "The Mack," overall I felt that exploiting women for financial gains was wrong. Despite my reservations and negative feelings, Belinda persisted, framing it in a way to make it seem like I was doing her a favor. I was really not interested and stopped going with her when she went to work, choosing instead to supervise the spot and make sure all was running well.

Occasionally, I would hit the stroll with her, she would turn tricks, bring me the money then after a few hours test me by saying, "I'm tired, can we leave now?" Following the lead of the character I saw in The Mack, I would say, "Hell no bitch, get out there and get me my money, I don't have time to play games with your ass!"

She would giggle and say, "Yes daddy, I'm about to get you your money!" then hustle off and come back a few hours later with twice as much money as she had the first time. And this would continue a few more times until I finally got tired and was ready to go. And every time we left she would look at me disappointed and shake her head. I knew what she was thinking. She wanted me to push her and make her stay out there until she was exhausted, but that just wasn't in me. I had far too much compassion to ever be a pimp but I liked spending time with Belinda. She was always schooling me to something new. She had so much potential to be something great yet she spent all her time chasing a crack high.

While I was making moves with Belinda, Dink was handling most of the business as Quan was in and out of the spot on an irregular basis. He was becoming more and more easily agitated, leading to arguments between the two of us and to him flipping out on whoever was working for us at the time. In a few weeks, Stankman, Hector and the rest of our Buffalo team started to ease away, eventually leaving no one to work the spots except for us.

Quan would say, "Fuck those bitch ass niggas, we need to get some real niggas up here anyways." With limited options, we took a trip to Rochester to see who we could recruit to come back to Buffalo and work the spots. Quan went and got two of Tee's younger cousins, both of whom I'd known for years from the Westside of Rochester and Wilson High school. They were both a few years younger than us but had been hustling for a long time and had heard the stories from Shawny and Tee about our out of town drug selling success and jumped at the opportunity to head out of town and make some real money with a real team.

We had been making more frequent trips to the Bronx and had amassed a team of soldiers that were ready to come up to Buffalo whenever we were ready. We grabbed Scatter Mooch, Kwame and Quan's uncle, a seasoned gangster, fresh off of a twenty-five year bid for murder spent almost entirely in New York's infamous Attica prison. Scatter was thin, dark skinned, missing several teeth and had one of the hardest, coolest walks I'd ever seen. He also spoke in a way that was so gangster that all the hardest dudes in the South Bronx would try to emulate his speech patterns, single handedly turning his neighborhood and surrounding neighborhoods, into a breeding ground for imitation Scatters! He would say "Yoooooooooaaa, my niggaaaaaa" in a long, drawn out way, making sure to over emphasize his thick New York accent. Then add rapid fire, "What-the-deal-with-that-shit-my-niggaaaaaaaaaaaaa?" No one sounded more like Scatter Mooch then Quan. In fact he took "Scatter talk" to an entirely new level, making it his own so much so that soon the young thugs were trying to emulate him!

We also brought a couple young dudes up from the Bronx, T-Low and Salsa, both of whom grew up around the game and were seasoned veterans when it came to hustling on the gritty street corners of the South Bronx. Kwame's cousin Ant-Live and a few others came up as well but they quickly returned to the Bronx, leaving Scatter, T-Low & Salsa to hold things down.

After getting them situated into one of the new spots on Wilson street, we put Scatter in charge of security, gave him access to an arsenal of weapons and let him ride up and down the street on a bicycle keeping his eyes open for anything that looked out of order. Scatter had a way of intimidating people and quickly established himself and without our knowledge, he started extorting the local drug dealers and eventually the customers. When one of the customers finally told me that Scatter was shaking him down and forcing him to smoke with him whenever he bought from us I told Quan who insisted on talking to Scatter himself. Soon after, the customer ended up in the hospital after Scatter brutally beat him down, sending a message to any other customer or drug dealer out there that if they snitched to us he would do the same thing to them.

Scatter's drug use started to seriously affect our money as customers started to prefer going elsewhere rather than having to deal with Scatter's threats. We ended up sending Scatter back to the Bronx but the damage was already done. He managed to alienate customers and create enemies with a lot of people all of which meant more problems and less money for us.

The stress was quickly surpassing the profits so I slid off to Rochester to see my daughter and clear my head. While I was there, I ran into Jennifer's brother at a local pool hall and he told me that she was in the hospital and had just given birth. In the course of a little more than two months, my responsibilities as a father had expanded from one child to three. The few short days I was in town, were spent arguing with Shatina, getting into a huge argument with Heather about my first son and finding out that I now had another son that just entered the world. To relieve my stress, I linked up with Puba, bought some weed and drinks and spent the next few days smoking and drinking until everything was a blur.

My son was born on January 27, 1994 and I spent the entire month of January as well as the next few months getting as high as I could get, often drinking until I passed out. I don't recall the first time I saw my son, but I do remember feeling like I was already a failure as a father. Out of all of my kids, he resembled me the most, looking almost indistinguishable from me when I was an infant.

Despite my issues with his mother, I immediately fell in love with the little dude. He had a smile that lit up a room and I could tell that he would be special. My relationship with my oldest son was a hit or miss often depending on whether or not Heather was in the mood to let me see him, which was understandable considering my inconsistency in his life. I had a daughter with a woman that would flip out to the extreme whenever the mood hit her, and my relationship with my newest child's mother made me less than enthusiastic about sticking around. Using the acrimonious nature of the relationships with my children's mothers as an excuse, I went back to Buffalo more determined than ever to make as much money as possible clinging to the hopes that money would somehow magically solve all my problems.

Laura kept telling me to chill out and move more slowly. She said that her contact downtown was telling her that I was hot and that they were watching me closely. I knew that I was being watched, which is why I had spent the previous month or so setting up new stash houses and preparing to move everything from Wilson street to a few blocks away. Even with all the moves, she kept saying, "Sometimes you got to look at the signs. Everything keeps telling ya'll to slow down. Just for a little while. I will take you out of town and you can just chill while I get some money for us, but please, just slow down."

Her words rang true in my ears and were pretty much in tune with my gut instincts. I knew she was right but between the weed and liquor clouding my mind and not wanting to return to Rochester to figure out how to be a father, I shook it all off and moved forward with my plans. I had everyone meet me at Laura's father's house across the street from Muhammad's corner store and right downstairs from my old spot. We always got together at least two or three times a week, usually to sit down and eat a dinner that Laura prepared. It was an opportunity to strengthen bonds and come together as a unit and had always been an important part of how we did business.

Laura had been staying with her father since she got back in town and I was usually there on most nights or would at least come through for dinner or lunch. On occasion, I had used the house to bag up small amounts of work or to count money but never really kept any serious amounts of weight or money there and never ever sold anything from the house.

T-Low, Salsa, Laura's father and I were all sitting around the living room as Laura was cooking when Salsa got up to use the bathroom and noticed a shadow move past one of the side windows. "Yo, something ain't right yo. Somebody is outside the window."

T-Low jumped up and peeped through one of the curtains on the front window overlooking the front porch. "Oh Shit, its 5-0, they are about to kick the door in!" I got up to run to the back bedroom but before I could get two steps off the couch, there was a loud "BOOM" followed by a cracking noise and three or four officers wearing bullet proof vests and carrying large assault rifles, rushed in from behind the door which was now in splinters.

"Get the fuck down, police mother fuckers, search warrant! Get down now or we'll shoot you in the fucking face!" An officer grabbed me, threw me on the ground and put his foot on the side of my face while another officer put his knee into my back, put his arm on the back of my neck and grabbed my arm placing a handcuff on my wrists. "Don't move mother fucker. We got you now 'C'! You piece of shit." Leaning down closer to me he whispered, "You should've worked with us you stupid mother fucker, we could have all got rich but you want to be a dumb nigger!"

When they finally let me up, I looked up to see the two detectives that had stopped me at least three or four times in the last few months. I knew who they were, everyone knew who they were. They had developed a reputation that started with them stealing money from drug dealers years back and morphed into what it was known for at that time, taking money and drugs from dealers that didn't work with them, pocketing the money and then selling the drugs.

The few times that they jumped out on me, one of them would grab me while the other one would jump out telling the officer that was acting like he was going to rough me up to "Chill out" or "take it easy." Then the 'good cop' would say, "Forgive my partner. He gets a little worked up when he runs into people in our neighborhoods that don't work well with us. We know who you are and I know that you know who we are so let's cut the shit. This is our block and you need to give up something of value to work on our block." Then the 'bad cop' would start going through my pockets, pulling out my usual wad of cash and slowly counting it before sliding a few hundred or sometimes a few thousand off the top then placing it back into my pocket.

Everyone knew these cops and everyone hated them but they had the entire city of Buffalo either kicking them back money or selling drugs for them. I found out later that they were both related, Paul and Gerald Skinner. Gerald was Paul's younger brother and he was always playing the 'bad cop.' He was known to have a serious temper and it was openly discussed that he would use the butt of his gun to split open someone's head or to cuff someone then viciously beat him after they threw them in the back of their unmarked car. Paul wasn't a saint, everyone used to talk about how he would beat people and I personally witnessed their handy work on more than one occasion. The entire narcotics squad was alleged to be crooked but the Skinners and their partner whom everyone called Acosta, were long known to be the worst.

The Skinner brothers where standing in Laura's father's living room, smiling from ear to ear as a few other officers broke picture frames, over turned furniture and tore food out of cupboards as they searched the house. One of the officers yelled from the back bedroom, "We got something, Paul come take a look." Paul looked at me and said, "We got your ass now, I told you, I told your dumb nigger ass!" He made his way to the back bedroom where he stayed for a few minutes before coming back out with a purse in his hand and a digital scale in his other hand.

"Well well, look at what we have here," he said, as he dumped the contents of the purse onto the table in front of me. A few thousand empty baggies fell out along with a large jar of powder that was used as cut when cooking cocaine and a few hundred bags of packaged crack. His brother laid me back on the floor and searched me again, this time pulling out the wad of cash from my pocket and placing that on the table with the rest of what they say was found in the back room.

"It looks like someone was trying to sell some coke!" Paul said loud enough for everyone to hear before bending down closer to me and whispering, "I told your ass the rules and your dumb ass just wouldn't listen. Now you and your little home boys are going to jail."

They put all of us into separate police cars and took us downtown to be booked. The following day they dropped the charges and released everyone except for me. I found out later that the Skinner brothers signed a warrant request stating that one of their confidential informants, or CI's, had purchased a quarter ounce of crack from me at the house on numerous occasions. The warrant also said that when the informant made the purchases, I had a nine millimeter hand gun in my waistband. I knew this was all bullshit as I had never sold any drugs directly from Laura's father's house and I had never kept any type of guns in or around the house either. The Skinners had a long established reputation in the streets for lying in order to obtain warrants and then using those warrants to steal money and drugs from the occupants of the homes that they entered.

As soon as I was released from jail I stopped by the store across the street from the house and Muhammad told me that two officers had come by the store a couple of times asking about me and telling him to make sure that he told me that they had come there looking for me. I knew that I had to lay low for a little while so I headed across town to the Westside. Within a day I set up shop in the predominantly Latino neighborhood a few blocks away from the Peace Bridge which took you from Buffalo and the United States to Canada. The neighborhood was known as the city's main hub for heroin and was teaming with what looked like walking zombies.

Heroin was a different high than crack. Crack made people anxious, gave them lots and lots of nervous energy while heroin slowed people down. I set up shop in a hard core junkie's house and he was the first person that I ever watched shoot up heroin. He also smoked crack or he would use powder cocaine to mix with the heroin doing what the junkies called, 'chasing the dragon.'

I paid him twenty or thirty dollars for using his place and he quickly converted the money into one of the small wax paper baggies of heroin. Heroin was usually sold in these small, semi-clear bags for $20 apiece, larger quantities were sold as bundles. In Buffalo, a bundle contained five $20 bags, or as bricks which were ten bundles. A bundle was going for $500 in New York City so a person could easily double their money simply by making the six-hour drive to Buffalo, but most people would add cut to the bags to stretch them and thus turn $500 into $1500 or $2000 depending on the purity of the initial heroin. The bags would always have a stamp on them to indicate to the user which heroin they were buying, sort of like a brand name similar to Nike or Reebok for sneakers.

At the time, all the junkies were looking for the bags with a red scorpion on them because there were reports in the news and all over the streets of people overdosing and dying from that particular brand. The more people that overdosed, the more demand for the product. There was no better marketing tool than to have someone overdose and die from a particular brand of heroin. After a death, everyone would rush to obtain that particular brand with the hopes of obtaining the best high.

Francisco, the owner of the apartment, went and copped a bag with the red scorpion on it and quickly rushed into the bathroom to get out his kit and prepare the heroin. He talked to me as he went through his process, removing an old spoon, tearing off a piece of a cotton ball, lighting a candle, emptying the powdered contents of the bag into the spoon, adding a small amount of water, then holding the spoon over the flame of the candle until the contents of the spoon started to bubble up. He started sweating profusely, eyes widening as he placed the piece of cotton onto the spoon, added a little more water then pulled out a dirty looking syringe from his back pocket. He placed the needle against the cotton and pulled back on the syringe, watching intently as the brownish looking liquid was sucked up into the syringe.

He grabbed a belt from his kit and quickly wrapped it around his arm, asking me to help him pull it and then secure it tightly just below his bicep, right above his elbow joint. He tapped at the veins starting to protrude in his forearm, and then tapped at a vein on the back of his hand, where he was finally able to find one that looked like it might receive the needle. His arm was covered in injection marks, scars and large, open scabs from his years of shooting up and the back of his hand looked only slightly better.

Noticing the grimace on my face he snickered and said, "Yea man, I've been shooting this shit up since I was fourteen. This shit is no bueno Poppi, I can't even find a good vein anymore. Last week I had to shoot up in my dick bro, that shit hurt like a mother fucker but it worked." I just shook my head and squeezed my legs together tightly at the thought of a needle being injected into a penis.

After a few minutes of trying over and over to get a vein to cooperate, he was finally able to inject the liquid into his hand. He took a deep breath, followed by a few short ones then his head dropped and drool started running from the corner of his mouth. He didn't look like he was breathing so I nudged him a little, needle still hanging from the vein in his hand, until he lifted his head slightly and slurred, "Yea poppi, this shit is good poppi, real good..." his voice fading to an almost undetectable low. He stood up, walked over to the toilet and started to throw up, heaving repeatedly until he finally sat back down. Sensing my concern, he snickered again and said, "I'm ok poppi, when that shit makes you throw up it means it is good! Real good!" His head dropped again and he nodded off for about ten minutes before lifting his head and slowly moved back towards the table with his cooking supplies then opened the other bag and prepared to do it all over again.

Francisco showed me an entirely new world. He introduced me to professional men and women, many wearing expensive suits and pulling up in high end cars; lawyers, business executives, as well as your regular impoverished hood folks, all of whom were junkies, each one buying at least four or five bags every single day. The money that I estimated was being made from heroin sales had to be four or five times what we made from selling crack. Heroin junkies had to have their fix every day or they would get physically sick. I found out later that heroin withdrawal can actually kill someone and the pain that addicts suffer when they don't have their fix is excruciating.

Quan saw what I saw and immediately made up his mind that on the next trip to the city, he would bring back some heroin. But before we had a chance to make another trip, the police ran up into the house we were working out of and arrested all of us again. As soon as I got out, I went straight back to the house that they raided, intent on retrieving the rest of the hidden drugs and knowing that they didn't find anything because I had everything safely hidden behind a light switch in the living room.

I had witnessed enough police searches to observe where they searched and where they never searched. They were hip to all the hollowed out cans of soup and whip cream containers and always seemed to look for hidden compartments behind walls and in the floors but they rarely thoroughly looked through the garbage and never took the time to remove any of the covers over light switches or outlets. There was always space behind a light switch or an outlet, usually large enough to drop a large bag of whatever you were hiding and easily retrieve it with the use of a coat hanger or something similar.

Right before the police raided the house, I unscrewed the plate covering the light switch in the living room, stuffed a few ounces of crack behind the wall under it and screwed the cover back into place. When the officers came in the house, throwing around furniture, breaking cabinets and roughing us up, I laughed as I watched the two biggest mouthed cops stand right next to the light switch, one of them turning the light off and on, as they threatened us and looked for drugs.

I recovered the bags from behind the wall and headed up the street to set up shop at another house. Two days later everyone else was released and they all met me at the new spot. The downtown jail was only a fifteen-minute walk to the house so they all walked straight there from the jail. We hugged, lit up a few blunts and went up to the pizza spot up the block to get a few slices and figure out our next move. I had become more and more distant from everyone, constantly wrestling with the growing feeling that I needed to leave the streets alone and go in another direction. I had no idea what I wanted to do but I had been seriously thinking about attempting to go to college. The few times I tried discussing it with Quan he would dismiss it, saying, "Ah nigga you just need to get this money, you're a hustler man, this shit here is what you were made to do!"

As everyone talked, my mind kept wandering back to the idea of school, to the idea of getting away and leaving all the drama and bullshit behind me. Francisco came busting into the pizza shop, "Yooooo, they just raided your spot man! The police are there right now, running through the whole spot. Ya'll better make a move, they were asking about you."

We all looked at each other and Quan ran out of the shop and around the corner, coming back a minute later, "Yo money, this shit is crazy yo! 5-0 is all over that house man!"

T-Low said, "Fuck this, I just got out of jail twenty minutes ago, this shit is getting crazy as hell." I immediately realized that this was a sure sign I couldn't ignore. I felt that I needed to leave that pizza shop and get the fuck out of Buffalo immediately. Quan said, "Yo nigga, this is part of the game. Shake that shit off and let's get back to work. We found a gold mine over here, we just have to get that Her-on and make some moves." I shook my head and said, "Naw man, I need to lay low for a while, I'm out bro, I'm out."

I had no idea what I was going to do or where I was going to go but I knew I had to do something different. Laura suggested that we go to Toronto for a while so we could lay low. She reached out to a few of her friends in Canada and we packed a bag and headed for Toronto. The drinking age throughout Canada was eighteen so as soon as I turned 18, a bunch of us would pile into cars or rent a limo and hit the bars and clubs on the Canadian side of Niagara Falls, drinking until we passed out.

As soon as I got to Toronto I immediately fell in love with the city. It was beautiful, clean and huge, full of diverse groups of people from all over the world. I spent hours walking around downtown and exploring the smaller neighborhoods that bordered the downtown area. I spent a lot of time hanging out in Chinatown, Yonge Street, Bloor Street, the Harborfront and Kensington Market. Laura would go to the large Bingo halls and play bingo for hours, usually winning a few hundred dollars but making much more money by picking the pockets and lifting the purses of the bingo players. She knew the city well and had enough hustles that money was never an issue.

We bounced around from hotel to hotel until we had enough money to hold us over for a few months and could head back to Buffalo. Laura left her newborn daughter with her sister while we were gone and the month we spent away from the baby was driving her crazy. I had spent more time away from my own children but being out of the country felt like I was much farther away than I actually was. Rochester was just across Lake Ontario from Toronto but it felt like it was half-way across the world. I had been fighting against the growing desire I had to spend time with my kids, to pursue a more stable life and get out of the streets. I kept telling myself that I hadn't accomplished my multi-million-dollar goals yet and felt like a failure every time I started to formulate any sort of plan that would lead me back to the square life. Most of the people that I knew looked at squares as being lame, as being unable to cut it in the streets, as losers that didn't have the heart, courage or ability to survive and thrive living outside of the system. I made up my mind to give it one last hard run and put a plan together that I knew would get me to where I thought I needed to be.

I went right back to work, organizing things and setting up a new spot. Everything was running smooth and the money was rolling in until I got stopped walking up the street by the police. I was clean, no drugs, nothing illegal but the officers ran my name and a warrant popped up so they took me straight downtown, booked and processed me and held me for a few days. I finally appeared in front of a Judge who was none too pleased with the fact that I had several different aliases, missed some court dates and they were still unsure as to what my real name was. He hit me with a high bail for the felony warrant and sent me back to jail to wait until my next court date which wasn't scheduled for another few months. I called Laura and told her what happened and eventually was able to get in touch with Shatina to tell her as well. I gave them both the name I was arrested under so Shatina could write me and so that Laura could put some money in my account and come visit. I sat back and tried to get as comfortable as possible, feeling that I wouldn't be getting released any time soon.

They moved me to a unit that had thirty or forty cells in it, all surrounding a common area where inmates could watch TV, play cards, socialize, etc. I knew most of the inmates in there and quickly got caught up on the latest news about who was snitching, who was running what inside and outside of the jail and who had beef with whom. I knew the guy that brought books to the pods twice a week so he hooked me up with some good reading materials and Laura brought me new books to read every week. I spent most of my time in my cell reading or talking with a few of the inmates that I knew from the Bronx and Rochester.

I also spent a lot of time writing and reading letters. I wrote Shatina almost every day and she wrote me back at least once or twice a week, occasionally sending me pictures of my daughter. Despite wanting to reach out to her, my ego wouldn't allow me to write Jennifer so I got updates on how my son was doing through my mother. I had plenty of time to think about my kids and the choices that I made that led to me sitting in a jail cell. I thought about all the times that my instincts tried to push me in another direction, about all the times I started to walk away and do something else, and about all the times I shook those feelings and thoughts off and just kept right on doing what I was doing. I listened to other inmates tell me their stories, about how drugs had destroyed their lives and taken them from their families, jobs and freedom.

I played chess with one brother that everyone called Shogun. He was probably in his early fifties, in good shape and well respected by everyone, including the correctional officers. He was one of the most intelligent people that I had ever talked with and every time we talked he opened my eyes to new things. He was the first person I ever heard break down the criminal justice system, I mean get into detail about how the system was the new form of slavery. He pointed out specific laws and then showed me how each one of those laws only had real effects on black people, specifically poor black men. I had heard people talk about the system before but he did more than talk, he supported his talk with tangible information, pulling out certain laws he had printed out and giving me academic studies that followed those laws. He turned me on to books by Amos Wilson and "The Miseducation of the Negro" by Carter Goodwin Woodson, as well as reintroducing me to Alex Haley's "The Autobiography of Malcom X."

The more we talked, the more difficulty I had understanding how this extremely intelligent, articulate, thoughtful brother with so much knowledge of self could be sitting in a jail cell. He looked me right in my eyes and said, "Young brother, I lose control in the streets. I always manage to find my way right back to cocaine and cocaine always manages to find her way right back to me." Then he dropped his head and shoulders and for the first time since I met him, looked as if he was defeated. After a few moments, he lifted his head. "Young brother, you have an opportunity to be who I am in here. All the good you see in me, you can be that out there! You have strength that I don't and I see you are smart as hell. Don't waste your life with the rest of these fools. I want to be able to point at the TV or pick up a book one day and say 'I know this brother right here! He made it!'"

His words weighed heavy on my mind and heart because I knew that he was speaking the truth. I knew that I could make something of myself but I just didn't know how or where to start. I felt overwhelmed and sitting in a jail cell, listening to everyone around me talk about schemes and plots to get over on the system made it easy to lose focus and get caught up in the faux macho bravado associated with street culture.

Before I knew it, I was headed back to court and my attorney was confident that they would reduce my bail but the Judge had a different idea all together. He refused to reduce the bail and set another court date another two months away. Before I could get down on myself my attorney told me that he spoke to someone from a new program and that they would come to talk to me about the program. He said if they accepted me that I could get released and be back on the streets in the next few weeks. He didn't tell me anything about the program, only said that someone would come to the jail to meet with me soon.

A week later I was called from my cell to the attorney visiting room where I met with a guy wearing a cheap suit and carrying a briefcase. He pulled out a large folder and removed a few papers from it, placing them in front of him and started to write as we talked. "So you are in here for drugs?" he asked, never looking up from his notes. "Yes," I said. "You are from the area?"

"Yes"

"Do you have a drug problem?" He said, finally looking up for the first time.

"Huh? A drug problem? Naw man, I don't have a drug problem," I said, showing my disdain for his question.

"Listen, we just got funding for a new intervention program for people with drug problems in the criminal justice system. The program can only help you if you are at least willing to take the first step and admit you have a problem. So again, I ask you, do you have a drug problem?"

I thought about his question again and asked, "What type of help can your program provide?"

"Well first of all, we can get you out of here and back home with your family, then we can get you into an excellent treatment program to help get you on the road to recovery. But we can't do anything unless you can take that first step and admit that you have a problem."

I thought about his words for a moment then said, "Hell yeah I have a problem! Now can you get me out of here?"

He smiled, wrote down a bunch of notes, stood up and said, "I will be in touch in the next 24 hours," then he tucked the folder under his arm and knocked on the door to leave the room.

A few days later, I received paperwork to sign so that I could be released from jail and into the supervision of this new program. I got released to Laura's address and went to meet with a probation officer who placed an electronic monitoring device on my ankle and told me that I had to check in with a day reporting program every morning. They gave me a box to plug into the phone line at the house. The box would send updates to the probation officer verifying my location every fifteen minutes. The box was supposed to be set so that if I went anywhere farther than the front porch of the house it would register that I was not home and I would thus be in violation of my probation agreement. From the first day we connected it, the box kept registering that I was not home when I actually was. The probation officer came to my house on three different occasions at odd hours of the night after he received a call from the machine saying I wasn't there and each time he found me home in bed. Eventually, he just stopped coming and even stopped calling, assuming that the alerts he received were in error.

The day reporting program was at a drug treatment facility. I met with a counselor who looked at my report and told me that I was going to have to attend meetings all day at the program, from 8am until 5pm, six days a week. After hearing his suggested program for me I said, "Listen, I don't have a drug problem. The man told me that if I told him that I had a problem he would get me released to this program. Look at what I was charged with when I was arrested. Does that seem like something a drug addict would have? All that money and all those drugs? Come on man you've been doing this for a long time, do I look like a crack head?"

He looked me up and down, re-read my file and gave me a look of uncertainty. I added, "Ask anyone of these hypes from the Eastside about me. They will all tell you who I am, I've never used cocaine a day in my life, I smoke weed and that's it." He got up, went into the other room and came back with one of the program participants that had been clean for the past thirty days and brought her into the office. She immediately recognized me and he asked her if what I was saying was true. She looked at me hesitantly and I said, "It's cool, tell him who I am." She confirmed everything that I had said.

He said, "Listen, I'm still going to have you come each day this week for the all day sessions and after that I will drug test you. If you come out clean we can move you down to once a week." Still dissatisfied I shook my head and went and sat down in one of the meetings that was in progress.

I looked around the room and realized that I knew most of the people in there, they were all customers of mine at one point or another. As soon as they recognized me they gave me a confused look, nodded their heads and went back to listening to what the speaker was saying. These meetings usually involved the members sharing their personal stories around drug use or telling the group how their day was going. When it was my turn to share I always passed and at the breaks three or four people would always come up to me and say, "Man what the hell you doing here? I know you ain't fucking with no crack! You got a drinking problem or something?"

I would sometimes explain what happened and they would shake their heads and say, "Man if they only knew who they had up in here!" One of them said, "Shit you could make a killing right here if you had anything! All these hypes up in here! Man listen, if you had something I would buy three or four right now!" then he broke out laughing. I laughed too but my mind started turning. The first of the month was the next day and the entire place had that nervous, excited energy that was always associated with a payday.

I couldn't hustle anywhere else, the police were watching my every move, often following me to and from the program. I was still sitting on plenty of crack I just had no way to safely get rid of it and I was quickly running low on money. I grabbed about fifty bags, hid them under my nuts and went to the program the following day and by the end of the first hour long meeting I sold everything. I called Laura and had her bring me some more. A few hours later, I sold that and repeated the process a few more times. I left there with a pocket full of money feeling like I just discovered an amazing new gold mine.

The following day, my counselor pulled me to the side and said, "Man I don't know what is going on, I've been working here for ten years and I've never seen so many people fall off at the same time before. It seems like the whole place is high as hell and half the people aren't even here today. I got to piss test you, everyone is getting tested today." He handed me a clear plastic cup and walked with me into the bathroom. I peed in the cup, handed it to him and went to my group. By the end of the week he agreed to have me come once a week to just check in and take a drug test. I'm not sure if someone told him what was going on or if he figured it out but the way he looked at me told me that he was suspicious of me so I was glad to be out of there.

I ran into a few of the people from the program on the streets and each one was right back into their old routine, looking like they hadn't bathed in days, eyes glossed over and out on the hunt to get some money for more crack. I hadn't really thought about what I had done. I was focused on the end result, the money that filled my pockets each day and the fact that I was able to get off my packages right under the nose of the police and the probation department. In that moment, I felt like I was the man, outsmarting the system by selling drugs at a drug treatment facility, it felt like something you would see in a movie.

Despite the rush I got from beating the system and making money when they thought that they had me down and out, my conscience started speaking to me and I couldn't shake the sight of seeing the same dude I sat in group with right back on the street chasing a crack binge that started because of me. I shook off my conscience, shook free from that little voice that was telling me that what I was doing was wrong and tried to convince myself that it was all part of the game.

I found myself having longer and more pronounced periods of introspection about my future, and the more I thought, the stronger my desire became to make some changes. I thought about my oldest son and how little time I had spent with him those last few years. I thought about my daughter and how she smiled and giggled every time I held her and how she would drop everything as soon as I walked in the door, follow me around non-stop and fall asleep in my arms. I thought about my other son and his goofy laugh, about the way he would bounce around and talk in gibberish and about how I would crack up laughing. And I thought about the conversations I had while I was in jail with Shogun, his words still ringing in my ears.

My desire to be with my kids was always intense and seemed

to be growing into a heavy, constant yearning that made my heart ache. I was spending more and more nights trying to fight back the tears associated with those feelings. I felt like I was failing them, that I was letting them down, that I was doing everything but taking care of them and I wanted to change my situation and more importantly change me. I was ready to embrace my desires to give and accept how warm it made me feel when I just made positive moves, when I acted out of the true depths of my heart.

I knew that the hard edge that I had worked so hard to develop was cracking. The natural warmth and kindness of my heart had been slowly eroding that tough exterior and I was tired of fighting against the change. I had no idea what I was going to do but I had been seriously thinking about trying to go to school, maybe enroll in college and see what I could do in that world. I was starting to regret dropping out of high school and was thinking that if I would have just stuck it out that I would have graduated from college by then and been on to doing something big. For the first time since I was a little kid I thought about what I wanted to be, beyond trying to make millions in the streets. The more I thought, the more I felt that the answer would somehow be found in school. I got so frustrated that tears would run down my cheeks as I thought about 'what if' and 'if I would have' scenarios.

In the middle of one of these deep thinking sessions, my probation officer called me and told me that I needed to come down to his office the next day. He said that when I was initially arrested the computers had some sort of problem and the finger prints weren't registering with everyone's mug shots so I had to come down to get fingerprinted again. In disbelief, I asked, "So you mean that they don't have my fingerprints?"

"That is what I said. Just come down here so they can print you again, besides, I need to drug test you anyways."

I hung up the phone and stood there for a moment, frozen by what he had just said. It was as if someone had heard my request, as if my tears had somehow opened up a magic door of opportunity and I was about to be sucked out of my world of despair, directly into what I had been asking for, a second chance at a new beginning! I knew that when they arrested me they booked me under another name. The officers found ID in the house, said it was mine and simply booked me under that name.

I thought, if they don't have my prints matched to my mug

shot and they don't have my real name I am out of here! I packed up a bag, told Laura I had to make some moves and that I would call her in a few weeks, cut off the ankle bracelet, which never worked correctly anyways, and jumped on the next bus to Rochester. I didn't want anything to do with anything negative anymore, I wanted and needed a clean break so I left all the drugs I had except for a half pound of weed, with the intentions of never coming back. I was nervous as hell and thought that it had to be too good to be true but my instincts were telling me to 'go' so I boarded the bus, sat in the back and smiled for the entire two-hour ride.

PART III

"If you Want to fly, you got to give up the shit that weighs you down. "- Toni Morrison

18 CLEANSING

I made it to Rochester without a clue as to what I was going to do or where I was going to stay. I knew absolutely nothing except that I was ready to make changes. Shatina was working overnights at a home health-aid type of job and I told her that I could watch the kids for her while she was working. This gave me an opportunity to spend quality time with my daughter as well as the other kids and gave me a place to crash on the nights she was working. When she came home I would usually have breakfast made, have the kids up and dressed and be ready to make a move out of the house myself.

I had grown leery of Shatina and her outbursts and I knew that she could go off at any moment but I was truly enjoying the time with the kids and I felt like I needed to make up for lost time. I had an overwhelming desire to do everything right in my life. I felt like I needed to give as much as I could and follow a path of nothing but positive actions and I felt that spending time with them was an important part of my path. The guilt that I still felt over messing with Shatina in the first place was heavy and I thought about Shawny daily, thinking about how I had let him down. I thought about Quan as well and how our bond of brotherhood was severely damaged by sneaking around with his little sister. I needed to make up for the wrong I saw in the situation so I walked on egg shells for a while, trying my best to simply be there for her and the kids.

I started looking for a job and within a few weeks found one that was perfect. I was hired to be the head chef at a small startup bar and grill all the way out in Greece, Rochester's largest suburb. I worked with the owner to develop the menu creating many dishes from the ground up. I always enjoyed cooking and my years in various kitchens taught me to work quickly and put out a quality product and I finally had a professional kitchen that was mine to run.

The only problem was the location of the restaurant. On the

days that I was staying at my mother's house I had to catch a bus from her house downtown then catch another bus to the very last stop in that part of Greece, then walk almost 4 miles from the bus stop to the restaurant. The entire trip would take anywhere from two to three hours one way but I was determined to do the right thing so I didn't complain. I jumped on the bus, walked to work and made it happen.

Shatina had a mini-van at the time but she rarely would offer to give me a ride and I would never ask. I was intent on making my own moves and doing it with or without anyone else's help. I started staying at Shatina's until I had to leave for work, usually in the early afternoon. It was easier to just make the five-minute walk downtown rather than having to take an hour long bus ride from my mother's house and it gave me more time with my daughter and the kids.

Eventually and despite the knots in my stomach telling me not to go there, we started messing around again which led to discussions about getting back together. My mind and heart were in a very different place. I was 100% focused on my ideology of doing all the right things. I wanted every aspect of my life to be filled only with what I considered to be positivity and it opened my heart to new hope in places where there was none before. I started seriously considering going to school and began meeting with counselors at MCC, the local community college. I prided myself on never being late to work or missing a day and I was ready to embrace monogamy and despite my reservations about her stability, felt that doing so with Shatina was the right thing.

For the first time since I was a kid I was optimistic about my future, believing that I could actually do something different with myself and put myself in a position to make a difference in the lives of those around me. I was open to the idea of love and family and felt like I had the solution to make up for my previous wrongs with Shatina, I was going to legitimize our relationship, I was going to marry her.

While my heart and mind were focused on moving ahead in life I wasn't blind to our history or to the problems I saw in Shatina. I very much believed that our marriage had no chance at lasting more than a year but I felt like it would buy me enough time with the kids to further solidify our relationships and hoped that perhaps, there would be a change in her, and she would miraculously mature and morph into a full blown version of the glimpses of beauty that I saw in her. At times, she was very loving, affectionate and caring, enough to give me hope that she was capable of putting forth an effort to really try to make things work. But that was always short lived and interrupted by sometimes violent outbursts and angry threats that would often lead to her telling me to 'get out of her house.'

Despite all the signs pulling and pushing me in another direction, I felt that marrying her was the right thing to do so on July 1, 1995, we were married. A month or so later she was pregnant and my life as a married man began. I found another job working an extra thirty to forty hours a week cooking and continued my full-time job running the kitchen at the restaurant in Greece. I was determined to start school and suggested that Shatina do the same so we agreed to alternate semesters, her going first, then me, then her, etc., so that we could both work towards obtaining our degrees at the same time while also being able to care for our growing family at home.

I knew that her success meant that it would make it easier for both of us as well as the kids so I rearranged my work schedule so I could take care of the kids while she was in class and coordinated with her mother for the times when there was a conflict. By the end of her second week she stopped going and withdrew from her classes. School was not something that she had any real interest in completing and the fact that she dropped out of school in the eighth grade, when she got pregnant with her first child, certainly didn't help.

Her failure at school led to more arguments as I believe she was hurt and upset with herself but refused to reach out to anyone for any type of help. Instead she would take it out on me and the kids, yelling and screaming and arguing over what appeared to be nothing. Fridays were the busiest day at my main job. We did a fish fry that brought in lots of customers because of the size and quality of the fish. I would usually start prep work early in the morning and by three in the afternoon we would be packed, first with the early bird dinners and by the time they cleared out, the regular after work Friday dinner and happy hour crowd.

One Friday, during the middle of the dinner rush she kept calling my job, demanding to speak with me despite the owner telling her numerous times that I was extremely busy. She finally told him that it was an emergency involving one of the kids so he took over on the cook's line while I took the phone call. I answered the phone to hear her say, "I'm sick of you, you could have taken my phone call! What if something was really wrong with the kids? I know you don't give a fuck about these kids."

I said, "What is going on? What happened?"

"I needed to talk to you but your dumb ass was playing games and not getting on the phone!"

Perplexed and anxious to get back to the line as I watched the orders coming in and piling up, I said, "If there is nothing wrong with the kids then I have to go, it's busy as hell here, you know Fridays are my busy days. I will call you when things slow down."

"If you hang this mother fucking phone up I swear I will call the police and give them the name that you used in Buffalo and I will tell your cracker ass boss all about your drug selling ass! Now what mother fucker??"

This wasn't the first time that she had brought up calling the police and telling them about my alias. There was nothing that I regretted more than writing her while I was locked up and allowing her to know the circumstances of why I left Buffalo. She knew that the prosecutor said I was facing a seven-year sentence if convicted and she knew how ecstatic I was at the seemingly miraculous fresh start I had been given. Any time things didn't go her way or I didn't bend to one of her requests, such as arguing with her on the phone about nothing while at work in the middle of a dinner rush, she would threaten me with exposure.

I had grown tired of her games and said, "Fuck it, you do what you have to do. I'm going back to work so I can earn this money to pay our bills."

She called back four or five more times, each time I dismissed the calls and tried to focus on work but I couldn't. Orders were coming up late, food was being overcooked, waitresses were yelling and I was just an overall mess. The owner, seeing my sloppiness, pulled me to the side to ask if everything was alright. "Yeah, I'm good, everything is alright," I said, "Just drama with my wife."

When I got home that night she continued to attack me, now furious that I hung up the phone. She screamed at me to 'get out,' that she wanted me to leave so I packed up a few of my things and headed to my mother's house. By this point my mother had seen me come and go several times and each time questioned why I continued to deal with the situation. And each time after a day or two, Shatina and I would talk, she would apologize and I would end up back at the house.

As I struggled to get my life moving in the right direction the rest of the world seemed to be mirroring the craziness I was experiencing in my relationships. OJ Simpson, whose arrest and trial had dominated the news, was preparing to receive the jury's verdict in his trial for allegedly murdering his wife and her male companion. I remember sitting on our bed, watching game 5 of the NBA Finals while my daughter sat in my lap, laughing and watching me as I watched the game. Patrick Ewing and my New York Knicks had finally made it to the finals and I was enjoying the game.

As I yelled at the television screen rooting on my team, a news bulletin flashed across the bottom of the screen stating that famous former NFL football player and movie star OJ Simpson was fleeing from the police on a California highway. The game was cut off and replaced by news anchors providing play-by-play analysis of the chase. I was furious, I couldn't believe they would cut off the game for a slow-moving car pursuit.

It seemed like the entire country was waiting for the OJ verdict. The case itself had exposed raw racial nerves and an entire population of African-Americans that were still on edge and trying to recover from the shock associated with the innocent verdict of the police officers caught on video beating an unarmed black motorist, Rodney King, almost to death. While Black America had always known the inequity associated with being black in America, the Rodney King video finally felt like solid, indisputable proof of the savage treatment black folks experienced daily.

When the Rodney King verdict was handed down an entire population of enraged and grieving black folks took to the streets of Los Angeles, taking their frustrations out around their communities. I remember the feeling of arrogance and sensing the silent 'high-fives' exchanged between many of the white males walking around after the officers were found 'not guilty.' I remember the looks that the local police officers gave black males as they rode by, their chests pushed out with grins on their faces sending the message: "Know your place Niggers! This is our world, we can do whatever we want to you and no one cares."

Throughout the trial, racial tensions grew deeper as police

officers and conservative whites shook their heads and pointed their fingers at the 'savageness of black men,' as exemplified by OJ. A black man killing a high society white woman in America would surely bring down a guilty verdict and a punishment that would work to deter any other black man from ever putting his hands on a white woman. When the verdict was finally announced, many in black America literally jumped up and down and celebrated the not-guilty verdict as if it meant that they themselves had been somehow proven innocent, while white America looked on with shock and disbelief as they wrestled with accepting the idea of a black man getting away with allegedly murdering one of their own.

The growing hostility between black and white America seemed to parallel the divide within myself. I once again found myself struggling to make sense of why there was so much hatred in America between the two groups of people that each constituted half of who I was. Yet I had no misconceptions about who America saw me as being. I understood completely that in the eyes of the police, the politicians, the Judges, my friends and many of my family, I was unequivocally a black man and as such, I was subject to all the hatred and oppression and outward anger that was being openly expressed because of the verdict.

During all the craziness and back and forth with both the country and my own personal life, I thought about what I could do to somehow contribute to changing the divided world while also keeping myself engaged. I thought about what I enjoyed while growing up and the few things that always brought me joy and figured that I should focus on something to do with working with kids or maybe sports. After doing some more research, I felt that I had found my perfect career choice, a job that would allow me to have fun while working with kids and I'd be able to wear sweatpants to work every day! I made up my mind to register in the physical studies program at Monroe Community College so that I could become a gym teacher.

When it was finally time for the new semester to begin at MCC I met with the financial aid department and academic counselors and spent hours waiting in line after line to register for classes. I was finally set to begin my first semester in college. Despite our agreement to alternate semesters and me still encouraging Shatina to re-enroll in the summer semester, she had no interest in school for herself, or more specifically in seeing me go to school. I registered to take the majority of my classes at the downtown campus so that I could either walk or catch the bus to school.

I jumped on a bus and went to the main campus to get my class schedule finalized and buy my textbooks. Then I jumped on a bus and headed downtown for my first day of classes. Walking in to the old Sibley's building, I was filled with a nervous pride. I couldn't believe that I was really about to start college. I made my way through the throngs of people to my first class, took a seat in the front row, took out my textbook and a notebook and pen and then started listening, taking notes and asking questions. At the age of twenty-four, I was officially a college freshmen.

19 CHICKEN'S COMING HOME

As the semester progressed, I found myself completely engaged in my classes. Any free time between working either job was spent reading and studying, usually in a quiet corner or empty booth in the bar at work. Studying at home was almost impossible and was sure to lead to Shatina starting an argument. My mother continued to ask me why I stayed in such a tumultuous relationship and I would just shrug my shoulders but I knew the answer to her question. I stayed because I felt like I deserved all the arguments and bullshit especially considering feeling like I never should have messed around with her in the first place. There was a large part of me that worked hard towards and hoped with everything that I had, that she would somehow change her ways and all the beautiful things I saw in her would bubble up to the surface and magically take control of her and her actions. She was now three or four months pregnant and I wanted to try to limit her stress so I took a lot more bullshit than I had previously accepted which in turn seemed to encourage her to push things further and further.

She started ending arguments by telling me that my daughter wasn't my daughter or she would grab the other kids and tell them that they didn't need to respect me because I wasn't their father. Arguments just kept progressing further and further until she started taking things to a new level and tried to physically attack me, leaving me to dodge her slaps and punches and retreat out of the house. With absolutely no thought in my mind to ever hit or fight her back, even in self-defense, I finally made up my mind that I had enough.

I planned to pack my things and leave and thought that the best time to do so would be between my classes. I would come home while she was gone, pack, grab my things and go back to class then head to my mother's house when my last class was finished. I left class and made it home, started packing and was just about finished when I heard the door open downstairs. Trying to avoid the argument that I was sure would take place, I quickly pushed my bag under the bed to hide my intentions.

She came upstairs and immediately started arguing with me.

"What the hell are you doing home? Aren't you supposed to be at your precious school right now?" I just shrugged and told her that I had to head back to class. She went into the closet to grab something and noticed that my clothes were missing. "Oh, so you think you are about to leave me? You ain't shit, take your shit and get the fuck out of my house!"

I went to grab my bag from under the bed and she rushed over to me and tried to kick me while I was bent down. I easily blocked her kick, stood up and headed for the door with my bag. She jumped in front of me and grabbed my shirt, scratching my chest and neck in the process. I grabbed her hands and held them, "Chill the fuck out, you want me to leave so I am leaving."

As soon as I let her go she came at me again, swinging wildly as I moved to the side, avoiding her slaps and punches. I looked towards the doorway and saw her oldest daughter and son standing there watching as she attacked me. I hated when the kids saw us argue and I would almost always either leave the house or try to get them settled in another room so that they didn't have to witness the nonsense. I said, "Go downstairs and turn the TV on. Your mom will be down in a minute."

"Hell naw, ya'll don't have to listen to him, he ain't your daddy! You stay right there and listen to your mother!"

Feeling things escalating and just wanting to leave, I grabbed the phone and said, "If you don't chill I'm calling the police."

"Call the police mother fucker, you the one wanted! Go right ahead, I bet your ass goes to jail!"

Feeling completely desperate, and emasculated, I dialed 9-1-1 and waited. When the operated answered I said, "I need some police assistance. I'm trying to leave the house and my wife is physically attacking me."

In the background, as she was still trying to punch, kick and slap me, she was yelling, "Hell naw, this mother fucker needs to get out of my house. He is trying to kill me and hurt my baby. I'm pregnant and he is trying to kill me."

I stayed calm, stayed on the phone and made sure that the operator could hear everything that was going on. She continued to yell, throw things and grab me, eventually ripping my shirt and adding a few more scratches to my face and chest. By the time the police arrived I had my bag and was on the front porch waiting. As soon as the officers pulled up and got out of the car she rushed outside and tried to make it look like she was crying even though she wasn't shedding a single tear. She was yelling, "This mother fucker has to go, I'm sick of his shit, he tried to hit me and my baby."

One officer pulled her to the side while the other talked to me. "Look man, I just want to leave. I was packing my stuff to leave when she came home and she started going crazy, hitting and scratching me, look, you see these scratches?" I said, showing him the marks on my chest.

The officer also pointed out that I had scratches on my chin which I wasn't aware of at that time and saw my ripped shirt. The two officers talked among themselves and then said, "Listen sir, do you have everything you need from the house? If so, you are free to go unless you want to press charges against her."

"WHAT? Hell naw, how that mother fucker going to press charges against me?? He is the one that beat my ass!"

The officer said, "Ma'am, this gentleman has been calm the entire time we were here. He has visible signs on him of an assault. If he hit you or attacked you there would be some signs for sure. Either calm down or I will take you to jail. Let him leave and let things calm down."

As the officer walked with me down the stairs, fuming mad, she yelled, "You just going to let his ass go like that? Well I'll tell you what, he has warrants on him! You better check you will see!" My heart froze, I closed my eyes as I dropped my head. The officer stopped me and said, "Give me a minute, let me just run your info and I'll get you on your way."

After a few minutes he came back and said, "You are all set to go, there aren't any warrants on you."

I looked back to see her standing on the porch with the kids, neighbors were now gathered on their porches and the sidewalks trying to see what the commotion was about. I took two steps up the sidewalk when I heard her say, "Naw, un uh, you got try this name, this is the name he has the warrant under."

The officer checked the name and said, "Can you take a seat in the car? I need to check out something else." My heart sank even deeper. I couldn't believe that she did that. She knew that I was facing a seven-year sentence and she had absolutely no hesitation in providing them with the information. The officer said, "Man I'm sorry but I have to take you downtown to check this out, there is a warrant under that name. They just have to run your prints and if it's nonsense then we'll let you go."

The officer shook his head and gave me a look like he was truly sorry for me. I dropped my head out of embarrassment that the woman that I was married to would act that way in front of the police, in front of the neighbors, but most disappointedly in front of my daughter and the kids.

They ran my fingerprints and my first arrest came up but nothing else. Then they read the file which provided a description of me. The officer contacted someone in the Buffalo police department and they sent two detectives down to try to sort everything out. The officers came with some photos and a large case file, tried to interview me but I told them that I needed a lawyer, and decided that they would take me to Buffalo to appear in front of a judge so that the judge could sort everything out.

They cuffed me, put me in the back of their unmarked police car and drove me to Buffalo in the middle of a snow storm which made the otherwise hour long drive take almost twice as long. I sat in silence the entire ride, watching the snow fall and thinking about how hard I wanted to start fresh. I thought about school and how much I enjoyed my classes and I made up my mind that no matter what, I wouldn't allow anything to mess up my opportunity to do something better with my life.

I sat in jail in Buffalo for two days before finally seeing the judge. When I finally got in front of the judge, my attorney was not present so the judge set another date three weeks away. I said, "Your Honor, I need to say something," to which the judge responded, "Sir I strongly advise you to not say anything until your attorney is present."

"Your honor I understand that but I really need to get back home so I can get back to school. I'm in the middle of my first semester of college and waiting three weeks will definitely ruin my chances to complete my semester." The judge sat back, raised his eyebrows and said, "You are a student?"

"Yes sir, I'm also the provider for my family, I work two jobs and my wife is a few months away from having our second child. I've worked very hard to get my life in order and I don't want to jeopardize my employment either sir."

With a pleasantly surprised look on his face, he said, "Can you provide proof of your employment and school?" The prosecutor interrupted saying, "Your honor, with all due respect, this is a drug dealer that has disregarded the rules of this court and we still don't know his real name or his true identity."

The judge responded, "We need to figure out who you are, but I am confident that if you can provide me the proofs I asked for we can work something out to get you back home and back to school, work and your family." The prosecutor was furious but the Judge set another court date two days later and said that he would personally reach out to make sure my attorney was present.

I knew the court had no idea that my wife was actually the one that turned me in and I prayed and prayed that he wouldn't somehow find out before our next court date. I figured I had nothing to lose by throwing everything I had on the table and seeing what the court would do. I made a bunch of phone calls, my mother helped get my school documents and work proofs together and I went back to court a few days later ready to see what was going to happen.

Just before we went in front of the Judge my attorney told me that the Judge was willing to accept a guilty plea to a felony count of possession of a controlled substance in exchange for five years of probation and no prison time. He said that they would release me immediately and I could be back in Rochester in a few hours. I quickly decided to accept the plea knowing that I would be able to return to school and hopefully get back to the life that I was trying to build. The repercussions of a felony conviction never really weighed heavily on my mind. I figured probation wasn't that bad, I had done it before and since I was actually working and going to school, I thought it would be easy.

Against the objections of the prosecutor, the Judge accepted my plea deal and told me that he was very impressed with the direction that my life was headed. I signed some documents, got information about the probation department in Rochester and jumped back on a bus headed for Rochester.

When I got back, I went straight to my mother's house and within two hours, there was a knock on the door. My mother opened the door to see a police officer standing there. He handed her an envelope and said, "This is an order of protection issued against you. Please read it over and be sure that you have no contact with the petitioner." Stunned, she opened the envelope and saw that Shatina had taken out an order of protection claiming that my mother was harassing her and asking the court to make sure that she did not contact her or the kids. The following day I received a copy of the order of protection that Shatina taken out against me, claiming that I assaulted her and referring to the incident with the police and that I was currently being held for a serious drug charges in Buffalo.

Following the language of the order of protection, I contacted the police and had them escort me to my house to retrieve my belongings. When we arrived at the house no one was home. The officers came inside the house with me and I saw a large pile of my things in the corner of the room. The only thing I was worried about retrieving was my school books and notes. As I rummaged through the neatly packed items I saw that all my belongings were there, everything except for my school books. The officers went upstairs with me and helped me look around the house but we were unable to locate any of my school items.

I got back to my mother's house and fought back the tears as I told her that everything was there except for my school books. "What am I going to do about my books and my notes?" She hugged me and said, "It will be ok, you'll find a way." I wanted to believe her, to embrace her words as the truth but I felt defeated. I sat down on the couch and thought for a long time, shook off my feeling of defeat and made up my mind to go to the school and figure out a way to buy more books.

I went to the school and asked for a print out of my classes but was told that I wasn't in the computer system so I went to academic advisement to meet with a counselor and try to resolve the issue. A black woman with a nasty attitude came out and asked me to come into her office. I sat down and explained to her what happened, told her about Buffalo, my troubled marriage, the phone call to the police, court, put everything on the table. The more I talked, the more her face dropped and eventually she started crying.

She said, "I am so sorry, no one is supposed to be able to withdraw you from your classes except for the student but I withdrew you from your classes."

Totally confused I just looked at her. She continued, "Your wife came here and she was pregnant and had the kids with her and her mother and she told me this story about how you beat her and were just sent away to prison for beating her and that you would be locked away for the next seven years. She had all your books and I

277

showed her how to sell them back to the book store. I am so sorry she seemed so sincere but now I see that it was all a sham. I am so, so sorry."

I just looked at her and shook my head. I knew that Shatina didn't want me to go to school but to go that far was surprising even to me. The counselor helped me get an emergency credit on my account enabling me to buy all my books back from the book store. I was able to buy back my actual books which was miraculous as I had highlighted and taken a ton of notes in the books. I got notes from classmates for the classes I missed and was right back into the swing of things.

Work was a different story all together. Shatina went to my main job and tried to get the owner to give her my paycheck. She told him that I was a drug dealer and that I had just been sent back to Buffalo for violating my parole and said that I had beat her which is why I was sent to prison. He refused to give her my check but when I sat down to talk with him he had already promoted the part-time cook into my position. He had a truly perplexed look on his face as I explained what happened and he just couldn't comprehend that I had once been involved with drugs. He gave me my final check and wished me luck and told me that he would give me a great reference if I needed one. Fortunately, Shatina hadn't paid a visit to my part time job which quickly offered me a full-time position and put me right back to work.

I had my first series of Family Court dates before the semester ended, the first few to address the order of protection which she eventually dropped when she realized that I was requesting a trial date to prove it was nonsense, and the next few to deal with the child support order she was now requesting for my daughter. She used court for child support as one of the many threats she would pull out whenever we argued or I didn't bend to her will. I had always taken care of my daughter. In fact I took care of all her kids, buying them clothes, getting them ready for bed, getting them dressed in the morning, doing all the things that I felt a father should do for his children, biologically mine or not.

In her mind child support was a form a punishment, a way of exacting revenge against a father when she got an attitude. I heard her brag about it to her girlfriends and even to me, about how she took a "Nigga to court and got that paper" and now he sees that she is not playing games. All of her girlfriends had the exact same attitude, that court was for punishing fathers and that they were "about to get paid." This was the mentality of an overwhelming majority of the women in the hood and almost every single father that I knew had gone through or was going through the family court system.

After the restraining order was dropped, and it became clear to her that I had no intention of rekindling any sort of physical or marital type of relationship, she started with the threats again but found that she no longer had any power. She couldn't threaten to kick me out because I no longer lived with her. She couldn't threaten to call the police and tell them about my past because I had already dealt with that issue and I would simply hang the phone up whenever she would start yelling or screaming or talking crazy. So, she turned to what she had left, keeping me from seeing the kids and hitting me with child support. She changed her phone number and moved without telling me or giving me any of the new information. For a month, I had no idea where my daughter was or what was going on with the pregnancy.

I was quickly learning about what my rights were when it came to the kids. The next time I saw Shatina was when I went to court for child support. They awarded her support based on my income at the time which I did not fight. The only thing I asked the court to do was please let me see my kids which led me to discovering that in the New York family courts, they separated child support and custody issues and required you to see two different Judges to deal with the issues. The child support court had nothing to do with custody and vice versa.

I pulled her to the side and asked her if we could talk for a moment. She rolled her eyes and sucked her teeth but finally agreed to sit down and talk. I told her that I wanted to see the kids, that us not being together had nothing to do with them and she begrudgingly agreed to let me see them later that day. She dropped all the kids off at my mother's house and we hung out for the day. When she came to pick them up, her oldest son started crying. He hugged me and said, "Can we stay with you?" which made the other kids say the same thing. She saw this and got instantly pissed off, yelling, "Get your asses in this car right now." She angrily buckled each child into their car seat then slammed the doors shut on her mini-van before walking over to me, belly now huge and bulging from being only a short time away from the delivery date of our child, and said, "Nigga you trying to turn my kids against me? I got a trick for your dumb ass. I bet you don't see any of my kids again mother fucker!" She jumped in the car, slammed her door shut and sped off. When I tried calling her the next day she had once again changed her phone number.

I went to the court clerk's office and asked them what I needed to file in order to see my children. The clerk gave me a packet of papers, told me to fill them out and make three copies, have the copies notarized then return them to the clerk so they could file them. The clerk said that it would take anywhere from two to three months before I would have a court date and gave me a number to call to see if I qualified for a court appointed lawyer. I called the number and was told that I didn't qualify because I didn't have an already pending court case. I was told to file the papers myself and once I was given a court date to call them back to see if they could appoint a lawyer.

I had no idea how to complete the paperwork so I just followed the instructional packet that came with the forms, made the copies, got them notarized and filed them with the clerk. I got a notice for the court date, had her served with a copy and was forced to wait until the court date before I could see my daughter again. I tried to include the other kids in my visitation and custody request but was told that I had no legal right to see them because they were not my biological children and I had not officially adopted them. Because our child had not yet been born, I also wasn't able to include him in the request and was informed that I would probably have to go through the entire process again once he was born.

As soon as Shatina was served she went ballistic, calling me and threatening to have her brothers beat me up, threatening to call Kwame because "You know that Kwame will kill you quick!" She bombarded my mother with phone calls, relaying the same threats to her to pass on to me until my mother just stopped answering the phone for a few days.

Meanwhile, I was attending classes, working and trying to save up enough money to buy a car and get my own place. I had to check in with my probation officer once a week and had to undergo random drug tests so I stayed away from weed, turning instead to cigarettes in the hopes that they would provide some sort of relief from the stress and was soon smoking a pack, sometimes two packs every day. My mind racing, I was unable to sleep at night, I had difficulty focusing and studying was almost impossible but I kept pushing forward. I was determined to not let anything get me sidetracked from finishing school.

As I learned more about the court process I decided it was time to also file visitation papers for my oldest son. I was seeing him more frequently but it was still on the whim of Heather and there were plenty of times when we didn't agree on things which would lead to her not letting me spend time with him. I was tired of feeling like I had to kiss her ass to be able to see my child and thought that the courts would provide a more stable and consistent visitation arrangement.

I was going through similar situations with Jennifer but it was not as extreme. She would get an attitude, I would go see her, spend some time with her, we would share some intimate moments and for the next few weeks or a month she would be cordial and I would see my son on a regular basis. She would get an attitude because we weren't spending time together and then the cycle would start all over again. We never got to the point of going to court; any time my son needed anything she would tell me and I would take care of it immediately and seeing him was not a problem unless we were going through the down side of our cycle.

I hadn't spoken to Shatina in over a month when my mother called me and said she was almost certain that Shatina had given birth. My mother worked at a school that sat directly behind the apartment building where Shatina's mother lived and as she was looking out of her office window she saw Shatina drive up and get out of her mini-van carrying a baby in a car seat, looking like her stomach was pretty much gone.

My heart felt like it was in the pit of my stomach. I knew that we were going through problems and I knew that Shatina would stoop pretty low as evidenced by her telling the police about my warrant and selling my school books, but I never thought that she would deprive me of my right to be there when our child was born. In that moment, any positive feelings that I had for her were replaced with pure disdain. For the first time, I accepted that she would never change, that all the negative things that I saw in her were actually who she was and not just bits of who she could be when she was upset or angry. All I could do was shake my head, not in disbelief but in disappointment in myself and deep regret for breaking the code of brotherhood and messing with her in the first place.

A few more days went by before she finally called me and told me that she had delivered my son on May 1, 1996, and that he was born healthy, with no problems or concerns. With absolutely no input from me she named my son on her own. I never even brought up her not calling me to tell me she was in labor or her naming our son without consulting me. I knew it was pointless and would only lead to more drama so I simply moved on, swallowed my anger and hurt and focused on doing what I could to make sure that I was a part of my son's life moving forward.

Between the money I had saved from working and the additional money left over from my student loans, I was finally able to buy a car enabling me to take classes at the main campus in the Westside suburb of Henrietta. I was still working my full-time job but really wanted to graduate on schedule despite starting my studies a semester behind the rest of my class. I spoke with the Dean of my program and received a waiver to take 21 credits in the upcoming Fall semester as opposed to the normal 12 credits. I filled my schedule with most of my physical education requirements as well as an anatomy and physiology course and I decided to take a black history course.

I accepted an internship at a local gymnastics center where I volunteered coaching athletes for the Special Olympics. I also secured a couple different student teaching assignments in a suburban elementary school, teaching physical education to kindergarten and first graders. I discovered that I truly loved working with kids especially the Special Olympic athletes. I left the gym feeling fulfilled, like I accomplished something and always looked forward to going back, feeling more like it was a privilege rather than work.

At the end of the semester I asked if I could continue working with the Special Olympics, even though my internship credits at the gym would be over. They gladly kept me on as the men's coach for the Monroe County Special Olympics. I had an amazing experience working with individuals with a variety of learning abilities. I learned techniques for helping students with varying levels of Autism and Down Syndrome and began learning a lot about gymnastics terminology and skills.

The athletes seemed to enjoy me almost as much as I enjoyed them and I started to build relationships with their parents. We exchanged information on what worked and didn't work with their children which they loved and helped me work more effectively with the kids. The gym owner eventually offered me a job working at the gym which I quickly accepted. She gave me a packet of papers to fill out, told me to bring them back with me so that she could officially put me on the schedule.

I couldn't believe that things were falling into place for me and I started feeling like I had found my true calling. I sat down and started filling out the application; name, address, work history, smiling and patting myself on the back as I wrote. I got to the end of the application and my heart felt like it was stuck in my throat as I read, "Have you ever been convicted of a felony. . ." For the first time since pleading guilty in that Buffalo court room I thought about the consequences of that day. I contemplated lying, just checking the "no" box and turning in the application but that went against my instincts and more importantly I didn't want to lie to the owner of the gym. I felt that I needed to check the "yes" box but couldn't help thinking that doing so would mean I would have to explain to her what happened and that I wouldn't get the job. I wrestled back and forth with that question on the application for the rest of the week and dreaded having to go back to the gym and turn in my application. A few sleepless nights later, I finally checked the 'yes' box on the application and figured that instead of writing about what I was convicted of I would talk about it with her, hoping that hearing it directly from me would make some sort of difference.

The owner asked me to come into her office, took my paperwork from me, placed it into a file with my name on it and said, "Congratulations! Here is the schedule, let me know if any of your class times here conflict with your class times at MCC and we will try to change them." Heart beating so fast that I could feel my pulse rushing up the side of my neck, I said, "I would like to explain why I checked 'yes' on the application."

Puzzled and not knowing what I was referring to she said,

"Yes to what?"

"I've been convicted of a felony, for drug possession. I'm still on probation for it now." I could feel the blood rushing to my face as it turned red from anxious embarrassment. She looked at me, seeing how extremely uncomfortable I was and said, "Did your crimes involve anything related to children or violence?"

I shook my head no and said, "Of course not." She handed me another form which granted the gym permission to do a background check and explained that she was only interested in any legal incidents that may have been directed towards or involved children. I told her that there were none but that I was involved in a custody battle for my kids with my wife and that was my only court involvement regarding children. We talked about the kids for a while and then she told me not to worry about anything. She reassured me that the job was still mine unless something came up in the background check that had to do with kids or violence.

For the next few weeks every time I came into the gym I felt as if it would be my last time. I felt that it was just a matter of time before she would call me into her office and tell me that I wouldn't be able to work there because of my conviction and that feeling remained with me until my last day working there more than a year later.

I was now forced to think about my chosen path as an educator and what types of hurdles might present themselves as I moved closer towards completing my degree and started to actively look for a job teaching. For the first time I thought, 'damn, I might not be able to teach.' I knew that I could go and talk with someone at my school to find out if my conviction would prohibit me from getting my teaching certification and finding a job but I couldn't bring myself to do it. I didn't want anything to discourage me from continuing to move in a positive direction. I just kept my head in the books, went to work, went to the gym, continued volunteering with the Special Olympics and kept my fingers crossed that all would work itself out in the end.

I was finally able to get a lawyer and focus on trying to fight for more time with my kids. I filed to establish visitation. Shatina filed for custody then I countered with a custody filing of my own and the battle began. She had already reached out to Quan on a number of occasions with the hopes of getting him to try to confront me. On occasion he would get all worked up about some lie she told him, and we would end up getting into an argument. I was astonished at how easily she could manipulate him into believing what she said especially considering that he was the one that had told me for years about how manipulative she was and about how she had tried to set up past boyfriends for beat downs, only to have them find out later that she had completely fabricated the story.

When that didn't work she decided to file yet another order of protection against me, this time stating that I pulled up next to her at a stoplight, took out a gun and threatened to kill her while the kids were in the car. She had one of her ratchet girlfriends vouch for her story and sign off on her declaration. I would have had a difficult time disproving her claim as the courts almost always took the word of the alleged endangered party except that the time and date she specified on her complaint conflicted with the time and date that I was at work at the gymnastics center where literally hundreds of people saw me and could vouch for my whereabouts. For the first time, I was happy that I had taken the time to talk to the owner about my personal situation and let her know about the custody battle and Shatina's unpredictability. She reassured me that she would provide testimony regarding my alibi during the time in question.

The court entered the temporary order without ever speaking to me, as she knew that they would, and ordered me to stay away from her and the kids until the matter was resolved. I went almost two months without seeing or having any contact with my kids before we could finally get to court and address the issues. By that time, she had cooled off and she withdrew the order before my lawyer had an opportunity to address the validity of her claims. I was furious and insisted that we attack the order and prove that she was succeeding in manipulating the courts to try to gain an edge in the custody battle but my attorney insisted that it was no longer an issue because she dropped the order.

Meanwhile I was going back and forth to court with Heather to try to work out some sort of stable visitation and custody agreement for our son. The legal battles were starting to wear me down and I was missing a lot of work and sometimes classes so that I could attend court or meet with my attorney. I remembered all the stories that women told me about how their kid's fathers weren't doing anything for them and never saw their kids and couldn't help wondering how much of that had to do with the resistance that was put up by the woman herself. I knew quite a few friends that were going through similar situations and had simply given up, thrown their hands up and said, "Fuck this, I don't need the bull shit," and walked right out of their children's lives. I started to envy them, wishing that my heart was built that way and that I too could just walk away but the love I had for my children took precedence over the bullshit.

One of the many hurdles to my visitation and custody cases was my previous criminal record. Shatina brought it up in court every chance she could, calling me a 'convict' and a 'drug dealer.' There were times when all I could do was hang my head, especially when I saw how the hearing examiner, similar to a Judge, looked at and spoke to me, with a total lack of respect and almost a defiance against my fight to be involved with my children. At one point, I was sitting in a court room by myself, waiting for the hearing examiner to call my child support case when the hearing examiner looked up and asked me for my name. I told him, he then shifted through some papers until he found the file for my case, at which point he quickly scanned through it then lifted his head and said, "Why are you here today?"

"I am requesting a modification of the child support order your honor. I can't afford to pay what the court is requiring me to pay now."

He looked through some more papers and said, "It says here that you are going to school full-time?"

"Yes sir, I'm working towards finishing my degree so I can get my teaching certification. I am hoping to be a teacher when I finish."

"And you are currently working full time?"

"Yes sir, I also work part-time teaching at a gym and I work ten to twenty hours a week student teaching as a requirement for one of my classes."

"Mr. Bost, this is off the record of course, but I strongly suggest that you give up on this school stuff and find yourself another full-time job. If you put the same time you are putting into school and student teaching into another full-time-job then you would have no problem meeting your child support requirements."

Stunned by what I just heard, I struggled to find the words to say anything in response. First I was confused, I had to replay the words he had just said over and over again in my head to make sure I didn't misunderstand anything. When I figured out that what I heard was in fact what he said, I went from confusion to intense anger. I wanted to say, "With all due respect, mother fuck you your Honor," but instead all I could muster was something like, "I am working towards trying to build a foundation for my future that will enable me to better take care of my family and myself and that requires education."

He just looked down and shook his head, saying in a completely disinterested, almost irritated tone, "Ok sir, we will hear your case in a minute." And as to be expected, he denied my request to modify the support order and instead added on more money for me to pay, making it clear that any future request would end the same way.

I was furious at what he said, telling me straight up to quit school and get another job. What type of advice is that to give a young father trying to establish a foundation to better take care of his children?! Unfortunately, my experience in that court room was representative of the norm. I was being kicked around and abused by the system which seemed to only be concerned with one thing, extracting as much money as possible from me and other fathers.

Child support hearings moved quickly and decisions were usually on the spot while custody and visitation cases could drag on for years. At that time, there were very few success stories from a father's perspective as the Judges still seemed to be heavily in favor of keeping kids with their mothers and putting fathers on an 'every-other-weekend-and-some-holidays' type of schedule with their kids. I was determined to remain as active as possible in their lives and despite the thoughtless advice of the hearing examiner, I decided that staying in school would be the most beneficial for the long term success of myself and my kids.

I was really enjoying being a college student. I could feel my mind expanding and was joyfully embracing learning new things, especially knowing that each class I took brought me closer to accomplishing my first academic goal of attaining my associates degree. As a physical education major I took the exact same core classes that the first year nursing majors took in addition to my physical education core classes. I took courses that taught us the fundamentals in sports such as football, basketball and baseball, and introduced me to new sports like tennis and racquetball. I also studied anatomy and physiology, sports psychology and took courses focused on education technics, which led to my student teaching positions.

I had to take a required course in statistics which kicked my ass big time. I had always struggled with math and found myself studying for at least twenty hours during the week leading up to each exam, only to find out later that I received a grade of a 'C' or a 'D'. While I struggled in my math course, I excelled in my English and history courses. My English professor, Ann Tippett, a bubbly, passionate, engaging woman, took an interest in me from the start and really encouraged me to continue to pursue my goals. Whenever she would notice that I was mentally somewhere else, she would take the time to talk to me after class and provide encouragement to stay focused.

Eventually, I felt comfortable enough that I began sharing aspects of my life with her, discussing some of my experiences and venting about my domestic issues. She was amazed that despite all the resistance I experienced from Shatina and the drama with the kids, along with working my full-time job and usually juggling a part time job, that I was able to still prioritize school and get fairly decent grades. She introduced me to her husband who was also an English professor, and he met with me a few times over a couple of months interviewing me for a book he was writing about adult students facing obstacles. I was thrilled to be recognized for my goals and was finally feeling like I was receiving some acceptance within the world I was now working towards being a part of. Her encouragement provided me with a much needed boost of energy that I was able draw from, for many, many years to come.

While I thrived in my English course, I found myself completely fascinated with my black history class. I was excited to take the class and I remember the first day, sitting in the very front row, listening intently in amazement as the professor started to speak. The Professor, Dr. John Walker, a thin, light skinned, grey haired gentleman, told us that he and his family had strong southern roots despite living in the Rochester area for a generation or more. He was one of the most articulate people I had ever heard speak, a minister and natural born orator, he delivered his lectures as if he were on the pulpit with passion and precision that captivated me as well as the rest of the class.

Dr. Walker took us on a chronological journey through slavery, introducing me to individuals that I had never heard of before; Nat Turner, Crispus Attucks, Gabriel and many other leaders of slave revolts. He opened my mind to look deeper at works by authors like James Baldwin, Richard Wright and Langston Hughes. I was blown away by what I was learning but more importantly, he provided insight into why I hadn't learned this before and gave hints, encouraging us to look deeper at the system we lived in and how it had historically failed black folks in this country.

I learned about the laws that were put in place to keep Africans enslaved, about the long-term effects of "Willie Lynch" type programing on black communities. He broke down the way skin tone was used to separate black folks as many of the lighter skinned slaves, most often products of the rape of black enslaved women by white slave owners, were used in the house doing domesticated work, while the darker slaves were used in the fields and usually received much more barbaric treatment.

Through his class I started to rethink my own identity and re-evaluate my experiences through a fresh set of enlightened eyes. I thought about my experiences at #37 school, being called 'white boy' and having to fight with the thugs in order to gain their respect. I thought about all the mothers of the black girls that I dated and how they would touch my hair and talk about "Having grand-babies with good hair." For the first time in my life I began to understand that my experiences being bi-racial were less personal then what I thought and more so related to the long standing programing experienced in the Americas.

The more Dr. Walker spoke, the deeper I listened, furiously taking notes and then re-reading the notes after class, pulling every book that he referenced and reading on my own outside of what was required for class. I was completely engulfed in learning and my entire focus had shifted, leading me to conclude that I had found a new calling. I wanted to teach history so that I could continue to research and learn but more importantly so that maybe I could inspire someone the same way that Professor Tippett and Dr. Walker had inspired me.

20 "THEY KILLED MY BABY"

While I was moving ahead, completely focused on changing the path of my life, many of my friends were still caught up in the streets. Puba was still heavily involved in the streets and had established himself as one of the main connections for large quantities of high grade weed. G dabbled in selling weed here and there but mainly still worked with Selector running the restaurant. Tee and his crew were pretty much the main coke connect for the entire Westside of Rochester and could always be seen riding around town in new cars while showing off wads of cash.

Quan went back to the Bronx and was hustling between New York City and Poughkeepsie, a small town about an hour to the north of the Bronx. Kwame teamed up with Kevin Chiles and a few other big time dudes from the Bronx and was lucky to make it out of a series of mass indictments handed down throughout the entire Soundview and Castlehill areas. One of the young dudes that came up under Kwame, Pistol Pete, had just been indicted for multiple murders and for running what would become one of the largest gangs on the east coast, the now infamous Sex, Money, Murder crew.

Whenever I ran into anyone that knew what I was involved in from my street days, they would always assume that I was still in the streets. I had always been low key and never flashed money or bought fancy cars or clothes. I liked the freedom that came with anonymity and was raised around old-school gangsters that stressed the importance of keeping your business private. Small cities like Rochester and Buffalo, where everyone knew everyone and people loved to talk about who had what, were especially difficult to make substantial amounts of money and remain under the radar.

I prided myself on always remaining the same. If I had a few hundred thousand dollars hidden away somewhere or if I was dead broke, carrying only a bus pass and lint in my pocket, I always looked and acted the same. So it was understandable for the people that truly knew me to think I still had some sort of street hustle. Till this day, despite having been out of the streets and drug sales for over two decades, there are still those who are convinced beyond a doubt that my current success and life achievements are somehow attributable to some type of street activity.

My transition into "square" life created a lot of distrust and uneasiness for my former peers. People from the hood and those that survive in the streets, tend to have a distrust for the mainstream system and anyone that is a part of that system or not in the streets. I understood the mentality as I was just a few years removed from being a part of society's underbelly. Despite working and going to school within the system, I still found myself distrustful of my new environment, creating an always present uneasiness within myself.

Many times, I was tempted with a proposition from my former peers who knew my reputation for being honest and trustworthy. They would offer me drugs on consignment knowing that I always repaid my debt and never cheated my partners. My street credit score would have been considered A+, a perfect 850 and there was always someone looking to enlist my business skills to expand their business. As is usually the case, when trying to cut away from a bad habit, I definitely had moments when I considered taking them up on their offers especially when I was dead broke and struggling. I would calculate how much I could make, go through a plan in my head to flip the package in the most efficient and profitable way, then fantasize about collecting and enjoying the money. But in the end, I always turned them down. I knew that it was my nature to give a 110% to anything I did and I wouldn't just flip one package but would go all the way in which was the exact opposite of where I saw my new life headed.

While I was truly enjoying my experience with school I was looking forward to the summer and a slow-down in my studies. To celebrate the start of summer, I planned a small Memorial Day BBQ for a few of my friends at my mother's house. We set up a card table in the driveway by the garage, fired up the grill and got some drinks. I cooked my usual side dishes and put a small radio in the garage. We all vibed to the music as we ate, played cards and just enjoyed the official beginning of summer.

I called Puba and told him to come through; we hadn't seen much of each other as I was busy with school and work, and he was still very much involved in his business in the streets. I tried to distance myself from what was going on in the streets which meant that it was difficult to hang out with Puba and some of my other friends that still ran in those circles. They knew that I was trying to do the school and work thing and respected my decisions to try to change my life so they would usually keep their distance, specifically if they were involved in something that could potentially get me in some serious trouble.

I stopped hanging around anything that could get me into trouble. It made no sense to risk getting caught up in someone else's bullshit when I wasn't even making any money with or around them. I no longer had as much in common with many of my old friends. I had to put in time at my job and school while they had all day to hang out, drink, smoke and chill. They didn't have to worry about a schedule or being somewhere on time or getting to sleep because they had to get up early.

There were definitely times when I was envious that they could still hang out and have fun but I knew deep down that I was making the right choice. I knew that I wanted a future that was bigger than the streets and I was growing to accept that moving towards that future meant moving away from some of the people that I cared about. It also meant learning how to balance the time in my day and working sixty hours a week, being an active father to my children and going to school full-time meant that I just didn't have time to hang out anymore.

Puba called me to ask what I was drinking then he showed up about an hour later with a gallon bottle of Hennessy. He handed me the bottle, we gave each other a hug as we always did and before I could walk away he said, "Man, are you going to open that bottle or what? What the hell are you waiting for??" We both busted out laughing as I went and grabbed two large cups and filled them up about halfway.

Since our early days of high school, Puba was the only one that could go drink for drink with me and still stand at the end of the night. We drank so many people under the table that eventually, people would see us coming and start heading the other way. G had given up trying to drink with us years before, after Puba and I had to carry him home and he ended up in bed for the next week, sick with a serious case of alcohol poisoning.

We sat down at the table and ate, drank and talked until it was dark. I was telling him how much I was enjoying school but that sometimes I missed making money in the streets. He said, "White boy listen. Man you are the smartest one out of everybody, you are making the right moves. These streets were never supposed to be for you. You have more potential than anybody. You are destined for big things, things way beyond this bull shit here!"

He told me about a store he was opening with Kip on Jefferson Avenue. Kip was planning on opening a second store, selling clothes, sneakers, mix tapes and various goods popular in the hood. Puba said he was going to partner up with our high school friend Terry St. John and they were in the process of building shelving and counters and installing phones and a security system. He wasn't ready to give up the streets all together but he hinted that he was growing tired of all the bull shit and wanted to start making some legitimate money.

We toasted to his words, took a drink of the straight Hennessy and talked some more. We laughed about the time I beat up the crack head outside of Jenks & Jones and about the times we would drop small pieces of paper on the floor and crack up laughing as Shaky would pick them up and try to smoke them. We laughed about the time Wade left us and we had to fight all the dudes from Black Mob by ourselves. We talked and laughed until he had to go then we hugged and made plans to get together the following weekend to go to the beach, grab some drinks and walk the pier.

A few days after the BBQ I got a call from Puba's mother. She said in a calm voice, "Jason, I don't know if you heard anything but people around here are saying that Craig was shot and he's dead. I haven't been able to get in touch with him since yesterday. They killed my baby."

I just listened and then said, "Naw, I haven't heard anything about that. Where did they say it happened?" She said, "On Genesee Street, at the apartments over by Brooks Ave. They say that the police are over there bringing out his body right now."

I jumped in my car and made my way down Brooks Ave. When I got close to Genesee Street, I saw the entire block in front of the apartment building cornered off with yellow tape and there were eight or nine police cars parked all around the block. I walked up to one of the guys wearing a suit, obviously a detective and asked him if he could tell me what happened. He said that someone had been killed in the building, so I asked if they knew who it was and he told me that they weren't sure, they were trying to ID the victim.

I explained that I had just received a call from a friend's mother and she was worried that the victim might be her son. He asked me to describe what her son looked like, I said, "A little shorter than me, dark skinned, a little heavier than me with a short, faded haircut." The detective said, "naw, it's not her son, this guy is much bigger, a lot heavier than that."

Breathing a sigh of relief, I thanked him and took his card and headed to Puba's house. Puba's sister was there along with his aunt, whom I was meeting for the first time. His mother, looking completely lost, gave me a hug and I told her about the detective on Genesee street. She said, "Baby, everybody is saying that it's Craig. They started telling me last night that someone shot him. I can feel it in my bones that that's Craig."

I gave his aunt the detective's card and she called him. After speaking with him for a few minutes she asked me if I would go with her to the morgue so we could take a look at the body and make sure that it wasn't Craig. I kept saying, "I know it's not him, I just don't feel it, let's go so we can put his mother's mind at ease."

His mother stopped me, "Jason, please steady yourself. I know that's my baby and I know that's your brother so be ready for what these people are going to show you." I hugged her again and reassured her that all would be well.

The morgue was located directly next door to my college. I had passed the building hundreds of times driving to school but never knew what it was until we pulled up into the parking lot and went inside. A worker buzzed us into the building then guided us to a small dark room decorated with only a few chairs set up randomly and placed against three of the walls of the room. On the fourth wall, there was a large window that started about waist high and went up just above my head. The window was covered in a dark grey curtain, completely blacking out the other side of the window except for a few rays of light fighting their way through the top and bottom of the curtain, making small shapes of light on the floor and ceiling inside of the room.

Puba's aunt kept saying, "Jason, I know its him, please just be strong for me." I nodded my head acknowledging her words but I knew that she was wrong. The man that brought us to the room came back in and closed the door then explained that the curtain would open and the body would be on the other side of the glass.

He said to take our time and let him know if we recognized the person on the table. "Are you ready?" he asked.

Puba's aunt nodded her head and grabbed my hand then the man knocked on the window. A second or two later, the curtain was pulled back revealing the body of a dark skinned man lying on the table, the length of his body running parallel to the length of the window. There was a dark blanket on top of him with the top portion pulled back revealing his face and shoulders. I breathed a sigh of relief and was getting ready to say, "Phew! It's not him! I told you that it wasn't him!!"

As I prepared to speak I felt her hand tighten around my hand as she leaned her body against mine to steady herself. She said, in a quiet, high-pitched semi-scream, "it's him, that's my nephew, that's Craig." I gave her a confused look then I looked at the body again, this time taking a big step towards the window. The man on the table was much darker than Puba and looked much heavier. I looked closer, finally seeing a resemblance in his cheeks. Then I looked closer yet, this time at his nose and his hairline and realized that she was right. It was Puba.

She pulled me closer to her, "Baby, it's ok, everything will be ok." I don't know what the man saw in my face but he quickly knocked on the window again and the curtain was closed. He gave me a few moments to register what was happening then gently asked me if I would sign a form indicating that I identified the body. I filled out the forms, signed them and handed it back then he gave me a card for another detective and told me that we should give him a call.

I thought about the conversation that Puba and I just had, how we laughed about old times and talked about the future. I was well aware of the life and death consequences of the streets. I saw Lamont put into the ground and I was there when Shawny was shot and when he finally passed. I had friends that died violently during high school as well as after. One shot after an argument in a dice game, another shot during a drug deal, yet another an innocent bystander hit by a stray bullet, and on and on and on.

I had become numb to the consequences of violence, matured in a way that no one should ever have to mature and I felt nothing but empty dullness. No pain. No tears. No hurt. No sadness. No anger, just numb.

Everything leading up to the funeral was a blur. We found out that Puba went to the apartment building to meet with a couple people that had been contacting him throughout the day. The rumor was that they wanted to buy a few pounds of weed from him but Puba was leery about dealing with them because he didn't trust them.

He was shot sometime around 9 p.m. the night before they pulled his body out of the apartment building. Someone said they heard a loud gunshot around that time and it seemed to match the coroner's time of death. Puba was shot with a shotgun at close range, a single blast to his chest. They said the injury was severe enough that there was little hope of him recovering even if they found him right after the shooting.

G was totally messed up after Puba's death. The friend that Puba was with came and told G that night, right after it happened, that something was wrong. He had dropped Puba off in front of the building then waited for him to come out which never happened. Instead four dudes came out looking around very nervously and hurried into a black Nissan Pathfinder then took off.

Then the friend took G to the apartment where they both went up and down the hallways calling Puba's name but heard nothing and no one in the building was willing to talk to them. When G found out that Puba was in the same building, in one of the apartments that they walked by as he called out his name, he couldn't take it and ended up breaking down completely. He took it personally, as if it was his fault and shouldered the weight of the incident even though he was nowhere close to the building when it happened. I believe he felt that if he would have been with Puba that he would have never gone into the building or that he would have been with him and somehow been able to prevent anything from happening.

While G withdrew, the rest of us mourned in our own individual ways. Even though our pain was personal to each of us we all stayed together for pretty much the next three or four days leading up to the funeral. Deidrick and Darius, Big Daryl's twin brothers along with Daryl, Shawn "Kool-Aid" Brown, Paul Griffin, Kip, G, and a host of others all gathered at Genesee Valley Park before the wake, each bringing bottles of liquor, cases of beer and enough weed for everyone to smoke ten or twenty blunts a piece. I hadn't seen EF in a few years and he even came through to show his respect and support.

We passed bottles back and forth followed by blunt after blunt after blunt, sipped and puffed, laughed and reminisced, all sharing stories about each other sprinkled in with stories about Puba. There was a genuine closeness between us all, a true familiar bond that was real and for the first time in many of our lives we openly said to each other "I love you bro," or "I love you fam," and declared our loyalty to each other as brothers.

My brother Calvin stayed close to me the entire time, watching as I interacted with my friends and observing the bonds and connection we all shared. On occasion, I would notice him looking on as we talked and laughed, and I saw wonderment in his eyes, a reflection of the respect that he had for our bond. Later, as I grew older and reflected on this moment, I realized that this was the moment that my brother made up his mind that he wanted the same type of brotherhood that he witnessed with us and I am convinced that it was definitely a factor in influencing him to make some of the decisions he would later make in his own life. As my little brother, he was greeted with the same love and respect from my friends as I was and he experienced the embrace of true brotherhood. While he had established a group of his own friends that all had the same sort of love for him, he had never experienced their presence in a time despair such as he was experiencing with Puba's death.

This was Calvin's first funeral, the first time that someone he knew was murdered and he was observing a ritual that many of us knew too well. Funerals, especially for the young, tend to bring out the best in people. They bring people together and help people forget old grudges at least temporarily, and make people come together in a truly supportive way. While the love and support was all genuine, it almost never lasted past the funeral. A few days or maybe a week later, everyone was back to leading their own lives, dealing with their own problems, all while still trying to cope with the recent loss.

By this point I was experienced at losing someone close, I had been to funerals for victims of violence and visited friends in the hospital as they laid there suffering from stab wounds or recovering from holes left in their bodies from bullets. I knew the pattern of death, the way people responded around it and how things always seemed to go back to the way they were soon after it was all over, even though we as individuals never really truly recovered. I too loved that closeness and cherished it in the moment more so because I knew it wouldn't last long, at least not in a collective group setting. I knew that might be the last time that all of us were together in that close-knit way until another one of us died then we would do it all again.

When someone dies as a result of violence and no one is arrested, it adds more depth to an already difficult situation. People are more on edge, more distrustful of outsiders and hyper-vigilant to any potential threats, real or imagined. Even before his body was found, there were rumors circulating about who may have set him up or even pulled the trigger and before he was laid to rest, small "seek and destroy" parties were formed; weapons were collected and a hurried plan was put together to try to find those thought to be responsible and to exact revenge.

At the age of 25 I had seen this all before and learned that the suspects in the moment weren't always the ones responsible. I heard of numerous people being shot and killed because someone suspected them of a loved one's murder only to find out later that they had absolutely nothing at all to do with it. One of the benefits of being numb was that it slowed down my thought process. With my emotions being almost non-existent, I could sit back and watch, take things in and not react on raw emotion. As they gathered up troops to head out to literally try to hunt down the alleged perpetrators, I fell back, stayed close to Calvin and a few others that were either in an emotional funk similar to mine or just not built for retaliatory behaviors, and just waited to see how things played out.

I went to spend time with my sons, watching them play and run without a care in the world, totally oblivious to my struggles or anything outside of their own little world. As my mind floated back and forth from reminiscing about times with Puba to the confusion and pain of the moment, through the love of my kids I began to regain my emotions. My love for them created an opening for the sorrow, anger and regret associated with Puba's death and my thoughts slowly and painfully began to humanize again.

I lifted Puba's coffin alongside Stephon "Twin" Dilbert, Paul Griffin, Kip and a few of our closest friends, and we placed him into the back of the black hearse. G was supposed to be a pallbearer as well but just couldn't find the strength to pick up his brother's coffin. We stood back, hands folded in front of us and watched as they closed the doors then we walked towards our cars in complete silence. As the funeral procession snaked its way around corners and through neighborhoods towards the suburban cemetery where Puba was to be buried, I marveled at how many cars followed, each one carrying people that knew and genuinely cared for and loved him.

We arrived at the cemetery, parked, then gathered at the back of the hearse to collectively lift the coffin and carry it to the already prepared open gravesite. We placed the coffin on top of large, grey strips that covered the top of the gravesite and then stepped back and listened as the minister began to say a few words about Puba before inviting everyone to take a flower and place it on top of the casket. Tears flowed down everyone's faces and sobs came indiscriminately from every direction as women hugged and comforted their men while others moaned in agony and pain.

I stood next to G and put my arm around him to help hold him up as his legs appeared to turn into useless pieces of overcooked spaghetti. He slouched down, sobbing, unable to regain his composure and I felt the heaviness of his body as I tried to hold him up. Someone else came and helped me keep him from falling as he went limp.

Eventually, people started to clear out while our core group remained by the casket. We put our arms around each other as one person would say their peace then slowly walk away towards their cars, open their car doors, then slowly drive away. I stayed until everyone had left; a few cemetery workers mulled about nearby, obviously anxious for me to leave so that they could start the process of covering the grave with dirt. I kneeled by the grave, bowed my head and shared my last words with my best friend and eventually gathered myself, stood and walked to my car and left the cemetery.

21 CONTRADICTIONS

I was offered a position working as a counselor in an on campus unsecured group home facility for youth. The campus had several cottages, each housing kids separated by gender, age and need. I was set to work at one of the houses with boys in their late teens, most of whom had legal problems, family issues, developmental and behavioral problems or combinations of all of the above.

I was excited to start but the day before my scheduled start date I came in to complete the necessary paperwork and once again found myself confronted with the question that had prevented me from moving forward with a number of jobs, 'Have you ever been convicted of a felony?' My heart sank as I made my way into the supervisor's office and started to explain my status as a convicted felon who was still on probation.

The supervisor, a middle-aged white man whose grey hair and rough appearance made him look much older than he was, told me that if I checked the 'yes' box the administration would surely not hire me. He suggested checking 'no' and said that it would remain between the two of us. I debated with myself for some time before finally checking the 'no' box and handing him my paperwork. The next day I started work but that application stayed at the back of my mind until the day I finally moved on to another job and then that question would once again create a problem.

Working with the kids at the group home kept me grounded. They were all street kids, most came from households where their parents had drug problems or were incarcerated and many of the kids started hustling at an early age, eight, nine, ten years old. Unlike myself, they had very limited opportunities and hearing about their struggles was heart breaking at times. Most of these young men had tremendous potential and intelligence and many even had a strong desire to do the right thing, they were just lacking role models and were wrapped up in the same sort of conditioned, imitative behaviors that once guided me towards the streets.

While I worked with them to help try to improve their decision making processes I couldn't help but recognize the hypocrisy, especially working with the youth that were on probation. I was still on probation myself and seeing my own probation officer once a month. During one of these visits, I was sitting in a chair in the large reception area waiting for my name to be called so that I could be buzzed through the back door and into the corridor that held all the probation officer's individual offices. I looked up and saw one of the kids from my group home come through the door, sign in and then look around for a seat. He took a seat a few rows behind me, put his head down, put his headphones on, turned on his Walkman and closed his eyes.

My heart started racing as I thought about the potential consequences of him finding out that I too was on probation. I nervously looked back, trying to determine if he really hadn't seen me or if he was trying to play it off. My probation officer cracked open the door and just before calling out my name he saw me and waved for me to come back. I hurriedly made my way to the door, stopping to look back as it closed and seeing that he still had his head down, nodding it to the music with his eyes closed. I shook my head, relieved that I didn't have to try to figure out what to say if he would have figured out that I was no different than he was, stuck in the system and going through similar legal issues.

As I put in overtime at the job and pushed ahead with school, my brother Calvin was steadily moving in the opposite direction. He had started hanging out more frequently in the city, around some of my friends, spending his days smoking weed and skipping school. They tried to steer him in the right direction, encouraged him to focus on school and kept him out of any serious trouble but his desire to be a part of the closeness he saw at Puba's funeral was driving him further and further away from what he was supposed to be doing. My mother was growing more frustrated with him and suggested that I take some time to talk to him so I bought an extra ticket for him to come with me and a few of my boys to a big concert out at Darrien Lake amusement park.

Calvin decided that he wanted to drink with us so he bought a variety of small bottles of liquor, jumped in the car and headed to the amusement park with us. Junior and G both tried to tell him that he shouldn't mix all the different types of liquor but he was intent on proving that he knew what he was doing so we all shrugged our shoulders and let him learn the hard way.

After an entire day of riding roller coasters in the hot sun and taking shots between rides, we finally made our way into the venue for the show. Before the first act hit the stage, Calvin had his head down, resting it on the chair in front of him, lifting it every few minutes only after he vomited. A few minutes later, Junior, who against his best judgment decided to help Calvin finish off his bottles, was doing the same. G, Paul and I all split our time between passing blunts back and forth, watching the show and cracking up laughing at the two of them.

As soon as we got back to the car Calvin said, "Man, I wish I would have listened to you, that was horrible!" I just nodded my head, "Lesson learned little brother. You better believe that I will never tell you anything wrong, no need for you to make the same mistakes I did. You have a lot of wisdom around you, take advantage of it whenever you can." He nodded then closed his eyes as he rested his head against the coolness of the car door and tried to stop his head from spinning.

Calvin was never a street dude; he grew up in suburbia surrounded by other suburban kids and always managed to find a good group of people to hang around. When he attended Camp Good Days & Special Times, a camp for kids with cancer and their siblings, he was also surrounded by counselors and other campers that genuinely loved him. His popularity in school kept increasing as people were drawn to his openly generous heart and extreme loyalty.

As soon as he found a way to get around, usually with one of his friends that had access to their parent's car or were fortunate enough to have their own car, he started making his way to the Westside of Rochester, stopping by my friends' houses and hanging out with Kip at his store on Jefferson Ave. They all kept him sheltered and never let him stray too far in a direction that could lead to any real trouble. He was everyone's little brother and everyone loved him to death.

While Calvin was out exploring the city and enjoying the life of an average teenager, I was stressed out dealing with more and more bullshit from Shatina and new issues with Heather. Heather was preparing to marry a dude named Joe, supposedly the same guy she had dated in high school and had been with off and on even before we were involved. The tension between us was slowly evaporating and I got to see my son on a regular basis. However as soon as she was married, the tension returned, fueled by the obvious disdain that her husband had for me.

I had no problem with him but he had a serious attitude every time he saw me. I wrote it off to him simply being one of those bitch-ass type of dudes and didn't think much about it until my son called me crying saying that Joe had whipped him because he allegedly talked back to him. I immediately called Heather to get her side of the story before I moved to confront her husband. She said that it wasn't as serious as he made it sound but admitted that he did use a belt to whip my son.

I was filled with instantaneous rage and it took me a few hours before I was calm enough to try to engage in a conversation with him about what happened. I called five or six times before I was finally able to get him on the phone and before I could even ask him about the situation, he said, "man listen, I ain't about to answer to you for what goes on in my house. If that boy gets out of line, he will get his ass whipped. Period."

Rage was now boiling over to the point where I could feel the veins in my head throbbing. Surprisingly, I managed to calm myself down, "I understand your position, it's tough to have issues in your household but we need to find another solution to resolving issues with my son. Why don't we sit down and talk?" My calmness totally threw him and he uneasily agreed to meet me at a public place so we could talk. I figured that a public place would help make him feel more comfortable but I knew that regardless of how many people were around, I was going to give him the beat down of his life!

He never showed up and after a few more days of calling and getting the run around I finally lost it and went to their house. I saw his car in the driveway and my son told me that he was home so I parked a few houses up the street and went to the side door and rang the doorbell. I heard him yell at my son, "Don't answer that fucking door, you don't touch the door in my house." My anger now boiling completely over, I started banging on the door, "Bring your bitch ass out here so we can talk. What kind of man hides in his own house and tells my son he can't answer the door? You are a straight up punk. What kind of man hides in his house like a bitch?"

I banged on the doors, knocked on the windows and after a few minutes got that feeling in my stomach, the one that always came right before the police showed up or something bad was about to go down. I got in my car and as I drove up the street I saw three or four police cars, lights on but no sirens, go flying by me, then stop in front of their house.

A few days later I was served with an order of protection that said I had to stay away from him, his job and Heather's house. All I could do was laugh. This dude talked so much junk about what he would do to me and how he would do it but when it came time to get busy he was 100% punk, a true softie. I showed my friends the order of protection and everyone cracked up laughing. Eventually I was able to laugh as well, especially when I found out years later the real reason for his attitude towards me and my son.

Heather didn't marry the Joe that she had dated in high school, instead she married another guy named Joe. This was the same Joe that was engaged and living with Amy-Lynn when I called her that night, and the same Joe that she put out of her house so I could blow her back out for the night. This was the same dude that sat down across the street and watched as I went into his fiancé's house and came out in the early hours of the morning after his fiancé and her mother made me breakfast. I heard that he even gave Heather the same ring that he originally gave to Amy-Lynn, the ring that she threw at him when she was beating his ass in her garage and kicking him out of her mother's house. Yep!, this was that dude. I called up G and a few of my other friends and told them and it became something that we all laughed about for years.

Seeing how stressed I was, a lady friend offered to take me to Niagara Falls for the night to relax and try to clear my mind. As we drove back, I got a frantic phone call from my mother. She told me that Calvin had been arrested and she had been trying to call me all night long. She told me that he was being accused of shooting someone in the face, another kid around his age that lived around the corner from my mother's house.

I couldn't believe what she was saying. Calvin had just turned sixteen-years-old a month or so earlier and was not even close to being any type of thugged out street dude. I couldn't even imagine him with a gun, let alone shooting someone. We found out shortly after that there was a confrontation at a house party between Calvin's friends and a group of other dudes. One of Calvin's friends suggested that they go get his mother's .22 caliber pistol and go back to the party to settle things. Between drinking and smoking and everyone being high, Calvin grabbed the gun as they pulled up to the party, put it out of the window and pulled the trigger.

I'm not sure what his intent was but I don't believe that he meant to shoot anyone. From what we were told, it sounded like they were just trying to scare the other group of dudes but the bullet left the gun and hit the other kid in his face, just below the cheek and miraculously exited through his open mouth. It didn't take the police long to track down everyone involved and there were plenty of witnesses that saw Calvin pull the trigger.

They sent him to the county jail downtown and eventually the attorney my mother hired was able to work out a plea deal. My sixteen-year old brother, the prankster of all his friends, the kid that everyone loved with the big heart, the most suburban, non-street smart kid you can imagine, was sentenced to three years in the New York State Prison system. At the time he started his bid he was the youngest inmate in the New York State adult prison system. My mother was sick; I doubt if she slept more than an hour a night through his entire court process and it wasn't until a year after his arrest, when he finally made it to the minimum security facility, that she finally started to look somewhat normal again. The bags under her eyes were slowly fading and she was able to hold a conversation with me for more than a few minutes without breaking down and crying.

When he was first locked up, my mother called me hysterically crying saying that he called her upset because some dudes were trying to press him into giving up his commissary (goods such as chips or juice that can be bought through an inmates account). She told him that he needed to tell the guards and let someone know so that they could help him. I was furious with her and tried to explain that he could get seriously hurt if he did anything like that. I tried to explain the philosophy behind 'snitching', telling the authorities about something that happens in the streets or in this case in jail. I tried to help her understand that this was not the suburbs, that his new surroundings were not dictated by the world she knew, that many of the rules that she had followed and been around her entire life were in direct conflict with how things were done in the streets.

In that moment, I wished that I had let Calvin hang out with me more, that my boys had let him stray a little farther away and experience some more of the streets. I was upset with myself for keeping him too close and trying to protect him from things as opposed to allowing him the space to see things for himself. In retrospect, I know that we did the right thing. I know that keeping him away from the streets and out of harm's way was the right thing to do. The last thing that I wanted was for him to experience any of the bullshit that I did, for him to get in any type of legal trouble or worse, end up a victim of violence himself.

All I could do was write him letters, accept his phone calls when he was able to use the phone and try to guide him through the system from afar the best that I could. He bounced around his first year or so, starting at reception in Elmira, the exact same prison that I rode by so many times as a kid, then he made his way to Hudson, Green and Ogdensburg and to a minimum-security spot way up north, close to the Canadian border just across from Montreal. My little brother was growing up in the system while I was fighting like hell to do everything in my power to stay away from anything that might lead me in that same direction.

While my brother was going through struggles as a teenage inmate, my mother along with Patrick, Reg, and my girlfriend at the time, watched me walk across the stage as I received my Associates Degree in Physical Studies at the MCC graduation ceremony at the Rochester War Memorial. Reg and I had slowly restarted our friendship from the situation with Heather and having him at my graduation was an indication to me of how much I was growing. I listened intently as they called all the names leading up to my own, until the speakers pronounced loudly, "Associates of Science, Jason C. Bost." I walked across the stage, shook the hand of the college president with my right hand and accepted my degree in my left.

I was too busy thinking about the next step in my journey to actually appreciate and enjoy the moment. I embraced my mother afterwards, and stopped to take pictures with Patrick and Reg, but my mind was already at SUNY Brockport and I was anxious to begin what I planned on being the final leg of my academic journey.

Kip was at the graduation ceremony to see his sister Kerri graduate and found me afterwards, greeting me with a big hug and tears in his eyes. He told me how proud he was and reminded me that he truly felt Puba was smiling down on us, assuring me that he could feel his energy. I thought about Puba, about how much potential he had and about how it was all buried right along with him. I had a deep desire to keep moving forward, motivated knowing that I was fortunate enough to still be alive while so many of my friends no longer had opportunities because they were gone, their lives cut short by gunshots and violence.

Shortly after graduating from MCC, I entered SUNY Brockport as a Junior. I lost some credits because I changed majors and had to go back and take a few extra 100 and 200 level history courses. In general, 100 level courses are freshmen or first year courses, 200 are second year, 300 third year, etc. MCC only offered 100 and 200 level courses as they were only a two-year school while Brockport offered all courses, even 500 and 600 level courses for those pursuing master's degrees.

My first semester at Brockport was spent researching and writing history papers, reading tons of assigned books and sitting in classes with professors that didn't seem to move me in the same way as Professor Tippett or Dr. Walker. I was getting bored with the subject matter and the constant issues with my children's mothers were starting to wear me down.

Shatina and I continued to battle in and out of court. She moved two or three more times, each time with me not finding out where she had moved until we went to court and I got the new address from the court papers. She had started seeing yet another new guy and went out of her way to throw her new relationship in my face, even going as far as bringing him to court with her for one of our hearings. Whenever I would pick my kids up she would have him come to the door and hand me my daughter, always saying to her, "Say good-bye to daddy," in reference to her boyfriend. My daughter was too young to understand what was going on or to know any better so she would giggle and say, "Bye daddy," and give her mother's latest boyfriend a hug as he handed her off to me.

Every few months I would show up and there would be a new guy at the door, usually grimacing at me and trying to look hard, probably with a head full of bullshit fed to him by Shatina. The same pattern would repeat itself, the new guy would hand my kids to me while she would make some daddy reference. I was furious and ready to have her and each one of those guys dealt with and seriously considered physically hurting a couple of these clowns, but I always managed to talk myself out of it. I hated bringing my kids back to that environment and spent many days in tears trying to gather myself, feeling like my heart was breaking as I thought about the things she said to my kids and the way she continually bounced strange men in and out of their lives.

Eventually, over time, I learned to shut out thoughts of my kids when they weren't with me. I trained myself to shake off the negative visions I had of them possibly being in harm's way and suppressed the instincts that were pushing me to go get them out of that house. I was learning to numb myself and dull my senses when my children weren't with me and as unhealthy as it was, it managed to help me survive and prevented me from having some sort of psychological breakdown or snapping and inflicting serious harm on Shatina and her boyfriends.

I talked with my lawyer about her behaviors, specifically her pattern of never staying in one apartment for more than six or seven months at a time; the introduction of various men to my children and her encouragement to have my children call them 'daddy'; her inability to hold a job or even look for a job, relying instead on welfare and child support and numerous other offenses that I felt surely would result in the court awarding custody of the kids to me. My lawyer, tears rolling down her cheeks, told me bluntly that we would need more to prove her to be unfit as a mother which was the only way the court would give custody to a father. She pointed out that the court had already commented on my criminal record and the previous restraining orders despite them being bogus.

She suggested that I settle the case and agree to a shared custody agreement that would provide me with consistent access to the kids. After speaking with Shatina's attorney and some negotiating, I reluctantly agreed to the average father's visiting plan. The kids would remain in the primary custody of their mother while I got visitation every other weekend and every Wednesday night overnight. I would get them for most holidays, including their entire spring and winter breaks.

We signed off on the agreement and put a temporary end to the custody/visitation portion of our legal battles. With the custody order in place I requested a modification of child support and asked them to reduce the support by the number of days the kids would be with me. Of course, the same hearing examiner that suggested that I quit school and find another full-time job refused to modify the order in my favor and instead provided me with another increase.

I felt defeated and decided to throw myself completely into school and work. When I wasn't in class, studying, or working, I started going out to bars and clubs and trying to party my stress away. We frequented all the hot spots, the clubs in the downtown area of the city that played mostly hip hop music and catered to mostly black crowds as well as the suburban clubs that were filled with primarily white crowds. Patrick preferred going to the Latin bars. He always had a thing for Latinas, since we were in grade school! Everyone knew him in those cramped little spots, bachata and salsa music blasting away.

When Patrick first moved back to Rochester from San Diego, we got an apartment together above a corner store on Monroe Avenue and Harwood Street. After about six months of hard-core partying, Patrick moved in with his mother and I moved into a small one-bedroom place on Bellwood Place, a dead end street off Goodman Avenue on the East side of the city. I bought some bunkbeds and set the attic up as the kid's bedroom even though they never slept in it, preferring to sleep in the living room or in my room with me.

My neighbor across the street, who everyone called Bear, was an easy going, good natured guy who was always ready to share a drink and pass a blunt. The street was relatively quiet except for us when we would cook-out and play music on the weekends. Bear, his name seemingly a reference to his size and demeanor, loved to cook and I would share cooking duties with him. He usually manned the grill, cooking ribs, steaks, and burgers, while I whipped up macaroni and cheese and other side dishes. Bear, dark skinned and easily weighing four hundred pounds, always had good weed and loved to drink so our cook outs were always lively.

I would hit the club with Patrick and sometimes Randy and his crew, then come home, walk across the street to Bear's house. Twin would always join us and we would drink gallons of Hennessy mixed with V8 Splash Tropical Blend, smoke, and eat until the sun came up. We all knew that there was something special about that summer. In just a few months, we had all developed a closeness that you normally only see among family or people that had known each other all their lives. We drank, ate and laughed all summer long, with each day better than the last.

I hated moving from that street but I knew I needed a bigger place. Patrick had finally saved up enough money to go half with me so we got a large house off of Jay Street with a large fenced in backyard and a driveway big enough for the kids to ride their bicycles and big wheels. I kept pushing forward at school, working towards completing my Bachelor's degree and finally received notice that I was eligible to participate in the upcoming graduation ceremony.

To celebrate graduating with my Bachelor's degree, we planned a big party at my house. I was still ten credits shy of completing my degree but the school allowed me to walk with my class in anticipation of finishing the final credits over the upcoming summer semester. Just like at MCC, I sat and waited until they announced my name, walked across the stage, shook someone's hand then took a seat and waited for the ceremony to end.

I was much more excited about the party scheduled to take place than the actual graduation itself. I felt like I hadn't earned the graduation because I knew I still had to go back and complete those last few credits but I was burnt out and had lost the excitement I once felt towards college. I was bored at Brockport. My history classes lacked the passion that I experienced in Dr. Walker's class and I continued to have problems trying to find a job in the education field.

I had great references, everyone seemed to love me at my student teaching placements but I would repeatedly encounter the same problem. I would interview, be offered an opportunity then be handed an application in which I would have to check 'yes' on the dreaded "Have you ever been convicted of a felony" question. I started feeling like I wasted my time going to school, that I was destined to be stuck at a dead end job or worse, eventually have to go back to the streets to make a living.

Just before my graduation, Twin and I made the four or five-hour drive upstate and picked up Calvin on the morning he was released from prison. He came home as a 19-year-old after doing almost three years in various prisons throughout New York State. He had grown taller and bulked up and his playful innocence was still there, just buried underneath some maturity and a new layer of distrust. He was paranoid in the way that all inmates are when they first step outside of prison. Freedom seemed like it felt slightly uncomfortable and despite being very happy to be out, he had uncertainty written all over his face.

We decided that he would come and live with me but he had

to first go to my mother's house until his parole officer cleared the move. We tried to have everything set up before he came home but the move to my house was slowed down in part because I was a convicted felon. While on parole, parolees are not supposed to have any contact with other felons so they had to give him special permission to live at my house. I wanted him closer to me so that I could keep an eye on him and hopefully provide some guidance to help keep him moving in the right direction.

While I thought about my brother and his reentry into the outside world, I sat through my graduation ceremony disappointed with myself. My ability to focus on school was slipping away and I found myself bored, just doing the bare minimum amount of work to make it through my classes and my grades reflected my lack of interest. I desperately wanted to teach and hadn't thought of any type of alternative plans so hearing that I might not be able to receive my teacher's certification because of my felony broke my spirit. I thought about how readily I accepted that plea deal and shook my head at my naivety. I had always heard old heads talk about the system and how it was designed to keep the black man down but I never really took them seriously. The exact same forces that many claim to be excuses for not succeeding were now having a tangible effect on my life and I was feeling the pressure.

Despite my loss of interest in school and growing disenchantment with the system, I was still ready to party! Bear, G and Twin spent the afternoon setting up a huge tent in my driveway under which sat a makeshift bar consisting of all kinds of bottles of liquor and a full keg. They set up four or five large speakers throughout the tent along with a scattering of tables and chairs. We opened a few bottles of champagne, rolled a few blunts and partied our asses off. For the rest of the night I forgot about my remaining credits, forgot about application questions and job searches, suppressed thoughts of the issues with my kids and just enjoyed the moment. Tim Ragland, Reg, Kip, Ozell, Vic and most of friends came through to celebrate along with my cousin Paul, my mother, my sister Nicole and Calvin.

It was good to have my brother home but I was starting to lose patience with him and we were starting to butt heads more and more frequently. He lacked focus and was spending most of his time running around with his friends and hanging out. I could not understand his desire to reclaim his lost teen years. I just wanted to see him go to school, find a job or do something that would work towards establishing a foundation for his future. Despite the increased tension between us, we enjoyed ourselves partying that night. We spent the entire night laughing and reminiscing and I enjoyed watching him party with Paul and some of their friends.

Watching G spin records all night reminded me of how much I enjoyed music and I soon re-focused my energy into trying to figure out a way to get more involved with music. After saving up some money I bought a set of turntables, speakers and enough equipment to build my own small recording studio. I started buying vinyl records again, building on my already extensive record collection. A few years prior, I worked with G in a small recording studio called Po' Boyz Music on Genesee Street. Denis Lee, the owner of the studio, taught G how to engineer recording sessions and I would sit in with G eventually learning enough to engineer my own sessions.

I wanted to see Denis turn his home studio style set up into a real business but he was content making a few dollars here and there from the local dudes that would rent out studio time. My vision was much larger and eventually I decided to try the studio thing on my own. At first I tried to emulate Denis by providing engineering services and renting out time for others to record at my house but then I came up with a new idea on how to utilize the equipment. I convinced G to make some mix tapes so that we could put them in stores. I started recording G spinning records live way back during our Jenks & Jones days and we made our first official mixtape a few-years prior, right after Puba was killed, using G's 4-track Tascam recorder.

The mixtape game was just starting to take off on a national level. Using the format that the original mixtape DJ's started, DJs like Kid Capri, Brucie B, Triple C, and Ron G., the new mixtape DJ's like Clue, Juice and Green Lantern started to commercialize their tapes. Originally, mixtapes were recordings simply made from the DJs live performances and then copied and given to friends or sold. These new DJs were taking new exclusive unreleased songs, mixing them together with other popular songs and adding their own 'tag' or 'drop' on the songs so that everyone would know where it came from. For example, DJ Clue would yell "Deee-Jaaaay-Clue, haa-haa" on the exclusive songs so that another DJ couldn't take the song from his tape and put it on their own.

DJ Green Lantern was from Rochester and had just started making some serious noise in the underground mixtape circuits. He took his tapes a step further, taking acapella or instrumental versions of original new tracks and mixing them with other acapellas and instrumentals. Sometimes he would produce original music and mix it with a series of scratches and mini-mixes to create an entirely new record that could only be heard on his mixtapes. He would also take words from various well-known records and scratch them together to make them say whatever he wanted, then string them together into long introductions that were also unique only to his tapes. Through his simple start with mixtapes, Green would go on to become one of the largest Hip Hop DJs in the world eventually becoming the tour DJ for Eminem and others.

I started reaching out to record labels and joined a few record pools in an effort to get access to the newest singles or unreleased tracks. I even reached out to Minnesota a couple times, asking him to send me some of the new material he was working on. My old crew from the Bronx, including Kwame and Minnesota, had been making a lot of noise in the music scene and dropped a few underground albums as the Money Boss Players or MBP. The group consisted of Lord Tariq, Big Ah, C-Dub, Eddie Chebba, Trey Bag and Minnesota and Kwame was their manager.

I hit the studio with them a few times during some of my runs back and forth when I was still in the streets and getting my supply from the Bronx. The entire crew basically transitioned from hustling in the streets to hustling music. Minnesota was producing records for everybody; Notorious BIG, Lil Kim, Junior Mafia, Big Pun and many other. He was starting to become the go-to producer for New York hip hop rappers when New York hip hop rappers were running everything. Lord Tariq teamed up with Peter Gunz and their single "Déjà vu, (Uptown Baby)" was blowing up the charts. Kwame had pulled me to the side a few times in the past and told me that I needed to focus on the music business and help him manage everybody but I wasn't ready. Many of my old crew were still dabbling in the streets and I was trying to keep my distance from any situation that might lead me back to where I had worked so hard to get away from.

I started to focus my time researching music, studying the game and trying to figure out how I could get my foot in the door without having to move to New York City. I was finally seeing my children on a regular, consistent basis and I was focused on them as well as trying to figure out a way to somehow still pursue my teaching goals. Twin, Bear and I tried to start a production company but that didn't last long. However in honor of them, I used the name we came up with, Bite 'Em Down Productions, when I finally started getting involved in bigger projects. I tried starting a record label with G and two of my other partners, but that quickly fell apart as they had their own ideas on how to do things and no one really had a clue as how to make things work.

Every weekend that I didn't have my kids I spent on the road, driving to cities like Albany, Syracuse, Buffalo, Baltimore, DC, Cleveland, Cincinnati, Detroit and Toronto, and linking up with the mom & pop music stores that sold mixtapes. I spent hours talking to store owners in their stores and watching as customers came in, browsed through the mixtapes and selected two or three to buy. I noticed that there were now at least ten to twenty different mixtapes at every store and saw that the customers usually bought the first mixtape they picked up. They were usually asking for the bigger name DJs like Clue and Green but if they saw a cover that caught their eye they would pick that up and at least look at the playlist on the back.

Seeing how the customers shopped, I started to design our CD covers myself. I got pictures of half-naked, sexy women in provocative poses, threw some big letters behind them along with featuring "DJ GNyce and JayBee" and made sure that we always had a few tracks that you couldn't find anywhere else along with one or two of the hottest records that were out at the time on the playlist on the back. By the time we released our third mixtape the stores were calling me and asking for more! I ran into Green Lantern at my man Dine's record shop in Rochester and he hooked me up with his distribution list which meant that I didn't have to visit each one of the stores. I could instead call them and arrange for the sale of the CDs on the phone, saving me lots of time and lots of money.

I was trying to get G's name out there and build his brand. He had always been dope' and till this day he is still one of the illest DJs I know but he started dragging his feet and taking too long to get the mixtapes done. I had deadlines to meet, I was setting up CD sales with the stores and promising them a delivery date and then I had to keep pushing the date back, waiting for G to finish the tape. Finally, I started doing it myself, I was nowhere even close to being on the level of G but I knew how to mix a little. I had a good ear for music and I knew how to work all the equipment and edit things down to make them sound better than they really were.

Trying to make the tapes, contact the stores, hit the road and sell the tapes, take care of my kids and hold down a job got the best of me and just as things were starting to take off I had to stop. I was pissed beyond belief with G for making me look foolish with all the people that I worked so hard to build business relationships with and we exchanged words numerous times. Actually it was more like I just cussed him out repeatedly.

I lost a lot of money on that equipment, CDs, travel, etc., but felt like I was heading in the right direction. I saw a future for myself in music but for the time I accepted a new job working at a community based organization focused on educating people on HIV, safer sex and sexual health issues. They hired me specifically to develop educational plans and implement those plans for high-risk youth and incarcerated adults.

It was the first time that I interviewed with anyone and had them tell me that my conviction was a positive for a job. As always, I was extremely anxious and expected the interviewer to give me that same look, sort of them trying to hide their disappointment or disgust with me. Instead the interviewer acknowledged my answer on the application and commented that it would help me gain the trust of the population with whom I would be working.

I was shocked and jumped at the job offer without even thinking about the salary. Fortunately, I ended up getting paid more than what I was making at my last job and the benefits were much better. I spent the first few months getting educated on various sexually transmitted infections, HIV, AIDS and male and female reproductive health. I received training to become certified as an HIV test counselor and started doing community outreach on the organizations outreach truck, handing out free condoms in the impoverished neighborhoods of the city including my old hood. I would have the driver go down some of the old blocks I used to hang on and stop when I saw some of my boys. Then I would slowly open the side door and watch them all get ready to run, thinking that it was some sort of undercover police van or something.

315

I would crack up laughing, then jump out and say, "Freeze mother fuckers, put your hands up and come get these free condoms!" They would all laugh, rush over and hug me saying, "Nigga don't do that shit JayBee! Man, we thought you was the police! Give me some condoms homie!" Someone would always add, "Aww man don't give him none JayBee, you know his soft ass doesn't get any pussy!"

While we laughed and joked, I handed out condoms and brochures with information about sexual health. Eventually, everyone in the hood knew the van and would start running up to it like they were chasing the ice cream truck when we were kids! I would usually give them something new every time I came through, condoms and some flavored lube, or condoms and female condoms, or condoms and dental dams. Each time, they would say, "Yo, what is this shit?" which was my opportunity to educate them to whatever the new product was, how it was used and how it could help protect them from the many infections associated with sex.

I created lesson plans and went into the same type of group homes that I previously worked, providing 45-minute to hour long presentations on safer sex, health and HIV. I started getting requests from some of the sororities and fraternities at the colleges and started to conduct trainings for their members and eventually was invited to teach HIV & AIDS education for a graduate level course at the University of Rochester and Rochester Institute of Technology. The professors would have me do an entire class on HIV developments or medications and I found myself standing in large lecture halls in front of classes of fifty, a hundred even two hundred students.

I loved teaching those classes. At the end of each session, I invited people to come up and exchange information, get my business cards and add me to their list of resources for research. It never failed; talking about sex to a room full of strangers always seemed to lead to two or three women giving me their number at the end and since we already broke the ice talking about sex, always made for memorable first dates!

One time, I did a presentation for one of the black sororities. There was a room full of fifteen to twenty beautiful black sisters, all educated and going to school trying to make something out of themselves. I was talking about discussing sex with your partner and the importance of getting tested for HIV and a few came up afterwards, flirted and asked for my card. A few days later I was doing HIV testing at our free clinic and one of the women from the sorority came in and asked me to test her.

Testing required a pre-test evaluation of risk which included asking questions about types of sexual behaviors, if they had anal sex, if they had multiple partners, used intravenous drugs, etc. She was very open about her sexual history and kept dropping hints about what she hadn't tried but wanted to try. I kept it very professional and despite how fine she was, ignored the flirtatiousness, swabbed her mouth for the HIV test and told her to come back in two weeks for the results. Two weeks later she came back, I took her into the private room, closed the door and gave her the results. She was negative. She breathed a sigh of relief then wrote her number down on a piece of paper and handed it to me.

Surprised, I looked at her and before I could say anything she said, "You told us how it was important to get tested and communicate with your partner. Well I got tested and you see that I am HIV free and I communicated every freaky thing that I have ever wanted to do. Now what I need you to do is help me make all that freaky stuff come true!"

I kept it professional and told her that I couldn't...man please! I went to her house and did my very best to make every single one of her freaky dreams come true! Those were some of the fantastic benefits of the job. A few weeks later, another one of her sorority sisters came in and then a few weeks later another. I felt that I was only doing my duty by encouraging them to get tested. Giving back to the community never felt so good!

I was truly a minority at the job. I was one of only maybe two other black folks that worked there, the other two were women and I was the only straight male in the entire organization. HIV was still primarily viewed as being a homosexual epidemic so most of the outreach and education workers, as well as management, were gay white men. I had always considered myself open minded and never had a problem with anyone because of their sexuality, religion or general beliefs, which came in handy at work as well as dealing with community events focused in and around the gay community.

One of my co-workers was a drag queen on the weekends, spending thousands of dollars to make custom outfits for his performances. When he found out that I was involved with DJing and music he asked me to make a few CDs for his performances. Usually just one or two songs spliced together, nothing fancy or complicated and he would pay me $150 for each mix! When the other drag queens heard his mixes, they all wanted me to do mixes for them as well. Soon I was doing four or five mixes a week, making an extra $500 or sometimes $1000 a week just doing 3 minute, two song mixes, usually incorporating Madonna, Cher or the latest pop or electronic music.

He kept inviting me to come to one of his shows and I kept saying, "Hell no!" As open minded as I was, I had no interest in seeing a bunch of gay men dancing around in drag. A few of my female co-workers told me that they loved going to the shows and finally a group of them convinced me to go. I grabbed Reg and my friend from high school Craig Norman, and we headed out but I didn't tell them where we were going until right before we walked in the door. Craig said, "Hell naw man, fuck that! I ain't going to no gay club! Especially not with both of you ugly mother fuckers!"

I convinced them to just give it a try for a few minutes. I wanted to pay my respects to the other drag queens that were paying for the music and show my support for my co-worker. We stepped into the club, probably looking like we were scarred out of our minds, went straight to the bar and ordered triple shots of Hennessy and Heinekens. I looked around and to my surprise the club was about seventy-five percent women! Naturally born women, not drag queens and they were all drunk as hell!

We downed our drinks, ordered a few more and when I went to pay, the bartender said, "Put your money away, whatever you guys want is on the house!" I looked up and saw this six foot five something chick wearing an outfit that looked like it came straight from Cher's closet with flawless makeup and perfectly done hair standing next to me. The bartender nodded and I heard her say, "Jason, you made it," in a voice deeper than my own! It was Pedro, my co-worker dressed in drag. By now I was feeling the Hennessy so I turned around, looked him up and down and started laughing hysterically. He started laughing right along with me and then led us to a reserved table right in the front of the packed club.

A few of the other drag queens came out and he introduced me to each of them just before the show began. He was the main emcee for the night and before the show started he came out, turned the microphone on, pointed to me and my table and said, "Ladies, if any of you are looking for a real man, this man right here is single, straight and in need of some attention tonight!" The ladies all screamed at the top of their lungs then within thirty seconds we were surrounded by about fifteen drunk, hot ass women, all trying to sit on our laps and buy us drinks!

I had been out with a lot of my homies chasing chicks but I never had a friend hook me up with so much ass so quickly! We drank, and drank, and drank, and then made our way to a limo parked outside where we drank some more with eight or nine fine ass drunk women there for a bachelorette party. We made our way back into the club and got bum-rushed again by different women. It was one of the greatest nights of my life! Who would have ever thought that we would end up surrounded by women, straight, horny women, at a drag show!

I was really enjoying my job and eventually got an opportunity to expand my program into the adult prison system. I was already working with incarcerated youth and youth in the various group homes but I also started going to Willard Drug Treatment facility, one of the only drug "Shock" programs in the New York State Prison system. I taught classes there for both male and female inmates. I found out a few years later that Quan was at Willard going through the shock program at the same time I was there teaching. He told me he heard that I was there and was sick that he missed me. It was one of many reminders of how much my life had changed.

I got an opportunity to go to Five Points Maximum Security Prison. Five Points was the newest prison in the New York State system and was state of the art. Every inch of the facility was monitored by cameras. I went through security, had my bag searched and went through a pat-down of my body then an inmate met me at the main reception area and walked me through the prison to my classroom. I looked around and thought about how different my life could have been, how I could have been one of the inmates sitting in the same class I was about to teach.

When I finished my presentation, I was peppered with questions and stayed an extra hour or so making sure to address each question. These were some intelligent brothers. These dudes were seriously on point. They asked questions that showed that they listened and although they might not have been knowledgeable about the subject matter at hand, they were far from being dumb. Some of them shared their stories with me, and some shared a brief breakdown of how long they had been locked up. A few of them were lifers, one of them had been locked up since the late 1970s and another had been in for ten years but still had another twenty years to go. A few were close to going home and one of them was from my neighborhood, an old head who I had never seen around because he had spent the last twenty years in prison.

I left there feeling completely refreshed, grateful that none of my past mistakes had landed me inside that prison and thankful that I was taking my life in another direction. I thought the entire ride home about what I'd done, the things I'd seen, the people that I'd lost and started to feel like I needed to do more, that while I was moving in the right direction, I wasn't where I was supposed to be yet. Little did I know how much my life would change in the next year.

22 MORTEM

I called my friend Jerome Turner and we decided to head up to Buffalo to hang out. We both needed some time to get away and clear our heads. He was going through drama at home and I was trying to sort out my thoughts and figure out my next move. We hit a few bars and I swung by a former girlfriend's house. She cooked for us and we had a few more drinks before we finally started making our way back to Rochester. By the time Jerome dropped me off at my house, I took off my clothes and lay down, it was about four in the morning. I closed my eyes and within a minute, started drifting off to sleep.

My phone rang loudly, startling me out of my sleep. I looked outside and saw Jerome's car still sitting in front of my house. I answered, "Aw man, what the hell did you forget?" and expected to hear him say he needed to use the bathroom or something but instead heard my mother's voice. She was crying hysterically. She was trying to tell me something but I couldn't understand what she was saying because of all the sobs and sniffles.

"Mom, what is wrong? I can't understand you. Slow down and tell me what's going on." She took a deep breath and finally, between long sobs said, "I think he's dead."

"What? Who's dead? Mom what are you talking about?"

"They shot my baby. They shot my baby in the chest. They shot your brother." Then the sobs got deeper and longer.

I froze as my stomach felt like it dropped all the way down to the floor. Did she say someone shot my brother? And that he was dead? I tried to convince myself that I heard her wrong, that I somehow mistook her muffled cries and sobs. "Mom, calm down. What did you say? Where are you?"

She took a deep breath and then, almost as if she was asking me, in a state of complete shock, she said, "I'm at Rochester General, in the emergency room, you need to get here right away." She tried to talk but was struggling to catch her breath, finally she said "Jason, I think Calvin is gone." Her words hung in the air and circled my head like a vulture, slowly and patiently circling its next meal.

I stood up and felt the blood rush to my head as the cloudiness of the alcohol and weed immediately and almost magically cleared. I grabbed my car keys, ran down the stairs, missing two or three on the way and landing with a loud thud at the bottom of the staircase. I pushed open the door, jumped in my car and sped all the way across town to the hospital, running full speed through red lights, hitting corners so fast that my tires screeched and the car felt like it might tip over. I pulled into the emergency room entrance, parked my car next to an ambulance and jumped out.

I noticed three or four dudes standing around the front entrance, looking disheveled and recognized one of them. He saw me and quickly turned his head, trying to avoid eye contact. I made my way through the sliding doors and to the nurse's station and told them that my mother had just called me. Before I could finish my mother came from behind a secured door, tears running down her cheeks, face red and eyes swollen from crying. She walked towards me looking almost like a zombie, like her body was there and her thoughts were directing her my way and she recognized me but her spirit was someplace else.

I rushed over to her and she looked at me confused. "Jason, I think they killed him. I know he's dead but I just can't believe it."

A doctor took us back to a private room and then my mother and the doctor told me that Calvin had been shot in the chest. They rushed him to the hospital and did their very best but they couldn't save him. He was dead. My mother filled me in with the few details she heard from the police as well as one of Calvin's friends that was with him at the time. She would cry hysterically then suddenly stop and just stare at the wall or at me or at the floor, then start crying again.

I hugged her and tried to comfort her but I could feel her anguish through her sobs. I could sense that there was nothing that anyone could do to help her with her pain. Her hurt was coming from a place that only she could understand, that only a parent that had lost a child could relate to. It was so deep and so sorrowful that I could feel it around her. It engulfed her spirit and shook her to her very core.

The doctor came in and started talking to my mother, offering to give her something to help calm her down while I stepped outside to speak with the three detectives that came to the hospital immediately after leaving the scene of the shooting. I was always uncomfortable around police, especially detectives and this time was no different. The older detective, I believe he was the Sergeant or a supervisor of some sort, a seasoned homicide investigator whose chiseled eyes seemed to pierce right through me, introduced himself and the other two officers. He explained that one of the detectives was the lead investigator and then started asking me a few questions about my brother.

I asked them if they could tell me what happened and they explained that Calvin was in an apartment when someone ran into the apartment and supposedly tried to rob the occupants. They said my brother was shot in the chest by one of the alleged robbers. They said it was a large caliber gun and he had survived for a while. He was actually trying to talk when the ambulance arrived but died at the hospital. They said Calvin's friend survived when he jumped out of a second floor window but he was in bad shape because it looked like he had broken his back.

They gave me a card and told me that they would talk to me some more in a few hours and that I should call them if I heard anything that may help. I nodded my head and then my mother and the doctor asked me if I wanted to see my brother. I looked at my mother, not knowing what to say. She pleaded with me in a low shaky voice, "Please come with me, please. I need to see him one more time." I put my arm around her and we walked into another room, one of those large emergency room type areas that you see on TV, with machines making beeping noises and wires and things everywhere. In the very middle of the room was a gurney and on it was a body. Everything was covered from the chest down with a white sheet and the head was propped up on some sort of soft block.

I noticed the spots of dried blood on the floor and saw discarded gloves with blood on them in the wastebaskets around the room. I felt my mother's hand squeeze my arm tight, much more tightly than I could ever imagine her having the strength to squeeze it. I looked up to see my brother laying there, eyes closed, looking like he was sleeping. My mother kept looking at me, almost as if she was trying to gain insight into reality and figure out if it was a dream. "Can I touch him?" she asked the doctor who nodded his head and exited the room as she reached for his forehead and slowly rubbed his hair.

I could tell that she was expressing her good byes and acknowledging to him for the last time that she loved him. "He's so cold, he doesn't feel real," she said, looking at me again as if she was asking me a question. "Do you want to touch him and tell him good bye?" she asked me. I shook my head no and we walked out of the room and into a deeper cloud of confusion and pain.

I called Patrick, Twin and a couple of my other boys and told them what happened. I told them about the dudes that were standing out in front of the hospital and that their vibe was off and a couple of my other homies came through with guns just to make sure that nothing more went down. This wasn't new to any of us. We had already lost many others to gun violence so we were programmed on how to move whenever something like this happened. Despite my grief and pain, I went into automatic mode, moving the same as I had before, taking precautions and setting up a perimeter around my family to make sure that nothing happened to anyone else.

In the moment, we had no idea who did what or why Calvin was really killed so we rounded up the crew. Unbeknownst to my mother, they came with some heavy artillery and we escorted my mother back home. By the time she was home and situated it was light outside so I started calling family members to let them know what happened. My mother had already called my sister Nicole who had moved out to Chicago, and she was already on a flight headed back home.

I called my mother's sister, my aunt Sandy next. Before I could even finish telling her, she started crying uncontrollably. Then I called my aunt Robin out in California and told her. We talked for a few minutes and after that I don't remember any more phone calls. All I remember is trying to keep my mother calm and watching her as her hands shook and she stared off into space. A few more of my boys came through the house along with some of Calvin's friends and slowly more friends started to trickle through the house in waves.

One of my boys stayed watch at my mother's house. I told him that at that point everyone was a suspect. We watched carefully as each person came to pay their respects, looking for signs that they might be fake or anything indicating that they might have been involved. Slowly, family started to arrive, my Aunt Sandy and Janice drove up from a few hours south of Rochester. My sister's flight arrived from Chicago. My Aunt Val came along with my cousin Paul. Paul took it hard. He had always been really close to Calvin, they were both only a few weeks apart in age and were more like brothers than cousins.

I called Heather and told her what happened and asked her not to say anything to my son. I wanted to tell him myself so I headed over there and we talked in my car sitting in his mother's driveway. I put my arm on his shoulder and told him what happened. He just looked at me and started crying. Then I repeated the same thing with my daughter, and my other sons, who were all still a bit young to totally comprehend the concept of death. They only knew that it meant that they would no longer see their uncle Punk, as they all fondly called Calvin. They cried as well. Seeing their tears broke my heart and I had to fight with all my might to keep the tears from flowing from my own eyes. I told myself that I had to be strong for them, show them that I was there for them so I swallowed hard and held it all back.

When I told G about Calvin he lost it and broke down crying uncontrollably. He still hadn't recovered from Puba's death and this was just too much for him to handle. When he finally got it together he got dressed and didn't leave my side for the next week or so. My cousin Mark came in from Albany and stayed close to me for a few days as well. People came in and out of my mother's house bringing food and drinks and trying to offer their support to my mother. A few of her friends along with my aunts, took over the house, organizing food and people while I started to make funeral arrangements.

None of us had slept. My boys all came through with bottles and bottles of liquor, beer and boxes of blunts and I spent that first night spinning records in my living room, drinking and smoking until I was super high. Jadakiss had a record out at the time called "We Gonna Make It." I played that record over and over and over again, non-stop for hours straight. I puffed on blunt after blunt. We all drank straight from one of the bottles of liquor and then passed it as I tried hard to lose myself in the lyrics and focused on allowing the beat to keep my thoughts as calm as possible.

The next morning as the sun rose and the birds started chirping, I was still playing that record, smoking, and passing a bottle of liquor around. I took a quick shower, went by my mother's to check on everyone then Twin and G drove me to a church to start making the arrangements. I entered the church and looked around and saw no one but I could hear a television playing down a hallway at the other end of the church. I walked down the hallway and entered this large cafeteria style room and saw six or seven people gathered around the television, all watching intently, no one moving or saying a word. One woman had her mouth wide open while another was just shaking her head saying, "Oh my Lord Jesus, oh my Lord Jesus."

They were so engulfed in the television that no one even noticed me standing there until I said, "excuse me, I'm supposed to talk to someone about a funeral service." An older man turned and walked towards me while the others continued to watch the television. He shook my hand and said, "I don't know what this world is coming to. Death seems to be all around us." I nodded my head thinking that he was referring to my brother then he looked at me and said, "You don't know what just happened do you?" I shrugged and he realized that, at least in my mind, whatever happened was no comparison to what I was going through in the moment.

The only other thing I recall about this meeting was the small argument that ensued when I told him that I didn't want any type of church music played and instead handed him a list of Bob Marley songs. All songs that my brother loved and meant a lot to all of his friends and my mother. Calvin turned everyone on to Bob Marley. He was a true fan and would often spend hours just listening to records like "Redemption Song," and "No Woman No Cry."

The minister tried to insist that we utilize their usual musical selection but after a short discussion, and an instant 'donation to the church,' suddenly he understood and agreed to use the music we selected. I made the arrangements with him then headed over to the funeral home to set up the wake and make sure his body was taken care of properly. When I walked into the funeral home, no one was around and I again heard a television playing in one of the back rooms. Once again, everyone was gathered around, glued to the television looking on in horror.

I met with the funeral director and made the arrangements but got into an argument with him about the obituary. He told me that they wouldn't be able to print what I wrote because there were too many letters and he told me that it would cost too much. Then he tried to nickel and dime me with added costs for miscellaneous items. Twin, hearing me raise my voice and seeing me get agitated, eased his hand down his side and was getting ready to pull out his pistol, sensing that I was real close to beating this dude's ass. Just as I started to move closer to him and Twin started to pull his hand out, I heard someone say, "Jason?" I looked back to see my friend Denise Williams standing there. Denise was one of my friends from Chandler Street, my boy Tracy's older sister. She said she wanted to be a mortician since we were kids and there she was, finally working as a mortician for the dude that was about to catch the beat down of his life.

She put her hand on my shoulder and told me she heard about my brother then nodded to the other mortician and told him that she would take care of me. Twin followed the dude out and into the next room but I called him before he put his hands on the guy. Denise took care of everything else. She was empathetic, caring and beyond professional. She even prepared my brother's body herself and made sure everything went smoothly at his wake. Years later, she would open her own funeral home and to this day, her business is thriving, I am sure in no small part due to her professionalism and ability to empathize with her customers.

When I made it back to my mother's house, she was sitting on the sofa watching the television. I sat down next to her and she looked up at me, totally bewildered and said, "Is the world coming to an end?" I looked at the television and watched as the news showed the second tower of the World Trade Center collapsing. People were covered in dust. Thick clouds of grey smoke floated around everywhere. People were screaming and running while some just sat and cried. It all seemed surreal. My brother was shot and killed on September 9, 2001, less than 48 hours later, I sat with my mother and watched as the World Trade Center towers came down in New York City.

While everyone was in shock and talking about the towers we were going through our own tragedy. The rest of the world watched and mourned as thousands of people died while we watched each other mourn over the passing of a single person, my brother. I realized that we were in the middle of a historic event but it was impossible to separate those towers from my brother. To this day, while the rest of the world remembers the Towers all I can do is think about my brother and relive making my brother's funeral arrangements.

When all the funeral planning was done and my mother had enough of her sisters and friends and family around, Twin, G and I drove out to Charlotte Beach so I could clear my head. G rolled up two super fat stuffy blunts and handed them both to me along with a liter bottle of Hennessy. I lit up the first blunt, hit it a few times then went to pass it to G and he said, "Naw man, that is all you bro," and then did the same thing with the Hennessy.

In the hood, there is a tradition that I believe goes back to Africa, in which libations are offered for the dead. Anyone that planned on drinking would gently tap a bottle of liquor or beer prior to opening it, then whoever opened the bottle would pour some out into the ground for our dead loved ones. We had been doing it for so long that it was often done without even thinking. I opened another bottle of liquor as I walked towards the pier then I stopped and started pouring some out. This time I thought about who I was pouring it for and what it truly meant and for the first time, I felt a connection to the earth, felt like my brother was somehow enjoying the drink with me.

I puffed on the blunt and closed my eyes. I could smell the semi-fishy air gently rolling off Lake Ontario and felt a slight breeze brush against my face. When I opened my eyes, I was kneeling and tears just started flowing down my cheeks. My tears slowly morphing into quiet sobs that eventually turned into loud, uncontrollable weeping. I sat down on the sidewalk right next to the parking lot and cried. I cried from a place that was deep within me. From a place that had been buried time and time again and had built up so much pressure that it finally just exploded.

I wept loudly and unashamedly with my head down, dropping the blunt and pushing the bottle of liquor to the side. I saw G and Twin standing there keeping their distance and giving me the space I needed to just let it all go. As I wept and sobbed I looked up and through cloudy eyes saw something white move in front of me. I wiped the tears from my eyes and looked closer and saw a seagull standing about ten feet away from me. I started crying again and watched as the bird slowly walked closer to me. I started talking to the bird, telling the bird about the pain I felt and crying even louder than before and the bird just kept getting closer and closer.

The seagull looked at me as if it could feel my pain. I felt empathy and saw true concern in the bird's eyes and I sat up and started talking to the seagull in more detail. The more I talked, the more the bird would look at me and inch closer and closer. I finally started to reach for the bird to put my arm around it and invite it to share a hug and it finally inched away a bit. I talked to that seagull and watched its eyes and felt a comfort that I hadn't felt in a long time.

I wiped my eyes and my nose, sat up straight, picked up the blunt, lit it again, took a deep pull, then stood up, looking around to see that the seagull was gone, nowhere to be found. I shook my head and laughed, mumbling to myself that I must be losing my mind then I got into Twin's truck and we drove off.

I kept thinking about that seagull, wondering if it was just something in my mind, possibly a manifestation of my broken heart that somehow only I could see. I asked "Twin, am I tripping or did you see that shit too?" He said, "Naw man, you ain't tripping, that was beautiful man." G chimed in saying, "I saw it too. Jay listen bro, you know that was your brother trying to tell you something."

Thinking that they were just fucking with me I said, "What did you see?" They both said almost at the exact same time, "That seagull!" I don't know if it was the much needed cry or the magic in the seagull but I felt like a burden was lifted off of my shoulders. I felt like my brother was somehow trying to tell me that we would be ok. Thankfully G and Twin both saw the same thing so I know it was real. To this day, whenever I think about that seagull I shake my head in disbelief and almost as if it is magic, that same feeling of calmness returns and calms my spirit again.

I don't remember much about the funeral or the burial but I do remember sitting in my mother's back yard and watching the different women that had all been a part of my life at one time or another. I looked at each one and thought about what I saw in her and I had one of those light-bulb moments when everything becomes super bright and clear. I realized that I had to change my path, I needed to change the type of women that I was dealing with. I felt like I needed to change my life and move in a different direction. I had been feeling that way for a while but my brother's death just really pounded home the need for change.

They say that when you experience a serious loss, be it the death of a loved one or otherwise, that you shouldn't make any major changes in your life for at least a year. You shouldn't change jobs, end or start a relationship, move, nothing. You should just sit still and allow yourself time to process. Fuck that, I was ready for a serious change. I was tired of seeing the people that I loved killed. I was tired of busting my ass to try to get ahead only to have someone throw my past in my face and consistently remind me of the mistakes that I made.

I was ready to get away from Rochester. I thought about all the times that I left. About how much money I always made. About how much better I always felt. I knew that I needed to get out of Rochester and I was feeling like I needed to be closer to or in New York City. I was starting to seriously think about making moves in the music business and saw that trying to do that from Rochester was going to be next to impossible.

I started to distance myself from all the women in my life, cutting each of them off one by one. For the first time, I saw that none of them would be able to provide me with what I was looking for. That what I needed was something completely different than anything that I had ever had before. I realized that I needed intellectual stimulation, someone that could open my eyes to new things and a new way of thinking.

In retrospect I should have taken the time to simply find myself. To figure out more about me and work on my weaknesses and flaws. But instead I jumped on one of the black dating websites and entered very specific search criteria, thinking that using filters would also magically filter out any of the bullshit that comes along with meeting people. I started corresponding with a woman and after a week or so of exchanging emails, each one getting longer and more detailed than the last, we finally exchanged phone numbers and began talking on the phone. I told her about my brother's death and she immediately offered a shoulder to cry on, empathizing with me as she told me that she too had lost a brother a few years prior to a drowning accident.

We started talking daily on the phone. Our conversations would last for hours and hours, often ending when the sun was coming up and each of us had to get off the phone in order to get ready to go to work. I hadn't done that since high school and the conversations seemed to have rejuvenating energy. We decided it was time to meet and chose Binghamton as a meeting place as it was half way between Rochester and her place in New Jersey. We met at a restaurant/bar and as soon as we sat down, I took her by her hand and told her that she was going to be my wife. She laughed and told me I was crazy but less than a year later, we stopped in that same town and took a walk on the same bridge that we walked on the first night we met, I got down on one knee, in the middle of a freezing, drizzling rain and snow storm, pulled out a ring and proposed to her.

Prior to the proposal, we decided that I would move to where she was living in New Jersey. She had a good job, earning a good salary and it was a lot easier for me to try to find another job down there than for her to try to do the same in Rochester. It would also put me just a few minutes outside of New York City and my instincts kept pushing and pulling me hard to get closer to the city.

I started looking for a job, scheduled a few interviews in Manhattan and again went through the same struggles with having to check that 'yes' box indicating that I had a felony conviction. Once again it ended up costing me a few job opportunities but in the end I was offered a position as the director of an outreach and peer education program located in midtown Manhattan. I knew that I needed to get out of Rochester, get away from the violence and separate myself a bit more from many of my friends that were still dabbling in the streets or simply not doing much with their lives. I knew that the move would provide opportunities for me to grow and better myself financially and professionally but all I could think about was my kids.

Per our custody visitation schedule, I finally started seeing them weekly. Every Wednesday I would pick them up from school, bring them home, cook them dinner, do homework with them, get them bathed and ready for bed and watch our TV shows together as we laughed and talked. 'Bernie Mac' was our favorite show and to this day we smile whenever we watch an old episode, not because the show is funny, which it definitely is, but because of the warm memories I have of sitting on the couch cuddling with my kids and laughing together as a family.

I struggled with leaving them but I knew that I had to do it to create a better situation for all of us. I sat them down and told them that I was going to move. My oldest son was about 13, daughter and other son were around 7 and my youngest son was about 5. My youngest was the only one that said anything. He looked me right in my eyes and said, "Will we ever see you again dad?" My heart broke. I couldn't fight back the tears as I hugged them all and said, "Of course. I'm not leaving you, I'm just moving out of Rochester. You will see me on the weekends just like always and the holidays. We just won't see each other on Wednesdays anymore." We hugged and talked and I think it took them all about a year or so of seeing me travel back and forth every other weekend, never missing a single visit, before they started to relax and feel like I wasn't leaving them for good.

23 NEW BEGINNINGS

I immediately got to work networking and reaching out to friends in and around the entertainment business. Randy's younger cousin Elijah, whom everyone called Vato, had moved to New Jersey a while before I did and he was staying with Carl Thomas, the R&B singer signed to Sean "P-Diddy" Comb's Bad Boy record label. E-Bass, another friend from Rochester, was making some serious moves doing production and instrumentation work for many of the industry's biggest producers and artists like Jay Z, Usher, Swiss Beats and many others. I started hanging out with Vato and E-Bass at Carl's house and through Carl I started meeting other artists and producers.

I linked up with my old street partner Minnesota who was still working with industry heavyweights like Lil Kim, The LOX and Mos Def. Kwame was still trying to convince me to work with him managing our old crew, the Money Boss Players, who still had a strong buzz from their earlier underground album as well as Lord Tariq's hit record with Peter Gunz. I also linked up with another one of my partners from Rochester, SMK, South Memphis King, who had long ago moved to Memphis and established himself as a go-to producer for many of the upcoming acts in the south.

While I started making contacts and working to learn the ins and outs of the music business, I was also working my regular job and learning more about the Manhattan that almost no one sees. My job provided services to homeless youth, most between the ages of twelve and twenty-two, who were living on the streets either in the midtown/Times Square area or uptown Manhattan area around Harlem. I worked from a separate office site but the main drop-in center for clients was located on 8th Avenue between 38th and 39th Streets.

The drop-in center was open from early in the morning until five or six in the evening and provided a place for kids to watch TV, socialize, participate in groups and get access to trainings, mental health care and other programs. My program focused primarily on youth sex workers with most of my kids being gay or transgender. My job working with the diverse population in

Rochester introduced me to a lot of gay and bisexual individuals but this was my first time working with and around transgender people.

Transgender people, or trans for short, identified as being different than their biological birth sex. The majority of my kids were trans females; they were born biologically male but identified as female. There were a few of them that 'passed' as female and you probably wouldn't even look twice at them if they walked past you on the street but most of my kids didn't pass easily. Some had five o'clock shadows, large Adam's apples, broad shoulders or other masculine features that made them quickly identifiable as males attempting to pass as females.

If you've ever seen a man dressed in women's clothing, even for mature, open minded adults, it can create a situation where without even thinking, you make a comment or just stare. People point, laugh, make fun of and in some cases, confront or become physically aggressive towards what they perceive as a man dressed as a woman. Almost all the kids in my program became homeless because their families would not accept them as being gay or trans. I had kids that were eleven and twelve-years-old living on the streets with absolutely no support from their families. With nowhere to go and no one to help them, almost all of the kids, even the straight kids, turned to prostitution to survive. Thirteen, fourteen, fifteen-year-olds selling their bodies to grown men and performing unthinkable sex acts for a few dollars just to get enough money to eat or buy shoes or a coat in the winter.

I provided group and individual counseling to the kids in my program as well as worked to try to link them with resources to help with housing, food, clothing and health care. Through the counseling sessions I learned about many of their stories and got an in-depth understanding of what they had to go through daily. They told me about abusive tricks, being sexually and physically abused by family members, about feeling rejected and unloved by their parents and families, and a foster care system that often seemed to punish them for their sexual or gender identities. While I never struggled with their issues directly, I could relate to their feelings of being an outsider through my own experiences being bi-racial, which helped me to truly empathize and connect with them.

I did outreach a few times a week, walking the streets of Times Square, learning all the places that homeless kids would congregate in the winter to keep warm. I did outreach in the area between 14th and 16th streets, in what used to be called the Meat Packing district. The kids would walk around and tricks would drive up and down the streets looking to pick them up to have sex with them in parked cars or back alleyways. I handed out sandwiches and condoms and invited them to come to groups or stop by the drop-in center. There were plenty of nights that I would ride the train home feeling guilty that I left them to fend for themselves for that night, tears in my eyes as I thought about the things they shared with me. As I sit here writing this, my eyes are tearing up and I can feel that knot in my throat thinking about some of my kids from that program and the things that they went through.

I remember coming home and sharing some stories with my soon-to-be-wife, trying to come to terms with a world that would allow children to be homeless and then becoming angry at the thought of all the men that would pick them up and use and abuse these kids. The first time I opened up and shared my day with her she told me that it was sad but said that she felt that it was God's way of punishing them for being gay. My mouth damn near hit the floor. I told her that there was no way any God would want children selling their bodies in order to make enough money to eat. It was one of the first times I remember thinking to myself that I was making a big mistake, that maybe we were just too different to make our relationship work.

Religion became a major point of conflict in our relationship. I was non-religious and felt that organized religion was more destructive than productive. I remembered all the studying I did about slavery and the Crusades and learning about how divisive religion was. About how millions and millions of people had died in religious conflicts. I had friends that were Muslim, Catholic, Protestant, Jewish and Hindu and I accepted them all for who they were.

I told her from the start of our relationship that I would never be 'converted' to Christianity but that I supported her faith and would never stand in the way of her going to church or practicing what she believed. I even went to church with her a few times and actually enjoyed the service until the preacher started talking about the importance of giving him money! One church asked all new people in attendance to stand up then as we all stood, the minister questioned us as to where our 'home church' was or if we were saved. When they got to me I said, "I don't have a home church. I am just here supporting my fiancé." The minister looked at the woman sitting on the stage next to me and they both gave me a look like they were disgusted with me before sucking his teeth and saying, "Well, we will pray for you," then moved on to the next person.

I went to another church with her that made every male in the church wear a suit and tie to Sunday service. I couldn't understand why it was important to dress up to go to church. I questioned whether the church would allow a homeless person or someone that couldn't afford a suit to attend and she told me that the church didn't feel 'those types of people' belonged. Her attempts to show me the beauty and greatness of her religion were failing miserably and were actually working to move me farther away from engaging in any type of religious affiliation. I told her that I would go to church with her if she found a church that accepted everyone; black, white, Asian, gay, trans, everyone. She told me that the Bible said that homosexuality was a sin and therefore no true Christian church would openly accept gay or trans people.

For the sake of our relationship we stopped discussing religion and focused on planning our wedding. I felt like she would come to realize that many of her beliefs had flaws and in time change her way of thinking. I believe that she too felt that I would eventually 'find Jesus' and become saved or embrace Christianity. We both went into it hoping and planning on the other person changing, a definite formula for failure.

A month or so before we were set to marry, I got an opportunity to travel down south and make the rounds meeting with various label executives and artists that were prominent in the Southern Hip Hop scene. After much discussion and debate with my fiancé, I quit my job with the plan of pursuing opportunities in the music industry full-time. She was against it and felt that I should focus on finding a better paying job in a more traditional industry. I convinced her that I would be able to find something that would enable me to earn more money than I was making at the time within the music industry if I could put all my time and effort into making it my future. I was gambling on a bet that had no guaranteed payoff but I had a plan.

I headed down to Memphis to meet up with SMK, one of my

partners from Rochester. He introduced me to my first real taste of the southern hip hop scene. Most artists in the south were making moves as independents, completely outside of the established music business systems. They were handling their own distribution, recording in their own studios or the studios of other artists in their town and they were teaming up with the hottest artists from surrounding cities and collaborating on songs. Then each artist would put out that song on their own projects.

Until then, like almost everyone else from New York, I had always thought of the south as being country. I envisioned slow talking folks in old beat up clothes, sitting on country porches in front of dusty red dirt roads. What I found was bustling cities with urban settings similar to what I saw in New York and I immediately noticed that while everyone did seem to talk a little bit more slowly, they were far from slow thinking.

The southern artists all seemed to support each other. Artists from one city would work with artists from another city, thus introducing each artist's fan base to the other and expanding their overall fan base. The south was like one really big spread out city. Memphis, Birmingham, Nashville, Atlanta, Little Rock, Mobile, all of the large cities in the south were separated from the next large city by only few hours' drive and each city had their own radio stations usually reaching hundreds of thousands of listeners.

Most artists would start working their own record in the local strip clubs. If it caught on with the strippers and the customers in the club, the DJs would usually start playing it in the mainstream clubs and eventually it would make its way onto the local radio stations. Sometimes if the artist had connections in neighboring cities, or enough money to pay the DJs and club promoters, the neighboring cities would pick up the song and start playing it as well.

I went to all kinds of hole-in-the-wall strip clubs and bars located hours outside of the main cities. On one occasion, we went to a club in Chattanooga, Tennessee, a few hours outside of Atlanta, and met up with some of the 'countriest' looking dudes I had ever seen. We went with them to the club to meet with a local radio promoter. One of them had his hair permed and straightened and was wearing a pair of bright green alligator shoes with a bright green suit to match. His front top teeth were gold and he was driving an old school Cadillac painted bright orange and sitting on

337

huge, 26" gold rims. I couldn't help but laugh when I saw them. I had never seen anything like it before.

SMK cracked up watching me laugh. "Man Jay, you ain't seen shit yet! Wait till we hit New Orleans and Mobile! Now those are some country ass Niggahs down there!" We went to another club and I watched and listened, soaking in the environment and quickly picking up on what records made the club react. Triple Six Mafia had a record out called "Tear the Club up" and when that record came on I thought the entire club was about to fight! All the women left the dance floor area while all the men eased back towards the wall and started giving each other looks like they wanted to rip each other's heads off.

As soon as the beat changed, the entire club started to walk counter clockwise, staring at each other. Then they started strutting and throwing their hands in the air towards each other as they crossed their feet. They bent down, jumped back up and then crossed their feet again. When the beat changed again, all in unison, they switched directions and started going the other way. I said, "We need to make a move man, these fools are about to go at it big time!" SMK was laughing so hard he had tears coming down his face. He said, "Man Jay, you are crazy! They not fighting, that's the Gangsta walk! That's a dance we do down here in Memphis man!" I watched for a few more minutes then started laughing myself. I had never seen anything like that in my life!

We made our way to Atlanta, stopping in Birmingham and a few smaller towns on the way, meeting with local artists and radio personalities in each one. We got to Atlanta one night about three or four in the morning and pulled up to a gas station to get some gas. Two beautiful old school cars pulled up right next to us and the driver in one of the cars jumped out, came over to our car and said, "SMK! Where you been at? I need some of those beats man!" SMK started laughing and then introduced me to the driver, who to my surprise was one of the biggest hip hop artists of that time, Ludacris.

In Atlanta, I met a bunch of up and coming artists, some of whom would later become some of the biggest names in hip hop, including Young Jeezy. I linked up with my man Vic, the first brother that put me on to the coke game back in Rochester and we hit up a few of the local strip clubs and hung out. In Atlanta, strip clubs were where everyone went to party, men, women, everyone.

If you wanted to do business in Atlanta, you had to hit up the strip clubs.

Atlanta was the first place that I saw entire neighborhoods composed of multi-million dollar houses owned and occupied exclusively by black families. For miles and miles there would be mansion after mansion with the newest Mercedes, BMW's, Bentley's or high end sports cars filling the driveways. Young, smiling, black children bounced around the front yards, passed balls back and forth, and rode bikes up and down the perfectly manicured lawns. All the images that I had seen of the blacks in the south usually showed black folks sitting on a ragged porch, wearing overalls with a piece of hay in their mouths, surrounding by a yard full of old, rusty cars and ugly, mangy looking dogs. Atlanta had a lot of run down hoods but it was also full of highly successful and intelligent black folks. It was truly a beautiful sight.

From Atlanta, we eventually made our way to Montgomery and Mobile Alabama before we stopped in New Orleans. In each city or town we passed, we stopped and met with the local mom & pop record store owners, exchanging information and connecting with the local artists, just like I had done when I hit the road selling mixtapes. We met with Ms. Rea, the owner of Peaches' Record Store in New Orleans, the biggest record store in the city. We also connected with some of SMK's old partners who were now making music and working with Cash Money Records and they showed us around New Orleans. I hung out in neighborhoods from the upper and lower 9th Ward districts, into the 17th ward, some of the poorest, roughest housing projects in the United States.

I also spent some time in Houston, Texas in the studio with Devan the Dude and a few of the A&R's at Rap-A-Lot Records. I was familiar with Devan's music from his appearances on Dr. Dre's album "The Chronic" but after meeting him, I became a huge fan. He was one of the funniest guys I've ever met, cracking jokes about everything and everyone. He pulled out a huge shopping bag size bag of weed, opened it up, handed it to me and said, "Man roll up until your fingers hurt, I'm about to see if you New York boys can hang with us country Niggas!" I rolled and we smoked until I couldn't take it anymore and of course he let me hear about it!

By the time I left the south to head home, I had made enough contacts with record stores, label people and artists and spent enough time studying their entire system that I was convinced the south was going to be running things for a long time to come. I saw the flaws in the system being used on the East Coast. The lack of support between artists in the same city. The inability to see the south as being much more than a bunch of "country Niggas" and a lack of interest in working with southern artists would eventually lead to the South's domination of the music industry.

24 MARRIED LIFE

Just before we got married, we moved from Jersey City to Newark, into one of the historical brownstone buildings on James Street. James Street was lined with brownstones, most built in the early or mid 1800's, and was known as one of the nicer streets in all of Newark. We had the second and third floors of the building with the first floor of the building occupied by a young brother that was attending Rutgers Law School and his roommate who was a recent graduate of Rutgers Law school working as an attorney in the entertainment industry.

Our building was only a few blocks from the Rutgers Newark campus as well as the campus for New Jersey Institute of Technology("NJIT"). Ironically, later in my life, I would spend considerable amounts of time at both NJIT and Rutgers Newark, but at that time school was the farthest thing from my mind. We also lived a few blocks away from the main downtown shopping area which was filled with small black owned stores and shops selling everything from incense and body oils to sneakers and urban fashion. Downtown Newark had a feel to it that reminded me of 125th Street in Harlem, always busy with black faces bustling back and forth as they exchanged conversation and goods.

Newark was and still is a "Chocolate City," a city that is composed almost exclusively of black residents. There were a lot of Latinos on the North side of the city and the entire Ironbound section, just south of downtown, was composed of all Portuguese, Brazilian and Central American immigrants. Besides those pockets of immigrants, Newark was all black and almost all ghetto. While Rochester had pockets of impoverished areas, Newark was one huge impoverished ghetto where drugs, gangs and violence were common place.

Marcel, Patrick's nephew, introduced me to a Newark native and artist named Michael "Script" Brown. Script showed me around the city, introducing me to hoods like Weequahic on the Westside, as well as neighboring cities like Irvington and East Orange. To an outsider, all the connecting cities looked like an extension of Newark, all similarly rundown and full of the various gangs and drug issues found within Newark itself.

Through Script I met a lot of young brothers, most were artists themselves and almost all were gang affiliated. Eli, Script's protégé, was a fourteen-year old MC from around Script's neighborhood. For his young age, Eli was a super talented lyricist and Script was teaching him how to channel his experiences in the streets into powerfully written poems. Eli was always joking around and making everyone around him laugh. From the first day I met him he never stopped talking about his goals to make it in the music business.

Eli dropped out of school when he was about thirteen, joined the Crips, one of the dominant gangs in his neighborhood, and started selling drugs, stealing cars and doing all the other things associated with gang life in Newark. Every time we got together I would talk to this young brother about life, about the ability to change, about taking his life in another direction but like me when I was younger, he couldn't see anything except for what was directly in front of his face. The only role models he had in his hood were all gang bangers and drug dealers and just like I thought at one time, he felt that they held the key to his future.

In many of the neighborhoods in and around Newark, stealing cars was a favorite past time. For many years, Newark was the car theft capital of the world and on any given night you would see young dudes from their pre-teens to early twenties, flying through the streets of Newark, running red lights, stop signs, whatever they had to do to disengage the police that were usually in hot pursuit. The ability to steal a car, get the police to chase them, then successfully lose the police and get away was held in high regard. I learned to drive extra careful whenever I was in Newark. Always slowing down even when I had green lights, just to check both ways and make sure there were no cars flying through the intersection. I witnessed a number of car accidents then watched as the occupants of the car cracked up laughing as they all ran and headed in separate directions, similar to the way we used to run from the police in my old neighborhood.

Script managed to steer clear of the gangs, stolen cars and drugs partly because of the influence of his father and grandfather who were both respected ministers and church leaders in their communities. He was a truly gifted artist and everyone in his hood respected his talent. The hood could be strange; it was full of violence, drugs and people willing to do anything to anybody in order to get ahead, but it was also supportive and protective of individuals that had talent or had an opportunity at making it out of the hood. Script was not only a gifted lyricist and MC but he could also draw which eventually led him to obtaining his college degree in graphic design. He had sketch books full of comic book characters, people, places and anything that his mind could envision.

I eventually agreed to manage Script and in the middle of finishing his first project, Elli was shot and killed. Fifteen-years-old and just starting to find himself and this young brother was murdered. Allegedly shot and killed by one of his own friends and fellow gang member. Script took it pretty hard but like me, he had grown accustom to death by violence. He also had grown numb to the pain associated with losing someone so young.

I started spending more time with E-Bass and Vato, going to studio sessions with E-Bass and networking with other industry heavyweights every chance I could. E-Bass was doing a lot of work with Roc-A-Fella Records and contributing to albums with Jay-Z, Memphis Bleek, DJ Clue, Cam'ron and The Diplomats and up-and-coming producers Just Blaze and Kanye West. Vato was working on Carl Thomas' new project and was starting to spend a lot more time around Puffy and the Bad-Boy camp. I started doing a lot of work with my old Money Boss Players crew, specifically with Tre-Bag, Eddie Cheeba and Minnesota, who had formed an affiliated group we called Boss Money. We ended up putting together a record deal with a new independent label based in Brooklyn and run by some Russian immigrants.

Minnesota, Cheeba, Trey and myself were spending almost every night at the label's brand new recording studio in Brooklyn where we started working on Minnesota's solo project. The label ended up signing Biggie's group Junior Mafia as well as an up-and-coming young comedian from Africa named Michael Blackson. I started hanging out with Lil Cease and Klepto from Jr. Mafia on a regular basis, spending hours together in the studio as they worked on what would become their second album, "Riot Music."

I took on Minnesota, E-Bass and Boss Money as official management clients. Most business was conducted late at night in clubs, bars or recording studios. Most of the recording sessions wouldn't even start until one or two o'clock in the morning so I was spending most nights away from home which was working out fine for me as my home life was less than desirable.

Not soon after I moved to New Jersey, even before we were married, I started noticing things about my relationship that didn't sit well with me. We were starting to clash on almost everything, from what type or color furniture to buy to what to eat for dinner every night. If I didn't bend to what she wanted then whatever issue was on the table would simply stay there, unresolved and waiting for one of us to back down. We started to have less and less physical contact and I was spending more and more time being frustrated and simply unhappy. In the middle of our newly developing hostilities, my oldest son was starting to have more serious issues at home and with school. I tried to convince his mother to let him live with me for years and she finally agreed.

I knew that he couldn't attend the public high schools in Newark. The school he was assigned to was notorious for gang activity and had just experienced a shooting inside the school itself. My wife did some research and talked to a few of her friends who recommended St. Benedict's, an all-boys private school a few minutes from our home in downtown Newark. We registered him for school, paid the tuition, bought him some uniforms and got him situated.

I have always felt like my son was ahead of where I was as a father. While I eventually started working on myself, trying to become a better person and developing myself as a man, he was always a few years ahead of where I was prepared to be as a father. I now had a teenage son in high school living with me and despite my excitement and desire for him to be close to me, I was struggling to get my bearings on our relationship.

He was going through adolescence and experiencing his own problems and I felt ill-equipped to help. I struggled to connect with him and find ways to help but didn't have the answers that he needed which left me feeling lost and embarrassed. I slowly, started to ease away from my responsibilities, often leaving my wife to fill in for me with simple day-to-day things like dropping him off at school in the mornings or taking phone calls from teachers when they called with a problem or updates. Understandably, she probably started to resent me for leaving her to handle the responsibilities of a child that was not hers and I can say now that I am truly grateful she stepped up and helped us both.

In my quest to find a way to bond, I discovered that we shared a love for music, especially hip hop. I began to bring him along with me to the studios some weekends and to hang out at Carl's house. When E-Bass was on tour with Kanye West for his "College Dropout" tour, I took him to meet Kanye West and hang out back stage at a big outdoor concert held at Rutgers University. As we walked through the backstage tent and grabbed some food from the spread that was set up for the artists, his jaw hit the floor when Kanye walked by and I introduced him. His very first concert and he was backstage hanging out with Kanye West, one of the biggest artists at that time. Kanye took the time to talk with him for a few minutes, asking him about school and how he liked living in New Jersey with me and my son was mesmerized! The look in his eyes was priceless. He was riding on an unbelievable high and spent the rest of the afternoon walking around smiling. He took pictures with John Legend, Kanye and a few other artists that were on the tour and smiled from ear-to-ear for days afterwards. For the first time in a long time I felt like a good father. I was finally able to provide something for my son that he needed and give him a father-son experience that would stay with him for the rest of his life.

His mother started to encourage him to move back to Rochester with her. It was the last thing he needed to hear as he had just started to get things moving in the right direction. He made the basketball team at his school, playing on a team that would later yield future NBA Champion J.R. Smith as well as another player that went straight from the high school team into the NBA. He was starting to finally get into a routine and showed signs of academic progress but wasn't comfortable with the strict structure that he had to follow at my house. His mother continued to coddle and baby him despite my protests that doing so would limit his ability to grow as a man.

Before the school year was over he moved back to Rochester. I was disappointed and angry with him and his mother but there was a small part of me that was relieved. Despite my love for him and desire to see him succeed, I felt ill-suited and severely unprepared to parent him at his age. I wasn't ready to be a father to a teenage son and I felt like I failed him. I felt as if I should have fought harder to make him stay and it is a regret that I carry to this day.

The joint parenting effort associated with my son seemed to bring my wife and I closer together. Since our earliest conversations she expressed her desire to have children, actually she specified that she wanted three or four kids. I loved my kids more than I can express but I had experienced so much drama with their mothers that I was completely turned off to the idea of having more children. I had grown comfortable with my youngest son being my last child and had already started counting down the days to when child support would be over. I was greatly looking forward to not having to be in contact with any of my children's mothers. As horrible as that sounds, that thought worked to calm me and gave me a measurable end to the drama. Many of my friends in similar situations coined the term "doing a bid," a reference comparing paying child support to doing a specified amount of time in prison. I assured myself that I only had a few more years to go on my first "bid" and that soon, my next "bid" would end as well.

The thought of having another child was frightening but I felt depriving my wife of her dream of motherhood would be selfish and wrong. She married me knowing that I had four children and I married her knowing that she wanted kids so I shook off my fears and we got to work on making one of our own. For the first time since before we got married we were back to laughing and being physically close on a regular basis. I hadn't realized how much I had missed being close to her, how attracted I was to her and how much hope I had that we could actually live happily-ever-after together. After a few months of trying she called me in tears and said, "I'm pregnant!" From that moment, I knew that we were going to have a boy. Everything inside of me told me so and everyone around us thought the same thing. I would have been happy with either a girl or a boy but I truly felt that this child was going to be another son, so much so that we only discussed names for boys.

My wife was riding on a pregnancy high, happy and always admiring her ever growing belly and I was finally starting to make a few dollars managing artists. I was focusing on working with music producers as their careers seemed to last longer and they were the first ones to get paid prior to a project being released. Producers with an established record like the ones I was working with were earning anywhere from five to forty thousand dollars for each track placed with an artist, depending on if the artist was on a major label or not. The problem was that it could take months before the artist would actually record a song at which point the producer would be paid half of their fee, with the other half of the fee paid right before the artist's project was released.

Many artists would record the song and then months, sometimes even a year or so would pass before the back-end payment would finally be paid. This meant that I could spend hours or weeks or sometimes months bouncing from studio to studio, sitting in on numerous recording sessions, politicking and networking left and right, and taking numerous meetings before a track might even be considered by an artist. My clients needed to be actively hitting up the studios, networking with artists and have numerous placements in the pipeline in order to sustain any type of steady income. I only got paid if my client got paid and I only received a percentage of whatever they were paid so I might have to wait six months or longer to receive a payment of a few thousand dollars.

With another baby on the way and a wife that was stressing me to get a regular paycheck I started looking for new ways to generate some income. I started learning about music publishing and did some research on how to reclaim past due money from unclaimed publishing. I managed to secure some publishing deals for a few of my clients which generated some nice checks for me and helped to keep my wife off my back for a little while longer.

Minnesota was doing a lot of work with Mos Def and we were in the studio almost every night working on Minnesota's solo project, Boss Money's project and Mos Def's new project. I was spending most nights bouncing from one recording studio to another, checking in with E-Bass as he worked with artists like Jay Z and Kanye West, and hitting the road doing occasional tour dates with Mos Def and Minnesota.

We got Minnesota a gig doing all the music for Russell Simmons' and Stan Lathan's "Def Poetry Jam" on HBO. I met all sorts of poets and artists through "Def Poetry" and got to learn a lot about how a television show was produced as well as got my first taste of television money! I had previously received checks from several major record labels that bounced, which was common practice in Urban music. Everyone was trying to screw over everyone else. But the money from television, movie and commercial work was paid in full and on time and we didn't have to wait months or years for a project to come out. As soon as we submitted the work and it was accepted, they cut the check.

We did some work on the Ali G show for Comedy Central and linked up with Dave Chappelle who asked us to produce some music for his original comedy special, "For What It's Worth" on Showtime. I finally manage to get E-Bass and Minnesota to do some work together and they ended up each co-producing the music for Chappelle's special which went on to garner an Emmy nomination.

While at the studio, I got a call saying that my wife had to go to the hospital because her water broke even though she wasn't due for almost two more months. I rushed to the hospital and she was placed on bed rest to try to slow the birth and give our unborn child more time to develop but the baby had other ideas and on March 4, 2005, she gave birth. I was there when my oldest son was born but missed the births of my other children and there was no way I was going to miss this one. I stood next to the doctor as he told her that it was time to push and watched in wonderment as she strained and moaned and pushed, attempting to help our child exit her body and enter this world.

The doctor stood between her legs and as she gave it another big push, the baby popped out suddenly, catching the doctor completely by surprise. The doctor had to literally catch the baby as the baby flew into the doctor's hands. Stunned, they quickly called for a nurse who wrapped the baby in a blanket and immediately started to clean off the face and suction out the mouth. Everyone waited to hear the cries of a newborn but instead the baby just looked around and started smiling! The nurses and the doctor all said that they had never seen a baby come out smiling before then the entire room froze as they looked at the baby, then looked at me. One of the nurses said, "Oh my god that baby looks just like you" to which another chimed in their agreement and then another.

I felt the tears welling up in my eyes as I looked at my newborn child then at my wife who was now also crying tears of joy. I realized that I hadn't heard anyone say "It's a boy," so I moved closer and looked between the baby's legs then my heart dropped. I went into a momentary panic as I realized that something was wrong with my son's penis. I looked closer and saw that my son didn't have a penis. I was stunned. I could feel my heart breaking. I mumbled out loud, "Where is his penis?" I couldn't believe that something was wrong with my son. My beautiful son had a severe deformity, then it hit me: He didn't have a penis because he, the son that I knew was a son from day one, was actually a she! I had a daughter. I said, softly at first, "It's a girl," then added more stridently, with beaming pride, "It's a girl!! We have a daughter!"

Prior to coming home from the hospital, she spent ten days in the neonatal intensive care unit for issues related to her six-week premature birth. The first time I put my hand through the small port in her incubator and rubbed her little finger she looked right at me, grabbed my finger and started smiling, melting my heart and solidifying an already indescribable bond.

After our daughter's birth, my wife stayed home from work for the short time provided by her job then I took over the responsibilities of taking care of our daughter on a daily basis. I spent considerable time with each of my children when they were born but this was different. I was home with my daughter every day. Bathing her, feeding her, dressing her, playing with her and watching her go through all the amazing changes that babies go through as they grow. I understood how fast children grew and having four older children helped me appreciate every milestone that she met and I made sure to document as much as possible by taking a ton of pictures and video.

We immediately decided that we needed to move to a community that felt safer for our daughter. I enjoyed living in Newark. I was only a three-minute walk to the express New Jersey Transit train, which only took about ten minutes to get to Midtown Manhattan. Newark had a ton of great restaurants and a quickly changing and modernizing downtown area but the Newark school system was horrible and crime was a serious problem. We knew we didn't want our daughter growing up in a city where gunshots could be heard nightly and drugs and violence were an everyday part of life so we started the process of preparing to buy a house in suburban New Jersey.

I started to think about all the things that my daughter wouldn't experience living outside of the city, the different set of hurdles she would have to overcome growing up a black child around mostly white people. While I was confident that she wouldn't have to worry about growing up hearing police sirens and gunshots or seeing dirty needles or crack vials laying on the sidewalk, I was worried about the damage that could still be inflicted by growing up in an almost exclusively white community. It seemed like no matter how hard I worked to escape it, no matter what income bracket I managed to achieve, the impact of race and racial identity was everywhere.

I looked at my daughter and held her close to me, feeling her warm, sweet breath against my cheek and I gently kissed her forehead. She smiled in her sleep and my heart sank as I thought about all the games that I had run on women in the past. I had the same thoughts when my first daughter was born. I thought about how men talked about women in barbershops and how I had participated in so many of those conversations in which we discussed and described women as only sexual beings. I thought about how many times I heard a woman cry because of something I had said or done. I thought about how women were paid substantially less than men for doing the same work and about how women had to fight for the right to vote. I thought about my mother and everything that I saw her go through in trying to raise her children. I knew that I had to do something more to make sure that the little lady in my arms got an opportunity to experience a different world and would always know that she had a father that was right there for her, ready to take on the world to make sure she was safe and happy.

I started to rethink my career choice after we bought our dream house and moved about forty-five-minutes to the west of Newark. An outsider looking in would have thought that I was living the American dream and in many ways, I was but I was growing tired of a lot of the nonsense associated with the entertainment industry. I worked hard to distance myself from the life that I once knew in the streets and while I hadn't sold drugs since I left Buffalo, I was surrounded by street culture and the same hood mentality that was associated with drug sales and violence.

Hip Hop itself came from the streets. I loved the culture, grew up in the culture and embraced the culture as a part of me. I loved hip hop but I had grown tired of the mentality that surrounded a lot of the entertainment people, many of whom were still affiliated with the same streets that birthed the culture itself. I was experiencing growing pains and wanted more than ever to remove myself from the negative behaviors and actions of "hood mentality." The same mentality that led to me being a convicted felon.

I put together a resume to see what type of job I could find in another industry. I gained a lot of experience putting together teams. I learned to communicate with and direct the various attorneys, accountants, A&Rs and other professionals working on our projects. I felt that I should be able to transition my skill set to another industry. While putting the resume together and talking with clients and colleagues about my strengths, a few of them told me something that I had not thought about. They pointed out that I had a unique ability to communicate and be comfortable with clients that came from some of the toughest projects in New York City. At the same time being just as comfortable and articulate when communicating with older, white executives, wearing suits and ties and sitting in big chairs in large corporate offices.

Many of my clients came from the hood and never had access to anyone that could show them how to manage money because no one around them ever had any money. I remember securing a publishing deal for a client and going to the publisher to sign the deal and pick up a check. The publisher gave us a check for $80,000 and my client demanded that the publisher pay him in cash! After much debate, the publisher finally sent two armed security guards to the bank and came back with $80,000 in cash. My client gave me my fee and put the rest into a large paper grocery bag, wrapped the bag up with some rubber bands then threw it in his backpack and we left.

I asked, "Why didn't you just get the check and put it in your account?" He said, "Two things: first I don't trust those crackers. I know that cash won't bounce! And second, I don't have a bank account. If I cashed the check at the check cashing spot, they would charge me a couple grand!" A few days later, I finally convinced him to let me go with him to open a bank account and showed him how to make deposits, check his balance, etc.

Sending my resume out was a rude awakening. I got a call about a job opportunity, spoke with an HR rep and had a great conversation then received an offer to come in for an interview. The rep sent me an application to complete and send back prior to my interview and when I read the application my heart dropped. I got that same feeling I had always experienced when applying for a job. I was hoping that he would somehow let me come in for the interview, knowing that if they just met me and spoke with me they would see that I was perfect for the job. After sending in the application which contained the exact same information found on my resume but also that little "Convicted of a crime" box, I received a phone call saying that the position was filled. I knew that was bullshit but what could I do but shake my head.

Determined not to let my past stop my progress, I started doing research on graduate programs and graduate degrees and decided that I wanted to try going back to school. I thought that going back to school and getting a Masters' in Business Administration would increase the odds of me securing a job outside of the entertainment industry. But before I could start working on a graduate degree I needed to finish my bachelors. I was told that I could take the courses I needed online and have them transferred back to Brockport so I could finish my degree from Brockport.

I was excited at the prospect of going back to school. I thought that it would be the best way for me to start working towards securing a regular job which I knew would thrill my wife. I was wrong. She was dismissive of my idea and told me that I should just try to find a job and not waste any time going back to school. I was stunned. I thought that she would jump for joy at my desired change but instead she gave me reason after reason as to why it wouldn't work.

There had been a lot of things troubling me about our relationship and although at the time I refused to believe it, I was starting to feel that she didn't want to see me grow. At business dinners or gatherings with her friends or colleagues, she would introduce me saying, "This is my husband, he's a stay at home dad." Then she would list her professional credentials and impressive job title. I didn't mind being a stay at home dad, in fact I loved being able to spend so much time with my daughter. Being there every day for her and watching her grow was amazing but I was irritated. My wife always failed to mention my achievements in the entertainment industry. It felt like she was attempting to put me down and diminish my accomplishments while glorifying her own. Maybe I was simply insecure or misunderstood but it happened frequently enough that it started to become a constant thought.

While I didn't have a traditional job I still managed to build a client roster that enabled me to work with clients on Emmy and Grammy nominated projects and Grammy award winning projects. I contributed to singles and albums that were certified Gold (500,000 units sold), Platinum (1,000,000 units sold), and even Diamond (10,000,000 plus units sold). Despite my successes, she almost never made mention of my work outside of raising our daughter.

I began to grow increasingly discontent with our relationship and I felt that she was as well. We almost never did anything together as a family. The time we spent with our daughter was usually separate and our physical relationship had dwindled down to barely bi-annual encounters. We spent a few times together as a family traveling to Europe and California, during work trips for her job. I was grateful for the opportunity to start seeing the world but secretly wished it had just been my daughter and I, or that I was there with someone else. Our differences were becoming more obvious and the divide between us began to deepen, especially once I told her that I had registered for the online classes to complete my degree.

I found that the online classes were much more difficult than classes in a traditional class room setting. I'm sure that being out of school for so long made a difference as well but I started off struggling with the work. I eventually got into a flow and managed to pass all four of my courses. Ten years after I initially started, I finally earning my Bachelors' of Science in history.

I started applying to graduate schools and I received a letter inviting me to come to New Jersey Institute of Technology for an interview for their Masters in Business Administration program. I went to the interview and was offered a slot in their upcoming executive MBA program. In order to make my acceptance official, they gave me an application to complete and once again my heart sank. I shook my head knowing that they would ask about criminal convictions and that as soon as I checked that "yes" box my opportunity at the school would disappear. As I read through the application, slowly making my way to the end, I breathed a sigh of relief. There were no questions about criminal convictions except one that asked if I had ever been convicted of a crime while receiving federal student aid. I couldn't believe that in less than a year I had decided to go back to school, finished my bachelor's degree and been accepted into a graduate program that seemed focused on accepting me based strictly on my previous positive accomplishments and not excluding me because of a conviction that was at the time, over ten years old.

25 BACK TO SCHOOL

While I had never been a fan of schools or the school systems, I had always enjoyed learning and I found myself reinvigorated and once again inspired by my business classes. Our class was small, less than fifteen of us in total and we took every class together. There was a strong emphasis on group work with the idea being that business normally involves working collectively with others towards accomplishing a common goal so they would have us break down into smaller work groups of three to four people per group.

I didn't mind the group work. I got along with all of my classmates and actually enjoyed spending time with them inside and outside of the classroom. We were a diverse group, six or seven Indian or Pakistani men and an Indian woman, an African woman from Senegal, an African man from Liberia, a couple down to earth white guys, an African-American-women from Virginia and me. Our backgrounds were all varied, some like the Liberian brother and a few of the Indians, had advanced degrees in science and others had degrees in business or architecture. Everyone was already working in professional fields and the diverse ethnic, cultural and professional experiences made for fantastic discussions that provided insight from a wide variety of angles.

I enjoyed the management courses but took a keen interest in the marketing courses. I had considerable experience with marketing and product roll outs from my work on various projects within the entertainment industry but I was surprised when we started discussing the four "P's" of marketing: product, price, place and promotion. We examined various case studies of companies like Walmart, with their amazing supply chain distribution system, and Nike, with their branding and promotional strengths, and compared them to companies like Google and Microsoft. As I studied and learned more about these businesses and the techniques they utilized, I realized that I had perfected and used many of the exact same strategies from my days in the streets. Like when I decided to stop trying to double my money off an eight-ball as everyone else was doing, diluting the product with cut and then taking shorts on the sales in order to compete, thus lowering my projected profits and putting me in the exact same situation as all of my competitors. Instead, I bagged up only $170 off a $150 investment lowering my profit margins to the bare minimum. I increased the volume of my sales and blew out my competitors by providing my customers with a higher quantity and superior product for the same price. I was able to take my competitor's customers, increase my cash flow and build stronger relationships with my suppliers, leading to large lines of credit that helped me to further grow my business.

I realized that when I decided to use vials while everyone else in upstate New York was still selling their coke in baggies, I differentiated my product by promoting it differently and establishing a sort of 'brand' mark that my customers would know and look for. These were the same types of business lessons that I took with me into entertainment and that I was now learning about in business school. I realized that I had already utilized most of the theories and techniques we discussed in class but that I just never knew what the techniques were called. While we discussed theory and academic study, I laughed to myself thinking that I had already seen the successful outcomes of most of these techniques in my own business practices.

Business school was teaching me the language of business and helping to increase my ability to communicate with other business professionals. I noticed that when I told people that I was working on my MBA, the attitudes of most of the business professionals changed; they became more friendly and open to dialogue and seemed more willing to look at me as a peer as opposed to "just another street dude in entertainment." I loathed their attitude change, knowing that I hadn't changed and that they should have recognized me for my ideas even before my MBA but I soon came to realize that adding a few letters to the back of my name could be a powerful tool in many circles so I began to restructure my views towards them and use it to my advantage whenever possible.

Besides enjoying my courses and my classmates, school offered an escape from the growing unhappiness at home. We decided to enroll my daughter in a pre-school program so she could start socializing with children and provide me with more time during the day to focus on getting school work done. I was hesitant to enroll her in school as I loved spending time with her.

She was the highlight of every one of my days and we had grown extremely close but as much as I enjoyed it, my wife hated it. I understood her feelings and used them as inspiration to better myself so that one day she might be able to stay home but I started to find it more and more difficult to empathize with her, especially with what appeared to me to be her growing open contempt for me trying to improve myself.

I hated the idea of taking my little princess to school but I was able to get my school work done as well as spend more time focused on handling business matters for my clients. I was even able to take some long weekends and hit the road doing some tour dates with artists my clients were working with whenever I didn't have weekend classes. I set up a few events in other cities to try to make some extra money as well as provide an excuse for traveling and getting away from the house. My man Fingers was working for one of New York City's biggest DJs, Funk Master Flex. Fingers had experience setting up club dates and getting sponsorship for the dates so we worked together to promote an event on our own. I was spending a lot of time in Toronto, networking and building with a few of the artists that Minnesota was working with and thought that Toronto would be a perfect spot to throw a party. I partnered with Fingers, my friend Josh from Newark and my man PK from the Bronx to set up a model search sponsored by one of the men's magazines.

Toronto was full of unbelievably beautiful women, world class beauties from all different ethnicities and countries. There were so many exotic women walking around Toronto that it felt like I was on a movie set. From Ethiopians, with beautiful caramel skin and long legs; to French Polynesian women, with almond shaped eyes, model like perfect faces and shy smiles; to gorgeous West Indian women from all over the Caribbean, with natural hair styles, curvy hips and full, magnificently perfect lips. The women in Toronto were down to earth and easy to approach. They were the complete opposite of New York women, with their "You better not say shit to me" attitudes! It was so easy to meet women in Toronto, all you had to do was say "hi," then engage in a genuine conversation and if the vibe was right it was on and popping! Being intimate once or twice a year just wasn't working for me so I had long since started stepping outside of my marriage. I had been all over the world and I couldn't think of any other place where there were more beautiful, intelligent and engaging women than Toronto, making a sexually frustrated, unhappily married man feel like a kid in a candy store!

At one of the events we had dozens of insanely beautiful women come out to take photos for a chance to win a spot in an upcoming urban men's magazine. After the photo shoot and interviews we had an after party where even more beautiful women showed up. The ladies outnumbered the men about five to one and with the owner and bartenders giving us free bottles we had an incredible evening. I met this exquisitely beautiful West Indian woman and we spent the night talking, laughing and getting very drunk.

I didn't know it then but I would soon find myself falling hard for Shanice. She was a few years younger than I was but carried herself in a way that made her seem much older. She had perfectly shaped full lips and high cheek bones that made her smile visible from across the room. Short but with long legs, full breasts, curvy hips and one of the most perfect asses I had ever seen! I was soon taking trips back and forth to Toronto just to hang out with Shanice and she had a lot of family in New York City so she started traveling to New York so we could hang out more frequently. We both shared a love for travel and she started surprising me with trips to places like Jamaica, Mexico and the Bahamas.

The more time I spent with Shanice, the more I realized how truly unhappy I was at home. She seemed to possess everything that I had been missing. She was an amazing cook, went out of her way to make me feel appreciated and provided support and encouragement for my educational goals. She was super feminine and always made sure her hair and nails were done and went out her way to make sure she always had sexy panties and matching bras. She exuded sexiness and made me feel desired and needed as a man and with her support, I started to seriously consider what I would do after business school and for the first time, I started thinking about pursuing a doctoral degree.

When I was an undergrad at SUNY Brockport, my grades were mediocre. I wasn't focused and didn't see the big picture but in business school I was a straight 'A' student, working hard towards making sure that I got the most out of each class and finally gaining some academic confidence. I started considering a doctoral degree mainly in urban planning but quickly got discouraged when no one contacted me after sending numerous emails and leaving countless phone messages at a number of the schools as I tried to gain more information about their programs.

I spoke with my business law professor about my frustrations with the PhD programs and she broached the idea of law school. She explained that a Juris Doctorate degree was similar to any Ph.D. but in law and would enable me to teach at the college level if that was my interest. It would also give me the added opportunity to become an attorney. She had worked as an attorney for over twenty years and told me that she was more than confident that I would excel in law school and more importantly, make an excellent attorney.

I smiled at the thought but I knew that if I had such a difficult time just trying to find a regular job, my felony conviction would definitely prohibit me from going to law school. After several conversations with my professor, I finally confided in her about my criminal past and told her that I knew that there was no way I would ever be admitted to practice law. She explained to me that my conviction would not prevent me from being admitted to practice in New York or in New Jersey! I was astonished and spent the next few weeks bombarding her with questions and conducting my own research, including contacting a few people that I knew in the court system and speaking with a few of my friends who were lawyers. Everyone told me the same thing, that my felony by itself would not disqualify me from practicing law.

My professor was a graduate of Seton Hall Law School and encouraged me to apply there. She said that she would write a letter of recommendation for me and help me prepare my application but first I had to take the LSAT, the Law School Admission Test. I found out the test was offered twice a year, signed up for the test and was set to take it a few months later. When I told my wife she just stared at me for a long time, not saying anything, then finally said, "Why are you wasting your time with that? You aren't going to be able to get into law school anyway, not with your record and besides, you have to take the LSATs and do well on them and I don't think that is for you." Once again I was left speechless. I told myself that would be the last time that I shared anything with her about my future plans as I was starting to feel that she would do everything in her power to shoot them down.

I bought a book to help me prepare for the LSATs but didn't

invest much time studying. My international business management course was preparing for a weeklong trip to Europe to meet with political leaders and business people to help us gain a well-rounded global view. We learned that almost seventy percent of the CEO's and top executives of US companies had never left the country but were trying to compete in a global marketplace and our program was determined to change that trend.

I had been to Europe before, to Italy, Switzerland and the Netherlands, with my wife and daughter but I was extra excited about this trip. We were visiting Vienna, Austria, and Prague in the Czech Republic and I scheduled a side trip, leaving my classmates when they were scheduled to depart to go home and instead stayed in Europe for an additional few days on my own. Shanice was flying over to meet me in Berlin for a day then we were going to Amsterdam for the rest of the week.

After spending the week with my classmates exploring Vienna and Prague, I jumped on a train to make the five-hour trip from Prague to Berlin. Shanice was waiting for me at the hotel in Berlin; we planned my train arrival to coincide with her flight so that we both got there at around the same time. I was growing closer to her. She had such a caring heart and I loved her easiness and her femininity. Seeing her standing there, smile lighting up her model like beautiful face, hands on her shapely hips as she greeted me with a goofy laugh, I couldn't help but feel warm and comfortable. Although we were all the way in Europe, in a strange hotel, I felt like I was home. Her arms around me instantly put me at ease, all of my stress melted away and quickly was replaced by warm feelings of joy.

I know now that Shanice enabled me to stay in my marriage much longer than what I should have. I stopped caring about not having sex with my wife, stopped trying to fix whatever needed to be fixed and simply shifted my focus to Shanice. We talked all the time. She proved to be an emotional crutch when I was feeling down, gave me boosts of confidence and stroked my ego when I needed it, and fulfilled my physical needs, giving me someone to fantasize about and look forward to spending time with. Other than my children, there was no one else that I would have enjoyed being in Europe with, so we set out to explore Berlin, laughing and soaking in the sights together.

We explored East and West Berlin, ate currywurst and falafel, and got drunk sipping on huge mugs of German beer. We got to see the old Berlin Wall as well as the Reichstag and the Berlin Television Tower. I love to travel and explore new cities and her love for travel added a boost of energy that kept us exploring until we were both exhausted. I rented a car and we drove the Autobahn from Berlin to Amsterdam. I always wanted to drive on the Autobahn and it was an amazing experience. I set the cruise control at around 180 Kilometers per hour, roughly 110 miles per hour, and sped all the way to Amsterdam, stopping along the way to get gas and explore a few of the older German villages. I thought I was going fast until a few Mercedes, BMWs and Porches flew by me like I was standing still!

We got to Amsterdam and unloaded our bags at the hotel, which was right across from the Central Train Station in the center of Amsterdam. I had been to Amsterdam before and couldn't wait to introduce Shanice to Pomfriters, the addictively good French fries that you top with peanut sauce, ketchup or any of the other options they offered. We grabbed some food, hopped on the train and did some shopping then made our way to the Red Light District to get some weed and relax. Amsterdam's Red Light District is named for the red neon lights on the inside of the large, full body length windows that line building after building. Prostitutes stand in the windows dressed in lingerie and high heels and wave at potential customers as they pass by. If you see something you like, you stop and they will leave their window, open a door and immediately start negotiating with you, trying to convince you to come inside and spend fifty or sixty euros to satisfy your sexual desires.

The first time I saw the Red Light district I was shocked. I had heard of it, seen images in magazines and movies, and listened to songs about it but actually seeing it in person was unreal. The windows were filled with beautiful women many of whom looked like they could be Playboy centerfolds and they were open to do just about anything if you had a few euros to share. I learned that there were side streets and alleyways that specialized in various types of women. One alley had beautiful dark skinned African women in the windows, another had all older women, and yet another that had only larger women.

Just outside of the alleyways were Coffee shops which sold marijuana, hash and mushrooms. Stepping into one of the dimly lit coffee shops you could pick up a menu that outlined all the various strains of weed available and their prices. They offered pre-rolled joints or weed by the gram and had a variety of edible weed products like cookies, brownies, cakes and candy, all infused with marijuana. I had never tried any drug except for marijuana but I convinced myself that I wanted to try mushrooms. I had always heard that a good trip on mushrooms could open your mind and increase your creativity but I was too scared so I opted to try some edible weed products first and if that went well, I'd come back later and try the mushrooms.

After speaking with one of the weed experts about the edibles, I bought a large brownie for five euros. The woman explained that I should eat about the same amount as I normally would smoke so I figured that the five-euro brownie must be about the same as a nickel bag of weed and I could smoke a nickel bag by myself with no problem. I bought a few grams of White Widow and some other super high potency weed and a couple of Blunts and we found a quiet place on one of the canals to sit and unwrapped the brownie. We each ate half, rolled up a blunt then jumped on the train to do some more shopping.

About thirty minutes later we decided to head back to the hotel as we were both starting to feel something. By the time we made it back to the hotel we were both extremely high but it was a different type of high, a high that I could feel radiating from the inside out. We made it to the room and I closed the door while she went and sat on the bed, then I stared at the door and my mind went completely blank. I stood there for at least forty-five minutes before I turned around and looked at Shanice, who was now sitting on the bed bent over with her hands folded across her chest, rocking back and forth shaking her head. It took me what felt like an hour to finally be able to speak, "God damn. . . I am high as a mother fucker!"

She just looked up at me, stopped rocking for a few seconds and tried to speak but ended up just laughing and then went right back to rocking and slowly shaking her head. I had never been so high in my life! After a few hours, my high was still intensifying and I was starting to get paranoid, worried about what was going to happen. At one point, I thought about opening the door and yelling "Somebody help me please!" but I talked myself out of it, knowing that there was nothing that could be done. I was super high and felt myself rising higher and higher and higher.

After about five hours, the high finally felt like it peaked and my intense anxiety was quickly replaced with ravishing hunger. Shanice was curled up in the fetal position humming quietly to herself but she lifted her head and nodded when I asked her if she was hungry. I tried to convince her to come out with me to grab some food but she couldn't manage to do anything but laugh and shake her head no.

Finally able to enjoy my high, I made my way around the corner and hit up the Pomfritter spot as well as a few of the sandwich shops that were filled with walls that looked like vending machines, all lined with tiny windows, each containing different types of snacks like burgers or hot dogs. I grabbed a couple of large juices and headed back to the room. As soon as I walked in, Shanice jumped up and grabbed some of the food and started eating like she hadn't tasted food in years. I was right behind her and within a few minutes we devoured everything, laughing as we looked at the empty food wrappers and containers strewn across the bed and the floor.

We woke up the next day both vowing to never, ever try edible weed products again! I found out later that we were only supposed to break off tiny pieces or take a small bite from the brownie, spacing it out over the entire day but we had eaten the entire thing all at once and paid the price. I gave away the White Widow and the other weed that I bought and have not had any weed of any kind since that day!

26 LAW SCHOOL

Following the advice of my business law professor, I signed up for the LSAT exam and went up to Rochester to take the exam. It was an all-day test focusing on logical and analytical reasoning and reading comprehension. The exam was timed and forced you to think and make quick choices or risk not having enough time to complete all the questions. I left the exam feeling somewhat confident but more so relieved that I had actually completed the exam and was a few steps closer to seeing if I had any real shot at getting into law school. When I took the test, I had to indicate where I wanted my scores sent so I did thorough research on schools before taking the exam.

I knew that I had to stay close to home and New Jersey only had three law schools; Rutgers-Camden, Rutgers-Newark, and Seton Hall. Rutgers Newark and Seton Hall were both located in downtown Newark and were closer than Rutgers Camden but there were also quite a few law schools in New York City, such as NYU, Fordham and Columbia. After researching the focus of each school as well as the cost, I decided that Rutgers Law-Newark was the best choice for me as it was considerably more affordable and ranked one or two positions above Seton Hall in the national law school rankings. Rutgers also had a strong focus on community and public law projects, things which I was very much interested in learning more about.

Thinking that my chances of getting into any law school, let alone Rutgers was very slim, I decided to send my scores to a few other schools even though I knew they were too far away to attend, reasoning that if one did accept me, I would at least be able to say that I got admitted. I sent my scores to the University of Michigan, Miami, Buffalo and the University of Connecticut. With the LSAT out of the way I started working on my law school applications. I sat down with my business law professor and she helped me put together an outline for my personal statement. The personal statement is one of the most important pieces of the application. It provides the school with a sample of your writing as well as insight into your personality. Strong writing skills are necessary in law school and there are no face-to-face interviews so they tend to place a heavy emphasis on the personal statement.

Even after being reassured multiple times by my professor as well as many of my attorney friends and people that worked with various judges, I was still highly doubtful that I would be admitted to any law school because of my criminal record. I figured that even if I was admitted there was no way that I would be able to practice law. My professor kept reassuring me that my crime was not considered to be a "character crime" and that they would consider the elapsed time as well as my accomplishments since the conviction.

I thought that the best way to address my concern was to make it prominent in my application. I decided to highlight it and then present them with what I had done since then to improve myself. I wrote my personal statement about being arrested and learning from the experience. I used quotes about change from Henry David Thoreau and emphasized my strong desire to change my life and never again revisit the choices that led to my previous arrests. I wrote it, rewrote it and rewrote it again, then had my professor proofread it and then I rewrote it some more until I finally felt that it was as good as it could get.

I included my transcripts from my associates degree, bachelor's degree and master's degree program. My undergraduate grades from my bachelor's program were less than impressive but I had a straight A, 4.0 average in my MBA program. I was also able to add a lot of my awards and accomplishments from the entertainment industry such as the Grammy nominated projects I worked on and the numerous Diamond, Platinum and Gold records I received for projects I worked on with clients. I double checked my applications and submitted them all, knowing that Rutgers Newark was the only school that I was actually interested in attending.

Just before the time frame for acceptance letters started, I saw a news report that a major university had mistakenly sent out twenty thousand letters of acceptance to individuals that were not actually accepted to the university! I shook my head and thought, "Damn, that must have really sucked!" Then a few days later, I received a letter in the mail from Rutgers Newark Law School. My heart started racing. I wasn't expecting to hear back from any of the schools I applied to for at least another month or so.

I carefully opened the letter then slowly read each word: "Congratulations on your admission to Rutgers School of law at Newark . . ." I lifted my head, rubbed my eyes then re-read the letter again, then again and again. I figured that they must have made a mistake just like the news reports I saw about the other university, so I called the admissions office and asked them if they could verify my acceptance. The woman on the phone laughed and said that I was the fourth person to call that day, then she reassured me and once again congratulated me on my acceptance into the Law School's evening program! The evening program courses took place at night, were usually attended by working professionals and took four years to complete instead of three years like a traditional law school day program.

I couldn't believe how far my life had progressed. I reflected on the challenges that I faced just trying to find a regular job and thought about how amazing it would be to become an attorney and start my own practice, not having to depend on anyone else to decide if they could look past my old criminal conviction and give me an opportunity. Then I thought about the reality of becoming a lawyer and once again felt an overwhelming doubt take over. How could I become a lawyer if I couldn't even get hired working as a cashier at most fast food restaurants because of my felony conviction? It just didn't seem like a realistic goal so I reached out to one of the Dean's at the law school and set up a meeting to discuss my concerns. To my surprise I was once again reassured that my offense would not prevent me from practicing law.

My MBA program was scheduled to finish in October but law school started in the middle of August which meant that I would have to balance both programs for the first few months. I was still doing some client management and had accepted a partnership opportunity with a friend of mine, Showbiz and Diggin in the Crates. Diggin in the Crates, or DITC, was an independent label that started in the early 1990's as a hip-hop group consisting of Showbiz & AG, Buckwild, OC, Big L, Fat Joe, Diamond D and Lord Finesse. DITC's office and recording studio were located inside of Headquarterz Studios, DJ Premier's mid-town Manhattan recording studio. I knew that business school, law school and work would be too much to handle so I made preparations with my clients and DITC to ease away from my professional responsibilities so I could focus on school.

Everyone was thrilled for me and proud as if they themselves were going to law school. I heard more than one of my friends and clients remark, "One of us made it! One of us is going to law school!" I realized that like me, most of my friends didn't know many, if any lawyers outside of the ones that they hired to assist with criminal or family court issues or to review contracts in the entertainment industry. No one trusted lawyers, in fact they would often say, "Man I need to hire a lawyer to watch my lawyer!" To make it worse, there were very few black attorneys especially in criminal or family law. I got pats on the back and a lot of "Yea man, I finally got a lawyer I can trust!"

I was still traveling back and forth to Rochester every other weekend to see my kids and bringing them down for Christmas, Spring break and summer vacation and I knew that finding enough time to study was going to be a problem. My children were priority number one so I knew that if I was unable to figure out a way to still spend quality time with them, law school wouldn't work.

I signed up for the minority student program, MSP, which required that participants come to school two weeks before everyone else. MSP provided participants with an overview of the law school process and showed us how to take notes, write a case brief and develop a study outline. For all the core law school classes, one hundred percent of your grade is based completely on your final exam. We learned how to read and brief a court case, taking the essential elements in the case and learning to understand how they might be applied to future cases or the court's reasoning in previous cases.

MSP helped familiarize us with the Socratic method of teaching, where the professor calls on a student then asks them question after question after question about the content being discussed, always pushing the student to elaborate on their position and thoughts. With the Socratic method, there is no simple "yes or no" answer; the focus is on the process to come up with whatever conclusion you present. We learned that many professors rely on a system of 'cold calling' students, randomly selecting students from the class and badgering them with questions whether they are prepared or not. One of the biggest lessons that came from our early MSP sessions was to always, no matter what, be prepared.

On the first day of law school, all the new students attend a swearing in ceremony. Rutgers has always prided itself on being the most diverse law school in the country and looking around the room it was obvious that diversity was important. There were almost as many women as men and while white faces still dominated the room I would estimate that at least one-third of the population was Black, Latino, Asian, Indian, etc. There were people of all different ages and, we soon learned, from all different professional backgrounds.

Some students were young, coming directly from undergraduate programs, while others such as myself were older and in their thirties, forties, fifties even sixties. The Dean started to speak about the diversity, mentioning that we had members of our class that were former NBA players, successful music industry executives (a shout out to myself), state troopers, detectives, medical doctors, accountants, and on and on. I looked around that room and felt like they must have made a mistake, a feeling that would become a part of me for most of my first two years of law school. There was no way that I belonged in a room with all those smart and accomplished people. I would find out later that most of my classmates felt the exact same way.

Traditional legal education is broken down into three years of classes. The first year, in which they refer to you as 1L, short for first year law student, every law school in the U.S is the same. Students take core classes which make up the basis for all future legal studies, starting with contract law, torts, legal research and writing, constitutional law, civil procedure, property and criminal law. Since I was going part-time and scheduled to finish in four years instead of three, my first semester started with two, four-credit courses, contracts and torts.

My contracts professor was switched at the last minute as my original professor was offered a position in the incoming administration as the Lieutenant Governor of New Jersey. My new professor was a smiling, jovial middle aged man with an immense vocabulary. Every time he spoke I felt dumb. I initially thought that there was no way I could make it through law school if that was how everyone spoke, but I came to understand that it was just this one professor and many of my other professors would roll their eyes when his name was mentioned as if to say, "Oh boy, yeah he always talks like that!" The first day in my contracts class, sitting right in the front row, I raised my hand to answer the very first question he asked the class. I gave a simple answer, referenced a case we read and provided a conclusion then sat back patting myself on the back for my brilliance.

The professor asked me a follow up question, then another and then another, and kept asking me question after question until I ran out of answers. He then proceeded to lecture the class although it felt more like he was personally lecturing me, for at least a half-hour on every single flaw in my answer. He walked us through the process to come up with the correct answer which to me seemed almost identical to the answer I provided in the first place. I slouched down in my chair and if I could have, I would have buried my face in my book bag and hidden it there. I spent the rest of the class looking at the clock, ready to jump out of my seat and run out of that room as soon as the class ended.

To my surprise, a number of my MSP classmates came up to me after class and told me that they didn't understand why he went in so hard on me then came right back and basically repeated my original answer as the correct answer. I felt a little better but still felt like I had made a serious mistake, or better yet, that the law school somehow made a mistake in accepting me. This continued for the next few weeks, one after another, my classmates and I got our asses handed to us in our classes. I found myself sitting in the back of the room slouching down and praying that they didn't call on me and, of course, like clockwork, out of the blue when it was least expected I would hear, "Mr. Bost, please help us understand the elements of the case," or "Mr. Bost can you contrast this case with the case we read last week?"

Just when I was feeling like I was the dumbest, most ill-prepared law student of all time the Dean of the law school called a meeting for all the 1L students. We sat around the atrium in the first level of the law school, many heads hung low, looking mentally worn out and then he spoke to us. He said, "I know that many of you are feeling like you don't belong here. That you are questioning your decision to come to law school and feeling like you are the dumbest person in the room." You could hear a collective snicker across the room and see heads nodding in agreement. "Well, I want you to understand something, we here at Rutgers hand-picked each and every one of you because we knew that you have what it takes to be successful law students, and more importantly, amazing lawyers."

Seeing that he now had all eyes on him he added that there were roughly three thousand and five hundred applicants for our class and out of them, only two hundred and fifty students were accepted. He told us that each of us made up one of those two hundred and fifty and there was no way he or anyone at Rutgers would let us do anything less than live up to excellence and succeed at the school. I lifted my head a little higher, looked around and for the first time thought, "Wow, maybe I do deserve to be here!"

While I was struggling through my first semester of law school, I was also trying to finish up my last few classes for my MBA program. When I shared with my classmates that I was doing both programs they all thought I was crazy. Doing both programs forced me to be highly organized with my time and provided almost no time for anything except for classes, studying, and time with my daughter and the kids. I would get her up, make her breakfast and take her to school then read cases until I had to pick her up from school then I would go to class at night and on the weekends, and in my down time study for finals and write papers for my MBA classes. I was exhausted but I felt like I was finally accomplishing something tangible with my life. I had measurable goals that were materializing daily, enabling me to feel like I was growing as a person and making more positive contributions to my children as a man. Graduate school provided a much needed boost to my psyche and law school made me feel like I had an opportunity for a newly optimistic future.

My oldest daughter's issues with her mother reached a breaking point and she decided it was time to come live with me. My wife was less than thrilled with the idea but I once again dismissed her feelings and moved my daughter to our home and quickly got her situated at the local high school. Although she never said anything to her or made any real indication that she didn't want her to live with us, my daughter felt the negative energy from my wife. Not knowing how to express what she felt at the time and seeing how busy I was with school, she just kept her nose down, went to school and tried to stay out of my wife's way.

In retrospect, I can understand some of the issues my wife may have had with my daughter living with us. I went from earning a few sporadic checks with my work in entertainment, to bringing home almost nothing and being a MBA and a law school student, leaving all the financial burdens on her shoulders. While she was earning more than enough money to take care of the household on her own, I think she felt taken advantage of with the responsibility of feeding another mouth. On top of the stress in our home, my daughter was having a hard time adjusting to life in a very different environment than where she came from. She spent a lot of time at the house with me previously while on vacations and during the summers but going to school in the community was a different situation. She was coming from a highly diverse performing arts school in an urban area with a total of only seven or eight hundred students and moving to one of New Jersey's second or third largest public schools made up of roughly four thousand kids with over ninety percent of them being white.

She told me that it was like something she saw in a movie. There were social groups made up of athletes, the jocks; kids that wore all black, painted their nails black and wore dark eyeshadow, she called them the goths; the yuppie, valley girl types, mostly composed of cheerleaders; the nerds; and of course, the druggies. She felt like she didn't fit in and to make things worse, as soon as I filed papers to stop paying child support because she was living with me, her mother started to pressure her to move back. After finishing half of the school year, she moved back to Rochester, just in time for a child support court hearing in which her mother was then able to say that I should continue paying support because she was now living back at home with her.

Despite my ongoing personal issues, I managed to finish my MBA program and make it through my first year of law school even though preparing for law school final exams was a serious challenge. We created outlines of all the material from class lectures, notes and reading cases, and utilized the outlines to study for the finals. The outlines helped organize the vast amount of cases and laws that we had to memorize and helped create a sort of a map through the material. We would pull any final exam that the professor had on file in the library and go over every question on the exam. Most of them consisted of one or two essay questions in which the professor provided a hypothetical fact pattern. We had to pull the relevant facts form the hypothetical and then apply the laws we learned to those facts, providing a conclusion that tied together the facts with the law.

To help study, I joined a few study groups, one with about

eight or nine classmates and another with four or five. I quickly found out who I studied well with and we formed a smaller group, originally with five of us. We would reserve a small room inside the law library and lock ourselves in for eight to fifteen hours at a time, usually discussing, debating and thoroughly going through the material.

I already felt as if I was the dumbest person in the classroom and being up-close and personal with my classmates only intensified those feelings. These were some of the most academically intelligent people that I had ever been around. They always seemed to understand the material at a deeper level or were able to point out issues that I didn't even think about. They expressed that they felt the same way about me, commenting that I added things to our study group that they never thought about. These study sessions helped develop trust among our group members and increased the admiration and respect that we all had for each other.

I was extremely nervous taking my first exam, which ironically took place on December 12, my birthday. I think we had five hours to complete the exam and as soon as the proctor said, "You may begin," all you heard was the click of keyboards and an occasional sniffle or cough, coupled with the shuffle of the exam papers. Everyone wrote furiously, most of us right up until the proctor said, "Please stop writing, the exam is now over." Hands would cramp, shoulders would be tense and most of us would come out of the exams shaking our heads and doubting ourselves. If we only had one exam we would head across the street to McGovern's, a bar frequented by practicing attorneys and law students or head to our lockers and pull out one of the bottles of liquor we all had stashed away, grab a glass, and have a few drinks. If we had another exam the next day or sometime that week, we would leave the exam, get something to eat and head into one of the study rooms for another eight to twelve-hour study session.

Being an evening student meant that we had to take classes during the summer so I spent a lot of time with my face buried in law books while my kids ran around and played at the house and in the pool. Even with all the studying, I still managed to spend a lot of quality time with my kids, and my daughter was still with me every day while my wife was at work. I felt like I was finally doing something that my children could be proud of and that my mother could smile about. Each time I finished a final exam, I would head home, take my large case book and place it on my book shelf. The shelf started off empty but at the end of each semester I would add two or three or four more case books, slowly filling it up and allowing me to visualize my progress.

Knowing that my goal was to eventually open up my own law practice I knew I needed to get experience practicing law as soon as possible. Law school was great at preparing someone to think like a lawyer and to analyze and focus on legal principles but it didn't do much to prepare you for the actual practice of law. Right after my first semester, I was able to secure a legal internship with a criminal defense attorney doing research for cases, drafting minor motions, meeting with and interviewing clients and making court appearances with the attorney.

The attorney, James Gizzi, had been practicing for almost twenty years and handled juvenile cases in Essex County, New Jersey, and adult criminal matters in Bergen County. The Essex County Family Court, which also handled the juvenile criminal cases, was a few blocks away from the law school so I was able to attend court dates when needed and then walk right up the street to attend class when I was done.

Through James, I met judges, prosecutors and other attorneys and discovered that most of the black judges and attorneys went out of their way to offer their business cards and extend invitations to contact them if I needed anything. Most of the judges provided words of encouragement regarding law school and the black judges in particular, took the time to ask me about my studies and always greeted me with a smile or a friendly gesture whenever I appeared in their courtroom. Without directly saying so, they made it clear that they respected my pursuit of a career in law and they understood how difficult it was to succeed in a field that had traditionally been and still was, dominated by white men.

I had long ago realized that I had advantages in many situations when dealing with people of color in the professional world. This was highlighted when we had a fourteen-year old client that was arrested for his fifth robbery with a weapon. When he came into court, his pants were sagging down, exposing his boxer shorts and I could see the red handkerchief he tried to hide in his back pocket. His arms were covered with tattoos that I immediately identified as being affiliated with the Bloods. The Bloods and Crips were the two dominant gangs in Newark and were broken down into smaller Blood or Crip sets depending on the neighborhood you were from. A few years before, E Bass and I started a small recording studio on South 18th Street in Newark on a block that ran directly between two competing Blood and Crip neighborhoods. The client's tattoos matched the same set signs I would see tagged in graffiti all over the neighborhood so I knew he was from around that neighborhood.

Gizzi, the client and myself all went into one of the small attorney meeting rooms outside of the courtroom and sat down to talk. Before the client could sit down I suggested that he pull his pants up and button his shirt so he could cover the tattoos on his neck. I explained that it wouldn't look good in front of the judge. He obliged and gave me a head nod acknowledging his thankfulness of my advice. Gizzi introduced me as his law intern then immediately started to tell the client what the Prosecutor was offering. The client looked at me as if to say, "What do you think?"

Knowing that Bloods often address each other as "Blood" or "Bro" I said, "you from around 18th street bro?" Looking surprised, he sat up a little, slightly straightening his posture and nodded his head yes. "Listen, this is your fifth arrest for robbing someone with a gun, maybe the stick-up game isn't your thing, it's probably time to find another hustle."

The client looked me in the eyes and said, "Man where you from? None of these people in here talk to me like you do." I told him I was from New York but lived in Newark for a long time and was familiar with his neighborhood. I spoke to him as if we were both standing on a street corner in the middle of the hood, changing my dialect from the proper, courtroom etiquette that I used with my classmates, the judges and other attorneys, and reverting to the language that I knew would be easily relatable to him. He explained what happened in his case and provided some useful information that he hadn't shared in his previous meetings with Gizzi. We were able to use the information to leverage a plea deal for the client and got him probation instead of the serious jail time he was facing.

As the client spoke, Gizzi looked at me and when we were alone said, "How the hell did you do that? I have represented that kid for the past few years and he has never said more than a few words to me. You got him to tell you his entire life story! I don't know what you plan on doing when you are done with law school but you definitely have a bright future in criminal law!" I laughed and said, "Man, he just doesn't trust you. To him you are just another white man with a suit in the system."

After a few more similar conversations, I finally opened up to Gizzi and told him about my criminal background. I told him a little bit about my experiences in the streets and with selling drugs and he said, "You are able to communicate with these clients from their perspective because you have been in their position before and they can feel that."

Through Gizzi, I found myself in a jail cell for the first time in decades. We were at the Bergen County Courthouse and we had to meet with a client that was being held in the county jail. As we walked around the courthouse, down some stairs towards a large locked basement door, my heart started racing. I knew that I had done nothing wrong but many of the same feelings I got whenever I found myself in handcuffs headed to be processed somewhere all started to resurface. I tried to calm my nerves by laughing it off and embracing the irony of the situation but as Gizzi pressed the button to have us buzzed in, my head started spinning.

We signed in on the attorney log book, walked through a metal detector with our brief cases then they gave us both visitor passes and directed us to walk through the main corridor with the holding cells towards the back room where attorneys meet with clients. As we walked past the various holding cells, each containing ten to fifteen inmates, all sitting or lying down on hard benches while some were spread out on the floor, I felt it all rush back to me. The smells, the sounds of loud inmate voices bouncing off the hard concrete and brick walls, the officers' keys jingling as they walked. It all felt eerily familiar.

Without even thinking or realizing it, I went into jail mode. I walked with my back closer to the wall and positioned myself so that no one could sneak up behind me. My face hardened and I looked into each cell intently, making sure not to dart my eyes away too quickly from anyone else's stare or to stare at them long enough as to give them a reason to confront me. One of the older inmates, a chiseled dark skinned brother that looked like he had spent a lot of time locked up, stared at me intently and said questioningly with a curious smile, "Man what are you doing here?" I felt that he could sense that I had been in his shoes before; he sensed my uneasiness as I passed and we both gave each other a head nod to acknowledge him being correct.

Here I was, clean, suit and tie, brief case in hand, walking through a jail to see a client that I was now representing, while the entire time I was thinking and feeling like an inmate myself. It was the most uncomfortable feeling and it wouldn't pass until well after I had walked out of the jail, got into my car and drove away. A few days later I told Gizzi how I felt and without hesitation he said, "Well get used to being on this side of the bars; you worked hard and you deserve it, hell they deserve to have somebody like you working on their cases! You are going to make one hell of a criminal attorney!"

By the time my first year was over I had developed relationships with a handful of truly amazing people. Veer Patel, one of my study buddies was a first generation Indian-American, born to Indian parents that immigrated to the US just before Veer was born. He was the valedictorian of his undergraduate class and seemed to know everyone, both students and faculty. My other study buddy who would turn out to be one of my very best friends, Chinyere Ofoma, who we called "Chichi", was born and raised in Nigeria before moving to the US to get her undergraduate degree at my Alma Mater, NJIT. She had worked as an IT consultant for some of the largest fortune 500 companies and had traveled the world before deciding to attend law school Chichi was tall, dark skinned, gorgeous, thick in all the right places and extremely smart. She could skim a case once and pick out every single important nuance then apply that case to some obscure point from another case that we read two months prior. Veer was also very sharp and the two of them combined to make me feel like slow, old and oddly out of place.

We took every class and studied for every exam together. Usually when you saw one of us, you saw all of us. My evening law cohorts were much more helpful with each other while the generally younger day students were more standoffish and academically competitive. The evening students realized that the classroom was just that, a classroom, and seemed to have a much better understanding of the importance in establishing strong networks so we all spent considerable time hanging out together both inside and out of the law school and assisting each other whenever we needed anything, school related or personal.

While I floated among the various small cliques of student groups, mingling with Black and Asian classmates, cracking jokes and grabbing drinks with my Indian and White classmates, and studying with Jewish and Latino peers, many of my classmates stayed mostly among their peer groups. As had always been the case, I was comfortable among all groups of people and they were comfortable around me. One of my white classmates pulled me to the side one day to ask me about the Minority Student Program. I explained to him about the tutors they provided and gave him the contact information for the program director. With a great deal of contempt, he said, "It all makes sense now. . . I knew there was a reason that most of these people got into school here, they had an advantage over everyone else."

I explained to him that MSP had nothing to do with the admission process and that anyone could have checked the box to participate, including him. I then pointed at various black faces as they walked by, saying, "That's Lisa, she did her undergraduate studies at an Ivy league school and has a master's degree. . ." Pointing to a young brother I said, "Mitchell right there, he was the valedictorian of his undergraduate class at Cornell, he received full scholarship offers from damn near every law school in the country." Pointing to two beautiful young sisters sitting together quietly studying I added, "Both of those young ladies right there scored in the 170's on their LSATs. I don't know anyone from MSP that had an advantage over anyone else because of the color of their skin."

He seemed unimpressed but admitted that he had gained a better understanding of MSP. Many of my classmates would come to me with questions about race and I always took the time to engage them in a conversation. I developed a philosophy that the only way to battle racism and stereotypes was through open, nonjudgmental communication. The more we talked about race, the more comfortable they were with asking questions about things that they really wanted to understand. I would question them as well, trying to gain insight into their cultural, religious and racial beliefs. From my Hasidic Jewish female friends, I learned about the importance of women always covering their heads and my Jewish male friends explained to me why men wore payot, those long curly hairs along their sideburns. I joked that I was going to become a Jew just so I could wear one of those big fur hats in the winter time! I joked with my Asian friends about their horrible driving and they in turn joked with me and openly asked me about black stereotypes. Through humor and patient conversations, we explored stereotypes and gained deeper understanding of each other.

While I was thriving in my academic pursuits, life at home was becoming more tense. I completely gave up on trying to reestablish any type of physical relationship with my wife. After years of being told "not tonight" or "I'm not in the mood," I conditioned myself to not be attracted to her. I focused on what I perceived to be her physical flaws, refused to let any type of desire for her enter my mind and instead focused on my attraction for Shanice. When Shanice and I weren't able to see each other I would hang out with a law school classmate or another female friend, always making sure that I came home with zero interest in being physical with my wife.

There were no longer arguments about sex or affection which helped ease some of the tension but we were both unhappy and I knew it was just a matter of time before we would have to call it quits. I tried to convince myself that I needed to hang in there for my daughter, that she needed to have both of her parents together under one roof but my daughter was watching us through her young, watchful eyes, and we were teaching her what unhappiness looked and felt like instead of showing her what love was about.

We tried marital counseling a number of times and when that didn't help, finally started talking about divorce. I figured that we could handle it on our own, saving money, time and the emotional toll that can be associated with the court process. She agreed and told me that she would prepare and send me a settlement agreement for my review. When I received the agreement, I knew that the odds of us working it out on our own were slim. She wanted to keep everything, every dime, the house, the cars, everything. But even worse, she wanted me to agree to every other weekend visitation with my daughter. I reminded her that I was the primary care provider for our daughter, that I got her up, fed her, got her dressed, took her to school, picked her up from school, bathed her and made her dinner every day of her life. I didn't care about the money or the house, I just wanted to continue to be there with my daughter every day as always.

I sent her cases to read, legal statutes dictating how divorce was handled in New Jersey and suggested that she read up to get a more realistic idea of how things would play out if we went to court. She sarcastically reminded me that I was only a second-year law student who didn't understand the law and I reminded her that the only legal work she had done in the past decade was contract work and that I had been dealing with family law issues for the past twenty years. Needless to say, we got nowhere and eventually just stopped talking about separating as well as anything else.

I had always been a private person and went out of my way to keep my business, good or bad, to myself, so much so that none of my family or friends knew anything about the problems I was experiencing in my marriage. I felt that sharing negative information with them about my wife would make them look at her the wrong way and even if we had rectified our issues, that they wouldn't forget about them and move on the same way I would. I had seen firsthand how families and friends could ruin relationships if they were let too deep inside of the inner workings of those relationships and I knew that the last thing we needed was outside problems exacerbating our issues. Initially, I was discreet in my outside relationships, trying to be as quiet as possible and keep things low key so that even though she was aware I was cheating, no details ever came back her way but eventually that changed.

When Shanice came to town I started doing more things with her and her family, going to weddings, family gatherings, short trips to the Caribbean, and whatever else she wanted to do. When she wasn't in town I had no problem going to dinner with female friends, sharing drinks at a bar or attending events with them as their date. Eventually one of my exes that I allowed to reenter my life went a little crazy when I tried to break things off with her and she contacted my wife, telling her that she had been spending time with me. This led to more arguing and seemed to push our already tension filled relationship over the edge as it appeared to be what we both were looking for, some sort of articulable reason to finally start what we both knew was inevitable.

Things sort of went back to the way they were except now I was very much aware that I needed to start developing an exit strategy. Law school was going well. I secured another internship and was again working on cases, this time personal injury and civil in nature and I was starting to find my groove in school. Studying was becoming easier and I found that my way of thinking was changing. Law school breaks you down then builds you back up as it erases years of thinking one way and replaces your well relied upon common sense way of thinking with logic based on legal principles, facts and disproving facts.

My youngest son was going through some issues with his mother and was starting to get into some trouble outside of school. His mother had threatened to put him out of the house and I used this as my opportunity to come get him so he could live with me. I told my wife what was going on and from the start she was completely against him living with us. Despite her objections there was no way I was going to turn my back on my son so I made plans to go get him from Rochester and bring him back with me.

I managed to make my way through my final exams even though I had absolutely no focus. After a series of arguments about my son and realizing that I could no longer take being in a marriage with someone that I had lost all attraction and respect for, I knew it was time for me to file for divorce. Instead of studying for finals, I was wasting time arguing with her and eventually I neglected my studies and began aggressively researching matrimonial law. After spending three straight days in the law library working on my divorce complaint, I had an attorney friend help me review everything and went and filed for divorce. My wife was beyond pissed when I had her served with the divorce complaint and the tensions in our home grew as she took out her anger on me every chance she got. Our marriage had technically ended a long time ago but starting the divorce and all the energy wrapped up with it took a toll on me that I wasn't anticipating.

Right after I finished my exams, I went to Rochester to pick up my youngest son and bring him back. I felt horrible that he was leaving one unstable drama filled situation and coming with me into a brand new one. He had just failed the seventh grade for the second time, mostly because he missed about half of his days in school. He told me that his mother had never pushed him or provided him with assistance with school; in fact, he confided in me that she had asked him to stay home with her on most of those days so that he could help her around the house. I knew that education was not a priority for her but I was furious to find out that she was a major reason why he was now looking at falling behind two entire grade levels. When I received his school records they confirmed that he had missed seventy to eighty days each school year for his last few years.

A friend recommended a private summer school program in Newark that would help him earn the credits he needed to officially pass the seventh grade as well as help him get the credits he needed to pass the eighth grade, meaning that if he completed the program he could be qualified to start school as a ninth grader after the summer. I discussed my son coming to live with us and again my wife protested. I had no intention of moving out of our house as I learned that might provide her with an advantage in the custody and property distribution aspect of the divorce, and I was still confident that despite our issues we could continue to live amicably together until we were able to finally work out terms to separate. To me, things were no different than they had been the past five or six years.

The night before my son was set to begin his summer school program, my wife kept trying to start an argument with me and I kept walking away. She followed me, yelling and screaming, as I kept reminding her that she should lower her voice so the kids didn't hear her. Eventually she cornered me in the laundry room, a small closet like room off the kitchen in the house, and tried to escalate the argument. I ironed my clothes, ignored her ranting and raving and tried to walk past her on my way to the kitchen. She pushed her shoulder into me slightly then yelled, "You just pushed me, you just pushed me, you are going to jail!" I shook my head and kept walking past her then I noticed that she had the house phone in her hand. She raised the phone to her face and started talking, "Yes, he just pushed me, send the police immediately. He is a convicted felon and he just pushed me."

Until that point, I hadn't noticed that the entire time she was following me around the house trying to start an argument with me, yelling and screaming, she had the house phone in her hand and had already dialed 9-1-1. Fortunately for me, I didn't argue back and continued to ignore her so all the 9-1-1 operator heard was her yelling and screaming. I went to my bag, grabbed the divorce complaint then went outside and sat in a chair in the driveway waiting for the police to come. Two white officers came, one spoke with me in the driveway while the other went inside and spoke with her. After both officers conferenced together, the one that had been speaking with me said, "Look, this is really a waste of our time. She said you brushed by her in the kitchen and now she is fearful that you will hurt her." The other officer added, "I know this is bullshit but she wants to file a police report."

I just shook my head and laughed to myself as I thought about how one of the divorce attorney's that I had met with told me that this would happen. He told me that if he was her attorney, he would tell her to do exactly what she was doing, to call the police and get me out of the house so she could gain leverage in the divorce. He actually suggested that I do the same thing; file a police report about one of the recent incidents where she had physically attacked me and get a restraining order to get her out of the house but I explained to him that I couldn't do that. I explained that we had a child together and I was still holding on to hope that we would be able to amicably work out the divorce agreement for the sake of our daughter. He was right, I should have listened.

She filed a police report based on me brushing against her, saying that she felt threatened. In order to protect myself, I did the same thing, alleging the exact same set of facts she put forth. At 3 a.m., the judge heard both sides via phone and ruled that I should leave the house with my son and that neither of us should have contact with the other. With no place to go, limited access to money as she had transferred money from joint accounts and made every attempt to take away all available resources, I got a hotel room and got my son settled in for two-hours of sleep before his first day of summer school. We were allowed to grab a few clothing items from the house before we left. Little did I know that it would be the only thing I would be able to get from the house for months to come.

The only thing I was truly concerned about was seeing my daughter. The longest we had ever gone without seeing each other was a week when I was traveling. All I could think about was her and what she must be thinking and what her mother was telling her. I repeatedly stressed to my attorney that she was my main concern. I wanted to ensure that she knew that I hadn't deserted her but even more importantly, I needed to know that she was safe, comfortable and happy.

Show gave me the keys to his place in the Bronx and my son and I stayed there until things were settled. Not wanting my son to feel like we were homeless and wanting to keep him busy, I started taking him to a boxing gym in the Bronx run by Aaron "Superman" Davis. I would take him to school in the morning, a thirty-minute ride into Newark if we drove or an hour or so on the train. He would go to school while I studied then I would pick him up, get us something quick to eat and he would hang out at the law school working on his homework while I was in class. When I finished class I reviewed his homework and helped him with anything that was problematic then we would head to the boxing gym in the Bronx before going to the apartment, cooking dinner and settling in for the night.

Routine and staying busy kept me from losing my mind as I constantly thought about my daughter. I grew more and more resentful and angry at my wife as I thought about the things she had done, fabricating a bullshit story and calling the police with a full understanding of the dangers a black man faced from the police, keeping my daughter from me, leaving my son and I with no clothes and nowhere to go. When I finally started telling people about what was taking place no one could believe it. They thought we had the perfect marriage, mainly because I never spoke bad about her or shared our issues with anyone. The only person that had any sort of inside scoop on the situation was Shanice but even she was surprised at how ugly things had gotten.

It took about a month of filing court motions, having her continually ask the court for adjournments and numerous court appearances but I eventually got to see my daughter for a short weekend and then I had to wait another few weeks before I could see her again. Being away from my daughter was killing me and my wife knew it and she used that to try to gain leverage in the divorce proceedings.

I found an apartment about thirty minutes away from my daughter's school and in one of the top school districts in the state so my son would be placed at a good high school. The first night we spent at the new place, we packed up the few things we had, bought a couple of pillows and some blankets, and camped out on the floor in the new apartment. We had nothing, no furniture, no clothes, no dishes, forks, plates, pots or pans, towels, clothes, absolutely nothing, and she refused to let me come get any of the furniture or belongings from the house. Despite having nothing at all, I felt relieved and bathed in the positive energy that was surrounding our new home. I hadn't realized how negative and unhealthy my relationship was but I could now physically feel it around me. I opened up a few lines of credit at a couple furniture stores, bought my daughter a bedroom set and mattress, bought myself and my son the same, and set out to slowly buy the things we needed. Within a few weeks we had furnished the apartment and bought all the essentials to keep us going, including new clothes for him and a few things for myself.

A few weeks after we were settled, my son said, "Dad, I don't know how you managed to keep going to school through all of that. You got me to school and only missed one day yourself." I had been so focused on getting things situated for us that I didn't give much thought to school for me or for him. It wasn't something that was an option, it was a mandatory part of our lives. Hearing his words choked me up as I realized that he recognized how hard those few months were for me, and more importantly he saw the emphasis that was placed on education. By the end of the summer, he had completed all of his seventh and eighth grade credits and was able to enroll as a ninth grader in high school.

As I prepared to start my third year of law school, I was still only seeing my daughter on an almost every other weekend schedule, going to court at least once or twice a month for issues related to my divorce and now I was going to court for custody of my son as well. As usual, his mother was moving slowly on doing anything for him. She wouldn't provide his insurance information which I needed for his school and was dragging her feet on sending his social security card. I filed a motion for custody in Rochester and eventually won full custody of my son.

For the first time out of the twenty or so years I had dealt with family court in Monroe County, the judge looked at me as if I was a positive human being and not just some convicted felon or alleged dead beat dad. The judge was highly impressed with the fact that I had earned my bachelor's degree, master's degree and was now in law school as a single parent and seeking custody of my son. He joked with me about law school and said he was going to be peppering me with questions using the Socratic method and I joked back that after driving all night to get to court, which I had done, and dealing with my law school professors, that I had no energy left for him! It was the first time I felt somewhat comfortable in family court, like I had finally reached some sort of equal ground in the eyes of the court.

My son's law guardian laid out my son's history prior to living with me; his attendance record where he missed an unacceptable amount of days one year and even more the next year; his failing the seventh grade twice; and his mother's lack of support for school. He also told the judge that my son had completed all of his seventh and eighth grade credits over the summer he spent with me and that he was now enrolled in one of New Jersey's better high schools and was doing extremely well as a ninth grader. The judge congratulated me, wished me well on my studies and granted me sole physical and legal custody of my son.

I left the courtroom and went straight to the clerk's office to file a modification request for child support, providing them with a copy of the custody order as well as proof of him living with me, and then stopped by G's house to give him the papers to serve on Shatina. G was always more than happy to serve her with papers. He couldn't stand her, especially since he witnessed her trying to run me over in his front yard and he almost got hit with the car in the process! He always served her with papers with a big ass smile on his face then laughed his ass off all the way home.

I told my son what happened and explained to him that I was about to take his mother to court so that I could stop paying her child support. He was surprised and couldn't understand why I would pay her support if he was living with me. I explained that the courts won't change anything unless you ask them to so I had to ask them for the change. He shook his head and said, "That's messed up that my mom doesn't just change it, she knows I live with you." I just shrugged my shoulders, not wanting to say anything negative about his mother in front of him. Then smiled after he walked away, knowing that he was starting to see some things for himself.

I scheduled my classes around my son's schedule, making sure that I would always be home when he got home from school so that I could help him with his homework. He had a lot of gaps in his education from the poor school system in Rochester, missing most of his last few years of school and not having any type of academic support at home. We would spend three to four hours a night working on homework, going back and learning things he hadn't learned before and reviewing what we did previously so that he wouldn't forget. It was frustrating for him, especially when his younger sister would come home with homework that was right at the same grade level we were working on for him. He took regular classes but I got him into a remedial math class and tutored him at home on the foundational stuff he was missing. He initially hated math but with the help of a really good teacher and the additional tutoring at home, he went from being a "D" or failing student in math to an "A" student. He was making straight "A's" in all of his classes and for the first time in his life he told me that he felt like he could be anything he wanted to be, that he could actually do something with his life.

I was feeling indescribable pride with him and what we had accomplished. Then his mother began to call him and things started to change. She hadn't spoken to him for months and it felt like as soon as I served her with child support papers, she started calling and I immediately saw a change in his behavior. One of his teachers called me and told me that he hadn't handed in homework assignments for the past few weeks and was no longer participating in class. When I confronted him about it he was dismissive, saying that it didn't matter anyways because he was going to go back to Rochester with his mother. I was floored and totally lost it, yelling at him and trying to get him to understand how terrible of an idea that was.

He said his mother told him that I was keeping him away from her and not letting her see him, which was complete nonsense. She hadn't made any attempt to even contact him until after she was served with those child support modification papers. I sat him down, handed him the child support papers and said, "Look, you are old enough to see things for yourself. I had your mother served with child support papers a few weeks ago. When did she first call you? Don't answer, just think about what I'm showing you. It says right here that you live with me and I have custody of you and that is why I am asking them to stop my payments, because you live with me. You know your mother; you know how she moves, think about this before you go too far."

He refused to look at the papers and continued to not turn in homework, not participate in class and basically protest having to live with me. Eventually, after a number of fairly serious issues came up. I had to put him on a bus and send him back to his mother. She won. She convinced him to come back to live with her and less than a week after we went to court for the child support hearing, my son was kicked out of his mother's house and living at a friend's house, a pattern that would continue off and on for the next few years until he eventually dropped out of school and ended up getting into some legal trouble related to an incident involving his mother.

Once again I found myself with final exams approaching and serious drama dominating my life. I managed to shut myself off from the rest of the world, bury my head in my notes and focus on learning as much as I could in hopes that I would somehow manage to do well on the exams. Law school was a lot of work but it offered an escape from my problems and allowed me to forget all the drama and nonsense for a few hours a day. While I was in class, and when I was able to focus and study I would get lost in the legal theory and principals and slip away temporarily from reality.

Even though I tried, I just couldn't find enough time to study as much as I needed to and often I would gamble and skip entire legal concepts, hoping that they wouldn't appear on the exams. I did this for my Constitutional Law class, completely neglecting to study anything involving the hot topic at the time, President Obama's Affordable Care Act. I was sitting next to one of my classmates, Zerlina Maxwell, and she was smiling to herself as she reviewed her notes. I asked her what she was smiling about and she said, "I know he is going to ask about the Affordable Care Act and I started following that last year when it was first proposed. I am going to nail this!"

I said, "Huh?? Man, I hope he doesn't ask about that or I'm screwed." Zerlina, one of my MSP cohorts and early study buddies, spent the next ten minutes breaking down the Act, the history of the Act and the constitutional challenges it faced. I listened as she went on and on, trying to take in as much as I could before the proctor said, "Ok, everyone remove your books. . . ok you can start."

I opened the exam, which consisted of three questions, two of which we had to answer, and the very first question was about the Affordable Care Act! I looked at Zerlina, who was smiling from ear to ear as she winked back at me, and smiled to myself, thinking, "I am one lucky mother fucker!" I tried to incorporate damn near everything she had just shared with me then moved on to the only other question that I knew anything else about. When I left the class, I gave her a huge hug and told her that she saved my ass! To this day I still owe her a big-time favor so if any of you know Zerlina, please thank her one more time for me!

27 REDEMPTION

I started volunteering for a law school program called Street Law. Through Street Law I went into the maximum security juvenile detention facility in Newark and taught juvenile inmates about the law, specifically on stop and frisk and search and seizure rights. I loved teaching and hadn't realized how much I missed working with youth in the community until I got involved with the program. I once again found myself going into a jail cell, and experiencing all the smells, sounds and emotions of being behind bars. After visiting the juvenile jail for a few months, that awkwardness faded away and I become more comfortable in my new role as an educator working behind bars. I only spent a total of about four or five months as an inmate in jail, and I can only imagine what someone that did a five, ten, or twenty-year bid would feel like going back inside in a non-inmate capacity with the ability to just walk right out. It must be uncomfortably surreal.

Giving back, especially to youth in need, kept everything in perspective for me and acted as a constant reminder to stay humble and allow karma to play a bigger role in my life. I discovered that my heart felt lighter and more open when I utilized some of the gifts that I was given to help others. I started looking for more opportunities to give back and was offered a spot on a small team that was preparing to travel to Israel to work on a project helping at-risk-youth. While I am far from a religious person, I have felt my spiritual side grow stronger and stronger as I've experienced more amazing events that I find hard to explain, and Israel was yet another example.

I got to spend a great deal of time in the city of Jerusalem where I sampled foods from both Jewish and Muslim cultures, prayed at the Western Wall, listened to the Muslim call to prayer, and laughed and got to know others involved in the program from Ben Hurion University as well as my own classmates. I spent time in the tomb that, according to many religious scholars, was the final resting place for Jesus, and visited Bethlehem and the site of His birth in Palestine. I was moved to tears many times, in the Jewish, Muslim and Christian quarters of the city and felt an amazing connection to the masses of people around me.

Missiles were literally exploding around us, mostly in the city of Ber' Sheba, where a rocket launched from the Gaza Strip hit an elementary school less than a mile from where I was staying. Fortunately, school was canceled for the day because of the missile launches and no one was hurt but that coupled with the constant explosions, some farther away than others, was enough to keep me well aware that I was in an active war zone. By day we attended workshops and meetings and managed to sprinkle in some sightseeing, and at night we partied our asses off. I met Jews from all over, including a number from Africa. I was amazed at the large population of African Jews and found myself engaged in conversations about race, religion, and everything in between.

They badgered me with questions about the violence they saw in America, especially about American gang violence, and asked me to explain the mentality behind black folks killing other black folks. I found myself unable to effectively articulate the historical depths of racism and the long-term effects of slavery on an entire class of people but I managed to summarize things the best I could. They struggled to understand how my fellow Americans could view me as being anything other than American. For the first time in a long time I talked openly about the struggles I faced growing up bi-racial in America. With tears in my eyes I told them about my first experiences moving from the white community, where I was called a Nigger behind my back, to the black community, where I had to fight on a regular basis because they called me a white boy. It was in that moment that I started to formulate an outline for this very book. Seeing their response to my struggles and hearing their own experiences convinced me that more discussions about race and struggle was needed.

As I was preparing to register for the first semester of my final year of law school, I received a notice from the school that my financial aid packet hadn't been approved. I contacted the federal loan provider and was told that they wouldn't be able to approve my loan for the year because my credit score had dipped substantially because of the financial strain of my divorce. I was struggling financially and had to use my credit cards to live in between receiving the extra money I took out each semester from my loans. I was still waiting for the marital assets to be released so that I could pay off some of my credit card debt and try to get things back on track but my wife was dragging it out, hoping that she could starve me out and gain an advantage in the divorce.

I called, emailed and reached out to everyone in the school and financial aid providers to see what could be done to help free up the money I needed to attend school. Of all the potential pit falls I envisioned, from my criminal background, to not being able to handle the work load, to going through a nasty divorce, I never once thought about finances becoming an issue. As the start of the semester grew closer and closer, I grew more and more desperate then finally had to give up after receiving a final notification from the loan providers.

I told my lawyer what was going on and we filed a motion to try to force the court to release some of the marital assets so that I could utilize the money to pay for school but my wife's attorney kept asking for, and receiving adjournments until the semester had already started and it was too late for me to register and join the classes. I was beyond distraught and for the first time throughout the entire process, went into a state of depression. Without the money from my loans I was broke as hell, working off a strict budget every week and trying to figure out how I was going to scrape together $20 to put gas in my car so I could pick up my daughter when it was finally my time to see her.

I reached out to a few friends and family to borrow money to help with bills and had to get creative with which bills to pay when. I eventually fell behind on my rent and had to go to court to fight a couple of eviction notices. I couldn't afford my car insurance and got a notice that they were going to cancel the policy. My car was also starting to smoke profusely whenever I drove it and was in desperate need of a new transmission.

I repeatedly tried to find jobs and once again ran into the same road block that had always been a problem, my felony conviction. I had never been one to give up or let the circumstances around me break me down but I was feeling close to hitting a breaking point. I spent day after day sitting on my couch, watching the fish in my daughter's small aquarium. I watched those fish so much that I began to recognize their individual personalities. I knew which one would be the first to go after the food when I placed it in the tank, which one was the bully, which one was passive and where each one liked to hide whenever they were spooked.

All I could think about was finishing my law degree on time with my class and it was looking more and more like that wouldn't be a possibility. When we eventually got our day in court, the judge was outraged that I wasn't able to continue with my education and chastised my wife for her role in preventing me from finishing my law degree. He finally ordered her to release enough money from marital assets for me to pay for my tuition so that I could get back into school.

A few weeks after I deposited the check and paid my tuition, the student loan provider contacted me and said that I could ask them to reconsider my loan, which I promptly did, and to my surprise, a few weeks later they approved my loan. I was able to use some of the additional money to pay back some of the people I owed, catch up on my rent and bills and finish paying my tuition. I still had to figure out how I could make up the classes I missed the previous semester and take enough credits to finish on time with my class.

I met with my dean who agreed to let me take sixteen credits, which was highly unusual in law school, enabling me to complete my program on time. I still had to work my schedule around my time with my youngest daughter as well as make sure I could get my oldest daughter who was now living with me, back and forth to her college classes. I was quickly learning the complexities associated with being a single parent but despite the challenges and difficulties, there was nothing that kept me more focused and driven than my kids.

I wanted to take a course being offered on starting and running a law firm as a solo practitioner but the course conflicted with one of my nights with my daughter. Usually, when I was in a pinch, I would bring my daughter to a few classes with me. We would sit all the way in the back of the large lecture halls and I would bring coloring books, crayons, books for her to read, small toys to play with and my old computer so she could play games and watch videos, anything to keep her occupied and quiet while class was in session. I would usually clear it in advance with my professors, who eventually all grew to love her. She was always smiling and if they let her, she would raise her hand in class and attempt to answer questions.

Most of my classmates, including myself, took notes on our computers so as you looked around the classroom, everyone would have their laptops open, screens up and fingers flying as they typed away. Of course with a computer in front of you, it was also not uncommon to get distracted from time to time and jump on social media or surf the web. During one class, everyone was quietly listening and typing away while my daughter and I sat in the back row. She leaned over to me and whispered in a voice loud enough for the entire class to hear, "Daddy, that man is playing the same game I like to play on his computer!" The entire class looked up, then looked at the guilty party and busted out laughing. The guy was so embarrassed that he turned bright red and looked like he wanted to sneak out of the classroom. Even the professor had to chuckle.

On occasion, one of my classmates would take her to get a treat from the small snack bar or take her outside to walk around. By my last semester, everyone knew my daughter and she would walk through the law school as if she were a student. Despite the level of comfort we had, I didn't want to take advantage of the situation but after explaining my dilemma to my Professor, who was also the Dean, he was adamant that I bring her with me so that I could take the class.

I applied for and was accepted into the school's Special Education Law clinic and had to set up a schedule that enabled me to work approximately twenty hours per week in the clinic. We worked under the supervision of two experienced attorneys who guided us through handling our own case load. I represented indigent clients that were supposed to be receiving special education services but for one reason or another, had problems getting those services. Through the law clinic I learned how to interview clients during the intake process, create and open new client files, calendar important court and legal deadlines, negotiate with attorneys from various school districts, write motions and briefs on behalf of clients and argue clients' cases in court. The law clinic functioned just like a law firm and provided us with invaluable experiences actually practicing law.

Between my classes, the law clinic and running around for events for both of my daughters, the semester flew by and before I knew it, I was handing in my last few papers and closing out my client files at the clinic in preparation for graduation. As graduation day grew closer, I began feeling more and more like something was going to come up to prevent me from graduating. It just all seemed surreal, how a high school dropout, one-time drug dealer and convicted felon, could change the direction of his life and make it that far. I started thinking more and more about practicing law and started to doubt myself and rethink if that was a realistic goal. I had hit walls every step of the way and had to fight at every level of the slow, steady climb from the streets to higher education and the professional world. I knew that I had more challenges in store and was unsure if I would be able to find the strength to continue fighting. I was feeling worn out and beat down, until my daughter wrapped her arms around me and said, "Daddy, I am so proud of you. You are going to be a lawyer!" Her words immediately lifted me up and any feelings of doubt were replaced with a new-found energy and pride. Once again my children managed to save me without even knowing it.

As the semester ended and I was provided with official notice that I had completed all the requirements to graduate, I started confirming travel times and making arrangements for family and friends to attend. I got fitted for my cap and gown and took graduation pictures at the school. I was still feeling like something was going to happen, that at any minute someone would grab me and say, "We are sorry but there has been a mistake." I knew I put in the hard work, I knew that I studied extremely hard for the exams and I knew that I deserved to graduate but I kept feeling as if it just couldn't be real.

On the morning of graduation, I drove to Newark, parked my car, put on my cap and gown and walked into the law school. I took a deep breath as I looked around at all the smiling faces, people hugging each other and taking pictures. I made my way towards a group of my friends and was immediately greeted with a round of hugs and handshakes. We were all beaming with pride, champagne bottles and glasses floated around while flashes from cell phones and cameras went off everywhere.

I looked up and around the school that had been my home for the past four years and thought back to all the time spent studying in the law library, to the countless days spent locked in the small study rooms that lined the upper floor hallways. I thought about the anxiety I felt going into my first few final exams and about how we would often leave class during the break, grab a quick drink of Scotch from DJ's locker, then head back to class, and how much more interesting the second half of those classes always ways! I thought about the times that I had to bring my son to school when he was going to summer school, or my daughter to class with me or have my oldest daughter wait in the atrium while I sat in class, and how I had watched them all grow up during the time I was in school.

I felt a tap on my shoulder and turned around to see Chichi standing there, arms open wide, tears in her eyes as she prepared to hug me. As we embraced, we whispered to each other how proud we were of one another and how amazing it was to have forged such an incredible friendship. Veer joined in the hug and the three of us stood there, patting each other on the back and grinning from ear to ear, proud of our individual and group accomplishment.

As I sat in the large concert hall at the New Jersey Performing Arts Center and looked around at my classmates, listening to the various speakers as they prepared to call our names, my mind raced with thoughts about the past. I wished that my brother could have been there to share my accomplishment, and I thought about Puba and how proud he would have been. I thought about Shawny and all the things that he taught me about people and how I still leaned on those things and utilized them almost every day.

As I stood up and prepared to have my name called, I looked back to the balcony where my family was seated and waved, hearing my princess scream "daddy!" through all the noise and voices. I laughed and fought back the tears I felt building up inside. "Jason C. Bost. . ." I stepped on the stage, accepted my juris doctor degree, looked out at the packed audience and finally breathed a sigh of relief. I did it. I did it!

I was greeted by hugs from my mother, my sister, Patrick, his sister Celia and his mother Liz were there as well. My man Fingers was there along with Eddie Cheeba and Show. Cheeba kept saying, "One of us made it! Jay you did it man, one of us finally made it!" As I slowly moved through the crowds, hugging and congratulating classmates, soaking in all the admiration from friends and family, I stopped and looked up at the blue sky over my head. I closed my eyes for a minute, took a deep breath and just absorbed the moment then my thoughts quickly jumped to my next goal and I realized that I was just getting started. I knew that I had more challenges to come, that the higher I set my goals, the more resistance I would face and I felt like I was up for the challenge. Bring it on world, bring it on because ready or not, here I come!

WHITE NIGGER

ABOUT THE AUTHOR

Jason Bost is a proud father to three sons and two daughters; grandfather to two grandsons and six granddaughters; college professor who holds a Juris Doctorate Degree from Rutgers School of Law in Newark; a Master's in Business Administration from New Jersey Institute of Technology; a Bachelor's of Science in History from State University of New York at Brockport; and an Associates of Science in Physical Studies from Monroe Community College. He is actively involved in volunteer work, focused primarily on individuals with special needs and at risk-youth and young adults. He participates in public speaking engagements focusing on race, culture and overcoming adversity.

CPSIA information can be obtained
at www.ICGtesting.com
Printed in the USA
LVOW07s2228121017
552173LV00010B/782/P